WORLDS WITHOUT NUMBER

J.L. THOMPSON

CFI
An imprint of Cedar Fort, Inc.
Springville, Utah

© 2022 James L. Thompson
All rights reserved.

No part of this book may be reproduced in any form whatsoever, whether by graphic, visual, electronic, film, microfilm, tape recording, or any other means, without prior written permission of the publisher, except in the case of brief passages embodied in critical reviews and articles.

This is not an official publication of The Church of Jesus Christ of Latter-day Saints. The opinions and views expressed herein belong solely to the author and do not necessarily represent the opinions or views of Cedar Fort, Inc. Permission for the use of sources, graphics, and photos is also solely the responsibility of the author.

ISBN 13: 978-1-4621-4204-0

Published by CFI, an imprint of Cedar Fort, Inc.
2373 W. 700 S., Springville, UT, 84663
Distributed by Cedar Fort, Inc., www.cedarfort.com

Library of Congress Control Number: 2021949105

Cover design by Shawnda T. Craig
Cover design © 2022 Cedar Fort, Inc.

Printed in the United States of America

10 9 8 7 6 5 4 3 2 1

Printed on acid-free paper

CONTENTS

FOREWORD v

INTRODUCTION 1

CHAPTER 1: The Creation and Function of the Universe 9

CHAPTER 2: Life as We Know It 53

CHAPTER 3: My Introduction to the Unknown 101

CHAPTER 4: Government Disclosure of UAP 144

CHAPTER 5: Latter-day Prophets Speak about
 Extraterrestrial Life 191

CHAPTER 6: Scriptural Spacecraft? 211

CHAPTER 7: UAP in the Sky 229

CHAPTER 8: Saucers on the Ground 266

CHAPTER 9: "Extraterrestrial" Visitors 292

CHAPTER 10: "Extraterrestrial" Abductors 308

CHAPTER 11: High Strangeness and the Extraterrestrial
 "Message" 344

CHAPTER 12: Church Member Close Encounters 366

CONTENTS

CHAPTER 13: The New Age 392

CHAPTER 14: Paranormal Properties of UAP 409

CHAPTER 15: Who Is Sending the Message? 429

CHAPTER 16:   Are UAP and Their Message a
          Satanic Deception? 451

CHAPTER 17: Conclusion 492

AFTERWORD 499

SELECTED BIBLIOGRAPHY 501

ABOUT THE AUTHOR 504

FOREWORD

It may surprise you to learn from this book that sightings of unidentified flying objects (UFOs), not to mention contacts with and even abductions by purported "space people," are much more common than their discussion in the mainstream media might lead you to expect—unless you have had a sighting yourself or have been contacted or abducted! Or perhaps you have studied the phenomenon, as James Thompson has. If not, you may also be surprised to learn the extent to which people who think a lot about UFOs have become enamored with the occult and the so-called New Age. What does it all mean to a Latter-day Saint? Brother Thompson has given that question much more thought than most of us, and he provides some highly perceptive insights in this volume.

From 1962 until about 1980, I gave the question of UFOs quite a bit of thought. Indeed, a book that I wrote, *The Utah UFO Display*, was published in 1974 (and is now long out of print). I interviewed about twenty UFO witnesses or groups of witnesses from a file of about eighty sightings that had been collected by Joseph Hicks, a junior high teacher in Roosevelt in the Uintah Basin of Utah. My goal was to be scientific. I considered the several explanations that had been put forward and concluded that none was sufficient, although all had some elements of truth or possible truth. Then, as now, many UFO sightings were misinterpretations of natural or conventional phenomena such as the planet Venus. A few were simply lies or hoaxes. Because they have been seen throughout history, they could hardly be secret weapons of somebody's air force. One can apply much psychology in understanding the witnesses, but mass hallucinations or other psychological phenomena cannot explain the UFOs. In my thinking, one could not scientifically eliminate the "visitors-from-another-planet" hypothesis, which was the main idea at that time—and the main target of UFO debunkers.

Nevertheless, as I delved into the various aspects of the UFO phenomenon, it became increasingly apparent that the UFOs could hardly represent true explorers from another world. For one thing, as Thompson describes, they wanted to be seen; they were putting on a display. I was perplexed by it all and concluded in my book that "they are putting on a show for our benefit. Why? What are they trying to prepare us for? What's the point of all this conditioning? One thing is certain: in a few areas of the world, such as the Uintah Basin, their display is having a powerful effect upon the collective thinking of the inhabitants. It is becoming the stuff of legend and folklore. Perhaps if we keep our minds open and remain patient, we shall someday know why."

After writing the book, I became increasingly disturbed about what was going on. The "contactees," as we called them then, were becoming more numerous, and their stories were becoming more difficult to shrug off. With such experiences, it became virtually impossible to maintain an objective, detached, scientific approach to the study of UFOs. My religious interpretations were becoming more important than science. But I could not accept the idea that our visitors were from Enoch's Zion, for example, or that they were angels who were preparing for the Lord's Second Coming. There were too many signs of evil, too much resemblance to spiritualism and other occult matters. It was easier to imagine that "false Christs, and false prophets," were showing "great signs and wonders; insomuch that, if it were possible, they shall deceive the very elect" (Matthew 24:24; see also Joseph Smith—Matthew 1:22).

I am amazed at the intensity with which the UFO phenomenon has become associated with contactee and abduction stories, which now seem paramount. There has been a profound influence on (at least) Western collective thought, which is increasingly involved with the New Age religion and the occult. The world is being taught an alternative to the return of the Savior!

FOREWORD

James Thompson has examined these matters in much depth. He provides some answers, tentative at least, to the questions that I posed at the close of my book—and he poses many questions of his own. As a legal writer, he knows the limitations of his knowledge and investigative abilities, not to mention the strange nature of the evidence, so he is never dogmatic. As a devout Latter-day Saint, he has a body of revealed knowledge—Father Lehi's iron rod—to hold onto, and that he does. His love of his Redeemer and the gospel message shine through in every discussion, and his probing of the enigma is as extensive and deep as that of any UFO researcher known to me. You have much to learn as you read these pages, and you can learn much from this volume. And perhaps you can help to restrain the flood of evil that is rising in the world. Read in the proper spirit, this book can help you do so.

Frank B. Salisbury, PhD (late)
Professor, Head of the Department of Plant Science,
Utah State University

What Others Are Saying . . .

"This is the largest story of our lifetime. The government has determined these are not of human origin. They're not Russian or Chinese. We don't know where they're from. They behave in a way that defies physics, and they are constantly buzzing our military installations. It is huge, and without shame we're going to stay on this."

—TUCKER CARLSON, "Tucker Carlson Tonight"
Fox NewsChannel, October 3, 2021

"In my youth, I read James's first book on the UFO subject, *Aliens and UFOs: Messengers or Deceivers?* I was always fascinated with the UFO/UAP and extraterrestrial subjects, but struggled with how such a strange reality could fit into God's plan. I credit James's book with helping me come to terms with these subjects that are sometimes frightening, but always intriguing. I was able to accept that our Creator is still in charge and that I am shortsighted to place limits on His ability to create. Now many years later, I've interviewed hundreds of UFO witnesses, recorded the stories of dozens of alleged abductees, traveled the world investigating and lecturing on the most prolific UFO cases, and I've even had my own incredible UFO sightings that I cannot deny. Overwhelmingly, the evidence suggests that the phenomenon *is* real. Something indeed *is* happening. While we may not presently know for certain what that something is or where it comes from, I firmly believe it will be made known to us in its proper time. I advise Church members not to fear. Just buckle up . . . because it's about to get interesting!"

—BEN HANSEN, TV host and personality

"James has chosen to explore a unique topic. If our planet really is being visited by extraterrestrials, how does that fit into the gospel plan? If it's all an illusion orchestrated by the adversary, what are we to think of that? James looks at these questions from a variety of angles that will, perhaps, only increase in importance as we approach the Second Coming of our Lord and Savior, Jesus Christ."

—CHRIS HEIMERDINGER, best-selling author
of *Tennis Shoes Among the Nephites*

INTRODUCTION

The universe is immense and vast. We as a species, as humanity, are in our early infancy of understanding and exploring it. God, our Heavenly Father, comprehends it completely—and He governs every particle and wave of the entire universe. Nearly thirty years ago I authored a book that discussed with members of The Church of Jesus Christ of Latter-day Saints ("the Church") the nature of creation and the life that God has created here. In that vein I shared the reality of "something" that was presenting itself in our airspace, commonly referred to as UFOs. I titled my original manuscript *Worlds Without Number*,[1] referring to the scripture in Moses 1:33 in which God our Heavenly Father declares, "And worlds without number have I created; and I also created them for mine own purpose; and by the Son I created them, which is mine Only Begotten." The ancient prophet Enoch confirmed this fact, telling us, "And were it possible that man could number the particles of the earth, yea, millions of earths like this, it would not be

---

1. My publisher changed the title to *Aliens and UFOs: Messengers or Deceivers?* (James L. Thompson, Horizon Publishers & Distributors, Inc., 1993), which was more to the point of the book, because they felt it would provide the potential reader with a better idea of what to expect. The late Professor Frank B. Salisbury, PhD, a Church member who was a leading scientist and university professor and had also examined the UAP phenomenon kindly provided a foreword. The scope of that work included various spiritual phenomenon as well. Two years later my publisher released a second book, a rewritten version of the first, with Church specific references removed: *Alien Encounters: The Deception Menace* (James L. Thompson, Horizon Publishers & Distributors, Inc., 1995).

a beginning to the number of thy creations" (Moses 7:30). And finally, we also learn from revelation that Jesus Christ is the creator of these innumerable worlds, and they are populated with God's children. "That by him, and through him, and of him, the worlds are and were created, and the inhabitants thereof are begotten sons and daughters unto God" (Doctrine and Covenants [hereafter, D&C] 76:24).

As a result of this direct revelation from God, members of the Church are nearly unique in their understanding and belief that we are not alone in the universe; that our Heavenly Father creates "worlds without number" and populates them with His "begotten sons and daughters." Other religions, especially those flowing from the Roman Catholic Church, including most protestant sects, have long been convinced that earth and its human population are God's only creation containing life. Those faiths have long informed their adherents that any claim of life outside of that found on Earth is false—a doctrine of the devil. Secularists likewise believe there is no life beyond our planet—or at least that was the state of matters when my original book was published. That belief was founded on the concept of evolution and how astronomically difficult it is to get life started on a planet. Of course, the prospect of ever being visited by intelligent life from another solar system would be infinitely rarer, under this rubric, because life-sustaining planets are so few in the universe, and the distances between them are just so vast, making it statistically impossible that we would be visited by one in our lifetime. Most scientists are still mired in this thinking.

Most Western philosophy has derided reports of intelligence elsewhere in the universe, including signs of life flitting about in our own earth airspace. "It's not true, because it's not possible," has been the mantra. And that refrain has been enforced with severeness. Anyone who claims to see a craft in the sky that is too advanced to have originated from our own technology is ridiculed as irrational, or disparaged as a liar. This prohibition has been enforced at all levels of society—especially within the ranks of those who are most likely to actually witness unknown technology—like military and commercial pilots, and radar and sensor array operators. Beyond that, let a witness claim that he saw a humanoid person exit such a craft, and the witness is shunned

INTRODUCTION

and scorned. This social enforcement system is fairly thorough and successful in its objective of hiding the facts from plain public view and keeping discussion to back rooms and the outskirts of society. This has been the situation, until recently.

So, where does this leave members of the Church? Unlike most Christian religions, and secularists for that matter, we believe it is certain that humanoid life exists in other locations. In fact, the Lord declares that the universe is teeming with life, created by Him, and that innumerable planets house human life, perhaps much like us. Do we then immediately believe the stories of alien craft flying around in our airspace and entering our seas? Is our acceptance of the millions of eyewitness accounts of UFOs, or UAP (unidentified aerial phenomena),[2] visiting our planet automatic? Perhaps not. But if so, then what does it portend for our lives on Earth? How does the knowledge that we are being visited by "others" affect the way we view ourselves—in the universe and in light of the gospel-centered life provided by our Father in Heaven? Does the presence of "others" in any way negate or change our relationship with our Heavenly Father? Or, does the fact that life exists throughout the universe necessarily indicate that unknown craft in our night skies belong to the others? And what of the "message" that the visitors appear to be sharing during their visitations with various people on earth? These are the very questions that we discuss in this work. Some of the possible answers may be even more surprising or even jolting than a simple yes or no to any of them. Therefore, a discussion about the true nature of the universe, as understood by the prophets and by scientists, should assist us in our understanding of what is, what may be, and what is not. A review of the nature of creation, universal mechanics, life, spirit, and consciousness should help us better understand who we are and who else is out there—and how we should proceed in light of recent government revelations about UAP in our skies.

---

2. UAP has become the preferred term of the US military and government due to the stigma associated with the term UFO. The irony is that it was the government and military that created the stigma through its own debunking and ridiculing campaigns, now finding they must destigmatize the phenomenon as they admit its existence.

Governments around the world have recently begun a process of disclosing the existence of UAP. The US government recently declassified and authenticated a number of videos recorded by our military purporting to be UAP hovering near our ships and racing at breakneck speeds through our airspace. Those videos were leaked to the public, sparking congressional calls for full agency reporting of any information they possess concerning UAP in our airspace, or in our seas as it turns out. As of this writing, the US government has essentially conceded the truth of UAP in our skies and seas. As a result of those admissions, these questions naturally arise: What are they? Whose are they? Why are they here?

First, it is important to understand a little about UAP so we comprehend the importance of these three questions. Many who are now forced to accept the existence of UAP cling desperately to the view that they must belong to "us." A cursory observation of the UAP tells us the following about them:

- Extremely high speeds; over 60,000 mph in our atmosphere
- Rapid acceleration; 0 to 30,000 mph in less than 1 second
- Sharp "V" turns, like hitting and bouncing a ping-pong ball
- Rapid acceleration and deceleration, creating thousands of g-forces
- No visible means of propulsion (no jets or propellers)
- No flight control surfaces (no wings or fins)
- Able to deactivate all weapons systems, including nuclear missiles in silos
- Move rapidly from space, to atmosphere, to water
- Create no discernible sound or heat during operation
- Extreme velocity and acceleration causes no sonic boom, or air disturbance

What do these characteristics mean? Our fastest craft travel at a modest 2,100 mph, at top speed. The absolute speed record is roughly twice that. Our rockets eventually attain an orbital speed of around 17,500 mph. Anything entering earth's atmosphere at those speeds burns up from the extreme friction—so we have to slow them dramatically as they re-enter and come toward the surface. Our only means of propulsion is thrust, created by a spinning propeller or by burning fuel to release hot exhaust gas, thus propelling the craft forward. If our craft were to take off or stop at UAP rates witnessed by our military observers, human occupants and even equipment would be instantly crushed (liquefied).

What are the implications of these UAP characteristics? They have propulsion systems that are thousands of years in advance of our state-of-the-art technology. Let's think about what that means. When Joseph Smith received instructions to translate the Book of Mormon, humanity read by gas lamps and traveled by horse and buggy. The steam locomotive was just coming into existence. Since then, the world developed electricity, the internal combustion engine, the airplane, radio and television, the jet engine, and the transistor, which eventually led to the microcircuit and computer. Those rapid advances in the short span of 200 years have completely transformed our world and the way we live and interact. If that progress were to continue at the same accelerated pace for the next 1,000 years, we *might* be able to produce a craft that functions on physical principles that negate the effects of gravity—as appears to be abundantly clear in the function of UAP. However, antigravity propulsion and the other characteristics that we observe in UAP may actually be 10,000, or even 100,000 years in our future. Perhaps more. If you ask most scientists about developing an antigravity propulsion system that enables us to travel to planets outside of our solar system and arrive within a few hours, or even years, they will tell you it is absolutely impossible—the laws of physics simply don't allow it. Therefore, craft visiting us from other planets beyond our own solar system are simply "impossible."

The "craft" that we see in our skies and in declassified military videos appear to possess technologies that would entirely change our life on earth if we owned them. Whoever wielded antigravity technology would instantly rule the world. Not only would the nation, a superpower like America, China, or Russia, who possessed these technologies have unlimited energy sources, but it would have extremely efficient transportation, food production, and construction capabilities—far in excess of all others. The technology would provide it with extreme economic and military advantages over other nations—and by extreme, I mean one-million-to-one ratios. If the United States possessed these technologies, we could immediately end hunger, poverty, and pollution, and focus our resources on humanitarian and democratic pursuits—all without any interference from hostile nations. We would immediately cease investing trillions of dollars annually into the old (obsolete) systems. If, on the other hand, one of those other hostile governments owned these technologies, they could threaten to deliver hundreds of massive ordnance super bombs simultaneously at major cities and strategic sites around the nation, and set them off without threat of counter-strikes. In short, whichever earth superpower controls this technology immediately becomes the only superpower and the only economic superpower. Because none of the world's superpowers are stepping up and claiming their place at the head of the table, and the Russians and Chinese are still trying to steal whatever technology they can from others, we must assume that the UAP are not any of us. Moreover, UAP with these advanced flight and propulsion characteristics have been observed and recorded for over seventy years, completely eliminating the possibility that they belonged to an earth superpower at that time—the superpower who possessed the technology would have avoided the hard economic times, complete with starvation, and would have avoided the space race and regional and global struggles for supremacy with such abilities.

With literally millions of eyewitness reports of extraordinary craft zipping through our airspace, and tens of thousands of close, personal encounters with those purporting to come from other worlds, what are we to understand about these phenomena and how they affect our comprehension of our universe? What is the significance of the carefully crafted "message" being delivered to thousands around the world by these beings in a perfectly choreographed presentation of that message? All of these issues are exacerbated and multiplied by the high strangeness of interactions with the "beings," the reproductive and genetic experimentation and the bizarre spiritism nature of the visitor messages. Compound these with the non-humanoid versions of the visitors, including insectoid and reptilian, and repeat encounters and experiences for many people, and you have a phenomenon that most feel is better kept hidden away—with leakers held in derision—not

INTRODUCTION

unlike the dark family scandal that is best left unspoken. Is it any wonder that our generals in the Pentagon decided decades ago that it is better to conceal the existence of UAP and their occupants, seeing that the high strangeness aspects of the phenomenon create many more questions than are answered?

Consider these matters with me for just a bit, and seek the inspiration of a loving God as we pick our way through the cluttered path of "extraterrestrial" visitations and contacts. In the end, watch carefully and seek the counsel of a wise and inspired prophet of God before making final decisions that alter any aspect of your life or understanding. Like me, you will probably conclude that because of absent official declarations on these subjects from God, through His prophets, it is impossible to "know" anything conclusive—it is impossible to say I have a "testimony" to bear about any such matter. I do not.

Personally, I have read scores of books on the subjects of the universe, the gospel, and UAP and "alien" visitors, reviewed thousands of hours of television and radio programming, and interviewed many eyewitnesses and analysts to provide the data utilized in our discussion. I have no personal ax to grind in presenting this material—I do not hold myself out as a ufologist, nor do I attend UFO conferences or conventions and the like. I am not a UAP experiencer, although like so many of you, I may have seen some things that make me wonder. However, I have been approached by many, including government intelligence personnel and Church members and leaders, who tell me, "James, you are right that they exist—I saw one come down, and it was completely clear what I was seeing." When a bishop or stake president looks you in the eye and solemnly recounts his close encounter with such a craft, you really must take stock of the phenomenon and give it the sober and comprehensive investigation it deserves. Moreover, when solid people tell you that they saw the "occupants" of the craft—some interacting with them, and some being abducted against their will—it puts a very serious burnish on the subject.

I tell you this: You personally know someone who has seen a UAP. Approximately 7 percent of Church members report seeing them clearly—unambiguously. That's 7 percent of 16.6 million members (as of this writing), or 1,162,000 Church members who have seen them.

This means that over a dozen members of your ward have seen a UAP, and perhaps one or two have seen a purported "occupant." These percentages hold true for all people, worldwide, resulting in thousands of sightings daily. The chances are, members of your family have seen them. If we begin to speak of these phenomena openly, we will discover that it is much more prevalent than any of us thought. I encourage all of us to begin speaking of these matters openly—robbing it of its hold over so many.

Nevertheless, I have prayerfully pondered and considered these matters at length, and have even personally experienced direct contact with non-human entities making claims that we all find to be interesting, if not extraordinary—or alarming. However, I do not recommend that you dwell very long on these subjects, nor make them your point of focus in your life in any measure. As we will see in our discussion, there is opposition in all things. Some is light, and some darkness. As we ponder the light, we perchance will comprehend portions of the darkness as well. To paraphrase Nietzsche, "If you stare into the darkness, the darkness will stare back at you." I have certainly experienced that truth, despite my best efforts to avoid it. Like so many of you, I am a battle-scarred warrior for Christ, and I fear that many of those wounds were inflicted as a direct result of my willingness to peer into the darkness, that I might prepare this report for you. I recommend that you maintain a spirit of truth and light in your life during our discussion of who and what is exercising such great influence over humanity as we approach the times that we have always referred to affectionately as the latter days.

CHAPTER 1

The Creation and Function of the Universe

If we wish to understand the nature of the universe, including how it functions in relation to our existence, then we must look to what is observable by scientific inquiry, as limited as our current ability to view it all may be, and what our Father in Heaven has revealed on the subject. Unfortunately, both sources of "truth" provide us with little usable information. With apologies to both science and revelation, we are still in our infancy of gaining knowledge about the vast universe and its beginning and function. We have recently developed space-based telescopes whose resolution surprised us to learn that many of the twinkling stars in the night sky are not stars at all—but entire galaxies, each containing 100 billion stars and perhaps as many solar systems.

We are not unlike a tiny ant floating on a small piece of wood in the middle of a vast ocean, who seeks to better understand the world in which he finds himself adrift. From our superior and enlightened vantage point, we smile at the little ant and understand that he will never be able to comprehend the world, the solar system, the galaxy, or even the tiny particles that make up the matter of his hunk of wood and the galaxies—because he has such a limited ability to view and understand things so much greater than himself. Sorry to tell you, but we are that ant in the big picture of the cosmos. However, for the purposes of our discussion, we are edified by a brief conversation of what it is we believe we know, and how it affects our relationships with Deity, humanity, and 'others.'

IN THE BEGINNING

"In the beginning," the revealed word of God commences, the Elohim (Gods) "created the heavens and the earth."

We learn a few things about the creation of this earth in the scriptures and in the temple. The Book of Abraham, which was received by the prophet Joseph Smith through pure revelation, appears to provide the most detailed and understandable account of the creation. The Genesis account, as well as that provided in the Book of Moses, which is essentially an inspired update of Genesis, provide much of the same information but from a different viewpoint at times.

However, before we launch into a full discussion of the days of creation, which would not actually add that much to our discussion of the creation of the universe and how it functions, let us pause and first realize that God has revealed precious little about the creation. In fact, He has revealed very little about most subjects. Allow me to clarify my meaning. God reveals what He wants us to know. That revelation usually comes through declarations to the prophets, although revelation can come to all of us, within our limited spheres of influence and authority. It can even come in the form of inspiration, through the Light of Christ, to those who have no particular grasp of the gospel and its importance. But all truth proceeds forth from the shining light of God, who possesses all truth and knowledge. We have a little understanding of who God is. We have a little understanding of what He has done and why He has done it. "A little understanding?" you might ask. But don't we have thousands of pages of detailed knowledge about God and His holy plan of salvation and exaltation? We do. But the problem is that the knowledge about God and His abilities and activities fill trillions and trillions of pages. Here's what God tells us: "For My thoughts are not your thoughts, neither are your ways My ways," declares the Lord. "For as the heavens are higher than the earth, so My ways are higher than your ways and My thoughts than your thoughts" (Isaiah 55:8–9)

There it is. It may be harsh, but it's the way things are. We are children. He is God. He may be our Heavenly Father, but He is God—He who is omnipotent, omniscient, and from everlasting to everlasting. Compared to God, we have very limited knowledge and even less understanding of that knowledge. I think that we may tend to tell ourselves that because the prophets have revealed a little more to us about God and His Son, Jesus Christ, and their work and glory, that we know a lot. We don't. Do we know more than others who reject the prophets? Yes, we do. How much more do we know? Let's say we know ten times more than others who know nothing of the restoration of all things in these latter days, just preceding the Second Coming of the Lord Jesus Christ. Ten times more sounds like a lot.

However, the problem is that the scale is much larger than we assume. If others have a knowledge and understanding level of 1, and we have a knowledge and understanding level of 10, then we feel quite comfortable and cozy in that superior position of intelligence. If the scale were 1 to 100, our position of 10 on the scale would be enviable. Take a deep breath, because in reality, the scale is closer to 1 to 1,000,000. "For as the heavens are higher than the earth, so My ways are higher than your ways and My thoughts than your thoughts." How much higher are the heavens than the earth? Much. Heaven is very far away. The heavens are very high above the earth. God's thoughts, ways, knowledge, and understanding are exponentially higher than ours. Before looking deeper into what we know from the revelations, let's first consider what secular learning tells us on these matters.

SECULAR VIEW OF CREATION

If you go into a science class, you will likely learn about the Big Bang Theory of creation. In that theory, which is usually presented as much more than just a theory, you learn that there was nothing in the beginning. There was a void. There was nothingness. There was no energy. No light. No sub-particles. No particles. No atoms. No matter. There was no underlying matrix holding all structures together and giving them form. There was no time. There was nothing whatsoever. FOREVER NOTHING. Then, after eons and eons of absolutely nothing, there was suddenly a gargantuan burst of "something" that nearly instantly produced incredible amounts of energy, gravity, and subatomic particles that arranged themselves into atoms and then molecules, producing all of the matter in our vast universe and exponentially expanded it with the ticking of time. That burst of something came from nothing—*creatio ex nihilo*. There was nothing to provoke the great burst of somethingness. There was no provocateur. From that burst of something from nothing came the trillions of galaxies, each containing a hundred billion stars and planetary systems. The only evidence of this burst of something is the manner in which the galaxies appear to be hurtling through the universe at very high speeds, from a centralized location, as if it were exploding matter from the point of a bomb that was set off 13.8 billion years ago.

If that's where matter got its start, then what do we learn in the classrooms about the origins of life? Roughly—here it is. There was nothing. No life. No biological tissues or animate matter anywhere. For billions of years there was nothing. Then, as one of those stony little planets sat quietly with percolating pools of hydrogen and other elements baking in the sun's radiation, suddenly, without provocation there was out of nowhere a single celled living organism. Where did it come from? Nowhere. It was just suddenly there—inanimate material transformed inexplicably into a living organism. It had never happened in the prior billions of years of similar circumstances, but now, suddenly, it happened. This single cell living organism had the intrinsic complex ability to absorb and process the energy it required, to multiply into replicas of itself, and congregate with those replicas, and eventually join together in a functional organism that eats, drinks, reacts, seeks better conditions, reproduces, and so on. This animated organism survived through replicating and multiplying generations and continued to reorganize itself into higher and higher life forms, until the day when it walked, then learned to talk, then text—the very pinnacle of intelligent communication.

Personally, I don't like this theory. It lacks logic and fails to meet the scientific criteria for a theory to become an accepted fact. Lest we become too heady in our rejection of such theories, let us remember—we don't know how it all began. We have no idea. Like Carl Sagan, the famed scientist who thought a great deal about these matters, we simply don't know what there was before there was something. "If the general picture of a big bang followed by an expanding universe is correct, what happened before that? Was the universe devoid of all matter and then the matter suddenly somehow created; how did that happen? In many cultures, the customary answer is that a God or gods created the universe out of nothing. But if we wish to pursue this question courageously, we must of course ask the next question: Where did God come from?"[1]

William W. Phelps, the scribe to Joseph Smith and Restoration insider, penned a song that sets forth the early leaders' curiosity on such questions. In "If You Could Hie to Kolob," the poet asks, if one could ever "find out the generation, Where Gods began to be? Or see the grand beginning, Where space did not extend? Or view the last creation, Where Gods and matter end?" This song always gives me a feeling of the eternities and the endless and wondrous nature of God, our Eternal Father. It also expresses the questions still posed by the spiritual and intellectual elite of the early restored Church. They simply didn't know. The Prophet Joseph Smith knew much more about the subjects, but he lacked the language or proper paradigm to express his understanding to the Saints of his time, as we will see.

As we begin to truly understand how the universe actually works, we also begin to comprehend how marvelous the creation actually is. There is so much more to it than mere happenstance and coincidental merging of atoms—trillions of trillions of trillions of trillions of tons of matter that erupted into existence from a singularity of nothingness, according to our brightest scientific minds. It's a little funny to think about this theory—that everything suddenly erupted from nothing—because in the early days of the Catholic Church, its leadership came up with the creation doctrine (dogma) *creatio ex nihilo*, which is Latin for "creation from nothing." Under this dogma,

---

1. Carl Sagan, *Cosmos.*

God created everything (except Himself) out of nothing. Apparently, He preexisted all matter and energy. During the Renaissance and the age of reason and scientific methodology, modern thinkers scoffed at the antiquated and simplistic notion of *creatio ex nihilo*. Then, as astronomers began to measure the expansion of the universe, which can be thought of like a giant explosion from a central point in space, they were stuck with the nagging conclusion that the entire mass of existence had to have begun at that single point. Hence, the Big Bang Theory. Like Carl Sagan, they had to deal with the question, what were things like a second before that explosion from a single point that is only a tiny fraction the size of an atom? And, how did that tiny pinpoint of nothing become the tremendous amount of something that fills the universe today? *Creatio ex nihilo*!

Professor Ron Hellings, PhD, a Church member who earned a doctorate in physics and spent twenty-five years as a research scientist at NASA, is well aware of the questions we are discussing in this chapter. He has said, "In the last 20 years, we have learned so much about the universe that we are now mystified and profoundly confused." Understanding that both scientific observation and revealed knowledge fall short of providing us with the real nuts-and-bolts of how the universe came into being, or how it actually functions, Professor Hellings warns, "This is no time for anyone to criticize anyone else's beliefs based on what cosmologists know."[2] Professor Hellings explains that "there are big problems with standard Big Bang cosmology," such as the "horizon problem" and the "flatness problem," both of which challenge the Big Bang's underlying principle of being a random and chaotic occurrence. Some alternatives like "inflationary cosmology" have been proposed to correct the problems, Dr. Hellings adds, which encompasses the ideas of "eternal inflation" of the constantly expanding universe, and "the universe becoming a multiverse."

Supporting the teaching of the Prophet on the subject, the first law of thermodynamics governs matters of creation and destruction of matter and energy, and can be summed up in three statements:

---

2. Aaron Shill, *Deseret News,* August 24, 2009.

THE CREATION AND FUNCTION OF THE UNIVERSE

1. **The law of conservation of mass:** Mass cannot be created or destroyed.
2. **The law of conservation of energy:** Energy cannot be created or destroyed.
3. **The law of conservation of mass-energy:** Neither energy nor mass can be created or destroyed; instead mass is conserved as energy or energy is conserved as mass. A combination of the law of conservation of energy and conservation of mass (based on $E=mc^2$ (energy mass equivalence).

The first two laws governed scientific thinking until the end of the 1800s, but then scientists began to understand that the two were actually interchangeable. As a result, the third law was developed, making better sense. For instance, when we take photons of energy in such a manner as to create matter out of it, we call this "matter synthesis." Or, we can easily convert mass to energy by burning wood, or splitting atoms.

With these principles in mind, Professor Hellings explains, "The inflationary cosmology would say matter-energy is conserved, everything is matter-energy and the multiverse can be infinite and eternal." Inflationary cosmology is no panacea, however, and Hellings says that "there are just a bunch of competing theories and no way to tell between them."

All of this informs us that scientists are doing their best to figure out the origins and functionality of the universe through observation and experimentation. In many ways they have made great strides—doubling from a 5 to 10 on our scale of 1,000,000. Again, they, like the ant floating aimlessly in the sea, are very limited in their ability to observe both the macro and the micro aspects of the universe. The point is that with everything we learn from scientific observation, and the revelations from God, we only know a small fraction of what there is to be known. Those who reject the revelations of God as originating from a real being of superior knowledge and intellect know much less and busy themselves trying to figure things out through observation only. Observation is good. Scientific inquiry is good. But to pursue knowledge of creation and how the universe works, without considering what the Grand Creator has told us about it, is akin to walking from the Pacific to the Atlantic wearing a blindfold. Let us consider what the Lord has revealed about the creation and functionality of our universe, and see if it can help augment our understanding of observable scientific principles.

GOSPEL VIEW OF CREATION

Again, in the beginning, the Elohim (Gods)[3] created the heavens and the earth. Which creation is this? Which heavens? Which earth? Is it the creation of the very first matter? Unfortunately, it appears that the creation outlined in Abraham, Genesis, and Moses, as well as the temple endowment, are figurative principles of the separate periods of creation of our own earth—although there may be some clues in the texts about the original creation generally. The scriptural accounts that we possess are based on the revelation given originally to the prophet Moses, who was specifically told that the account pertains only to the creation of this earth and its specific inhabitants. "But only an account of this earth, and the inhabitants thereof, give I unto you. For behold, there are many worlds that have passed away by the word of my power.

---

3. Those who were involved in the creation are said to be the Elohim, meaning Gods, whom we recognize as the Father and the Son, plus other noble and great intelligences that existed before the earth was formed. Abraham tells us, "Now the Lord had shown unto me, Abraham, the intelligences that were organized before the world was; and among all these there were many of the noble and great ones; And God saw these souls that they were good, and he stood in the midst of them, and he said: These I will make my rulers; for he stood among those that were spirits, and he saw that they were good; and he said unto me: Abraham, thou art one of them; thou wast chosen before thou wast born. And there stood one among them that was like unto God, and he said unto those who were with him: We will go down, for there is space there, and we will take of these materials, and we will make an earth whereon these may dwell" (Abraham 3:22–24; see also Abraham 4:1). President Joseph Fielding Smith wrote: "It is true that Adam helped to form this earth. He labored with our Savior Jesus Christ. I have a strong view or conviction that there were also others who assisted them. Perhaps Noah and Enoch; and why not Joseph Smith, and those who were appointed to be rulers before the earth was formed?" (*Doctrines of Salvation* 1:74).

And there are many that now stand, and innumerable are they unto man; but all things are numbered unto me, for they are mine and I know them" (Moses 1:35).

The account of the creation of this earth is given in creative periods—sometimes called days. They are not days. They are not thousand-year periods. They are very long periods of time during which certain preparations of the earth are made. The periods of creation are separate, with long periods of development and percolation in between. Then, when the creators return to initiate the next phase or period of creation, the first thing they do is check their previous phase of work, to see how it has developed during their long absence. They say of this period of absence between the "days" of creation, "And it came to pass that it was from evening until morning that it was night" (Abraham 24:19). So, if we wish to understand how God created, or at least "organized the elements" to create our earth and populate it with human and animal lifeforms, it is helpful to get a clear idea that the creation accounts in the scriptures are merely figurative and only offer short-hand information about the actual processes and occurrences of creation.

To explain that during the creative periods various organs of the planet were being prepared to eventually support lifeforms that would later be introduced, in Abraham we read about the fifth creative period:

> And the Gods said: Let us prepare the waters to bring forth abundantly the moving creatures that have life; and the fowl, that they may fly above the earth in the open expanse of heaven. And the **Gods prepared the waters** that they might bring forth great whales, and every living creature that moveth, which the waters were to bring forth abundantly after their kind; and every winged fowl after their kind. And the Gods saw that they would be obeyed, and that their plan was good. And the Gods said: We will bless them, and cause them to be fruitful and multiply, and fill the waters in the seas or great waters; and cause the fowl to multiply in the earth. And it came to pass that it was from evening until morning that they called night; and it came to pass that it was from morning until evening that they called day; and it was the fifth time. (Abraham 24:20–23; emphasis added)

Also, as we noted above, the work accomplished in this fifth creative period, like each of the respective periods of creation, is only the *preparation* of the waters, so that the waters could eventually sustain life. Likewise, in the sixth creative period, it is the *preparation* of the earth itself to eventually sustain life. Although the creators are preparing the waters to bring forth sea life and sea fowl during the fifth period, no final sea life or fowl are being created or introduced into the waters during the fifth period. This is true of all of the creative periods.

These creative periods are phases of preparation of the planet to eventually receive and sustain life. In addition to this, we learn that there are at least three steps in the process of creation: 1) all things are created first in the mind of God (His plan), then 2) are created in spiritual form, before they are eventually 3) created (organized from unorganized matter[4]) in our tangible world. In Moses we learn a little more about the spiritual phase of creation, after God has conceived and planned (created) things in His mind. "And every plant of the field before it was in the earth, and every herb of the field before it grew. For I, the Lord God, created all things, of which I have spoken, spiritually, before they were naturally upon the face of the earth. For I, the Lord God, had not caused it to rain upon the face of the earth. And I, the Lord God, had created all the children of men; and not yet a man to till the ground; for in heaven created I them; and there was not yet flesh upon the earth, neither in the water, neither in the air" (Moses 3:5).

These three separate types of creation further complicate our understanding of the process of creation, as we make appeals to various scriptures to better comprehend it. It can be understood—but a thorough understanding of these principles is not really germane to our present discussion. What we really want to know is how the universe came into being, and how it is structured, and how

---

4. We receive little guidance about the nature of unorganized matter. As we discuss later, unorganized matter may not refer to raw elements floating in the cosmos, but energy that has not yet been converted into mass. In the case of living creatures, we know that their mass is additionally infused with their organized spirit element, thereby animating them, resulting in a "living soul."

it functions, to help us better understand what is and what is not happening in our universe.

Another aspect of the length of time of creation that we don't really know that much about is how long the periods of creation were. There is no indication in the scriptural record, and each period of creation could have been much longer or shorter than each of the other periods. They may have been thousands, millions, or even billions of years each, with equally large periods of time (night) separating the periods. The only indication of the age of the earth, or possibly of a system related to the reign of God, is found in the *Times and Seasons*. Therein, William W. Phelps, the editor, referred to the "records found in the catacombs of Egypt," passing on some information he claimed to have originated with Joseph Smith concerning the age of what he termed "this system." He said that "eternity . . . has been going on in this system, almost two thousand five hundred and fifty five millions of years."[5] That number is how they said 2,555,000,000, or 2.555 billion years in those days. Whether "this system" refers to our earth, our solar system, our galaxy, one of the higher orders of systems comprising our universe or the universe itself, or possibly Heavenly Father's eternal kingdom, we have no answer. What is so unique about the statement is that in Joseph Smith's day, no one spoke of the age of the earth or the universe in terms of billions of years. No one. Not even the most agnostic of scientists. Some thought that perhaps the age of the earth was tens or hundreds of thousands of years—or millions at the most. Now, scientists guess, based on their perceived status of the universe's expansion since the moment of the Big Bang, that its age could be at least 2.5 billion years, with most guessing it could be in the 13.8-billion-year range.

WHY GOD DOES WHAT HE DOES

The work and the glory of the Father are outlined in this passage of scripture, as revealed to Moses: "And the Lord God spake unto Moses, saying: The heavens, they are many, and they cannot be numbered unto man; but they are numbered unto me, for they are

---

5. *Times and Seasons*, V, January 1, 1845, 758.

mine. And as one earth shall pass away, and the heavens thereof even so shall another come; and there is no end to my works, neither to my words. For behold, this is my work and my glory—to bring to pass the immortality and eternal life of man" (Moses 1:37–39). The multiplicity of worlds and their many generations of existence and progress is very clear in this revelation, and we see that everything God does in this regard is centered in the progress of His children—with the goal of their eternal life as the crowning achievement of His work. He creates a world, not unlike our own earth, and He populates it with His spirit offspring. Generations of His children live and die on the planet, and when all who are assigned to that telestial orb for their personal period of temporal probation have completed their sojourn on its surface, it passes into its next phase, having fulfilled its telestial purpose.[6] We will discuss what eventually becomes of such a planet below.

Born of the Light

The process by which God actually creates is hinted at in the following scripture: "Behold, I reveal unto you concerning this heaven, and this earth; . . . by mine Only Begotten I created these things. . . And I, God, said: Let there be light; and there was light. And I, God, saw the light; and that light was good. And I, God, divided the light from the darkness" (Moses 2:1–4). There is "light" at the center of all creation. It is the light of truth, the "Comforter," which is the glory of the celestial kingdom, and it provides the promise of eternal life to the children of God. This light emanates from the presence of God,

---

6. Concerning the "passing away" of planets, President Joseph Fielding Smith explained that this does not indicate that planets die or disintegrate:
"HOW EARTHS PASS AWAY. This passing away does not mean that earths grow old and die, becoming cold, lifeless bodies, wandering through space, perhaps to disintegrate, be broken up and in some unknown manner be recreated, by some natural force working on the energy in the universe. We have every reason to believe that the passing away of an earth simply means that it will undergo, or has undergone, the same definite course which is destined for our earth, and the Lord has made that perfectly clear. This earth is a living body. It is true to the law given it. It was created to become a celestial body and the abode for celestial beings" (D&C 88:17–26, Isa. 51:6–7; Ps. 102:25–26 [*Doctrines of Salvation*, Vol. 1, 72]).

through His Son, and fills the immensity of the created universe. It specifically fills the sun, the moon, and all of the trillions of stars, in that it is *in* the sun, the moon, and the stars, and that it is the source of the light which they radiate, and is the very power by which they were created. It's a lot to comprehend, but read with me.

> This Comforter is the promise which I give unto you of eternal life, even the glory of the celestial kingdom; Which glory is that of the church of the Firstborn, even of God, the holiest of all, through Jesus Christ his Son—He that ascended up on high, as also he descended below all things, in that he comprehended all things, that he might be in all and through all things, the light of truth; Which truth shineth. This is the light of Christ. As also he is in the sun, and the light of the sun, and the power thereof by which it was made. As also he is in the moon, and is the light of the moon, and the power thereof by which it was made; As also the light of the stars, and the power thereof by which they were made; And the earth also, and the power thereof, even the earth upon which you stand. And the light which shineth, which giveth you light, is through him who enlighteneth your eyes, which is the same light that quickeneth your understandings. (D&C 88:4–11)

We note that Jesus Christ is the medium through which the Father creates and fills all things with life and light (see Hebrews 1:2). The scripture expressly tells us that the Father "is in the bosom of eternity, who is in the midst of all things." These are not just passive words of praise and honor. These are descriptions of who God is, where He is, and what He does. To a limited extent, they are also a description of *how* He does them. Now let's look at the remainder of the passage, which is extremely instructive on the manner of creation: "Which light proceedeth forth from the presence of God to fill the immensity of space—The light which is in all things, which giveth life to all things, which is the law by which all things are governed, even the power of God who sitteth upon his throne, who is in the bosom of eternity, who is in the midst of all things" (D&C 88:12–13). Is God sharing with us His grand secret of creation and governance? Is there a light that emanates from God that creates the matter of the universe and governs its functionality? Are all universal laws encoded in this light? God is very specific in telling us that the Light of Christ, which is an aspect of His Spirit, which we often read that emanates from the personage of God and gives light, revelation, intuition, and understanding to all life—and not just those who receive the more specific gift of the Holy Ghost—is the medium by which He governs and gives form and function. The Light of Christ emanates from God and "fills the immensity of space" and gives life, and gives substance and order (governs all things). We will discuss the nature of this light below, but for now, it is important to understand that it is by a form of light that God extends His influence and power throughout the universe (see John 1:5; 8:12).

The scriptures provide a very interesting insight into the principle of how this eternal light emanates from God. According to God, He speaks the word, and the light emanates and organizes unorganized matter (see Hebrews 11:3). First, as we have already read, Jesus Christ is the medium through which the light, called by God the Light of Christ, is delivered to every particle and reach of the universe. Christ, the first creation of God the Father and the Firstborn of the Father—as such, a God in His own right—is called "The Word" by the prophets. "In the beginning was the Word, and the Word was with God, and the Word was God. The same was in the beginning with God. All things were made by him; and without him was not any thing made that was made. In him was life; and the life was the light of men. And the light shineth in darkness; and the darkness comprehended it not" (John 1:1–5). This Word (through the light or medium of Jesus Christ) is spoken (broadcast) by the Eternal Father, and the Light (creative—organizing—governing wave) emanates throughout the expanse of the universe, permeating and giving life and structure to every particle and object. "And by the word of my power, have I created them, which is mine Only Begotten Son, who is full of grace and truth. And worlds without number have I created; and I also created them for mine own purpose; and by the Son I created them, which is mine Only Begotten" (Moses 1:32–33).

The Nephite prophets likewise understood this principle, as exemplified in this explanation of God's power and ability to control the earth and His other creations. "For behold, by the power of his word man came upon the face of the earth, which earth was created by the power of his word. Wherefore, if God being able to speak and the world was, and to speak and man was created, O then, why not able to command the earth, or the workmanship of his hands upon the face of it, according to his will and pleasure?" (Jacob 4:9). God utilizes the same language in revelation to the Prophet Joseph Smith: "All things whatsoever I have created by the word of my power, which is the power of my Spirit. For by the power of my Spirit created I them; yea, all things both spiritual and temporal—First spiritual, secondly temporal, which is the beginning of my work; and again, first temporal, and secondly spiritual, which is the last of my work" (D&C 29:30–32).

This power of God, to speak the word and organize and govern all of His creations, both animate and inanimate, spiritual and matter, is the true answer to our questions about creation and organization—although it still doesn't really tell us how it all began in the very, very beginning of existence. What the scriptures tell us is that in the beginning was God, our Eternal Father. God declares, "I am that I am." He introduces Himself thus: "Behold, and hearken unto the voice of him who has all power, who is from everlasting to everlasting, even Alpha and Omega, the beginning and the end" (D&C 29:30–32). And similarly, the Prophet says of Him, "By these things we know that there is a God in heaven, who is infinite and eternal, from everlasting to everlasting the same unchangeable God, the framer of heaven and earth, and all things which are in them" (D&C 20:17).

ETERNAL NATURE OF ELEMENT

The Prophet Joseph Smith received important information from the Lord about the eternal nature of the elements and the relationship of matter and spirit. He said: "The elements are eternal, and spirit and element, inseparably connected, receive a fulness of joy" (D&C 93:33). He also clarifies, "There is no such thing as immaterial matter. All spirit is matter, but it is more fine or pure, and can only be discerned by purer eyes; We cannot see it; but when our bodies are purified we shall see that it is all matter" (D&C 131:7–8). Therefore, our bodies are made of matter, and our spirits are made of matter—eternal elements.[7] Obviously, gold atoms are much heavier than hydrogen, which is much heavier than spirit element, but all are matter just the same. Joseph Smith explained, "The spirit of man is not a created being; it existed from eternity, and will exist to eternity. Anything created cannot be eternal; and earth, water, etc., had their existence in an elementary state, from eternity."[8]

Speaking on the concept of *creatio ex nihilo*, Joseph Smith explained: "Now, the word create does not mean to create out of nothing; it means to organize; the same as a man would organize materials and build a ship. Hence, we infer that God had materials to organize the world out of chaos-chaotic matter, which is element. Element had an existence from the time [God] had. The pure principles of element are principles which can never be destroyed; they may be organized and reorganized, but not destroyed. They had no beginning and can have no end."[9]

Jesus Christ tells us something of the eternal nature of God, Himself, humans, and the elements: "I was in the beginning with the Father, and am the Firstborn. . . . Ye were also in the beginning with the Father; that which is Spirit, even the Spirit of truth; . . . He that keepeth his commandments receiveth truth and light, until he is glorified in truth and knoweth all things" (D&C 93:21–23, 28). God pre-existed all things, and Jesus Christ, the Firstborn Son of God, was in the beginning with the Father. But not just them—all people were in the beginning with them. In what form we will discuss below, but the importance of the eternal nature of humans should never be

---

7. Parley P. Pratt, an early Apostle, wrote, "Matter and spirit are the two great principles of all existence. Everything animate and inanimate is composed of one or the other, or both of these eternal principles. Matter and spirit are of equal duration; both are self-existent, they never began to exist, and they never can be annihilated. Matter as well as spirit is eternal, uncreated, self existing. However infinite the variety of its changes, forms and shapes; eternity is inscribed in indelible characters on every particle" (*History of the Church* 4:55).

8. *History of the Church*, 3:387.
9. *History of the Church*, 6:308–309.

underestimated. The relationship of the elements and light (and truth), both of eternal existence, is further elucidated in the following passages. Herein, we learn of the very important nature of light upon element and how the more light we receive from the source, God, the higher caliber of eternal being we can become. "Man was also in the beginning with God. Intelligence, or the light of truth, was not created or made, neither indeed can be. All truth is independent in that sphere in which God has placed it, to act for itself, as all intelligence also; otherwise there is no existence. . . . For man is spirit. The elements are eternal, and spirit and element, inseparably connected, receive a fulness of joy; And when separated, man cannot receive a fulness of joy. The elements are the tabernacle of God; yea, man is the tabernacle of God, even temples; and whatsoever temple is defiled, God shall destroy that temple. The glory of God is intelligence, or, in other words, light and truth" (D&C 93:29–36).

Adding to our understanding of these principles, Elder Orson Pratt of the Quorum of the Twelve Apostles commented: "The materials out of which this earth was formed, are just as eternal as the materials of the glorious personage of the Lord himself. . . . This being, when he formed the earth, did not form it out of something that had no existence, but he formed it out of materials that had an existence from all eternity: they never had a beginning, neither will one particle of substance now in existence ever have an end. There are just as many particles now as there were at any previous period of duration, and will be while eternity lasts. Substance had no beginning; … the earth was formed out of eternal materials, and it was made to be inhabited and God peopled it with creatures of his own formation."[10]

LET THERE BE LIGHT, AND MATTER

We have been considering the relationship of light, elements, and spirit, and how light emanates from God to give life, substance, structure, and order to the universe. Since my first publication on this subject nearly thirty years ago, scientists have made major discoveries in

---

10. *Journal of Discourses*, 19:41.

the field of particle physics. The Higgs Field was first theorized, then demonstrated to exist through decades of experimentation using the Large Hadron Collider (LHC) at CERN near Geneva, Switzerland. The Higgs Field was theorized to permeate space and excite subparticles into a structure giving them mass. In 2013 the Higgs boson, an elementary particle in the Standard Model of particle physics produced by the quantum excitation of the Higgs field was successfully produced, proving the theory true. On December 10, 2013, two of the physicists, Peter Higgs and François Englert, were awarded the Nobel Prize in physics for their theoretical predictions. Interestingly, many have come to call the Higgs Boson the "God Particle."

God is the Supreme Creator, the First and the Last, and the Author of all that exists. We look around and see the world, all living things, the solar systems and galaxies, and realize that they are marvelous and inexpressibly impressive. They are all living in harmony and balance, at all levels—from the subatomic particle/wave[11] to the atom, molecule, and all the way up to the super galaxy. Like children, we are only now beginning to understand the vastness and complexity of the universe, and the vibrational resonance "dance" that all matter and energy share. We are in the kindergarten of quantum physics and quantum mechanics, the next level of scientific knowledge that underlies what we believed we knew about the structure and functionality of the universe.

At the most basic level, we have long understood that energy, in its many forms, is waves at various frequencies. This includes white

---

11. There have been extremely interesting observations made on the subject of the nature of light—whether it is a wave or a particle. Scientists have argued back and forth for hundreds of years, because at different times and under different circumstances, it sometimes acts like a wave and sometimes like a particle—but at all times as if it is imbued with its own reality-possibilities/trajectory decision-making intelligence. The field of quantum physics was essentially born when it was discovered that during scientific single particle double slit experiments, light would act as a wave until it was observed by a human, and then it would begin to act like a particle. Yes, when under conscious observation, electrons are "forced" to behave like particles and not like waves. This 100 percent repeatable experiment shocked scientists and opened profound and distressing scientific dialogs about human consciousness and its ability to control energy and the elements.

light, infrared light, heat, sound, and so on. Mass, or matter, on the other hand, we have thought to be made up of particles—atoms of elements that we find on the periodic table. As we have seen, God has revealed that light (traditionally thought of as a wave of energy) actually interacts or bonds with the elements, in ways that are unclear to us—including scientists. God declares that He is Light. What type of light? We don't know. In fact, there are many types of light—an infinite number of types—all of which are determined or categorized by the frequency of their vibrational or resonance rate and the depth of the wave. In addition to white light and the others we just mentioned, there are x-rays, gamma rays, microwaves, and so on. In fact, there are billions of types of light, each just slightly different because its frequency (vibrational rate or resonance) is slightly varied from the next. They are all energy (what we have always thought of as waves), but we have come to understand that some waves interact with particles, and in some instances, provide their structure and tangibility. What I mean by this is that certain light frequencies are known to interact with various types of atoms—hydrogen, helium, carbon, oxygen, and in fact, every atom on the periodic table. Light waves are understood to interact with the atoms to stabilize the electron cloud shapes around atoms. In other words, light interacts with elements to produce solid matter—the universal glue that holds molecules together.

Now, when we read that creation begins with, "Let there be light," it certainly takes on greater importance in our understanding of the structure of the universe. "Let there be light" is the English translation of the Hebrew יְהִי אוֹר (yehi ʿor). The Hebrew phrase יְהִי אוֹר consists of two words; יְהִי (yəhî) is the third-person masculine singular jussive form of "to exist," and אוֹר (ʾôr) means "light." When God speaks the Word, as we have discussed above, and the Light of Christ is shined or broadcast throughout the immensity of existence, the Light interacts with the atoms (unorganized matter or element) and actually stabilizes the eternal elements, and gives them shape and substance, thereby literally creating mass throughout the universe. Whether the emptiness of space or the center of a red giant star, it is all the same from God's viewpoint, because as He declares, "There is no space in the which there is no kingdom; and there is no kingdom in which there is no space, either a greater or a lesser kingdom" (D&C 88:37). All locations throughout the universe are governed by the Light of Christ that emanates from God, giving shape, form and substance to the elements and the cosmos. "And unto every kingdom is given a law; and unto every law there are certain bounds also and conditions" (D&C 88:38)

When the Light had been broadcast from the Father of Lights, and filled the great expanse, He declares, "And I, God, saw the light; and that light was good" (Moses 2:4; see also Genesis 1:4). Yes, the light was good. Not because we could see. It was good because it gave order to the cosmos and structure to the elements of the universe, as well as life to the animate creations of God, and understanding to mankind everywhere. "And the light which shineth, which giveth you light, is through him who enlighteneth your eyes, which is the same light that quickeneth your understandings; Which light proceedeth forth from the presence of God to fill the immensity of space—The light which is in all things, which giveth life to all things, which is the law by which all things are governed, even the power of God who sitteth upon his throne, who is in the bosom of eternity, who is in the midst of all things" (D&C 88:11–13). What do we know about this light that emanates from the presence of God and fills the universe and organizes (gives structure to) the elements? Is this light related to the Higgs field we discussed above? We don't know the light's vibrational rate. We don't know anything other than what the scriptures and prophets have told us—that it is, and that it successfully fills the universe and permeates all things that are. We know that it is a Comforter to humans and communicates knowledge and wisdom to the souls of men and women. We know that it is a direct link to God, the Father. We know that it emanates through the power and persona of the Son of God. Consider with me the deeper meaning of the concepts of light, truth and spirit in the following three revelations from the Lord in light of our expanded understanding of the Light of Christ.

> He comprehended all things, that he might be in all and through all things, the light of truth; Which truth shineth. This is the light of Christ. As also he is in the sun, and the light of the sun, and the power thereof by which it was made. (D&C 88:6–7)

For the word of the Lord is truth, and whatsoever is truth is light, and whatsoever is light is Spirit, even the Spirit of Jesus Christ. And the Spirit giveth light to every man that cometh into the world; and the Spirit enlighteneth every man through the world, that hearkeneth to the voice of the Spirit. (D&C 84:45–46)

That which is of God is light; and he that receiveth light, and continueth in God, receiveth more light; and that light groweth brighter and brighter until the perfect day. . . Wherefore, he is possessor of all things; for all things are subject unto him, both in heaven and on the earth, the life and the light, the Spirit and the power, sent forth by the will of the Father through Jesus Christ, his Son. (D&C 50:24–27)

Indeed, creation, order, and life emanate from the presence and person of God, our Eternal Father, through the medium of that holy light. Even the New Testament prophets understood His power and force in sustaining and governing every aspect of the universe. "He is before all things, and in him all things hold together" (Colossians 1:17). "Hold together" is a beautiful expression of the principle of divine creation. Also, seeing how Joseph Smith was so attuned to these high principles, vindicated by modern science, provides an unambiguous witness of his divine calling.

STRUCTURE OF OUR UNIVERSE

We have come to understand the bulk configuration of the universe thus:

1. Our earth has a moon in its orbit, and is one of eight planets that orbit a star, which we call the Sun. This system of a star surrounded by planets is called a solar system. The solar system is held together by gravity, holding the moons in orbit around the planets, and the planets in orbit around stars.
2. Our solar system is one of approximately 100 billion solar systems that swirl in a spiral or elliptical galaxy. Gravity holds the 100 billion stars in place, and it is now thought that a giant

black hole resides at the center of our Milky Way galaxy, creating the gravitational pull on the swirling mass of stars.
3. Our galaxy *may* be one of many galaxies that swirl in a super galaxy or other super structure.
4. All of the galaxies throughout the immensity of space constitute our universe. We can see approximately 100 billion galaxies at this point in our technological ability.

When I first published on these subjects nearly thirty years ago, science had not yet confirmed the presence of any planets in orbit around stars outside of our own solar system. I predicted in that work, based on what the prophets have revealed about the composition and structure of the universe, that numerous planets would soon be discovered. Of course, that prediction was borne out, and as of this writing thousands of planets have been confirmed to exist outside of our solar system. Some scientists now believe that nearly every star has planets in its orbit.

There are other components to our universe than stars and planets. There are materials floating through space, like gas, dust, nebulae, meteor fields, lone comets, and so on, although the bulk of our universe is structured with the stars in galaxies formation, as far as we can see. We are told that the universe is expanding, rather rapidly, giving rise to the Big Bang theory, although the method of expansion does not seem to support the exploding universe model. Instead, the expansion appears to be occurring everywhere at once, in all directions, despite a general outward push from a central location. For a broader examination of this particular phenomenon, an appeal to "red shifting" and "expanding universe" will produce fascinating results. Scientists tell us that the universe is mainly space, with extremely large volumes of matter, plus extremely large volumes of what they term "dark matter." Dark matter, so called, is a substance hypothesized by some scientists to help solve the mathematical problems inherent in the Big Bang theory. The presence of dark matter causes me to think that perhaps the prophets understood all along in their attempts to articulate the existence of "matter unorganized."

The spaces between stars are vast. How vast? The nearest star to our own Sun is Proxima Centauri—a small, low-mass star located

4.2465 light-years from the Sun in the southern constellation of Centaurus. That 4.24 light-year distance represents the time it takes light to travel from Proxima Centauri to the Sun, or vice versa. That's 4.24 years, blasting through space at the blistering speed of light. Most stars are vastly farther away. How fast does light travel? We speak of it in terms of miles per second—186,000 miles per second, in fact. This means that light can travel entirely around the circumference of the earth about 7.5 times in a single second. How many miles per hour is that? It is 670,616,629 mph.[12] That's 670 million miles in a single hour. Multiply that by 24, and multiply that by 365. Now multiply that by 4.24, and you get the distance to Proxima Centauri. The distance to other stars can best be comprehended by a look at our galaxy—which is 100,000 light years across. The average distance between galaxies is about one million light years, making it a long trip, even at the speed of light, from one end of the known universe to the other. Yes, the light that we see from a star on the other side of our own galaxy left the star tens of thousands of years ago and is just arriving at our eyes. The stars from distant galaxies take much longer to arrive. In fact, many of the stars that we see in the night sky haven't existed for millions of years—but the light they emitted prior to their death is just now arriving.

Having said this, we are immediately discouraged at the hope of traveling to other planets outside of our own solar system. The sad truth is that even at the unattainable speed of light, most of the closest planets would require a trip of at least hundreds of years—if not thousands or tens of thousands or more. Is it possible for us to travel faster than the speed of light? Most scientists tell us no. The very laws of the universe make the prospect impossible. So then, how is it possible for earth to be visited by anyone not from here? This is precisely why most scientists adhere tenaciously to the view that even if there were intelligent beings living on other planets, it would be impossible for them to travel the vast distances across space to put on midnight displays in

---

12. Please always feel free to double-check my math. Anyone who has ever received a law firm billing statement knows that those trained in law often have substandard math skills.

our own skies—and they scoff at anyone who professes to have seen such a display.

Don't despair if you are a fan of interplanetary space flight and dream of the day when we might visit other worlds, or citizens of other worlds might visit us. We know that the physical "laws" of the universe as we currently understand them don't always apply—not under all circumstances. How do we know this? It is clear from the prophets that God, His Son, angels, and translated beings travel to this planet from those vast distances, and somewhat frequently. Even we ourselves traveled here from a great distance, to participate in our mortal sojourn on this planet. Before we consider how such travel might be accomplished, and how many beings might be traveling to earth to visit humanity, let us first consider what the prophets have shared with us concerning the structure and function of the universe.

Father Abraham discerned the structure, order, and composition of the universe by means of the Urim and Thummim—a device that allows prophets to obtain knowledge from God. In the following revelation given to the Prophet Joseph Smith, Abraham explains what he learned about the structure and function of our universe, making inquiries about it through the sacred device:

> And I, Abraham, had the Urim and Thummim, which the Lord my God had given unto me, in Ur of the Chaldees; And I saw the stars that they were very great, and that one of them was nearest unto the throne of God; and there were many great ones which were near unto it; And the Lord said unto me: These are the governing ones; and the name of the great one is Kolob, because it is near unto me, for I am the Lord thy God: I have set this one to govern all those which belong to the same order as that upon which thou standest. And the Lord said unto me, by the Urim and Thummim, that Kolob was after the manner of the Lord, according to its times and seasons in the revolutions thereof; that one revolution was a day unto the Lord, after his manner of reckoning, it being one thousand years according to the time appointed unto that whereon thou standest. This is the reckoning of the Lord's time, according to the reckoning of Kolob. (Abraham 3:1–4)

THE CREATION AND FUNCTION OF THE UNIVERSE

We have all heard this scripture quoted, and on those occasions, it was usually in the context of the time differences, if any, between earth and the place where God resides. What interests us more, for the purposes of this discussion, is the explanation about many great stars being located near where God resides, the greatest of all was nearest the residence of God. I have often heard detractors mention that members of the Church believe that God lives on a planet named Kolob. An important fact that we learn from this scriptural passage is that Kolob is not the celestial planet on which God dwells, nor a terrestrial planet on which Enoch dwells. Abraham is told that Kolob, the greatest star, is part of that group of stars near the residence of God and that those stars are "the governing ones." The Lord tells Abraham that Kolob is not only "nearest" unto God, clarifying that it is not God's abode, and Kolob is not a planet—it is a "Kokob, which is a star . . . the greatest of all the Kokaubeam," signifying stars. We can infer, however, that there are planets near Kolob: "And thus there shall be the reckoning of the time of one planet above another, until thou come nigh unto Kolob, which Kolob is after the reckoning of the Lord's time; which Kolob is set nigh unto the throne of God, to govern all those planets which belong to the same order as that upon which thou standest" (Abraham 3:9).

The amazing truth that we learn from this scripture is that Kolob is near the throne of God in the vicinity of several other great governing stars, but nonetheless, it "governs all those planets which belong to the same order as" Earth. Do you see the issue? Our traditional view of the universe tells us that planets, moons, stars, and galaxies are governed by the gravitational pull of nearby bodies, and possibly black holes. Proximity is essential to the traditional view of universal mechanics. This scripture informs us that earth is governed by Kolob, along with a number of other planets under the great star's control—that are not in proximity to Kolob. In other words, Kolob governs Earth and other planets, although it is nowhere near them. When I first discussed this principle nearly thirty years ago, we had to take the truth of the revelation on pure faith, because it didn't make that much scientific sense at the time. Now, however, with the development of quantum theory, we are beginning to understand the principles associated with quantum entanglement—where we find particles (photons) being influenced by consciousness, and simultaneous effects on paired particles that are nowhere in the vicinity of one another.

CLASSES OR CLUSTERS?

In rendering "translations" of Facsimile No. 2 accompanying the Book of Abraham,[13] Joseph Smith revealed that there exists not only classification and hierarchy among the planets and stars, but that groups of stars and planets are organized into "orders," as indicated by the above passage. As the scripture clarifies, Earth, and all other planets of its order, are governed by Kolob. The word "order," of course, is not defined for us here, and we cannot tell from the scriptures if order indicates a class or family of planets or a general location of concentrically clustered groups of planets. Because some of the governing stars and planets could be located in the same general location—somewhat near God's celestial planet—we could infer that the former definition (classes) is descriptive of some of the orders. That definition doesn't work for planets and stars located far away from the governing ones, as in the case of Earth and Kolob.[14]

The fact that Earth belongs to Kolob's order indicates two things: there must be something uncommon or unique about the Earth because it belongs to what appears to be a distinguished order; and, there exist other orders, of which Earth is not a member.[15] We have little information regarding these observations other than to note that this earth enjoys the distinction of having the Savior live His life here. This Earth

---

13. We should note that Joseph Smith was a prophet, seer, and revelator, not an Egyptologist. He did not actually "translate" the Book of Abraham or the Facsimiles in the Book of Breathings, but instead utilized them as a catalyst to receive revelation. The Book of Abraham and the interpretations of the facsimiles are revelations received by the prophet. See *The Message of the Joseph Smith Papyri, an Egyptian Endowment*, chapter 1.
14. We should not entertain too seriously the possibility that our own Sun is Kolob and that we live near the seat of God. Kolob is the greatest of all of the governing stars, the greatest of all the Kokaubeam, and our own Sun is one of the smallest types of stars—therefore, disqualified from consideration.
15. Although the existence of this fact may seem obvious, its significance will vary with a definitive answer to the question, how do the "orders" of planets vary?

THE CREATION AND FUNCTION OF THE UNIVERSE

Facsimile 2, Book of Abraham

Figure 2 of Facsimile 2

is unique of all of God's Creations because of these truths.

Joseph Smith's translation of Figure 2 (Facsimile 2) supports the idea that the great governing stars and planets regulate groups of planet "classes" or "families" rather than concentric clusters: "Fig. 2. Stands next to Kolob, called by the Egyptians Oliblish, which is the next grand governing creation near to the celestial or the place where God resides; holding the key of power also, pertaining to other planets; as revealed from God to Abraham, as he offered sacrifice upon an altar, which he had built unto the Lord."

The global body Oliblish, which is next to Kolob and second closest to God, regulates a group of planets not associated with Earth. Many commentaries on the Book of Abraham appear to indicate that these governing systems are merely moons revolving around planets, planets revolving around suns, and solar systems revolving around larger systems, until we arrive at galaxies revolving around systems at the center of which are "the governing ones." The fact that the governing ones are clustered near the celestial planet of God and their disparate governed systems are far away from God's abode indicates that this is not the case—not entirely, anyway. In other words, the concentric nature of the commentaries' theoretic systems does not allow for the grouping of the governing ones near God's planet, with their governed systems being far away in space, not near one another. However, the concentric nature of our solar systems and galaxies provides for partial correctness of this traditional theory. The breakdown of the theory comes in the non-concentricity of the entire system of universal governance.

THE MEASUREMENT OF TIME

To aid in our understanding of the nature of the universe, Joseph Smith rendered translations of the hand-drawn facsimiles that accompanied the Book of Abraham. These translations bear strong witness of the divine calling of Joseph as a prophet, seer, and revelator, as well as provide us with valuable information regarding the order of the universe.

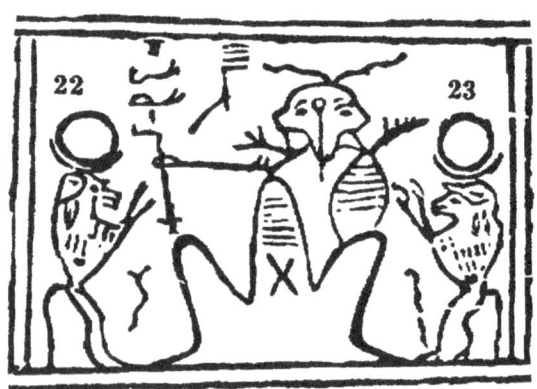

Figure 1 of Facsimile 2

THE CREATION AND FUNCTION OF THE UNIVERSE

The translation of Figure 1 of Facsimile 2 of the Book of Abraham confirms much of what has already been discussed in the scriptures treated above. "Fig. 1. Kolob, signifying the first creation, nearest to the celestial, or the residence of God. First in government, the last pertaining to the measurement of time. The measurement according to celestial time, which celestial time signifies one day to a cubit. One day in Kolob is equal to a thousand years according to the measurement of this earth, which is called by the Egyptians Jah-oh-eh."

The correlation between a "thousand-year celestial day" and a "cubit" is illustrated by Hugh Nibley in his explanation of Figure 4 (Facsimile 2): "The sky-vessel is called 'the ship of 1000 cubits long,' suggesting the designation of the above celestial Sokar-ship as 'also a numerical figure, in Egyptian signifying one thousand.' (Fac. 2, Fig. 4.)"

Figure 4 of Facsimile 2

The space/time relationship is elucidated in Nibley's statement, "Clement of Alexandria, an Egyptian, says that the ship symbol signifies 'that the Sun, taking its way through the sweet and moist air begets time, and hence is a symbol of time' (Strom., V, XL7, 41, 3; Hopfner, Fontes, p. 371)."[16] "Fig. 4. Answers to the Hebrew word Raukeeyang, signifying expanse, or the firmament of the heavens; also a numerical figure, in Egyptian signifying one thousand; answering to the measuring of the time of Oliblish, which is equal with Kolob in its revolution and in its measuring of time."

The translation of Figure 4 (Facsimile 2), the one-thousand-cubit solar bark signifying one thousand years of time to a day of time, informs us that Oliblish also measures time in like manner as Kolob. Unfortunately, we are no more enlightened concerning time relativity, but we are informed a little more regarding the structure of the universe.

---

16. *The Message of the Joseph Smith Papyri, an Egyptian Endowment*, 137–38.

I have sometimes listened while Gospel Doctrine instructors, and others, have assumed that there exists a difference in the comprehension of the passing of time between beings of these various classes of planets and stars, at, for instance, a "1 day:1,000 year" ratio—or other ratio, depending on the number of revolutions, and so on. A possible explanation of the principle is that the Kolob class (or classes) of planets and stars revolve at a much slower rate, and the passing of time is universally comprehended as one thousand years (as we comprehend them) per revolution.[17] However, the former explanation could be true—that is, "Earth class" beings could live or comprehend a thousand years in the same real time a "Kolob class" being lives or perceives a day. Different dimensions of existence could experience the passing of time at different rates.

All of this presupposes that God even experiences time (and space) in a way like man does. The truth is, we do not know the answers to these time/space questions, especially from God's viewpoint. Throughout the centuries, theologians, philosophers, and scientists have attempted to discern the relativity of time throughout the universe. We might assume that these are unrevealed mysteries and our preoccupation with them will prove unfruitful. We discuss these issues here, however, because they are raised in the UAP/alien visitation literature to a large extent. Again, before we can intelligently judge the validity of such "alien" assertions, we must garner all of the intelligence that God has revealed on the subject, no matter how little, as in this case. Some small amount of enlightenment may be had by H. Donl Peterson, who quotes Elder James E. Talmage and others in his book, *The Pearl of Great Price, A History and Commentary* (pp. 113–14). Therein, Elder Talmage and others briefly discuss measurements in units of time among the various orders and planets. The reader may find it enlightening. The representations are not definitive, however.

---

17. When the scriptures speak of revolutions of stars or planets, we lack information concerning whether "revolution" refers to the body revolving on its own axis (rotation) or orbiting around another star or planet. This is made apparent from Joseph Smith's translation of Figure 5 of Facsimile No. 2, discussed below.

THE CREATION AND FUNCTION OF THE UNIVERSE

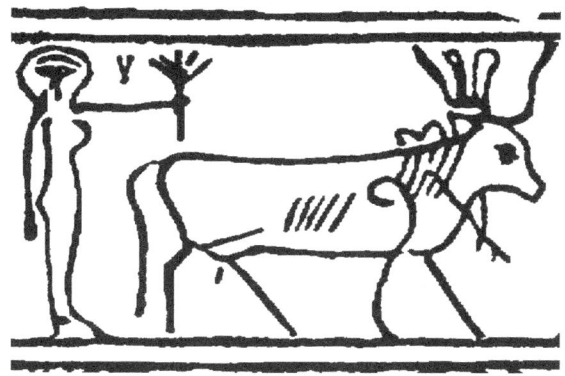

Figure 5 of Facsimile 2

HOW THE "GOVERNING ONES" GOVERN

The translation of Figure 5 is possibly the most interesting and confusing of all of the explanations of Facsimile 2 because it appears to be rooted in quantum physics and mechanics.

It appears to teach us concerning the organization of governing stars and planets and their governed groups. "Fig. 5. Is called in Egyptian Ensih-go-on-dosh; this is one of the governing planets also, and is said by the Egyptians to be the Sun, and to borrow its light from Kolob through the medium of Kae-e-vanrash, which is the grand Key, or, in other words, the governing power, which governs fifteen other fixed planets or stars, as also Floeese or the Moon, the Earth and the Sun in their annual revolutions. This planet receives its power through the medium of Kli-flos-is-es, or Hah-ko-kau-beam, the stars represented by numbers 22 and 23, receiving light from the revolutions of Kolob."

Figure 5 is said to represent Ensih-go-on-dosh, a governing "planet," defined as a "star." This instructs us that the words "star" and "planet" are sometimes used interchangeably to signify "star." The Egyptians believe it to be the Sun, although we receive no specific endorsement of their belief. The translation further informs us that Ensih-go-on-dosh, or possibly the Sun, "borrows" its light from Kolob, through a governing power or medium called Kae-e-vanrash. The structure of the sentence implies that this Kae-e-vanrash "governs fifteen other fixed planets or stars," among which are our own Sun, Earth, and Moon.

The last principle we learn from Figure 5 is that the Sun (Ensih-go-on-dosh) receives its light indirectly from Kolob, through Kli-flos-is-es or Hah-ko-kau-beam (note the plural suffix "beam"), either a star with two names, or two distinct stars, one of which is the intermediate transferor of light and power. As we said, however the medium operates, it is interesting to know, though modern science might not accept the principle, that these orders of stars from the governing to the governed are linked in a way that power and energy are circuited through them from the greater to the lesser, regardless of their relative position in space or proximity.

OTHER DIMENSIONS OF EXISTENCE

Are there other dimensions of existence outside of our own telestial plane? We know something about the vibrational rates of light (energy) and element (matter, or mass). We know that light combines with "matter unorganized" to stabilize it and give it substance and form, and combined they vibrate at a given frequency. For millennia prophets have attempted to explain how God, angels, and spirits live in the same universe that we do but appear to exist in a "dimension" different than our own. One of my favorite experiences from the Old Testament is when the prophet Elisha was assisting the king of Israel in his battle with the king of Syria, warning his king through the gift of prophecy. When the king of Syria learned about Elisha's gifts, he set out to destroy him and sent his army to encompass the city and take Elisha. Elisha's servant was quite frightened, but Elisha told him not to fear. "Therefore sent he thither horses, and chariots, and a great host: and they came by night, and compassed the city about. And when the servant of the man of God was risen early, and gone forth, behold, an host compassed the city both with horses and chariots. And his servant said unto him, Alas, my master! how shall we do? And he answered, Fear not: for they that be with us are more than they that be with them. And Elisha prayed, and said, Lord, I pray thee, open his eyes, that he may see. And the Lord opened the eyes of the young man; and he saw: and, behold, the mountain was full of horses and chariots of fire round about Elisha" (2 Kings 6:14–17).

THE CREATION AND FUNCTION OF THE UNIVERSE

First, it is comforting beyond words to receive another testimonial that the Lord is with His faithful servants and will support and uphold them as they serve Him. In this case, the servant of Elisha, like most of us, could not see the help that had been provided by a loving Father in Heaven. The prophet Elisha was well aware of God's deliverance, however, and seeing with his spiritual eyes, he knew that there was no contest between the army of Syria and the army of God. To alleviate the fear of his servant, Elisha asked God to open his servant's eyes, that he too could view what Elisha saw. "And the Lord opened the eyes of the young man; and he saw." We aren't sure what process was involved in the opening of the man's eyes, but God was quite willing to "open" them, through whatever mechanism is involved in changing telestial matter to comprehend terrestrial or celestial matter—or spiritual element. We certainly have numerous examples of this same principle being employed during the Latter-day Restoration of All Things, a few of which we discuss below.

Departed people, for instance, live in the spirit world. Is that the same level of existence as the angels or God? What we mean by this is, do the departed spirits that dwell in the spirit world have the ability to view angelic visitors in their natural state, or do departed spirits, like us, need to be "changed" to see the angelic messenger?

We have referred to the spirits (perhaps wave) of mankind, which occupy the same space as our material (particle) world and bodies, and are separated at the time of death—at which time the mortal body is separated and decays, but the spirit body continues to exist intact, perhaps in another dimension. Or, is it in our own dimension, but they vibrate at a rate that is higher or lower than our own? The prophets have described the spirit world, which occupies the same space as our own world, and we cannot readily interact with those who pass on to that dimension of existence. These things were utter foolishness to scientists, of course—until they began to detect and mathematically posit that different objects of different material types may indeed occupy the same space at the same time—oblivious to one another.

I'm not suggesting that our current understanding of quantum science is sufficient to prove the existence of the spirit world, but I find it very interesting in our discussion of alternate dimensions of existence based on resonance, or frequency of vibrational rates, that the word used by the prophets and apostles to describe being transported from this earthly plane to another plane of existence is "quickened." "For Christ also hath once suffered for sins, the just [Christ] for the unjust [humanity], that he might bring us to God, being put to death in the flesh, but quickened by the Spirit: By which also he went and preached unto the spirits in prison [spirit world]; who formerly were disobedient, when once the Divine longsuffering waited in the days of Noah" (1 Peter 3:18). It is more than interesting that the apostle explained to us the process by which Christ went to those who had dwelled in the spirit world since they died in the Great Flood. He could have said that Christ was killed and His spirit remained alive, and He went to visit those in the spirit world. He didn't say that. He was clear that Christ's spirit was "quickened by the Spirit" and taken into the spirit world.

For those who may think that we are focusing too closely on a subject that doesn't merit the study, allow me to share that while I was a missionary in Northern Italy, my companion and I came across a couple of young priests from the Greek Orthodox Church. Because they were bright and kind to us, I asked if they would do me a favor and explain a scripture to me—because I didn't speak or read Greek. They were happy to accommodate me. I opened my Italian Bible and read the above scripture. Then I asked them to explain to me the passage "being put to death in the flesh, but quickened by the Spirit: By which also he went and preached unto the spirits in prison." They opened their Greek Bibles and followed along. At first, they just confirmed that what I read was accurate. Then I asked about the meaning behind the terms and concepts like "quickened by the Spirit" and "preached unto the spirits in prison." They immediately began to see, for the first time in their careers, that this was a very profound subject. We talked for half an hour, and they wrote out the actual translation of the passages for me so I would always have them—something that had taken on significant meaning for them as our discussion progressed. Christ, in His state of being separated from His earthly tabernacle, being quickened by the Spirit, which was unmistakably a quickening spirit external to Himself, was amazing to them. The fact that in that state He was sent to preach the gospel message of redemption to the millions who had been disobedient and died in the waters of the Great Flood was not lost on them in the least. It was profound. It *is* profound.

Did the quickening of Christ by the Spirit (Light or Intelligence) change His nature or spiritual constitution and prepare Him to enter and interact with a different plane of existence and its inhabitants? In science and religion, we keep coming across the subject of different dimensions of existence that seem to share the same space. To the extent it is a true principle, let's first consider what dimensions are, in theory at least. Dimensions can be thought of as expanded units of existence. For instance, a two-dimensional world would be flat—like a television screen. If life were to exist in that flat 2-D world, 2-D people would need to navigate around each other and objects much like the old Pacman. If we expand that world, inflating it, we would have a snapshot of a 3-D world. It is easy to envision such a world, because it is essentially like our own. However, our third-dimension world is expanded by the presence of time, giving it fluidity. This time-expanded 3-D world is actually a fourth-dimensional world. If there is a fifth-dimensional world, we would need to construct a theoretical model to enable us to envision what it would be like. In the same way a 1-D world is expanded or inflated into a flat 2-D world, and a two-dimensional world is expanded or inflated into a 3-D world, which is expanded or inflated by time to produce a fourth-dimensional world—we must envisage an expanded or inflated 4-D world, producing a 5-D world.

Can we, in our fourth-dimensional world, see or interact with those who are of a fifth-dimensional world or sixth dimensional world? The answer is yes—but in a limited manner, absent some sort of linking or bridging ability. Let's think about the reasons for this. In a novella[18] by Edwin Abbott, he posits citizens of a 1-D world, a 2-D world, and a 3-D world, and how travel and interaction between the three worlds is perceived by the visitor and the visited. In practical terms, if an ant (3-D being) were to visit the 2-D world, a 2-D world citizen would only observe the point where the ant intersects with the 2-D world—

---

18. Edwin Abbott, *Flatland: A Romance of Many Dimensions* (London: Seeley & Co.), 1884.

perhaps a thin 2-D layer of its six tiny feet. Although the 3-D ant can perceive nearly all of the 2-D world and its citizens, the 2-D citizens perceive only a disturbing intrusion of six unfamiliar "things" into their world. Any attempts to communicate with members of the 2-D world would be entirely indecipherable to the 2-D citizens, and the point of communication would be unlocatable in their estimation. Think how it would appear if a fifth-dimensional personage were to present himself to a regular man, going about his business in our world. The location and composition of the 5-D personage would be indecipherable to the man. Attempts to communicate would seem surreal, and it would seem to the man that the communication was originating from his own thoughts. Keep this in mind.

Of course, even though the possibility of the existence of other dimensions may very well explain the existence of the spirit world, it may be overreaching for the purposes of our discussion. In fact, spirits are made up of a very fine element that cannot be seen by the heavier elements of the human eye. Perhaps the spirit world is simply our own fourth-dimensional world, where spirits walk among us but we simply can't see them—like nitrogen or oxygen. Or, perhaps we need a different type of light source to observe them with our eyes—much like we use infrared light to "see" heat emanating from animals or humans in the dark of night. These are only thoughts—not solid science or doctrine. Personally, I believe the spirit world is in another dimension.

The prophets have been clear in their teachings about the location of the spirits of men and women who leave their mortal body behind and enter the world of spirits. Following are some enlightening statements by President Brigham Young. "Here the inquiry will naturally arise, when our spirits leave our bodies where do they go to? . . . They do not pass out of the organization of this earth on which we live. . . . But where is the spirit world? It is incorporated within this celestial system. Can you see it with your natural eyes? No. Can you see spirits in this room? No. Suppose the Lord should touch your eyes that you might see, could you then see the spirits? Yes, as plainly as you now see bodies, as did the servant of Elijah. If the Lord would permit it, and it was His will that it should be done, you could see the spirits that have departed from this world, as plainly as you now see bodies with your natural eyes."[19]

President Young also taught, "When you lay down this tabernacle, where are you going? Into the spiritual world. . . . Where is the spirit world? It is right here. Do the good and evil spirits go together? Yes, they do."[20] Parley P. Pratt, a close associate of the Prophet Joseph Smith, similarly taught that the spirit world occupies the same space as our temporal world. It is instructive, I believe, in that he appears to indicate that there is more of a difference in the two worlds than mere vibrational level or weight of element—but there are multiple spheres of existence as well as a "veil" that separates the two worlds. "As to its [the spirit world] location, it is here on the very planet where we were born; or, in other words, the earth and other planets of a like sphere, have their inward or spiritual spheres, as well as their outward, or temporal. The one is peopled by temporal tabernacles, and the other by spirits. A vail is drawn between the one sphere and the other, whereby all the objects in the spiritual sphere are rendered invisible to those in the temporal."[21] This appears to be different dimensions.

Harold B. Lee, a prophet of the modern era, affirms the teachings of earlier brethren on the location of the world of spirits: "Where is the spirit world? Is it away up in the heavens? That isn't what the scriptures and our brethren explain. They have told us the spirit world is right here round about us, and the only spirits who can live here are those who are assigned to fill their missions here on earth. This is the spirit world. And if our eyes could be opened we could see those who have departed from us—a father, mother, brother, a sister, a child."[22] What we learn from these explanations of the nature and location of the spirit world is that it exists in the same space as our own earth, but we cannot see it or interact with it without some sort of change occurring to our faculties. What sort of change might be necessary to enable us to see and hear into other realms? I

---

19. *Journal of Discourses,* 3:368.
20. Ibid., 3:369.
21. *Key to the Science of Theology,* 129–130.
22. *The Teachings of Harold B. Lee,* 58.

had a personal experience when I was a very young man, and it left me with many questions about the subject. I share that experience in a later chapter. I have also received the personal testimonies of others, some close family members, and close Church associates, one of whom gave me my patriarchal blessing. These received visitations from loved ones from beyond the veil. One observable characteristic of all of these experiences was that the observer was able to view the person or environment of the "other world" while still observing the objects and environment of our own world.

QUICKENED VIBRATIONAL RATE

As we saw above, there appears to be a quickening involved in the process of seeing or interacting with beings of a different composition or dimension. We know this is true for us to see God, or to withstand His holy presence: "The veil shall be rent and you shall see me and know that I am—not with the carnal neither natural mind, but with the spiritual. For no man has seen God at any time in the flesh, except quickened by the Spirit of God. Neither can any natural man abide the presence of God, neither after the carnal mind. Ye are not able to abide the presence of God now, neither the ministering of angels; wherefore, continue in patience until ye are perfected" (D&C 67:10–13). This passage says that not only do we need to be "quickened by the Spirit of God" to see God, but also to see angels. There are a number of additional instances of "quickening" in the scriptures as well, and they all indicate that God's power elevates men, in various stages of progression (see Romans 4:17; Romans 8:11; Ephesians 2:1; 1 Timothy 6:13; John 5:21; 1 Corinthians 15:45; John 6:63; and Romans 8:11).

It's not hard to see a pattern in these descriptions of transforming matter (particle + wave) to an elevated state of existence. The light (Spirit) of God quickens the mortal body (particle/wave) to elevate its existence or vibrational resonance to a higher level—perhaps a different dimension. I also find it interesting how the Apostle Paul described his experience as he was overcome by the Spirit of God and quickened to another plane during a revelation experience. He refers to himself in the third person. "I know a man in Christ who fourteen years ago was caught up to the third heaven. Whether it was in the body or out of the body I do not know—God knows. And I know that this man—whether in the body or apart from the body I do not know, but God knows—was caught up to paradise and heard inexpressible things, things that no one is permitted to tell" (2 Corinthians 12:2–4).

In this elevated state, while quickened by the Spirit, Paul could not perceive whether he was still part of his body or not. An understanding of this principle becomes important to us as we begin to examine interactions with beings who claim to be human, or non-human, or from other worlds. Which worlds? Some claim to be flesh and blood humans or humanoids from distant planets. Some are plainly insectoid or reptilian. Others claim to have evolved beyond the need of a physical body and float in the aether of the universe. Others appear to be extra-dimensional beings, entering our world through portals or small openings in the veil that separate us. Is there any truth to any of these assertions? Has God revealed anything about these other purported forms of life? We discuss all of the forms of life revealed to the prophets below to discern if there is room in God's created universe for such beings. What are we to make of highly advanced beings that look like praying mantises and have extremely high intellect but no compassion? Are these made in the image of God? Are they animals with high intellect? Are they genetic mutations—half human and half insect or reptile? Are they psychic projections from an unseen predator? Within the boundaries of knowledge that God has provided, many of these seem more like theater than the actual creations of God. Yet, we occasionally discover some unexpected fact—some surprising detail, as the veil is drawn back just enough to catch a glimpse of what may lay just on the other side, in a usually unseen world.

A GLIMPSE INTO ANOTHER DIMENSION

I was in the seventh grade, and we had just moved to a new town. There were two very pretty girls in my grade, Mary and Chris,[23] and they invited me to walk with them to the house of some boys from school. I knew the two boys in question and agreed to walk with the girls. As

---

23. The names have been changed for reasons of privacy.

we arrived at the house, we walked up the driveway that led to the back yard. The detached garage was on the right, and there was an open walkway to the left leading into the back yard. The boys were on the grass near a camping tent—the older A-frame canvas type. The boys greeted us, and we spoke for only a moment. They mentioned something about some beer they had brought out. The four of them headed toward the open front flaps of the tent and invited me to join them. I was somewhat apprehensive about it, assuming that they intended to engage in activities that were inappropriate for me, so I politely declined the invitation. The girls said they would see me the next day at an event I knew about, and told me goodbye as the four of them opened the flap on the tent and entered it. I said okay and turned and started to take a step toward the driveway to leave. I suddenly remembered that I couldn't attend the event the next day because of something else I had planned, and decided to just pop my head into the tent and tell them about it so they wouldn't think I had stood them up the next day.

I had just planted my foot and taken only a single step away at that point, so I stopped and turned immediately and took a single step back toward the tent. Because the last of them had just disappeared through the front flap of the tent only one or two seconds earlier, I thought it would be okay to just open the flap and correct my statement—which had only been three or four seconds before that. I lifted the right flap and looked in, and was surprised that I couldn't see anyone inside. The tent was only about five feet across at the front, and I assumed it was about eight feet deep, so I gave my eyes a few seconds to adjust to the darkness inside because it was fairly bright outside the tent—a clear day with blue skies. Within a few seconds I could see what was inside the tent, and it was not what I had expected at all.

I could see far back into the tent, and it seemed to be hundreds of yards. There was a ravine, and I could hear water running down below as if there were a creek and small waterfall. Trees and plants covered the hills on the far side of the ravine, and it rose and went on for at least a few hundred yards as it rounded the top of a hill. It was a little dim in the sky above the treetops, as if it was evening there. I was shocked, to say the least, and wondered how it was possible to see a vast outdoors scene inside that small tent in the back yard. I looked up where I could see outside of the tent, and everything was perfectly normal. I saw the trees in the yard and the birds on the power lines. I looked around and saw how small the tent was, looked at the grass in the yard, saw a few toys that belonged to children, and I looked over at the house. Everything was perfectly normal. I looked back inside the tent, and the scene was exactly as it had been before. I stuck my head in farther this time, making sure I was actually seeing the panorama of a forested ravine and hillside.

For the first time I looked down, and I saw a young woman with very light skin and long dark hair sitting there, directly before me, facing away from me. She was unclothed, and her hair flowed over her shoulders and down her back beautifully. I was shocked. I had never seen anything like her before. I assumed it was Chris at first, because it actually resembled her, but that was impossible because I had seen Chris fully clothed and walking only ten seconds earlier. This young woman was the only person I could see now. No one else was around. There was no sign of my friends. I looked over her head at the forest[24] scene in the distance, hearing the sounds one would expect to hear in an active wooded area, and noted how it must be the end of the day in that world, because there was just a little evening light left. I looked back down at the girl in front of me and confirmed in my mind that she was there; real, alive, unclothed, and absolutely stunning.

I fully realized how impossible this all was, and sniffed the air to see if maybe there were drugs present and I was hallucinating. I only smelled fresh, humid air. I looked back outside at the well-lit afternoon blue sky, and again looked around at everything I could see—to make sure I was seeing normal things in their normal context. Not a single thing seemed out of place or abnormal in any way.

I looked back inside the tent and saw the young woman. Then I looked over at the other side of the ravine and took one last look, scanning the entire panoramic vista one last time, noting everything in great detail to ensure there was nothing vague about it. It was all there, in three-dimensional full

---

24. My first impression was that it was a forest; the type that was common in Oregon, my home. However, I noted unfamiliar trees and bushes, interspersed, that looked more like palms and tropical plants. It was much later in life that I saw forests with mixed foliage like this.

detail—the sights, sounds, smells, and humidity in the air. It was as real as it was impossible. I knew instinctively that whatever this was, it was not for me. I looked down at the girl again, and something told me that it wasn't Chris. There was something slightly abnormal about her. I focused a couple of seconds to determine what it might be and noticed her skin had a slight glow. It was beautiful but not normal.

I glanced back up to the other side of the ravine, then took a step back as I looked at the scene, and closed the flap of the tent. I looked around the back yard and surrounding areas again, taking everything in—the sky, the birds, the power poles and lines, the grass in the yard, the houses next door—checking my perception of reality. All of that had happened in only fifteen or twenty seconds, and it was all so fresh and confusing that I had no idea how to process it.

I turned and started to walk away from the tent, making a mental note of everything I saw, heard, and felt. I kept thinking that there must be something wrong with my perception—because what I had just viewed and experienced was absolutely impossible. I looked around at everything, checked everything, touched everything—and it was all perfectly normal. I looked back and saw that the tent seemed completely normal—just an old camping tent standing in the back yard where I had talked with my friends and seen them enter just thirty seconds earlier. The grass was normal, as well as the sky and lines between the poles and the houses beyond the fence. Normal, normal, normal. I touched the house as I walked by it, running my hands along the chipped paint on the wood siding, and I reached down and touched the water spigot on the side of the house next to the driveway. I scuffed my shoes on the cracked cement and looked up at the windows in the side of the house. When I got to the sidewalk and street, I touched the cars, feeling the smooth paint and chrome trim and the side mirrors, all to see if there was anything off about my perception. Nothing was abnormal at all.

The thought of the girls slipping me drugs of some kind came to mind, but I couldn't think of any way that could have happened—plus, there were no signs of any distorted perceptions outside of the tent. Everything seemed exactly as it should to me. I wasn't having a psychedelic trip. I touched everything I passed all the way home, and touched my own arms and hands and face, just to check my own reality.

When I arrived at my house about ten minutes later, I immediately told my mother everything that had just happened to me—and I told her before I did anything else, because I knew it was important that I make a record of the experience before I fell asleep that night so I could never wonder if it had been a dream. Later that afternoon I shared the highlights of my experience with my friend Alex, and he said that he believed me, as strange as it was, but didn't know what to make of it. The next morning, I asked my mother to repeat back what I had told her about my experience, and she told me everything I had shared. Every couple of years we have discussed the event, and she has always confirmed that she recalls it.

I have thought about that experience many times, wondering what it was and what it meant. Was there a message in it for me? There must be, because only a supernatural being could have created the extraordinary full panoramic glimpse into another dimension, the portal to which was there at the door of that tent. I saw my friends at school on Monday, and none of them said a word about me looking back into the tent after they disappeared through the front flaps. I had no doubt that they would have thought me mad had I mentioned what I experienced. I was sure that to them, they went into a very normal tent and drank and smoked and did whatever else kids of that time did inside a closed tent. Imagine my surprise decades later when I read the Harry Potter books and watched the movies, seeing how author J. K. Rowling had included tents whose inside dimensions were much larger than the outside. I wondered if she had experienced the same type of event but assumed she had only invented it as a literary fancy.

So . . . what did it mean? Who revealed that faraway land to me in such vivid detail inside the tiny confines of an old tent? No answer ever came. The only thing I ever knew for sure was that my instinct was correct—whatever that was, no matter how fascinating and alluring, it wasn't for me. I was correct to turn and leave immediately. I've always had the distinct feeling that if I had remained, it would have been the end of me somehow. Perhaps it was a baited trap—set by a predator. If so, it was a very powerful predator. I felt fortunate to be raised in a manner that taught me to walk away from such traps. If it was something else—a lesson to be learned—it escaped me. However, if nothing else, it taught me once and for all that there is much more to this life than we perceive with our five senses and that there truly is a very thin veil that separates us from other worlds. For me, that included the spirit world as well, providing me with a very solid "knowledge" of the absolute reality of the spiritual realm. That extended to angels and Christ and God—all of which I have been fortunate to never doubt.

Perhaps the dimensional portals we hear about are like the one I looked into. Windows into other realities or dimensions of existence. Doors that lead to other lands, through . . . what? . . . natural wormholes? I don't know how that could possibly function. The math says no. I only have my own experience to guide me, and even that gives me little usable information other than to share my concrete testimony that I have seen with my eyes and heard with my ears, and know that there are such portals. If that is of value, then it is my gift to the world. I have not had a similar experience since my youth, and I don't know who it was that facilitated my glimpse into another dimension.

DO MANY PLANETS EQUAL INTERPLANETARY TRAVEL?

The standard works leave no room to doubt that life exists on other planets. They make clear that many billions of planets, possibly many more, exist in our universe—planets peopled with children of our Heavenly Father, humans that appear essentially like us.[25] Regarding questions of interplanetary communication and travel, the standard works shed little light beyond that which is discussed above. However, latter-day prophets and apostles have commented on the topic and have assured us that such interplanetary communication and travel exists at some level or another. We know for sure that the possibilities of interplanetary communication and travel are greatly enhanced by the sheer number of planets populated by humans. Seeing in our own history that 100 years can elevate humans from horse and buggy to space flight, there is little difficulty in assuming that other planets, more righteous perhaps, have enjoyed longer bursts of technological revelation, thereby enabling interplanetary visitation. We examine these possibilities in the chapters that follow.

---

25. "And God said, Let us make man in our image, after our likeness" (Genesis 1:26).

CHAPTER 2

Life as We Know It

THE FIRST BEINGS

Who was present in the beginning of existence? Many of the personages were discussed in chapter 1. In this chapter we have a candid discussion about the life that fills the universe and those whom we know to exist in the eternities. Such a candid discussion may not be for the faint of heart, but let us maintain a spirit of profound respect as we make mention of some, whose existence or high calling are usually not mentioned in the spoken word.

God was the first of all. When asked, "Whom shall I say sent me?" God responded, "I am that I am."[1] As far as we are concerned, there was no one and nothing before God. In saying this, we must understand that the prophets have taught that God became a God through His efforts and intelligence and that He, as we, springs from a long line of beings much like ourselves—only exalted. However, in the "system" in which we live—whether that means galaxy, universe, or other system of creation or existence—He is the Grand Creator and

---

1. "I am that I am" is a common English translation of the Hebrew phrase אֶהְיֶה אֲשֶׁר אֶהְיֶה, 'ehyeh 'ăšer 'ehye—also "I am who I am," "I will become what I choose to become," "I am what I am," "I will be what I will be," "I create what(ever) I create," or "I am the Existing One."

Governor. He is the very first of all, and before Him there was nothing and no one. He spoke the Word, and creation came into being. He is the Father of Lights (see James 1:17; D&C 67:9). Likewise, God says of Himself, "Behold, and hearken unto the voice of him who has all power, who is from everlasting to everlasting, even Alpha and Omega, the beginning and the end"[2] (D&C 29:30–32).

This system began with God, the Eternal Father. The Prophet Joseph Smith declared by revelation, "By these things we know that there is a God in heaven, who is infinite and eternal, from everlasting to everlasting the same unchangeable God, the framer of heaven and earth, and all things which are in them" (D&C 20:17). The Prophet also taught that God, the Eternal Father in Heaven, does not stand alone in His divine position at the head of eternity but that He rules with His eternal companion at His side. Elder Dallin H. Oaks of the Quorum of the Twelve Apostles confirms, "Our theology begins with heavenly parents. Our highest aspiration is to be like them." In 1909, the First Presidency affirmed that "all men and women are in the similitude of the universal Father and Mother, and are literally the sons and daughters of Deity." Again, in 1995 the First Presidency and Quorum of the Twelve Apostles declared in "The Family: A Proclamation to the World," that "Each [person] is a beloved spirit son or daughter of heavenly parents, and, as such, each has a divine nature and destiny."

In addition to Heavenly Parents, the Firstborn Son was with God, the Father, from the very beginning. "In the beginning was the Word, and the Word was with God, and the Word was God. The same was in the beginning with God" (John 1:1–2). Jesus Christ Himself declares it: "And now, verily I say unto you, I was in the beginning with the Father, and am the Firstborn;" (D&C 93:21). Jesus Christ also reveals to us: "Thus saith the Lord your God, even Jesus Christ, the Great I Am, Alpha and Omega, the beginning and

---

2. We understand that these declarations are often delivered by the Son, when stating His Divine authority to speak for, and in behalf of the Father. Although they also apply to the Son in every regard, they are actually descriptions of the high and holy status of the Father.

the end, the same which looked upon the wide expanse of eternity, and all the seraphic hosts of heaven, before the world was made; The same which knoweth all things, for all things are present before mine eyes" (D&C 38:1–2). These scriptures tell us that Jesus Christ, the Great Jehovah,[3] was in the beginning, and was the Firstborn, and that He was a God—one of the Elohim (Eternal Gods of Creation and Dominion).[4] Of course, the fact that Jesus Christ is the Firstborn indicates that He was not actually in the very beginning with the Father—He was "born" at some point after the Father came into existence. However, we must realize that when speaking of those associated with God, including His eternal companion, and His Firstborn Son, and His countless spiritual offspring, the scriptures indicate that they all existed in one form or another from all eternity to all eternity. Before we discuss all of those, let us first remember that other member of the Godhead.

Something we also learn from revelation is that God was coupled with another Holy Being when He became Supreme. That personage is the third member of the Godhead—the Holy Spirit, also called the Holy Ghost. He is the Comforter who delivers light and communication from God and Jesus Christ through His own spiritual medium. We know very little about this personage and His beginnings or existence. All we know is aspects of His divine calling and that He has not received a body. We are unaware if He will ever take upon Himself a tangible, physical body of flesh and bones.

In addition to these three holy members of the Godhead and our Heavenly Mother, we were in the beginning with God—all of His spiritual offspring. The Lord tells us, "Ye were also in the beginning with the Father" (D&C 93:23). To a large extent, we have already discussed the eternal nature of spirit element and how all spirit offspring of God existed in some "unorganized" spiritual form before being "born" or begotten spiritually of Heavenly Parents. We know very little about this—only that it is. But Abraham informs us:

---

3. In Hebrew יְהֹוָה Yəhōwā, a popular vocalization of the Tetragrammaton יהוה (YHWH).
4. In the Hebrew Bible, Elohim (Hebrew: אֱלֹהִים) meaning Gods (plural).

Now the Lord had shown unto me, Abraham, the intelligences that were organized before the world was; and among all these there were many of the noble and great ones; And God saw these souls that they were good, and he stood in the midst of them, and he said: These I will make my rulers; for he stood among those that were spirits, and he saw that they were good; and he said unto me: Abraham, thou art one of them; thou wast chosen before thou wast born. And there stood one among them that was like unto God, and he said unto those who were with him: We will go down, for there is space there, and we will take of these materials, and we will make an earth whereon these may dwell. (Abraham 3:22–24; see also Abraham 4:1).

Abraham specifically calls the offspring of the Father "intelligences that were organized before the world was." These intelligences obviously existed in an unorganized form before they were organized. All intelligences were spirit element, as we have discussed above, in that primordial pre-organized state. In this sense, God, the Son, and all sons and daughters of God have existed eternally, from everlasting to everlasting. It is this organizing process that correlates to being "begotten" by the Father and Mother. Abraham also informs us that there were souls that were good, and some were even great and noble. The great and noble ones God said He would make His rulers. Rulers of what? We discuss this concept below. Jesus Christ confirms what we have read thus far and tells us something of the eternal nature of God the Father, Himself, and humans. "And now, verily I say unto you, I was in the beginning with the Father, and am the Firstborn; And all those who are begotten through me are partakers of the glory of the same, and are the church of the Firstborn. Ye were also in the beginning with the Father; that which is Spirit, even the Spirit of truth; . . . He that keepeth his commandments receiveth truth and light, until he is glorified in truth and knoweth all things" (D&C 93:21–23, 28).

Christ's first declaration confirms how long we have existed—that we were "in the beginning with the Father." We then note Christ's pronouncement that "all those who are begotten through me are partakers of the glory of the same." Partakers of what glory? The "same" refers to the previous statement, that He is "the

Firstborn." There is unspeakable glory in that holy office. Yet, we of His spiritual offspring who "are begotten through" Christ will partake of that same wondrous glory and become members of the "church of the Firstborn." What qualifies us to partake of that same glory? Jesus Christ reveals that if we keep His commandments, we will receive the necessary "light and truth." As we have learned in our discussion thus far, light and truth are not limited to receiving information—it is so much more than that. It is receiving the light that emanates from the Father, through the medium of the Light of Christ and of the Holy Ghost, and internalizing that light and allowing it to permeate our being and organize our souls into celestial beings. It is receiving the light, obeying His commandments (refraining from evil and affirmatively seeking to do good), receiving the required ordinances, seeking Him, and striving to be like Him that bring us to the "unity of the faith, and of the knowledge of the Son of God, unto a perfect man, unto the measure of the stature of the fulness of Christ" (Ephesians 4:13).

The following explains that the spiritual offspring of God are eternal, independent beings, filled with light and truth—like our Father. We act for ourselves, and either receive the light or reject the light, resulting in the eternal course we pursue.

> Man was also in the beginning with God. Intelligence, or the light of truth, was not created or made, neither indeed can be. All truth is independent in that sphere in which God has placed it, to act for itself, as all intelligence also; otherwise there is no existence. Behold, here is the agency of man, and here is the condemnation of man; because that which was from the beginning is plainly manifest unto them, and they receive not the light. And every man whose spirit receiveth not the light is under condemnation. For man is spirit. The elements are eternal, and spirit and element, inseparably connected, receive a fulness of joy; And when separated, man cannot receive a fulness of joy. . . The glory of God is intelligence, or, in other words, light and truth. (D&C 93:29–36)

Element and spirit element are eternal. They always existed, although in the beginning, in unorganized form, and God explains that combined element and spirit element receive joy. When combined "inseparably," they receive a "fulness of joy." True intelligence, which is the glory of God, is to receive and assimilate into our soul (combined spirit element and physical element) light and truth. We, through our souls (combined physical and spirit bodies), are the "tabernacle of God," or the "temple" where God dwells and is manifest.

On April 7, 1844, Joseph Smith took the podium to speak in what would be his last conference of the Church. He asked the 2,000 Saints in attendance for their "profound attention" and explained that he desired to speak about the spirits of men and women, due to the tragic loss of a good friend and Church member, King Follett. In the sermon, Joseph taught about our divine nature and eternal progression. He told the Church that "if men do not comprehend the character of God they do not comprehend themselves." Some in the audience had never heard the revelations about the eternal nature of humans or that God "was once as one of us." Joseph Smith taught that "all the spirits that God ever sent into the world" were "susceptible of enlargement," having the capacity to become like God their eternal Father in the eternities, and that the essential part of every person is coeternal with God, as we have discussed herein. This is when the entire Church learned the principle, "As man now is, God once was; as God now is, man may become." He explained, "God himself was once as we are now, and is an exalted man, and sits enthroned in yonder heavens! . . . It is the first principle of the Gospel to know for a certainty the Character of God, and to know that we may converse with him as one man converses with another, and that he was once a man like us; yea, that God himself, the Father of us all, dwelt on an earth, the same as Jesus Christ himself did."[5]

This eternal progression of the soul until it reaches celestialized perfection is further illustrated by the Prophet: "Whatever principle of intelligence we attain unto in this life, it will rise with us in the resurrection. And if a person gains more knowledge and intelligence in this life through his diligence and obedience than another, he will have so much the advantage in the world to come" (D&C 130:18–19).

---

5. *Teachings of the Prophet Joseph Smith*, 345–46.

THE FIRST ESTATE

Of all of the offspring of the Eternal Father, there were many great and noble ones, and many average ones, as well as many below average children. The great and noble are most likely those enumerated in positions of authority in the premortal world. "Where wast thou when I laid the foundations of the earth?" the Lord asked Job. "When the morning stars sang together, and all the sons of God shouted for joy?" (Job 38:4, 7). The Apostle Paul writes to the Ephesians, "For this cause I bow my knees unto the Father of our Lord Jesus Christ, Of whom the whole family in heaven and earth is named" (3:14–15). Yes, the family of God resided together in the heavens before the foundations of the earth were even laid, and most were gathering light in various quantities while others favored darkness. Those who were very faithful were given power and made leaders in the eternal order of the holy priesthood—granted authority to act in the name of God. In Alma we learn, "And this is the manner after which they were ordained—being called and prepared from the foundation of the world according to the foreknowledge of God, on account of their exceeding faith and good works; in the first place being left to choose good or evil; therefore they having chosen good, and exercising exceedingly great faith, are called with a holy calling, yea, with that holy calling which was prepared with, and according to, a preparatory redemption for such. . . . Thus they become high priests forever, after the order of the Son, the Only Begotten of the Father, who is without beginning of days or end of years, who is full of grace, equity, and truth (Alma 13:3–9).

In that premortal life, many of the sons and daughters of God were thus taught and prepared for futurity. "Even before they were born, they, with many others, received their first lessons in the world of spirits and were prepared to come forth in the due time of the Lord to labor in his vineyard for the salvation of the souls of men" (D&C 138:56). The Lord declares, "And they who keep their first estate [premortal existence] shall be added upon; and they who keep not their first estate shall not have glory in the same kingdom with those who keep their first estate; and they who keep their second estate [mortal existence] shall have glory added upon their heads for ever and ever" (Abraham 3:26).

First in order of the great and noble high priests after the Order of the Son of God was the archangel, Michael, whose name literally means one "who is like God." Michael was second in preeminence to the Firstborn. Of all that was done, it was Michael to whom the Father and the Son turned and gave instruction, and he caused it to be accomplished.[6] Bruce R. McConkie taught that Michael, "by his diligence and obedience there, as one of the spirit sons of God, he attained a stature and power second only to that of Christ, the Firstborn. None of all our Father's children equaled him in intelligence and might, save Jesus only."[7]

Joseph Smith revealed that Michael, as all of God's offspring who kept their first estate, or were faithful enough in the premortal life to merit coming to earth in mortality and gaining a temporal body, was the person Adam—the first man. He additionally taught of Michael, "The Priesthood was first given to Adam; he obtained the First Presidency, and held the keys of it from generation to generation. He obtained it in the Creation, before the world was formed, as in Gen. 1:26, 27, 28."[8]

---

6. We must bear in mind that Michael is assigned to this planet, Earth. Many of the "great and noble ones" enumerated in our scriptures likewise are recognizable as those who appertain to this earth. We do not know if the high and holy calling of Michael, and others, is universal in its application, or if it is limited to this earth and those assigned to it. We likewise do not understand the universality of matters discussed below pertaining to the presentation of the plan of salvation and exaltation, and the acceptance of it by two-thirds of the spirit children of God, and rejection of it by one-third of the heavenly hosts—whether those hosts were all of the spirit offspring of God assigned to billions of worlds like our own, or if the discussion is limited to those assigned to our single planet. We likewise do not know if Lucifer, who became Satan, is the leader of a universal rebellion of all of God's children, or only those assigned to our earth. For our purposes, we know that God says, "For behold, this is my work and my glory—to bring to pass the immortality and eternal life of man," (Moses 1:37–39), when speaking of the innumerable worlds that are populated with His children. The implication appears to be that percentages and forms remain somewhat constant throughout all of creation – and Satan passively excuses his deceptive and destructive behavior as being identical to that which is committed in other worlds.
7. McConkie, *Mormon Doctrine*, 16.
8. *Teachings of the Prophet Joseph Smith* [hereafter *Teachings*], 157)

Abraham was specifically told that he was one of the great and noble spirit sons of God in the premortal world. Others are mentioned, like Gabriel, who lived out his earthly sojourn as the faithful high priest and father of the post-diluvian world, Noah. Many spirit children of God served their fellow brothers and sisters in many capacities during their pre-earth existence. We learn through revelation that many of these spirits ministered to human mortals on earth in their capacity as messengers from God, or angels. Gabriel, for instance, after his death as the prophet Noah, ministered to Daniel (Daniel 8:16; 9:21); to Zacharias (Luke 1:11–19); and to Mary (Luke 1:26–38). We learn that ministering angels who come to the earth after their own death, but before their resurrection, are called "the spirits of just men made perfect" (D&C 129:3; Hebrews 12:23).

We learn through the scriptures and modern revelation that the spirits of men and women, as well as animals, greatly resemble their mortal bodies when they eventually take upon themselves these tabernacles of flesh. Joseph Smith explained, "That which is spiritual being in the likeness of that which is temporal; and that which is temporal in the likeness of that which is spiritual; the spirit of man in the likeness of his person, as also the spirit of the beast, and every other creature which God has created" (D&C 77:2). The premortal spirit Jesus Christ spoke to the Brother of Jared and explained that humans are created in the general image and likeness of Himself. "Seest thou that ye are created after mine own image? Yea, even all men were created in the beginning after mine own image. Behold, this body, which ye now behold, is the body of my spirit; and man have I created after the body of my spirit; and even as I appear unto thee to be in the spirit will I appear unto my people in the flesh" (Ether 3:15–16).

The disciples of the crucified Christ went to prepare His body for burial, only to find angels, whom they reported to look like men. "And entering into the sepulchre, they saw a young man sitting on the right side, clothed in a long white garment; and they were affrighted" (Mark 16:5). These angels often appeared in their glory, which radiates wondrous light. "And, behold, there was a great earthquake: for the angel of the Lord descended from heaven, and came and rolled back the stone from the door, and sat upon it. His countenance was like lightning, and his raiment white as snow" (Matthew 28:2–3).

GRAND COUNCIL IN HEAVEN

As part of our first estate, our Heavenly Father convened a grand council, and the Firstborn Son presented to all of God's spirit children the plan of salvation and exaltation.[9] Following His plan, Christ explained that we could become like our Heavenly Father. When Jesus Christ presented God's eternal plan to the waiting hosts of heaven, we were informed it would necessitate us leaving our heavenly home for a time and descending to earth in a telestial, fallen state. After living our lives, we would die and be resurrected, and if we fulfilled the plan successfully, we would receive all power in heaven and on earth and become exactly like our Heavenly Parents, begetting spirit children within our own eternal kingdoms (see D&C 132:19–20).

Under the plan, God would provide a planet for us where we would live and prove ourselves (see Abraham 3:24–26). He explained that we would walk by faith instead of knowledge during our earthly sojourn, so a veil of forgetfulness would be placed over our minds to conceal our prior experiences and memories. This would be necessary so we could exercise our own agency, to choose good or evil, without being influenced by our prior experiences with our Heavenly Father. We learned that we would have trials in our lives, including illness, injury, loss, poverty, betrayal, pain, disappointment, failure, sorrow, death, and grief. But we understood that these would be given to us for our experience and our good (see D&C 122:7). The plan would provide us with a path to receive a fulness of joy—as experienced by our Heavenly Parents. We were informed that not everyone of us would become like our Heavenly Father, but some would finish in telestial or terrestrial worlds where they would spend the rest of the eternities. Some, we were warned, would be lost. In any case, all would fall short of the glory of God, and as such, a Redeemer would be required. This Savior, we were assured, would be provided to expiate for all transgression,

---

9. See *Teachings of Presidents of the Church: Joseph Smith* [2007], 209, 511.

to pay the price for our sins, so long as we were willing to subject ourselves to the requirements of the covenant with Him.

Who would be the chosen Savior of all the hosts of heaven? Our Father asked the congregation, "Whom shall I send?" (Abraham 3:27). Jesus Christ, the Firstborn said, "Here am I, send me" (Abraham 3:27; Moses 4:1–4). Christ was willing to come to the earth and take upon Himself the burden of all sin and transgression, and all of humanity's ills. He, like our Heavenly Father, understood the absolute necessity of allowing each son or daughter to choose for themselves, exercising faith in the choices they made. He understood that only in that manner could we learn and grow, and ultimately prove ourselves worthy of celestial exaltation. Jesus Christ said, "Father, thy will be done, and the glory be thine forever" (Moses 4:2).

FALLEN SPIRITS

Not all of the spirit sons and daughters of God were valiant in seeking the light and growing to become like Him. There were those who looked on the power of the Father and were jealous of His dominion. They conspired to take it—by force. The plan of salvation and exaltation was presented to all of the sons and daughters of God, through which they were given the opportunity to progress through various stages of development, eventually becoming like their Heavenly Parents—in character, power, dominion, and glory. We read that "the morning stars sang together" (Job 38:7; see also D&C 128:23), rejoicing at the prospect of obtaining such a glorious existence. Lucifer, a Son of the Morning, designated the Light Bearer, obviously held a high and noble position among the great and noble sons of God. With all that we've learned about the importance of light—that it is the means by which all things receive their creation, form, substance, governance and intelligence—it must have been an unspeakable honor to be called the Light Bearer among all the sons of God. Yet, there was a flaw in that magnificent being. He hungered for power and authority—that which he had not earned by his own effort and merit, but that which God the Father had accumulated by His efforts. Lucifer saw his opportunity to rebel and steal the kingdom of the Father. Lucifer sought to be God, without earning the power and authority—to take by force that which belonged to another—the greatest of all.

Joseph Smith renders a more accurate version of the revelation, which tells us: "And there was war in heaven" (JST, Revelation 12:7). Yes, Lucifer spread rebellion throughout the hosts of heaven, and one-third[10] of God's spirit children followed him into combat. The rebel forces were immediately opposed by those faithful ones who stood on the side of the Firstborn, and of God the Father: "Michael and his angels fought against the dragon [Lucifer]; and the dragon and his angels fought against Michael" (Ibid.) The scripture then declares, "And the dragon prevailed not against Michael." Lucifer lost the war—he and his staggering number of rebellious followers were defeated. For them, there would be no continuance in that divine realm. There would be no plan of salvation and exaltation. "Neither was there place found in heaven for the great dragon, who was cast out; that old serpent called the devil, and also called Satan, which deceiveth the whole world; he was cast out into the earth; and his angels were cast out with him" (Ibid., 8)

Of this horrific tragedy, the prophet Isaiah mourns, "How art thou fallen from heaven, O Lucifer, son of the morning! how art thou cut down to the ground, which didst weaken the nations! For thou hast said in thine heart, I will ascend into heaven, I will exalt my throne above the stars of God: I will sit also upon the mount of the congregation, in the sides of the north" (Isaiah 14:12–13). The Lord speaks of the event thus:

> That Satan, whom thou hast commanded in the name of mine Only Begotten, is the same which was from the beginning, and

---

10. Again, we do not know if these numbers apply to all of the spirit children of Heavenly Father, or just those assigned to this earth. If just those who appertain to this earth, then we infer approximately 35 billion spirits followed Lucifer in rebellion, and 70 billion followed the Savior and Michael. These numbers are based on Church Family History Department estimates of a 100–billion-person cumulative population of this earth during its six thousand years of temporal existence. If the one-third applies to all of the spirit children of Heavenly Father, then the numbers easily climb into the "without number" range—trillions upon trillions.

he came before me, saying—Behold, here am I, send me, I will be thy son, and I will redeem all mankind, that one soul shall not be lost, and surely I will do it; wherefore give me thine honor. But, behold, my Beloved Son, which was my Beloved and Chosen from the beginning, said unto me—Father, thy will be done, and the glory be thine forever. Wherefore, because that Satan rebelled against me, and sought to destroy the agency of man, which I, the Lord God, had given him, and also, that I should give unto him mine own power; by the power of mine Only Begotten, I caused that he should be cast down; And he became Satan, yea, even the devil, the father of all lies, to deceive and to blind men, and to lead them captive at his will, even as many as would not hearken unto my voice. (Moses 4:1–4; see also D&C 29:36)

We note that God says that Satan became "the father of all lies, to deceive and to blind men." Something that is extremely important for all of us to understand is that this campaign of lying and deceiving is a full-time, full-pressure offensive. Satan is "anxiously engaged," and he employs the services of all of those who followed him in rebellion, and every tool and artifice at their disposal. What is their aim? It is to make you, and those you love, release your grip on the iron rod—the word of God, that leads to the pure love of God, which provides eternal life. His only goal is to get you to release it just enough so that he can distract you and get you to wander in another direction. Because this campaign is so prolific and pervasive, and so difficult to discern, so many are distracted and led astray—especially in the era where Satan exercises nearly exclusive control over media, news, social media, and education. There is barely a voice left that speaks the eternal truths that lead to exaltation in the kingdom of God. Satan lies and deceives, with an incessant drone of half-truths and outright falsehoods, to blind us so we can no longer see the immense beauty of the eternities. It is the method of deception that we discuss at length herein. The theater of delusion.

In the New Testament, the Savior recounts the episode as an eyewitness to the event: "And the seventy returned again with joy, saying, Lord, even the devils are subject unto us through thy name. And he said unto them, I beheld Satan as lightning fall from heaven" (Luke

10:17–18). Lucifer fell and became Satan, drawing a full third of all of Father's spirit children with him. The Apostle John, in the book of Revelation, called him "Satan, which deceiveth the whole world" (Revelation 12:8). Moses tells us that Satan is "the devil, the father of all lies, to deceive and to blind men, and to lead them captive at his will" (Moses 4:4). Joseph Smith records in scripture:

> And this we saw also, and bear record, that an angel of God who was in authority in the presence of God, who rebelled against the Only Begotten Son whom the Father loved and who was in the bosom of the Father, was thrust down from the presence of God and the Son, And was called Perdition, for the heavens wept over him—he was Lucifer, a son of the morning. And we beheld, and lo, he is fallen! is fallen, even a son of the morning! . . . who rebelled against God, and sought to take the kingdom of our God and his Christ—Wherefore, he maketh war with the saints of God, and encompasseth them round about. (D&C 76:25–29)

In this we learn that Satan makes war on the Saints—those who endeavor to follow God—you. Indeed, he makes war on all of the children of God who did not follow him in the rebellion against the Father. Regarding those children who come to this earth and are overcome by Satan, abandoning their eternal course to become like their Heavenly Father and subject themselves to Satan, the Prophet explained that those who know the truth and receive the testimony of the Holy Spirit and then deny the truth will be condemned to eternity in that place prepared for Satan and those who followed him (see D&C 76:30–38).

Satan and the third part of all of the spirits of heaven who followed him seek to destroy the plan of salvation and exaltation by destroying the souls of God's children who stood on the side of the Savior in the war in heaven. They have continued that war, following God's children here to the Earth, as we seek to live our mortal lives and gain an eternal inheritance through obedience to the requirements of the gospel. Satan and his followers, unembodied spirits who will never receive mortal tabernacles of flesh, hate all humans and seek to destroy each and every one of us in any way possible. The ancient prophet Nephi tells us, "Wherefore, men are free according to the flesh; and all things are given them which are expedient unto man. And they are free to choose liberty and eternal life, through the great Mediator of all men, or to choose captivity and death, according to the captivity and power of the devil; for he seeketh that all men might be miserable like unto himself" (2 Nephi 2:27). To thwart the plan for our salvation and exaltation, Satan and his followers do everything in their power to lead us away from righteousness. They seek to "discredit the Savior and the priesthood, to cast doubt on the power of the Atonement, to counterfeit revelation, to distract us from the truth, and to contradict individual accountability." They attempt "to undermine the family by confusing gender, promoting sexual relations outside of marriage, ridiculing marriage, and discouraging childbearing by married adults who would otherwise raise children in righteousness."

Let us stop for a moment to ensure we have a clear understanding of the true nature of Satan and his followers. As we said earlier, according to Church estimates, there are at least 35 billion of these demonic spirits on the surface of the earth—at least five for every living human—and these demonic spirits have just one object in focus: to destroy the soul of each and every son and daughter of God who has come to earth and been tabernacled in flesh. They hate us. Their animosity is boundless. Satan is the accuser, the liar, the deceiver, and he and his minions use every device at their disposal to twist, obfuscate, deceive, and lead astray. They do everything possible to stop the work and glory of the Lord, as related by the Prophet Joseph Smith in his account of his first attempt to pray vocally to Heavenly Father. "I kneeled down and began to offer up the desires of my heart to God. I had scarcely done so, when immediately I was seized upon by some power which entirely overcame me, and had such an astonishing influence over me as to bind my tongue so that I could not speak. Thick darkness gathered around me, and it seemed to me for a time as if I were doomed to sudden destruction . . .not to an imaginary ruin, but to the power of some actual being from the unseen world, who had such marvelous power as I had never before felt in any being" (Joseph Smith—History 1:15–16).

Christ, His Apostles, and disciples contended with many evil spirits during their ministries, and by the power of the holy priesthood they cast many of those spirits out of the humans whom they infested, commanding them in the name of Jesus Christ to depart. Similarly, the early missionaries to England were met with satanic opposition as they first arrived, moved into their new lodgings, and prepared for their first baptismal ceremony. Following is the account of the first seven missionaries in Preston, Britain, in July 1837, taken from their journals, books, and discourses. We follow the narrative offered by President Heber C. Kimball:

> A vision was opened to our minds, and we could distinctly see the evil spirits, who foamed and gnashed their teeth at us. I saw their hands, their eyes, and every feature of their faces, the hair on their heads, and their ears, in short they had fully formed bodies. We gazed upon them about an hour and a half. We were not looking towards the window, but towards the wall. Space appeared before us, and we saw the devils coming in legions, with their leaders, who came within a few feet of us. They came towards us like armies rushing to battle. They appeared to be men of full stature, possessing every form and feature of men in the flesh, who were angry and desperate; and I shall never forget the vindictive malignity depicted on their countenances as they looked me in the eye.[11]

When Christ spoke to the spirit entity that had possessed a young man, He asked the entity's name and the entity "answered, saying, My name is Legion: for we are many" (Mark 5:9). After receiving this information Christ listened as the spirits begged Him not to send them out of the country: "And all the devils besought him, saying, Send us into the swine, that we may enter into them" (Mark 5:12). Christ granted their request, and they entered into the 2,000 swine, "and the herd ran violently down a steep place into the sea" and drowned.

In this regard, allow me to proffer my personal witness of the reality of corporeal possession by these demonic entities by sharing an experience I had some time ago. A sister in the gospel requested that I perform a priesthood ordinance, and I agreed. Sensing I should do so, I took her hand with my left hand and raised my right arm to the square, and as I

---

11. *Journal of Discourses,* 3:229.

took a breath and opened my mouth to begin the ordinance, the sister immediately turned her head toward me and began to speak. I noted this and hesitated so I could hear what she had to say. As she spoke, I was at first quite confused. The voice I heard was not hers. It sounded like multiple people speaking in unison, and the voices were all quite ugly and hateful—mostly male, it seemed. The first words that came out were shocking. The demonic choir of voices began, "You priesthood men of God think you are so . . ." and they ranted and raged at me for nearly two full minutes, berating and chastising, accusing and reproaching. They were specific in telling me that the sister was theirs and that there was nothing I could do to save her from their grasp. Their message was one of hatred—they specifically hated me, and they hated all priesthood holders and all members of the Church. They were clear that they would stop at nothing to destroy every last one of us. While the voices spoke through her, the sister's face contorted with the words, and I was transfixed on what I was witnessing. I could see and hear the pure loathing, the limitless evil manifesting from her snarling lips, as the voices spoke in multiple, simultaneous tones that her female throat was incapable of producing. It was the same type of demonic voice that we often hear in movies, including deep diabolic bass voices at the same time as fiendish high-pitched voices—which detail made me wonder in the moment how sound producers knew what the voice of this demonic legion sounded like. I had heard of such experiences but never thought that I would be a personal witness of one in my life. I blessed the sister and referred her to her bishop and other priesthood leaders for counseling and spiritual guidance.

I learned from that experience that Satan knows my name. He knows me, and he knows you. Your name is written indelibly in the Book of Life, and he is determined to erase it through his diabolical machinations. Like many Church members, I have suffered countless attacks since that time, personally, and through my vulnerable family members and associates. Hence, the "battle-scarred warrior" status of our being. We all suffer the attacks of the evil one, and his 35 billion foot soldiers, all bent on our personal and real destruction. Of this, you have my personal eyewitness. He attacks us through those things that we care most about—loved ones, friends, career, and society. He strikes at the heart of what is truly important in this mortal life—family and obeying the commandments and receiving the ordinances of exaltation. He is a liar, the very father of lies, and every word that proceeds from his filthy mouth is either an outright lie or a cleverly disguised half-truth calculated to lead us astray (see Ether 8:25; D&C 93:25). In Father Lehi's vision of the tree of life and the iron rod that leads to its wondrous fruit, the sons and daughters of God are mocked and dissuaded from continuing their steadfast journey to the fruit, or love of God, by the deceit and lying words of the evil one, his demons, and those mortals who echo his lies in their own spewed philosophies. I hear the lying voice every day—on the television, radio, newscasts, lecterns, social media, and internet—spewing the same lies that Satan has always told in his tireless effort to undermine the plan of salvation and exaltation for the children of the Father. I easily recognize the evil voice—the defamations meant to loosen our grasp on the iron rod that leads to eternal life. The voices are clever and often entertaining and filled with wit. They sound delightful and inviting. Yet, they are disguised so we can't see who truly speaks them—their progenitor, the malicious father of all lies.

We will revisit this discussion of diabolical deceit, counterfeit, psychic projection, and sophistry as we scrutinize and discern the beings who present themselves in various forms to deliver messages from other realms. Before that, we must better understand the plan of redemption of our God and Savior, and the truth and light that lead to eternal exaltation in the Kingdom of Heaven. The truth—actual truth—is the standard by which we must measure all messages and presentations. Indeed, the Savior declares, "Truth is knowledge of things as they are, and as they were, and as they are to come; And whatsoever is more or less than this is the spirit of that wicked one who was a liar from the beginning" (D&C 93:24–25).

THE SECOND ESTATE

When God presented His plan of salvation and exaltation, we who did not rebel and kept our first estate prepared for our mortal lives on earth. The Lord said, "And we will prove them herewith, to see if they will do all things whatsoever the Lord their God shall command them;

And they who keep their first estate shall be added upon; and they who keep not their first estate shall not have glory in the same kingdom with those who keep their first estate; and they who keep their second estate shall have glory added upon their heads for ever and ever" (Abraham 3:25–26). Not all who professed to be on the side of the Savior were honest in that public choice. Some were inwardly evil but remained silent in their opposition to the Savior's plan because they realized that Lucifer could not succeed in his insurrection. Some were mediocre in their commitment to the principles underlying eternal progression and ultimate exaltation, while many were absolutely committed to fulfilling the terms and conditions of the plan and receiving a kingdom like that of our Heavenly Parents. All of these, in their varying levels of commitment and ability, come to earth with veiled minds and take upon themselves mortality—clothed in bodies of flesh and blood. They live their lives according to the faith they exercise and the choices they make. Then they die, and their spirits are "quickened" and enter the spirit world, while their bodies return to the earth to await their reunion with their spirit in the resurrection.

Adam and Eve came to Earth first. Adam was Michael, the archangel, who had been instrumental in the Earth's creation and was second only to the Firstborn Son of God, the great Jehovah. Eve, too, was a great and noble spirit daughter of God. Together they came to earth and were placed in the Garden, east in Eden. "And the Gods formed man from the dust of the ground, and took his spirit (that is, the man's spirit), and put it into him; and breathed into his nostrils the breath of life, and man became a living soul" (Abraham 5:7–8). "And the Gods took the man and put him in the Garden of Eden, to dress it and to keep it. And the Gods commanded the man, saying: Of every tree of the garden thou mayest freely eat, But of the tree of knowledge of good and evil, thou shalt not eat of it; for in the time that thou eatest thereof, thou shalt surely die. Now I, Abraham, saw that it was after the Lord's time, which was after the time of Kolob;[12] for as yet the Gods had not

---

12. This indicates that the earth was created in the vicinity of the great star Kolob and was still in that location at the time Adam was placed into the Garden of Eden.

appointed unto Adam his reckoning (Ibid., 11–13). "And the Gods said: Let us make an help meet for the man, for it is not good that the man should be alone, therefore we will form an help meet for him. And the Gods caused a deep sleep to fall upon Adam; and he slept, and they took one of his ribs, and closed up the flesh in the stead thereof; And of the rib which the Gods had taken from man, formed they a woman,[13] and brought her unto the man (Ibid., 14–18).

Their bodies were of a terrestrial level, not telestial as we are now. They were immortal, imbued with the ability to remain forever in that paradise, without predator or disease of any type to end their blissful lives. Plants had already been introduced to the earth, but somewhat simultaneous to the arrival of human life the scriptures tell us that animal life was introduced as well. "And out of the ground the Gods formed every beast of the field, and every fowl of the air, and brought them unto Adam to see what he would call them" (Ibid., 20–21). Again, we have very little understanding of the processes involved in providing temporal bodies for all of the animals, as well as Adam and Eve. In the early parts of the last century there was quite a discussion among Church leaders about the merits of the theory of evolution, and if any part of the theory is factual, how much? The Lord provided little revelation on the subject, so the brethren were free to speculate, trying to decide if any or all parts of the theory of evolution fit within the parameters of the revealed gospel. Many felt that God may employ evolution as a means of the creative process, given the long periods of time involved in the six creative periods and those periods of "night" between them. Some felt that the scriptures indicate that life, in any form, was introduced in the last creative period, precluding the gradual formation of the final forms of life that were introduced into the world around the time of Adam. As we have noted, God's ways are much, much higher than our ways, and we actually enjoy very little understanding of His processes. What we do understand is that

---

13. Some latter-day prophets have explained that the act of taking a rib from the body of Adam to create a body for Eve is a figurative description of what was done by the Elohim. We can speculate that some form of genetic cloning may be part of such a process, but our understanding of such matters is truly in its infancy.

animals[14] are created somewhat similarly to humans—they are spirits that are "breathed" into the mortal bodies prepared for them. Together, their spirit element and mortal body element make up a living soul, which will be separated at death, and reunited in an exalted state in the resurrection.

When placed into the Garden of Eden, Adam and Eve were given simple commandments. One commandment was to refrain from partaking of the fruit of the tree of knowledge of good and evil. We understand that there were actual plants and trees in the garden and that Adam and Eve were free to partake of their fruit. The tree of knowledge of good and evil is represented to be a real tree whose fruit had the ability to introduce the seeds of mortality into the bodies of Adam and Eve. Some theologians have speculated that sexual sin was the actual fruit of the tree of knowledge of good and evil. We disagree, because Adam and Eve were married and were given commandment to "be fruitful and multiply, and replenish the earth."[15] We know that the language regards reproduction, because it is the same language used when they became mortal and actually began to bear children. "And Adam knew his wife, and she bare unto him sons and daughters, and they began to multiply and to replenish the earth" (Moses 5:2).

Satan entered into the garden paradise, and through his deceitful, cunning lies, he eventually convinced Eve that partaking of the fruit

---

14. Joseph Fielding Smith taught, "Animals do have spirits and . . .through the redemption made by our Savior they will come forth in the resurrection to enjoy the blessing of immortal life" (Joseph Fielding Smith, "Your Question: Do Animals Have Spirits?", *Improvement Era* 40, January 1958, 16). Bruce R. McConkie said that the Savior's "ransom includes a resurrection for man and for all forms of life" ("Seven Deadly Heresies," speech given on 1 June 1980). Elder Tad R. Callister wrote, "The Atonement fully extends its redemptive powers to this earth and to all forms of life thereon to the extent necessary to save them from physical and, where necessary, spiritual death" (*The Infinite Atonement* [Salt Lake City: Deseret Book, 2000], 87).
15. "And the Gods said: We will bless them. And the Gods said: We will cause them to be fruitful and multiply, and replenish the earth, and subdue it, and to have dominion over the fish of the sea, and over the fowl of the air, and over every living thing that moveth upon the earth" (Abraham 4:28)

would endow her with benefits that the Father and Son were hoarding to themselves. She partook of the fruit, then convinced Adam that because she had done so, she must be exiled from him and they would not have the opportunity to fulfill the commandment to multiply themselves in the earth. Adam understood their predicament and knowingly partook of the fruit of the tree of knowledge of good and evil. Their bodies transitioned from a terrestrial level to telestial, and they became mortal. We have no idea how long Adam and Eve were in the garden. It could have been a very short time or millions of years—or much longer. There is no indication given through revelation. We also have no idea what was happening in the rest of the world during the time Adam and Eve were in the garden. We only know that by the time of their expulsion, the entire world was in the fallen telestial state, with death and disease common throughout.

In their fall from terrestrial to telestial, Adam and Eve also became fertile by that same process, thereby enabling them to fulfill the commandment to multiply. When they were expelled from the garden, they began to have children. The Fall of Adam and Eve and their expulsion from the garden was an epic event in the lives of our mortal progenitors with far reaching results, and merits a fuller discussion; but it is beyond the scope of our present discussion. Children came to Adam and Eve, "and from that time forth, the sons and daughters of Adam began to divide two and two in the land, and to till the land, and to tend flocks, and they also begat sons and daughters" (Moses 5:3). At this point, all of the myriad spirit children of our Heavenly Father began to come to earth and take upon themselves physical bodies, and go through the process of choosing between good and evil. First hundreds arrived, then thousands, then millions as they multiplied exponentially.

While in the garden, Adam and Eve were visited directly by the Father and the Son. Satan also intruded in that paradise, apparently communicating with them through the body of a serpent. When they fell and were expelled from the garden and forced out into the fallen telestial world, they were no longer visited by the Father, but only by the Son and angels. To point their minds toward the Savior, He who would help them and their children to overcome the effects of the Fall, God sent angelic messengers.

> And Adam and Eve, his wife, called upon the name of the Lord, and they heard the voice of the Lord from the way toward the Garden of Eden, speaking unto them, and they saw him not; for they were shut out from his presence. And he gave unto them commandments, that they should worship the Lord their God, and should offer the firstlings of their flocks, for an offering unto the Lord. And Adam was obedient unto the commandments of the Lord. And after many days an angel of the Lord appeared unto Adam, saying: Why dost thou offer sacrifices unto the Lord? And Adam said unto him: I know not, save the Lord commanded me. And then the angel spake, saying: This thing is a similitude of the sacrifice of the Only Begotten of the Father, which is full of grace and truth. Wherefore, thou shalt do all that thou doest in the name of the Son, and thou shalt repent and call upon God in the name of the Son forevermore. (Moses 5:4–8)

Adam and Eve accepted the judgments of God and were faithful in fulfilling the requirements of the Lord. They were righteous and immediately set their feet on the path toward eventual exaltation.

> And in that day the Holy Ghost fell upon Adam, which beareth record of the Father and the Son, saying: I am the Only Begotten of the Father from the beginning, henceforth and forever, that as thou hast fallen thou mayest be redeemed, and all mankind, even as many as will. And in that day Adam blessed God and was filled, and began to prophesy concerning all the families of the earth, saying: Blessed be the name of God, for because of my transgression my eyes are opened, and in this life I shall have joy, and again in the flesh I shall see God. And Eve, his wife, heard all these things and was glad, saying: Were it not for our transgression we never should have had seed, and never should have known good and evil, and the joy of our redemption, and the eternal life which God giveth unto all the obedient. And Adam and Eve blessed the name of God, and they made all things known unto their sons and their daughters. (Moses 5:9–12)

With their understanding of the necessity of the Fall and redemption through the eternal sacrifice of the promised Savior, Adam and Eve taught their children everything about the plan of salvation and exaltation, and how to overcome the effects of sin and death through the Redeemer's Atonement. They taught them the gospel and administered the ordinances that lead to salvation and exaltation. Satan, however, went among the children of Adam and Eve and deceived them, telling them that he too was a son of God, and instructing them to worship him.

> And Adam and Eve blessed the name of God, and they made all things known unto their sons and their daughters. And Satan came among them, saying: I am also a son of God; and he commanded them, saying: Believe [the gospel] not; and they believed it not, and they loved Satan more than God. And men began from that time forth to be carnal, sensual, and devilish. And the Lord God called upon men by the Holy Ghost everywhere and commanded them that they should repent; And as many as believed in the Son, and repented of their sins, should be saved; and as many as believed not and repented not, should be damned; and the words went forth out of the mouth of God in a firm decree; wherefore they must be fulfilled. (Moses 5:12–15)

Satan's lying and deception has never changed. In his effort to undermine and destroy the plan of God, Satan deceives the people of earth by telling them half-truths and lies, taking them in small steps and large leaps away from the truth and light of the Father and the Firstborn Son. In the end, he always sets himself up as the counterfeit Messiah, the replacement redeemer, and demands that the people worship him instead of God and His Son. Remember this, because we hear it in the messages of many beings who deliver communiqués to humanity from other worlds.

TYPES OF LIFE

A review of the types and forms of life up until this point in our discussion begins with God the Father, the first of all, followed by others associated closely with the Godhead—the Holy Spirit, Heavenly Mother, and the Firstborn Son. We also have the spirit offspring of our Heavenly Parents, who are "organized" into spirit element individual personages of male and female through some process centered in the creative abilities of the Heavenly Father and Mother. Our understanding is that the Firstborn, Christ, is one of these and stands at the head as the First. Of the remaining spirit offspring, two-thirds stood on the side of the Firstborn in the War in Heaven, championed by Michael, second only to Christ, thereby keeping their first estate and qualifying themselves to come to earth to receive mortal bodies and to eventually be resurrected. They are before their earth life, pre-existent spirits.

The remaining one-third of the spirit children are those who rebelled with Lucifer and were cast down to the earth to become Satan and his demonic followers whose only focus is to thwart the plan of God for His children (the two-thirds) by destroying their souls one at a time through deception and temptation. Plants and animals also cover the earth providing food, oxygen and numerous other resources to enable life on the planet.

Also, death has entered the earth, and thousands or even millions of children are beginning to come into this mortal existence, many of them dying from various causes. Their spirits are being separated from their bodies and entering the world of spirits. As far as we understand it, the spirit world is a plane of existence that parallels our earthly plane of existence, occupying the same space as our earth, but that world and those spirits who are assigned there exist at a different vibrational rate than our own, or possibly in a different dimension—like the fifth or sixth dimension.

Some of the spirits have not yet had an opportunity to come to the earth for their mortal experience at this point in our discussion but are sent as ministering angels. This assignment is reserved for the most valiant and advanced of the spirit children of God. We just read the scripture that says, "And after many days an angel of the Lord appeared unto Adam, saying: Why dost thou offer sacrifices unto the Lord?" (Moses 5:6). Who was this angel? Because it was within days of Adam being expelled from the garden, we assume it was before any humans had been born and died, so the only candidate is a pre-existent spirit son of God—someone who would one day be born through Adam's lineage.

After men and women began to die and their spirits moved on to the spirit world, some of them were allowed to come to people on the earth as angelic messengers from God. We are never quite sure about the nature of the various angelic messengers mentioned in the Old Testament (before the Resurrection), but we know that they were either pre-existent spirits or spirits separated from their bodies and awaiting the resurrection—what the prophets term "just men made perfect" (see D&C 76:69; 129:3; Hebrews 12:23). An example of this type of angelic messenger would be the angel Gabriel being sent to the virgin Mary. Gabriel, prominently mentioned as one of the most faithful and valiant of all of the angels, served out his mortal existence as Noah, the great prophet.[16] He had not been resurrected before the birth of Christ but had lived and died. Therefore, we understand that he came to Mary in his spirit form, performing that most holy assignment from God to announce to Mary that the Son of God, the Savior of the world, would issue from her womb.

Are there other types of life that we have not mentioned yet? Yes—at some point we know that certain men and women who had attained to perfection in their unity of the faith were translated.

TRANSLATED HUMANS

The standard works say little else about other worlds and their inhabitants generally, but we do learn a few things about one group of people that left this planet to live on another—the people of Zion.[17] Many Church members assume that if there are extraterrestrial visitors that come to our planet, they could be translated beings ministering to Earth from other planets. And perhaps in our search for extraterrestrial life it is important to establish scripturally the existence or nonexistence of human life on foreign worlds, so we endeavor here to pinpoint what happened to Zion and its inhabitants.[18]

---

16. *Teachings*, 157.
17. I highly recommend an article prepared for the *Ensign* magazine by Professor Hugh Nibley that was serialized in thirteen parts: "A Strange Thing in the Land: The Return of the Book of Enoch," Part 1–13; 1975–77.
18. Some latter-day prophets and apostles have alluded to the possibility that another group or groups of people have likewise been taken to another planet, such as the ten lost tribes of Israel.

As the Lord revealed to Enoch his earthly ministry and the eventual results thereof, Enoch was privileged to see his own future. "And it came to pass that the Lord showed unto Enoch all the inhabitants of the earth; and he beheld, and lo, Zion, in process of time, was taken up into heaven. . . And after that Zion was taken up into heaven, Enoch beheld, and lo, all the nations of the earth were before him; And there came generation upon generation; and Enoch was high and lifted up, even in the bosom of the Father, and of the Son of Man; and behold, the power of Satan was upon all the face of the earth. . . . And Enoch beheld angels descending out of heaven, bearing testimony of the Father and Son; and the Holy Ghost fell on many, and they were caught up by the powers of heaven into Zion" (Moses 7:21–27).

This passage, when analyzed with other verses in Moses 7, helps us gain an understanding of where Zion is. Enoch testified of events that were yet future to him. He said Zion would be "taken up into heaven,"[19] although he failed to identify the exact final location of Zion. In this passage Enoch himself was taken to "the bosom of the Father," and the Lord said to Enoch, "Behold mine abode forever." These statements, however, were made in connection with Enoch's visit to the throne of God, at which time he was shown all things pertaining to the kingdoms of God—past, present, and future. The scripture, standing alone, does not necessarily indicate that Zion was taken to God's bosom or abode—only that Enoch beheld God's bosom or abode.

The scripture is further enlightening because it indicates an ongoing connection between Zion and the Earth, even after Zion is taken. This it does by suggesting that others were translated to Zion after its removal and that angels continued to travel between Zion and the Earth. President Spencer W. Kimball confirmed this by answering the question: "Is man earthbound? Largely so, and temporarily so, yet Enoch and his people were translated from earth, and the living Christ and angels commuted."[20] The above passage also indicates another phenomenon, of which we have little information.

---

19. In The Book of the Secrets of Enoch, Enoch describes ten heavens, all with varying qualities of life.
20. *The Teachings of Spencer W. Kimball*, 445.

It tells us that other humans who received the Holy Ghost "were caught up by the powers of heaven into Zion." Who are these people? We hear frequently of a handful of prophets and apostles who were translated—Moses, Elijah, John the Revelator, the three Nephites, and others. However, there was another city of Saints who, like the Zion of Enoch, established their own order of righteousness and eventually were taken up as an entire city.

There was a great and marvelous man who held the high priesthood, around 2,000 years before Christ. He was called Melchizedek and was very much like Father Enoch, in that he was extremely righteous, and he established a colony of righteous followers that eventually grew into a city called Salem—located where the current city of Jerusalem is established. After Father Abraham rescued his nephew Lot, he learned that his brother had been taken captive and he rescued him and his people and their possessions. The kings of the region were solicitous, hoping to turn away Abraham's disfavor, but the King of Salem was a good friend to Abraham. The Prophet Joseph Smith received an expanded account of the meeting between these two great prophets of God, and although the passage is a little long, I encourage you to read it carefully, because it reveals so much about Salem, Melchizedek, Abraham, Enoch and Zion, and the state of those who become translated.

> And Melchizedek lifted up his voice and blessed Abram. Now Melchizedek was a man of faith, who wrought righteousness; and when a child he feared God, and stopped the mouths of lions, and quenched the violence of fire. And thus, having been approved of God, he was ordained an high priest after the order of the covenant which God made with Enoch. . . . For God having sworn unto Enoch and unto his seed with an oath by himself; that every one being ordained after this order and calling should have power, by faith, to break mountains, to divide the seas, to dry up waters, to turn them out of their course; To put at defiance the armies of nations, to divide the earth, to break every band, to stand in the presence of God; to do all things according to his will, according to his command, subdue principalities and powers; and this by the will of the Son of God which was from

before the foundation of the world. And men having this faith, coming up unto this order of God, were translated and taken up into heaven. And now, Melchizedek was a priest of this order; therefore he obtained peace in Salem, and was called the Prince of peace. And his people wrought righteousness, and obtained heaven, and sought for the city of Enoch which God had before taken, separating it from the earth, having reserved it unto the latter days, or the end of the world. (JST, Genesis 14:25–40; compare Genesis 14:18–20; see also JST, Genesis 9:21–25. The rainbow was the token of God's covenant with Enoch, and Zion will return when a righteous people on earth are ready.)

Abraham was highly desirous to remain among the people of Salem, but God had another mission in mind for him and commanded him to perform His holy errands first. By the time Abraham returned to the site of the holy city it was gone, as well as all of its inhabitants. They had been translated. Abraham greatly lamented his loss and sought for a Salem-like people all the remaining days of his life. The site of the city of Salem was left bare after its translation, and a people called the Jebusites eventually built a city there called Jebus. King David took over the city and eventually built Jerusalem on that most sacred of sites. Regarding the destination of the translated city of Salem, we are not told if it was taken to be with the Zion of Enoch to the "bosom" of God, or if it was taken to another planet. We mainly hear about Enoch's Zion in subsequent revelations.

We also learn more about Zion and its people and status in other ancient writings that have slowly come into our possession. An interesting example of ongoing communication between Zion and the Earth is illustrated in the Dead Sea Scrolls.[21]

> An extremely unusual son was born to Lameck. The child's body was white as snow, with parts as red as a rose. His long hair was white as wool, and his eyes were piercing and brilliant. He was able to talk immediately and, according to Lameck,

---

21. This is not, of course, canonized scripture that is necessarily accepted as containing true doctrine by the Church. However, the passage is instructive, and the reader is free to determine the value of the information.

apparently conversed with the Lord. Lameck, concerned and disturbed, wondered if the boy were his own or possibly had been conceived by one of the "watchers" or "sons of heaven."[22] He discussed the matter with his wife, BatEnosh, who swore that the boy was Lameck's. Lameck took his problem to his father, Methuselah, who in turn sought counsel from his father, Enoch, who previously had been taken (translated) into heaven. Enoch told Methuselah to assure Lameck that his son had been sent from God to do a great work on the earth and that his name should be called Noah.[23]

This passage raises a question that has been hotly debated among scholars and many ufologists, especially those of the "ancient alien theorist" bent as are ubiquitous on television programs. Before discussing the merits of the "watchers" theories, let's continue with our treatment of Enoch's Zion, which was taken up off of Earth.

Zion's process of reaching the above-indicated state of perfection was not quick or easy, as we learn from Moses: "And all the days of Zion, in the days of Enoch, were three hundred and sixty-five years. And Enoch and all his people walked with God, and he dwelt in the midst of Zion; and it came to pass that Zion was not, for God received it up into his own bosom; and from thence went forth the saying, ZION IS FLED" (Moses 7:68–69).[24] We cannot tell from these scriptures precisely where God planted Zion and its inhabitants. This latest passage suggests they were taken to the Lord's "bosom." This is supported by Enoch's own statement, "And thou hast taken Zion to thine own bosom, from all thy creations, from all eternity to all eternity; and naught but peace, justice, and truth is the habitation of thy throne; and mercy shall go before thy face and have no end" (Moses 7:31). Still, none of these

---

22. The concept of giants being born to normal human women impregnated by "Watchers" or "Sons of Heaven" is quite controversial among Christian scholars and ufologists alike. We discuss it in greater detail below.
23. *Christ's Eternal Gospel*, 155 (rendering parallel translations from The Book of Lameck, The Book of Noah, and The Book of Enoch from the scroll "A Genesis Apocryphon," the Dead Sea Scrolls).
24. See also, D&C 38:4; Genesis 5:24; and Hebrews 11:5.

scriptures absolutely points us to the precise location of Zion, or of God's "bosom," if Zion is there.

This actual event of translation of the city of Zion along with its geographical surroundings and underpinnings, being physically removed from Earth and taken elsewhere, is affirmed in modern scripture also. God declares that Enoch and the people of Zion were "separated from the earth" and that God "received" them to Himself: "The God of Enoch, and his brethren, Who were separated from the earth, and were received unto myself—a city reserved until a day of righteousness shall come—a day which was sought for by all holy men, and they found it not because of wickedness and abominations" (D&C 45:11–12; see also Inspired Version, Genesis 14:32–34).

Brother Hugh Nibley provides the following descriptions of the people of "Zion" and their elevated state of living in his *A Strange Thing in the Land: The Return of the Book of Enoch*, Part 12:

> The Mandean writings equate Zion to heavenly 'firmaments, habitations, worlds, and Jordans', giving the most vivid and appealing descriptions of such holy places, which, they say, are to be enjoyed only by the "spirits of good people . . . the wise and the prudent of the families of Abel, Seth, and Enoch." There the Saints live without discord or dissension; they are angelic beings, wise and gentle, without malice or deceit, constantly visiting each other. . . . They are vast distances removed from each other, but through their common Lord and God they all share a common glorious awareness of each other. All are incorruptible and hence without death; they do not grow old or wear out; their nature is unfading. . . Magnificent buildings stand beside tranquil seas; flowing springs give life-giving water. Everything vibrates with joy. The wants of the people are few. They move through the air by an effortless power of flight.[25]

Through latter-day revelation we also learn that the city of Zion will return to the Earth—to the city of New Jerusalem in Jackson County, Missouri—at the time when "a day of righteousness shall come." Of that glorious day, "the Lord said unto Enoch: Then shalt thou and all

---

25. Citing Van Andel, 115.

thy city meet them there, and we will receive them into our bosom, and they shall see us; and we will fall upon their necks, and they shall fall upon our necks, and we will kiss each other" (Moses 7:63; JST, Genesis 9:21–25). Both of these scriptures further reinforce the fact that Zion is with God, but again, we receive no qualification what it means for non-celestial beings to be "with God."

Although in all of the above descriptions we learn that Zion and its surrounding countryside is somewhere with God, we cannot be sure if it is physically "with" God, or physically "near" God, on a nearby planet. Of the planet on which God resides, modern scripture informs us, "The angels do not reside on a planet like this earth; But they reside in the presence of God, on a globe like a sea of glass and fire, where all things for their glory are manifest, past, present, and future, and are continually before the Lord. The place where God resides is a great Urim and Thummim. This earth, in its sanctified and immortal state, will be made like unto crystal and will be a Urim and Thummim to the inhabitants who dwell thereon" (D&C 130:79). God's planet is a celestial world. Our limited understanding of the doctrine of translation informs us that translated beings are raised from a telestial existence to a terrestrial (immortal, but not resurrected) state. We can safely assume that the city of Zion and the portion of the earth taken with it was likewise elevated to a terrestrial state. The obvious question is, are terrestrial beings living on a terrestrial portion of Earth somewhere off-world, compatible with a celestial world and beings, for an extended period of time? Other than our understanding that in the eternities beings of a higher order may minister to beings of a lower order, but not vice versa.[26] We cannot venture an informed guess about their compatibility. We know from Moses that "Enoch and all his people walked with God, and he dwelt in the midst of Zion" (Moses 7:69). But again, this is a case of a being of a higher order ministering to beings of a lower order.

It is possible that Enoch and his city dwell "near" God's celestial planet instead of on it. We learn from the writings of Father Abraham

---

26. See D&C 88:81–91.

that there exist planets and stars near God's dwelling place, as Abraham instructs as he sets out the hierarchy of the planets and stars. Abraham says among the great stars was Kolob, the greatest and nearest the planet on which God resides, and there are "many great ones" near it, which "are the governing ones" (Abraham 3:1–17). Although no definitive answer is found in these scriptures concerning the exact dwelling place of Zion, our reasoning that Zion is on one of the planets near God instead of with God on His own celestial planet appears to be supported by Joseph Smith's explanation of the process of perfection of translated beings. The Prophet explains, "Many have supposed that the doctrine of translation was a doctrine whereby men were taken immediately into the presence of God, and into an eternal fullness, but this is a mistaken idea. Their place of habitation is that of the terrestrial order, and a place prepared for such characters He held in reserve to be ministering angels unto many planets, and who as yet have not entered into so great a fullness as those who are resurrected from the dead."[27] This statement apparently eliminates any possibility that Zion is on God's celestial planet because translated beings are not "taken immediately into the presence of God," but to a "place of habitation" of a "terrestrial order." Therefore, God's "bosom" seems to be either figurative language for "a godly place," or a place or planet in space near God. This lengthy discussion about Zion and Salem and individually translated people is calculated to demonstrate that this Earth is visited by beings from Zion and beings from God's presence. Therefore, we know that beings from at least two other planets visit here, although we are unsure of the frequency of those visits.

All of these "regulations" regarding the status of translated beings do not take into account the changed status of Zion and its inhabitants at the time of the Lord's resurrection. We learn through revelation that all of these beings, translated before the resurrection, were with Christ in the morning of the first resurrection and have received the "fulness" of which Joseph Smith spoke above (D&C 133:54–55). This, of course, does not change the initial status of these translated persons as we have

---

27. *Teachings*, 170.

discussed them, but it could change their current status regarding the abode of Zion. They could now be celestial beings, living on their Zion planet, or even on God's planet. However, we know that Zion and its inhabitants remain as a single body and will return to the terrestrialized Earth as an intact city, and will unite with New Jerusalem, a city built on the American continent by the Saints. This indicates that there could be a continued "terrestrial" status for Zion, "an Holy City, that my people may gird up their loins, and be looking forth for the time of my coming; for there shall be my tabernacle, and it shall be called Zion, a New Jerusalem. And the Lord said unto Enoch: Then shalt thou and all thy city meet them there, and we will receive them into our bosom" (Moses 7:62–64). The changing of the location of the Lord's "bosom" and "abode" to New Jerusalem on this Earth in the near future are further indications that such words are not used as literal pinpoints of God's celestial dwelling place, but are figurative terms indicating a quality of life and continual communion with God.

THE WATCHERS

Some Christian scholars believe that the "sons of God" mentioned above were a certain class of angels set on earth after Adam's Fall as Watchers,[28] even protectors, some of whom became renegades and began indulging in inappropriate earthly activities. As indicated above, the concept of strange babies (and giants) being born to normal human women impregnated by "Watchers" or "sons of heaven" is quite controversial among Christian scholars and ufologists alike. Some modern ufologists believe that these sons of heaven were large humans from another planet, who, during a mission to Earth, impregnated many earth women, resulting in the birth of giant human children. Our first indication of the enigma is found in Genesis 6:4, which reads: "There were giants in the earth in those days; and also after that, when the sons of God came in unto the daughters of men, and they bare children to them, the same became mighty men which were of old, men of renown."

---

28. See Daniel 4:13, 17.

As we discussed, Noah's father, Lameck, was worried that Noah may have been the offspring of one of these "sons of God." He asked his father, Methuselah, for his counsel about it, and Methuselah sought counsel from his translated father, Enoch, who assured them the very special child was Lameck's. We are left to ask, who were these "sons of God" who impregnated the "daughters of men"? There is in the ancient book of Enoch a class of beings named the Watchers. They are thought of as "angels" who were sent to Adam after his expulsion from the garden to teach him how to live temporally and spiritually. So little information has survived about these beings, if they actually existed, that we must rely on uncanonized sources for most of our information. We discuss them here, however, because of their nature—seemingly angelic, yet human enough to develop passions and take human women as wives and impregnate them. In the book of Enoch, and the section therein titled The Book of the Watchers, we learn that hundreds of Watchers were sent to Earth by God to instruct and assist Adam and Eve. As the human couple bore children, who began to pair off and raise families, then tribes and villages, a group of 200 of those Watchers were enticed by the beautiful young human women and desired to take them as their own wives. Such a thing was strictly forbidden by God, but Satan came among them as Azâzêl and promised the 200 errant Watchers that if they would switch their allegiance to him, he would give them the desire of their hearts. "And Semjâzâ, who was their leader, said unto them: 'I fear ye will not indeed agree to do this deed, and I alone shall have to pay the penalty of a great sin.' And they all answered him and said: 'Let us all swear an oath, and all bind ourselves by mutual imprecations not to abandon this plan but to do this thing.' Then sware they all together and bound themselves by mutual imprecations upon it. And they were in all two hundred; who descended in the days of Jared on the summit of Mount Hermon."

As they completed their pact with their new master, Satan, the 200 Watchers took their pick of wives from among the beautiful human women, who became pregnant with their babies. The babies of these unions were quite abnormal, resulting in what scholars term

Nephilim[29] (from Genesis) or Anakim/Anak (giants). The resulting babies had insatiable appetites and are described as "great giants, whose height was three hundred ells: Who consumed all the acquisitions of men. And when men could no longer sustain them, the giants turned against them and devoured mankind. And they began to sin against birds, and beasts, and reptiles, and fish, and to devour one another's flesh, and drink the blood."

The Pearl of Great Price relates, "There also came up a land out of the depth of the sea, and so great was the fear of the enemies of the people of God, that they fled and stood afar off and went upon the land which came up out of the depth of the sea. And the giants of the land, also, stood afar off; and there went forth a curse upon all people that fought against God" (Moses 7:14–15). The giants persisted until the time of the Great Flood: "And in those days there were giants on the earth, and they sought Noah to take away his life; but the Lord was with Noah, and the power of the Lord was upon him" (Moses: 8:18).

The Bible also tells us about the giants in the lands that "the Emims dwelt therein in times past, a people great, and many, and tall, as the Anakims; Which also were accounted giants, as the Anakims; but the Moabites call them Emims" (Deuteronomy 2:10–11). There came a time when the giants dwindled in numbers among the people, until, "For only Og king of Bashan remained of the remnant of giants; behold, his bedstead was a bedstead of iron; is it not in Rabbath of the children of Ammon? nine cubits was the length thereof, and four cubits the breadth of it, after the cubit of a man" (Deuteronomy 3:11). Compare the size of Og to Goliath: "And there went out a champion out of the camp of the Philistines, named Goliath, of Gath, whose height was six cubits and a span" (1 Samuel 17:4). Whatever unit of measure we attribute to the cubit

---

29. The Old Testament Hebrew word for giants used in Genesis, is "nephil" or "naphal," which they say literally means "the fallen ones," or "those who are fallen down." They infer from this that these are beings who came from a higher level. A look at a Hebrew and Chaldee Dictionary (see *Strong's Exhaustive Concordance of the Bible, Dictionary of the Hebrew Bible*, 79, words nos. 5303–5307) reveals that nephil is often translated as a "feller," and naphal means "one who has failed or has been overcome."

and span, Og was 50 percent taller than the giant Goliath, who was much larger than natural men.

The Book of the Watchers tells us that the 200 fallen Watchers began to teach men to do evil, instructing them in weapons and war, technologies, and the cunning arts, which would eventually lead to their destruction.

> And Azâzêl taught men to make swords, and knives, and shields, and breastplates, and made known to them the metals of the earth and the art of working them, and bracelets, and ornaments, and the use of antimony, and the beautifying of the eyelids, and all kinds of costly stones, and all coloring tinctures. And there arose much godlessness, and they committed fornication, and they were led astray, and became corrupt in all their ways. Semjâzâ taught enchantments, and root-cuttings, Armârôs the resolving of enchantments, Barâqîjâl, taught astrology, Kôkabêl the constellations, Ezêqêêl the knowledge of the clouds, Araqiêl the signs of the earth, Shamsiêl the signs of the sun, and Sariêl the course of the moon.

It's striking how many of these "arts" remain at the fore of society, even today—leading to the same problems of godlessness, war, sexual sin, false religions, and spiritual practices and general corruption. When these problems, and many more, escalated to a point where the children of God being sent to earth were finding themselves in societies and families where they had little or no chance of fulfilling their mortal purposes and regaining the presence of the Father, He finally decided the corruption was too systemic and had to be stopped—rooted out. God gave the mighty angel Gabriel instructions concerning the Nephilim and the imprisonment of the Watchers.

And to Gabriel said the Lord: "Proceed against the biters [bastards] and the reprobates, and against the children of fornication: and destroy the children of the Watchers from amongst men [and cause them to go forth]: send them one against the other that they may destroy each other in battle."[30] We are unsure what happened to the Watchers and

---

30. The Book of Enoch (Charles), 10:1–15.

their children, the giants or Nephilim. The scriptures speak somewhat about these matters. Moses sent twelve spies to search the land of Canaan, who returned with news of the land being consumed by giants, making his spies seem like "grasshoppers" in comparison. "And they brought up an evil report of the land which they had searched unto the children of Israel, saying, The land, through which we have gone to search it, is a land that eateth up the inhabitants thereof; and all the people that we saw in it are men of a great stature. And there we saw the giants, the sons of Anak, which come of the giants: and we were in our own sight as grasshoppers, and so we were in their sight" (Numbers 13:32–33).

These events transpired during the epoch when Moses led the children of Israel, so it was long after the Great Flood. Therefore, if the giants discussed throughout the scriptures are related to those who were reportedly produced by the union of the fallen Watchers, perhaps translated beings, with human women, then their race somehow survived the Flood. In fact, the only real sources we have for the existence of the fallen Watchers and their giant offspring are non-canonical, so we cannot speak to their actuality with authority, notwithstanding that the canonized scriptures actually speak frequently of "giants" in those times. The subject will arise later in our discussion, because there are many who believe there is clear evidence that "Watchers" and "Nephilim" have always been among us, while their off-world tribes often visit our earth.

One last instance of a translated being that may become germane to our discussion of unusual visitations and apparitions is Cain, the son of Adam. We learn in Genesis and Moses that God had rejected Cain's offering because it was not made in faith (see Moses 5:5–8, 18–26), and that Cain killed his brother Abel (see Genesis 4:8–14; Moses 5:32–37). The Lord set a curse and a mark on Cain (see Genesis 4:15; Moses 5:37–41), and Cain entered into an unholy covenant with Satan (see Moses 5:29–31). Although we have never learned all of the details of the mark and curse that the Lord put on Cain, we have the account of Elder David W. Patten's alleged encounter with Cain in 1835. According to a report found in *The Life of David W. Patten, The First Apostolic Martyr*, Patten rode along the backwoods road on his mule and was on his way to visit with Abraham O. Smoot in Tennessee when he encountered "a very remarkable personage who had represented himself as being Cain who had murdered his brother, Abel." The apostle recounts,

> I suddenly noticed a very strange personage walking beside me . . . for about two miles. His head was about even with my shoulders as I sat in my saddle. He wore no clothing but was covered with hair. His skin was very dark. . . . He said that he had no home, that he was a wanderer in the earth. . . . He said that he was a very miserable creature, that he had earnestly sought death . . . but that he could not die, and his mission was to destroy the souls of men. I rebuked him in the name of the Lord Jesus Christ and by virtue of the Holy Priesthood, and commanded him to go hence and he immediately departed out of my sight.[31]

Elder Patten related the experience to President Smoot when he arrived at the house, and President Smoot later shared the experience in exact detail in a letter to President Joseph F. Smith, then a member of the First Presidency. After receiving the letter, President Smith shared its contents with the Quorum of the Twelve. Elder Abraham H. Cannon commented at the time that he had "always entertained the idea that Cain was dead," but now changed his views on the matter. It appears that the First Presidency and the Quorum of the Twelve accepted the account as true.[32] The recollection of Patten's encounter is cited in President Spencer W. Kimball's *The Miracle of Forgiveness*.[33]

Although there are a number of additional accounts of such a creature presenting himself to other Church leaders around the world, including Hawaii, none is adopted as canonical by the Church. Therefore, the experience is relegated to the category of lore by many researchers. We mention it in our discussion because we know there

---

31. Lycurgus A. Wilson, *The Life of David W. Patten, The First Apostolic Martyr* (Salt Lake City: Deseret News Press, 1900) 45–47.
32. Ibid., 45; "Diary Excerpts of Abraham H. Cannon," Thursday, November 9, 1893, L. Tom Perry Special Collections and Manuscripts, Harold B. Lee Library, Brigham Young University, Provo, Utah.
33. Deseret Book, 1969, 127.

was a Cain, that he was cursed, and that he did bear a mark—so there is a high likelihood that a creature did present himself to Elder David W. Patten and that it was either Cain or a demonic imposter. If it was indeed Cain, then his longevity and self-proclaimed inability to end his life indicate that there is another state of translation, which does not elevate to a terrestrial status but does make immortal in sin. If the creature was an imposter, then it is interesting that there are many who claim to see flesh and blood cryptids (unknown animals) that match the same general description. These animals, male and female, old and juvenile, whether flesh and blood or mere presentations (psychic projections) from an unknown being, or visitors from another dimension or planet, have appeared to tens of thousands who have seen them in clear, unmistakable detail—much as Elder Patten. We know that the encounter related by the apostle indicates the existence of a type of being somewhat unique in our list of beings in the universe. It causes me to wonder if there are other types of beings of which we have no knowledge.

RESURRECTED BEINGS

We have thus far considered the types of life that exist in our universe. They are the Godhead and the spirit children of God, including those spirits who kept their first estate and those who rebelled and were cast down to the earth without the opportunity to receive a mortal body or to ever receive resurrection and a kingdom of glory. In their pre-existent state, the spirit children of God await their mortal probation, and some are sent to earth to deliver messages and assistance—these we term angels. The third of the hosts of heaven who followed Lucifer are malignant spirits and appear as demons and deceiving beings of every type. Satan himself appears as an angel of light to deceive and obfuscate (see D&C 129:4–9). There are humans who come to earth and receive a physical body to complete their mortal lives. There are also the spirits of men and women who have lived, then died, who sometimes visit the earth as disembodied spirits to enlighten and deliver messages of truth and encouragement. They await their resurrection but are the spirits of "just men made perfect," so they are not confined to the world of spirits as are most of the dead. There are also translated beings, those who have lived and who were elevated to an immortal, terrestrial state, without tasting of death. Those who were translated before the resurrection of Christ were resurrected and elevated to a celestial glory at the time of Christ's resurrection. Those who were translated after the resurrection await their resurrection at the Second Coming of Christ when the dead are raised from their graves and brought to stand before the judgment bar of Christ. We consider the status of resurrected beings below. Other translated beings may include cursed people like Cain, or Watchers, who are said to be sent to assist humans in the beginning, just after expulsion from the garden, as in the case of Adam and Eve, to teach them how to grow and gather food, build shelters, worship God, and all things necessary for their support and well-being.[34] If Watchers do exist, then they, as every other type of living being we have considered thus far, can be valiant and obedient to do God's will, or can be lazy and rebellious, resulting in a fall from their status or potential status.

---

34. The non-canonical writings that provide much of our "information" about matters that occurred before the Flood tell us that the faithful Watchers were very much involved with Noah in the building of the ark and preparing for the preservation of humanity and the animals during the deluge. The indication is that the biblical representation of a crude vessel made from gopher wood and the leading of animals onto the great bark is a mere allegory for what actually occurred. In fact, there may have been superior technology involved, and the time that Noah, his family, and the genetic inventory of the planet were "adrift" may have been much, much longer than a mere year. I tend to believe that the ark was technologically sophisticated, as was the world that Noah left buried in the waters, and that much time was spent in stasis while the earth underwent cleansing and planetary upheaval. "And now the angels are making a wooden [building], and when they have completed that task I will place My hand upon it and preserve it, and there shall come forth from it the seed of life, and a change shall set in so that the earth will not remain without inhabitant" 1 Enoch (Ethiopic) 66:2. Noah and his family eventually disembarked their craft, leaving behind in the cleansing waters all of the technology and evil that had been taught to the world by the fallen Watchers and Satan. Noah and his family were commanded to never reveal what had existed in the world before the Flood, but Ham's wife Egyptus disobeyed, giving rise to the secret knowledge of the Egyptians and the rebirth of the occult.

At the time of Christ's death, He went to preach to the spirits in that portion of the spirit world that we call spirit prison—where those who have not yet attained a celestial status can learn and repent, and receive the ordinances of exaltation vicariously. After three days in the spirit world, Christ was resurrected, and many of the Saints who had died and were ready for celestial glory were resurrected with Him (see Mosiah 15:20–25). Resurrection is the reuniting of the spirit with the body[35] in an immortal state, no longer subject to disease or death and coupled with glory, except in the case of those who receive the second death and are condemned to outer darkness with Satan. Because of the Fall of Adam and Eve, we are all subject to physical death, which is the separation of the spirit from the body. Through the Atonement of Jesus Christ, all people will be resurrected and saved from physical death. Again, every person who has ever taken a mortal body will be resurrected. This includes babies who took only a single breath, as well as the most righteous and most evil of all humanity. Yes, Cain and Hitler will be resurrected. This is salvation, which comes through the Atonement of Jesus Christ, as a free gift to all humanity, who kept their first estate. "For all the rest shall be brought forth by the resurrection of the dead, through the triumph and the glory of the Lamb . . . even Jesus, to be crucified for the world, and to bear the sins of the world, and to sanctify the world, and to cleanse it from all unrighteousness; That through him all might be saved whom the Father had put into his power and made by him" (D&C 76:39–42).

However, there are varying levels of glory in the resurrection of the dead—the telestial, terrestrial, and celestial. The Apostle Paul compares the three degrees of glory, from the greatest to the least, typifying

---

35. Many wonder about the ability of the body to be reunited with the spirit in the Resurrection, due to the unavailability of most of the body's mass after death and decay. In fact, some bodies are consumed in fires, or eaten by animals, and so on, with little or nothing being left behind. The prophets have assured us that the body is a unique collection of eternal elements, which can be separated but not destroyed, and that the constituents of matter that will be reunited with the spirit in the resurrection are unique to that body and will be collected in a single unit of fine element in the resurrection. They will obey the voice of the Lord and will reassemble themselves into the body.

them as the sun, moon, and stars—as those three bodies differ from one another in brightness and glory (see 1 Corinthians 15:40–41). Christ explains that there are many levels of glory in the resurrection, although He refers to each, including the lowest in the telestial kingdom, as mansions. "Let not your hearts be troubled; for in my Father's house are many mansions, and I have prepared a place for you; and where my Father and I am, there ye shall be also" (see D&C 98:18, 59:2, 72:4, 135:5; John 14:2; Ether 12:32, 34, 37; and Enos 1:27).

The Prophet Joseph Smith and Sidney Rigdon were enabled to see enough of these three worlds to provide a description of what they beheld, at Hiram, Ohio, February 16, 1832. First, the Prophet described the telestial: "And again, we saw the glory of the telestial, which glory is that of the lesser, even as the glory of the stars differs from that of the glory of the moon in the firmament. These are they who received not the gospel of Christ, neither the testimony of Jesus . . . who deny not the Holy Spirit . . . who are thrust down to hell . . . who shall not be redeemed from the devil until the last resurrection . . . who are liars, and sorcerers, and adulterers, and whoremongers, and whosoever loves and makes a lie" (D&C 76:81–88, 103). The telestial is a kingdom of glory but of relatively low glory. Those who inherit it were not valiant, but even relatively bad during their lives. In the end, they accepted Christ as the Savior and bowed the knee[36] to Him.

Next in glory are those who inherit the terrestrial world. "Behold, these are they who died without law . . . who are the spirits of men kept in prison, whom the Son visited, and preached the gospel unto them, that they might be judged according to men in the flesh; Who received not the testimony of Jesus in the flesh, but afterwards received it. . . who are honorable men of the earth, who were blinded by the craftiness of men . . . who receive of his glory, but not of his fulness" (D&C 76:71–79). The terrestrial glory is populated with good, but unvaliant people, who were kind, generous, and even religious during their lives, but who never fully embraced the gospel of Christ or received the ordinances of exaltation.

Those who receive all of the ordinances of exaltation and take upon themselves the name of Christ and His holy priesthood, and

---

36. Romans 14:11; Philippians 2:10; Isaiah 45:23; Mosiah 27:31; D&C 88:104.

overcome all things and fully embrace the Savior and His eternal gospel receive a celestial inheritance and become like their Heavenly Parents in character and dominion. "They are they who received the testimony of Jesus, and believed on his name and were baptized after the manner of his burial . . . and receive the Holy Spirit by the laying on of the hands of him who is ordained and sealed unto this power; And who overcome by faith, and are sealed by the Holy Spirit of promise, which the Father sheds forth upon all those who are just and true . . . who are the church of the Firstborn . . . into whose hands the Father has given all things . . . who are priests and kings, who have received of his fulness, and of his glory; And are priests of the Most High, after the order of Melchizedek, which was after the order of Enoch, which was after the order of the Only Begotten Son. Wherefore, as it is written, they are gods, even the sons of God" (D&C 76:50–70, 92–95).

We also read that many messengers of God are resurrected beings. History is replete with the experiences of those who have received the ministering of angelic beings who were resurrected men. These resurrected messengers include, among others, Moses, Elijah, and Moroni. The Prophet Joseph Smith records a visitation from the resurrected ancient prophet in great detail.

> I discovered a light appearing in my room, which continued to increase until the room was lighter than at noonday, when immediately a personage appeared at my bedside, standing in the air, for his feet did not touch the floor. . . . Not only was his robe exceedingly white, but his whole person was glorious beyond description, and his countenance truly like lightning. The room was exceedingly light, but not so very bright as immediately around his person. . . . After this communication, I saw the light in the room begin to gather immediately around the person of him who had been speaking to me, and it continued to do so until the room was again left dark, except just around him; when, instantly I saw, as it were, a conduit open right up into heaven, and he ascended till he entirely disappeared, and the room was left as it had been before this heavenly light had made its appearance. (Joseph Smith—History 1:30–43)

This vision is instructive about the nature of such beings and about the manner of their appearance to mortals. The nature and function of the light that attended the visitation is likewise instructive and fascinating.

Finally, there are those who are lost in the process of the plan of salvation and exaltation. These are the sons of perdition, who come to earth and obtain a physical body, receive a sufficient understanding of the power of God, and accept it along with the direct testimony of the Holy Ghost, but deny Him. They live and die, then suffer the buffetings of the evil one while in the world of spirits, and are eventually resurrected—but then are sent away with Satan and his rebellious angels into outer darkness for all eternity (see D&C 76:31–38, 44–46).

IN HIS OWN IMAGE

This is the last of the types of living beings that are revealed to us. There are also plants, animals, planets, and heavenly bodies.[37] These, however, are separate from the intelligent race of God types of life considered in our discussion: premortal spirits, living mortals, disembodied spirits,[38] unembodied spirits,[39] translated persons, and

---

37. "And it came to pass that Enoch looked upon the earth; and he heard a voice from the bowels thereof, saying: Wo, wo is me, the mother of men; I am pained, I am weary, because of the wickedness of my children. When shall I rest, and be cleansed from the filthiness which is gone forth out of me? When will my Creator sanctify me, that I may rest, and righteousness for a season abide upon my face?" (Moses 7:48). "Since all creatures and the plants and trees of the earth were created spiritually, we discover that not only man is entitled to the resurrection but every other living thing that suffered the fall through Adam's transgression. So we learn that this mortal earth, like all on its face, is growing old, and eventually shall die, be cleansed, and then come forth a celestial world and everything will be restored to life never to die again" (Joseph Fielding Smith, *Presidents of the Church Answers to Gospel Questions* 4:130–131).
38. Spirits that have lived, then are separated from their bodies in death.
39. These are technically premortal spirits, but I name them separately because they are divided into those who kept their first estate and those who did not. Those spirits who followed Lucifer and became subject to Satan are unembodied and will never receive bodies.

resurrected persons. Each of these types of living beings interacts with mortals at various times and in various ways—some nobly and with honorable intentions, and some deceitfully, to draw mortal men and women away from God and His Son, and the exaltation they offer all God's children.

This sums up life in the universe as God has revealed it to us, and we see that intelligent life is all the same race—the race of God—but in varying levels of progression through that life. Are there no other forms of life mentioned in the scriptures or by the prophets? Not that we're aware of. However, we have discussed the possibility that Watchers may exist, as an example of types of life that may exist, but are not declared by the prophets. Even Watchers, however, would seem to fit within the category of sons of God, in one phase of their eternal existence or another. What of the purported children of the Watchers—the giants, or Nephilim? If they exist, what are they? Do they have spirits? If so, are they normal spirits, the offspring of Heavenly Father, or are they some sort of bastard spirit, plucked from unorganized spirit element to animate an unsanctioned being?

Also, could there be other types of lifeforms? Are their biomechanical bodies, cloned or genetically created, that act as avatars for living beings, or for unembodied spirits like those who followed Satan? The acquisition of bodies is certainly paramount to those demonic hordes, and they likely have access to the science and technology to make that desire a reality—to a limited extent. Are there mechanical or biomechanical bodies that house artificial intelligence creations? In this vein, could a human society have accidentally unleashed an AI that wiped out its creators and eventually decided to create various types of bodies, based on actual creatures it encountered throughout the cosmos? Could this be why the creatures that are said to abduct and study humans are very interested in our emotional makeup and "humanity," and why they communicate nonverbally and leave the recipient with an overwhelming perception of high intelligence without any spark of conscience or compassion? We know there are animals and plants. Are there other lifeforms than these? Are some animals highly intelligent—acting like humans, but still of the animal classification? Are there "other" genetic experiments that have rendered partial humanoid results—perhaps the insectoid or reptilian races that are purported to visit and often cruelly abduct humans? Are there other types of animal hybrids, humans genetically paired with sea creatures, amphibians, serpents, or fowl? Should we make anything of the assertion that Satan spoke through a reptile? What of the cryptids that appear to slip in and out of our dimension of existence, which resemble large hairy men, panthers, winged creatures, large canines, or change their appearance and disappear on demand?

We could easily dismiss all of these thoughts as nothing more than sophomoric nonsense or academic exercise and never give them another thought—except for the fact that someone or something is going to a lot of effort to convince us that these things are precisely what is happening in the universe. Many "others" and "visitors" appear in these forms, and some project images of themselves that vary from encounter to encounter. What are we to think of these? Are they deceptive? Are they dangerous? Are they demonic? Or are they simply lifeforms in their many varieties? Are all lifeforms in the universe created by God? We must assume so. Are there forms of life the prophets have not revealed to us? Is there intelligent life that is not in God's likeness? Or, is a six-foot tall, extremely intelligent praying mantis or reptilian with powers of telepathy also in God's image? I wish this were merely academic exercise, but in fact, these are questions that present themselves in bold, horrific living color in the lives of many thousands of people. We lack certain understanding of some of these principles, and our natural recourse is to attempt to make all reports fit into what we assume is the full picture of life in the universe. However, just because God has revealed many things to us through His prophets, doesn't mean He has revealed everything to us. We just don't know the answers to many of these "varied lifeforms" questions.

Here's an important question, to which the Lord *has* revealed the answer: Do the children of God live successive lives, with the same spirit being born and reborn as humans, men and women, and various types of animals, all as asserted in theories of reincarnation? No. There is no place in God's plan of salvation and exaltation for this philosophy—it is a doctrine of deceit spun diabolically by the father of lies. Any person or entity that teaches the doctrine of reincarnation is either mistaken, having been beguiled by the evil one, or in the case of unknown beings, is purposefully lying to lead you astray. This understanding provides a key by which we may unlock the messages of many beings who encounter humans, as we shall see.

The spirit children of God are sent to innumerable earths to live their mortal lives. What are those billions upon billions of planets like? What are those mortals like who populate those planets? We learn that God creates with variety, so there could be a wide array of variability in the inhabited planets and those who live on them, although He declares that His children are in His general likeness (see Ether 3:15–16). What is the likeness of humans? Are we eight feet tall, or three feet? Are we white, pink, brown, or red? Are we covered with hair, or bald? Fat or thin? Are our eyes round or narrow? Is our skin smooth or wrinkled? Are we peaceful or violent? What is human? All of the above.

How varied can people be, yet still be a spirit child of God and be created, spiritually and physically in His image? We aren't sure what the outer boundaries are of creation. Therefore, if we were to encounter a son or daughter of God who hails from another world, we aren't sure how that person might appear.

What about insectoids, or reptilians? In the following chapters are descriptions of many who present themselves to us as the sons and daughters of God, and many have a message for us. We will examine the nature of those visitors and their messages, and try to discern together who and what they may be.

CHAPTER 3

My Introduction to the Unknown

Brother Stambul, an investigator of the Church in my mission, had invited a group of us young missionaries over to his home to see some unidentified flying objects (UFOs[1]). He asked us to arrive just before dusk because dusk was the best time to see UFOs from his balcony. Bolzano, where I was serving, is a beautiful Germanic town in Northern Italy, just south of the Austrian border. I briefly discussed Stambul's invitation that day with my missionary companion, Stan Harter. We decided to take Stambul up on his offer, but the topic did not occupy too much of our attention for the remainder of that day.

At the predetermined rendezvous time, Stan and I, along with a couple of other missionaries in our district, were punctual, and there was just enough time to exchange a few pleasantries and consume some Italian biscotti before Stambul suggested we should go out on the veranda. The small group stepped out into the evening air. The city lay still in the eventide shadows of the eclipsing Dolomite mountains towering around us. We spoke in hushed tones, politely scanning the darkening sky—watching for UFOs.

---

1. Recently termed unidentified aerial phenomena, or UAP, by the US government.

Two minutes had not passed when Stambul spoke in his casual Italian voice: "Oh look, there's one now." He pointed above us. We looked up and watched as a pinpoint of light shimmered its way slowly through the twilight. I surveyed the object as it glimmered, moving in an almost straight path over us, quivering slightly every five seconds or so as if it had hit some ice and veered from its course momentarily. My quiet observation was disturbed by the commotion of others in our group, pointing and exclaiming. I looked at Stan and exchanged a smile—it looked like a passing satellite to us.

Another of Brother Stambul's "UFOs" flew over within five minutes, and we thanked him as we departed, suggesting that although the objects may have been satellites, who could tell for sure?

STAN HARTER

As Stan and I walked to our next appointment, we talked a little about the subject of UFOs. After I mentioned that our stake patriarch at home had told us about a close encounter that a member of our stake had related to him in confidence, Stan took a deep breath and confided, "I saw one, *Anziano* [Italian for "Elder"]." I was very attentive and asked him to share his experience with me. He agreed, and I was very impressed as I listened to the detail and consistency of his experience as he recounted it, and his obvious sincerity. It had occurred just a little over a year before he entered the mission field, as he was preparing, so it was very fresh in his memory. I had sat beside my missionary companion for hundreds of hours as he taught the gospel to those we encountered and bore his solemn testimony of the veracity of our message. Now, I felt that same spirit of truth as he shared his experience with me. At the time I published my first book on this subject, I asked Stan, then a successful business attorney in Southern California, if he wouldn't mind sharing his experience with my readers. He agreed, and sent me this account.

> When I was still in high school in the mid-1970s, I was dog-sitting for a family acquaintance. She was completely blind and the dog was her seeing eye dog. To keep the dog in peak performance, it was necessary for me to take the dog on a rather long

MY INTRODUCTION TO THE UNKNOWN

walk and put it through a series of exercises each day. Demands being what they were in those days, the only time I could engage in such activities was at night. It was while I was on one of these walks that I had my UFO experience.

On that particular night we had walked to an area where there was a lot of new construction but very few occupied structures. There were no artificial lights to obstruct the view. The sky was clear and afforded quite a spectacular view. As I recall, my mind was not on the view, however. In fact, I believe I had my eyes closed at the time trying to get the full impact of being guided by a seeing eye dog. The dog came to a sudden stop which caused me to open my eyes. I followed the dog's eyes and saw a saucer-like object hovering in the air. The craft had fixed lights on the top and the bottom with rotating lights around its perimeter. In the desert air at night, sounds carry for a great distance. The craft, however, did not emit any audible sound.

The craft continued to hover in a uniform pattern for a period of about 30 seconds, then it made a very quick movement to one side, returned to what seemed to be the original location, and made a very quick vertical move, disappearing from my view entirely. The dog continued to watch the sky for a moment and then continued on as though nothing had happened.

I note the details about the craft and its accelerations and velocity. Stan reports that it was shaped like a disc, and was just hovering. It was the classic two saucers placed one on top and the opposing one on the bottom. He says the lights on the top and the bottom were fixed—not moving, while lights in the center part were rotating around the perimeter. It was very close to him—a couple of hundred feet, he reported to me, and he was very confused how it made absolutely no sound whatsoever. When he shared the experience with me, he explained that it was hovering over one of the new homes being constructed in the development. Stan recounted how when the craft finally made a move from its original hovering position, it was a very fast, nearly immediate dart to the side—a few houses away from where it had just been, and it stopped immediately in its new position. Of course, the g-forces involved in that level of rapid acceleration and deceleration are impossible for any technology developed by our engineers and scientists, because not only would occupants of the craft be immediately smashed against the interior walls, but the equipment inside and the structure itself would be crushed. Stan says that after a few seconds, the craft repeated the move in reverse and zipped back to its starting position. After remaining in that position for only a few seconds, it accelerated upward and out of sight in just a second or two. Again, that level of acceleration creates g-forces that would destroy any metal structure or machine created with any materials available then, or now.

Because of the encounter that Stan[2] shared with me and his solemn testimonial regarding its actuality, I began to think about the nature of these craft, who might occupy them, and why they show themselves in our skies. I was fairly well versed in the scriptures and knew that our Heavenly Father tells us of His children on myriad planets like Earth. I had been raised on a steady diet of sci-fi movies and television programs that softened me to the idea of interplanetary visitors, so the phenomenon wasn't shocking to me. When I returned from my mission, I looked into the case that our stake patriarch had mentioned to our youth group and obtained some details about the matter from the patriarch's adult son, Tim Grossnickle, who had actually interviewed the brother on the long bus ride to the Oakland Temple, before our own Portland Temple was constructed.

UDO WARTENA

Tim Grossnickle interviewed Udo Wartena about the encounter shortly before Udo's death, which occurred just before I performed the research for my first book, so I was unable to interview Udo myself. I obtained the details from Tim and recounted Udo's experience in my first book. After publication, Brother Wartena's encounter experience

---

2. During the terrorist shootings of December 2, 2015, in San Bernardino, California, I reached out to Stan Harter to ensure that he and his dear family were nowhere near the incident, which had occurred somewhat near his law office. I was saddened to learn that Stan had passed of natural causes just two weeks earlier.

was republished widely. It was utilized as a case presented by MUFON[3] and was published in the March/April 1998 issue *UFO Magazine* without my permission. MUFON referred to Udo Wartena's experience as "the most significant humanoid contact case on record."

After the experience was reprinted so many times, researchers with access to remote documents were able to locate a 1980 personal letter from Udo to US Senator John Glenn, who had been a US astronaut, the third American in space, and had the distinction of being the first American to orbit the Earth, circling it three times in 1962. The year 1980 was very difficult for America due to the global energy shortage. Because Middle East oil suppliers were severely curtailing oil shipments to the United States, Americans were waiting for hours in long lines down the block from gas stations, trying to get to the gas pump before the station ran out of fuel and closed for the day. It was a horrific time for the United States, and Udo Wartena well understood that America was in need of a different energy source. Because he had learned about the energy source utilized by the craft he encountered, he shared the information with Senator Glenn in the hope that the United States could build on the data and develop the technology. Following is the text of Udo's letter to Sen. John Glenn. His encounter experience takes place as he mined for gold in the remote regions of Northern Idaho.

> In the forepart of May 1940, I had gone upon the mountain and found a glacier deposit. And from all indications had every possibility of carrying values. As I was working part-time for the Northwest Mining Co., I could only prospect on my days off. So it was into the summer before I could prove the ground. There were a lot of large boulders to move but when I got to bedrock, I found some fine gold.
>
> As I would need water for washing the material, I figured it was wise to bring the water down to where I could use it. . . . I still had some large boulders to move and while doing this one morning I heard a noise. Like that of a high flying plane, as army planes flying over, from Great Falls. At first I didn't

---

3. The Mutual UFO Network, "An Analysis of the 1940 Udo Wartena Case. Discovering the Alien Agenda," (Warren P. Aston, 1997).

take much note, but as the noise continued, I thought a car had driven up. So I got upon higher ground. I saw, where I had put the dam in the main ditch, a large (I will call it ship). It looked like a blimp, only more pointed on each end, and not as thick through the middle. About 35' thick, better than 100' long. As I stood there, a stairway was let down and a man came down this and started walking towards me. As I was somewhat more than interested, I went to meet him. He stopped when we were about ten or twelve feet apart.

He was a nice looking man, seemingly about my age, 35 or more. He wore a light gray pair of coveralls, a tam of the same material on his head, and on his feet were slippers or moccasins. He asked me if it would be alright if they took some of the water. I could not see why not, I said sure. He then gave a signal and a hose or pipe was let down. His English was like mine, but he spoke slowly, as if he was a linguist. He asked me what I was doing. I explained this to him. He asked me if I would be interested to come aboard. As he seemed an intelligent and pleasant person, I figured it would be interesting.

As we got closer to the ship, I noticed that it was round, like two dinner plates, one inverted over the other. It seemed to be made of metal. As I look back and compare, it seemed like stainless steel, though not bright or shiny. The ship appeared to be about 35' thick and well over a hundred feet in diameter. When we got into the ship, we entered into a room about twelve by sixteen feet, with a close fitting door on the farther end. Indirect lighting near the ceiling, and nice upholstered benches around the sides.

There was an older man in the room, plainly dressed and with white hair. It was then that I noticed that the younger man also had white hair. Somehow I believe they knew who I was, but they did not introduce themselves. Perhaps if they had, I may have been a bit upset. The younger man asked me what I would be interested in. So I first asked why they wanted this particular water. He said the water is good, as if they had gotten the same before, and it was convenient.

After we had entered the ship, I had noticed that the sound I had heard outside, was hardly noticeable, except what came

MY INTRODUCTION TO THE UNKNOWN

up the stairwell. So I asked him what caused the noise or humming. He said this would be a bit complicated, but he would try to explain so I could understand. He said as you noticed we are floating above the ground, and though the ground slopes, the ship is level. There are in the outside rim of the ship two flywheels, one turning one way and the other the opposite direction. He explained that this gives the ship its own gravitation, or rather overcomes the gravitational pull of the earth, other planets or the sun or stars. And though this pull is light, we use this gravitational pull of the stars and planets to ride on. He went into somewhat greater detail on the power development by these two flywheels. He mentioned something about them developing an electromagnetic force. As this was quite new to me and he realized that, but he saw I had gotten the picture, so he stopped.

I asked him where he got the energy to run the ship. He said from the sun and stars, and he would store this in batteries, though this was for emergency use. I also asked him what their object was or purpose in coming here. Well, he said, as you have noticed, we look pretty much as you do, so we mingle with you people, gather information, leave instructions, or give help where needed. I would have liked to ask him more about that, but didn't feel this proper, so let it ride at that. While we had been talking, a light had come on, apparently signaling that the water had been taken care of.

When I felt it was time for me to leave, I mentioned this. He asked me if I would be interested in going with them. I said that I thought it would be interesting to go with them but it would inconvenience too many people. Later I wondered why I had said that. As I started to leave, they suggested that I tell no one, as no one would believe me at that time, but in years to come I could tell about this experience. When I walked away from the ship, they raised the stairway, and when I got a couple of hundred feet away from the ship, I turned around. A number of more portholes had opened up and though I could see no one, I felt sure they saw me. Anyway, I waved at them.

The ship then rose straight up, then while circling slightly it continued going straight and in a very short while was completely out of sight. As I didn't have a watch, I did not know how long

I had been with them. It was around noon so it must have been about two hours from the time I first saw the ship.

This whole experience was so overwhelming that I did not go back to work. I kept going over in my mind all that had happened. I went back to where the stairway had been and though it hadn't gone into the soil, the grass was crushed down. . . .

I have wondered at times if this could have all been in my imagination. But then again I saw the impression of the ship in the grass. Then over the years a number of things have come to mind. The explanation of how this ship moved, seemingly not affected by earth's gravitational pull. From what the man told me at the time and what has come to me since, I believe I am not too far from an answer to this. It is for this reason I am writing to you. No doubt with the help of some other minds, the answer will be forthcoming.

We have just about reached the stage where we need a different type of air transportation and this is the answer. I feel confident that you could put me in touch with some people who could help to this end.

Udo Wartena, West Linn, Oregon—1980

I was quite amazed to locate this personal letter explaining the details of his close encounter with these "men" who look the same as we do, and who were happy to show Udo around their craft and explain their technology to him. I have prepared a graphic of the craft's means of generating a gravitational directional field, and only wish Udo had given additional details about this in his letter to Senator Glenn, having stated, "He went into somewhat greater detail on the power development by these two flywheels. He mentioned something about them developing an electromagnetic force." As with many aspects of what Udo saw and heard in those two hours on the craft, Udo had no point of reference and no language to explain what he learned. In subsequent decades he saw and read things that helped him explain what he had witnessed that day—like stainless steel, jet engines, electromagnetic fields, etc. The gravitational force field described by Udo is a type of torsion field generation that was pursued by Nazi scientists, as well as Russian scientists in the 1980s—perhaps inspired by Udo's

MY INTRODUCTION TO THE UNKNOWN

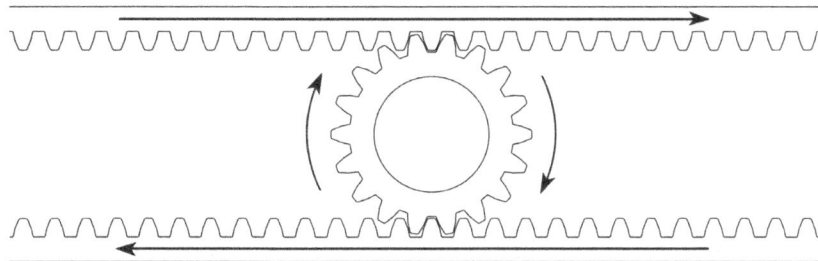

Example of "double flywheel" rack and pinion system, where top flywheel is powered to spin to the right as lower flywheel is powered to spin to the left by a common gear turning in the center. This system is said by some, including Udo Wartena's visitors, to be at the heart of generating antigravity fields when certain energy frequencies are applied.

letter to Sen. John Glenn. A number of groups claimed to have various levels of success with the technology—but no one, as far as we know, has successfully developed it.

In his personal interview about the experience with Tim Grossnickel, Udo shared a few additional details about the two-hour encounter. Tim relates the pertinent portions of the interview from memory as follows:

> Tim: Do you remember talking to my father about your experience while mining for gold in the remote regions of Northern Idaho?
>
> Udo: Yes. Your father was the first person I ever told about it.
>
> Tim: Why did you wait so long to share your experience?
>
> Udo: Who would believe what I experienced? Over the years I read some of the other accounts in the newspapers and magazines and realized that some of the same things happened to others. But some of them told of strange looking creatures. I doubted them, because the people on the UFO that I saw were just like us, and very nice chaps.
>
> Tim: What actually happened? How did you know the ship had landed?
>
> Udo: My mine shaft was nearly vertical and was over 30 feet deep in the ground. I had built up a sluice stream nearby to wash out the gold. I heard something like a big truck, or like a jet

engine, but this was before the time when I had ever heard such a sound. I came up my shaft to look, and in the meadow was a saucer shaped craft supported on legs.

A man was pulling down a hose to draw water from my stream. I did not feel the least bit of fear and I walked toward the man. He came and shook my hand, apologizing that they had not known that I was in the area. It was not their custom to interrupt or allow themselves to be seen. "Why not take water from the lake?" I asked.

"This water is more pure and free from algae," he answered, and invited me to see his ship.

He was such a pleasant fellow. I asked his age—he was quite handsome and youthful, appearing to be middle-aged. His companion on board looked slightly older, but was also in very good health. They answered that one was about six hundred years old as we measured time, and the other was over nine hundred years old. They knew over five hundred languages and were learning ours, and improving upon them all the time.

They had come here "to monitor the progression and retrogression of our societies," he explained. They live among us from time to time.

I asked if they knew of Jesus Christ, and if they held the Priesthood. "We would like to speak of these things," he responded, "but are unable. We cannot interfere in any way."

"Where did you come from," I asked. "We live on a distant planet," he replied, giving its name and pointing in its direction.

The love, or comfort I felt in these men's presence was remarkable. I was invited to be examined with an "x-ray-like" machine, which when passed over me could record what impurities were in my system.

The ship was propelled with two rings or discs about three feet wide and a few inches thick, which circled the inside perimeter of the ship next to "battery/transformer-like" units all around the outer wall. Rods separated the discs (turned by motors), causing the discs to move in opposite directions. A force was generated which overcame the gravitational pull of the Earth, or any other planet they were on. They focused on a distant star and used its energy to draw them through space at speeds greater than the speed of light. My host specifically mentioned "skipping upon the light waves."

They invited me to accompany them on their journey, but I declined—I was driving to Portland the next day for my wedding; I didn't want to leave them though.

Upon leaving the ship and standing by a rock some distance away, I heard the same loud noise as before as the craft lifted, rotated with sort of a wobble, brought up the landing gear, and began to rise slowly. It went faster as it rose until it disappeared at great speed. An energy had permeated the area and I lost all my strength for some hours. I was unable to walk. When my strength finally returned I walked back to the base camp.

Udo returned annually to the mine for a few years following the incident but never saw the craft or its occupants after that. He related that he always wished that he could have seen them again. Udo was so reluctant to speak of the incident that nearly five decades passed before he shared it with his wife—only after discussing it with his own patriarch. Tim Grossnickle describes Udo as a shy, pleasant, Scandinavian immigrant—a carpenter by trade. He trusts the word of this high priest and reports that Udo related this account to his father in a "humble and matter-of-fact way, having a relationship of friendship and trust with him."

Udo Wartena's experience is truly phenomenal. Of course, we don't know positively that it actually occurred. There are a few possibilities. Udo could have made the encounter up when he reported it to Senator John Glenn and his own stake patriarch. We are each free to use our best judgment about that possibility. I tend heavily toward believing that Udo believed he had the encounter, and didn't just lie about it decades after the event, asking his patriarch to keep it in confidence for the first few years. Is it possible that although Udo truly believed his encounter happened, it may have been a dream? Perhaps, like Stan Harter's experience could have been a dream. Or those of hundreds of thousands of others, including thousands of Church members, could be a dream, although that seems highly unlikely to me. In Udo's case, the daytime nature of the encounter and his double-checking the ground to ensure he had not dreamed it or hallucinated it due to a bad can of prospector's hash, remove it from the dream category for me. It is significant that he recounts that the visitor was human, shook his hand, spoke Udo's American English perfectly, and answered all technology questions but refrained from answering gospel questions—due to their non-interference policy, not unlike the "Prime Directive" of *Star Trek*.

The propulsion system explanation of "skipping upon the light waves" is extremely interesting, in that Udo had absolutely no knowledge or understanding about such technology or propulsion theories at the time, but decades later we find others who say they have experienced close encounters with "visitors" proffering similar explanations. The torsion field antigravity propulsion system is likewise fascinating, especially given the early date of the discussion. Subsequent treatises on torsion field physics have appeared in the literature, the most prevalent (albeit difficult to prove) perhaps being the rumor of the Nazi Bell (Die Glocke),[4] which was a heavy metal bell-shaped chamber surrounded inside the outer skin with narrow flywheels spinning at high speeds in opposite directions in a bath of red mercury energized to extreme levels with electricity. When American troops stormed the underground development facility, the Bell was missing, although the labs and power generation equipment were intact. Interestingly, a "craft" answering the same general description of the Nazi Bell (a large upside-down acorn) suddenly impacted in the woods outside of Kecksburg, Pennsylvania, on December 9, 1965. Many local citizens report that they saw the strange craft in the woods, but military trucks moved in immediately and put the device on a truck and covered it, then hauled it away, denying that anything had landed in the

---

4. In his 2001 book *The Hunt for Zero Point*, Nick Cook wrote that claims about Die Glocke originated in the 2000 Polish book *Prawda o Wunderwaffe* (*The Truth About The Wonder Weapon*) by Igor Witkowski. The book, written twenty years after Udo Wartena's letter to Senator Glenn, describes claims of a Nazi engineered device that was "a glowing, rotating contraption" rumored to have "some kind of antigravitational effect" that made it fade into time warps, and was part of an "SS antigravity program" for a flying saucer called the "Repulsine." Cook claimed an SS official named Hans Kammler was in charge of the project, and may have eventually traded the technology to the US military in exchange for his freedom.

woods. Interestingly, the scars in the trees remained for several years and were frequently broadcast to television audiences. Although the military denies everything, the physical description of the craft and the nearly precise date of twenty years following the disappearance of Die Glocke from the Polish Nazi research facility make us wonder if someone had hurriedly piloted the device out of the facility in 1945 in a dimensional time-space warp, and instantly reappeared in 1965. Of course, we understand that these types of speculation take us far afield from straightforward gospel discussions about the nature of the universe and nuts-and-bolts unidentified craft that appear in our skies, but the technology described by Udo Wartena actually seems to give some credence to the ability of "quickening" the vibrational rate of a field surrounding a physical craft, allowing it to slip from our dimension of existence into another—possibly a fifth or sixth dimension—then slipping back into our own dimension seconds or decades later.

HOW MANY PEOPLE ENCOUNTER THE UNIDENTIFIED?

I was around seven years old and had the assignment to feed the chickens, even early on Saturday mornings. We had a detached garage at the end of the short driveway beside our house, and the chicken coop was attached to the back of the garage. I walked out of the side door of the house into the brisk morning air and took the thirty or forty steps up the gravel driveway toward the open wooden door of the garage. I saw the open bag of chicken feed on the right side of the garage, near the door, and walked in. I noticed a little mouse in the feed, just at the top of the bag, and as I looked at it, a surreal feeling started to overtake me. I wondered why the mouse looked a little funny, more like a shrew, with a teardrop shaped body, head, and ears. It seemed a little strange to me and I got closer to see it better.

As I looked, I got the feeling that someone was watching me from behind, so I turned around and saw a very small man standing there in the driveway, about ten steps behind me. He was only my height, which was very rare in my experience, and his face was quite dark and very wrinkled. He wore dark glasses and was dressed in a small brown overcoat with warm clothes underneath, and he wore a brown fedora hat, which wasn't unusual for men at that time. He was, by far, the oddest man I had ever seen. I thought it was weird that such a strange little man would be standing in my driveway, but I wanted to be polite, so I walked back toward him and he began to speak to me. He knew me—at least he knew who I was and things about me. He came to give me a message, he said, and I was intrigued that such a strange, small, very old man would know me and have "an important message" specifically for me. I listened carefully as he delivered his message. He told me that I was very special, and that they had been watching me. He told me that I was being prepared for events that would occur when I was much older. There would be global strife, including wars and natural cataclysms, he said, and I would become a leader of my people and help them through the strife that was coming to the earth. "A leader of your people," he said specifically. He told me to be attentive and to prepare for that day.

    I immediately thought that I should get my parents and let them know that something really strange was happening, so I headed toward the side door of the house. I looked back and the little man was gone, so I went inside and found my mother in the kitchen. I told her everything that had just happened, and she looked at me curiously, then walked quickly to the side door and looked out. She came back in a moment and said she could see no one outside. I was already beginning to feel a heavy fatigue wash over me, and I could hardly keep my eyes open. "Okay," I said. "I don't know who it was, but he was really weird," I said. "I'm really tired," I added. She looked at me carefully, then told me to go lie on the sofa in the living room. I lay there for a moment thinking about what had just happened. The next thing I knew was that I opened my eyes and everything seemed about the same. I was refreshed, and it was a little late in the morning. I thought it was strange that I had gotten so tired so quickly and had to take a nap—something I had not done since I was a toddler. I went to find my mother, and she was getting my sister ready for church. "Church?" I asked. "Why are you doing that? It's Saturday."

    "No, it's Sunday," she corrected. "You slept all day yesterday, and all through the night. I didn't know if I should call a doctor or something."

    I was really confused and suddenly wondered if maybe I had just been sleeping and dreaming the little man episode. "Did I come in and tell you about that weird little man?" I asked her.

"Yes, you did," she confirmed. "And that was yesterday morning. And you've been sleeping all of this time. I thought maybe you were really sick or something, but you seemed okay. You were just sleeping and wouldn't wake up when we tried."

I thought about the little man and his message for the next seven or eight years, sometimes asking my mother to confirm that I had actually told her about him before I fell asleep—to confirm I hadn't dreamed the experience. She always said I had told her about it, and how odd it was that I slept my Saturday away—something I would never do. The weight of responsibility I felt at that young age was a little burdensome, and the oddness of the little man and his message caused me to wonder how he knew about me and about "the future." I wondered who my "people" were, or would be. When I wrote the first book on the subject of strange visitations and encounters, I had no memory of the visitation from the little man, and listened to witnesses describe small men with messages, and it struck me as odd that most of us never have such an unusual encounter, yet these particular experiencers had been "selected" to receive such a visitation. A few years after the book was published the memory of the little man in the driveway thundered back into my consciousness, and I could hardly believe that I could have so thoroughly forgotten the experience—especially when I had studied and written so much on the subject. I was shocked and called my mother to ask if she recalled it. "Yes, of course I remember it." She was equally surprised to learn that the memory had completely left my mind for those twenty years, then suddenly reappeared. In fact, I had always enjoyed very clear memories from my earliest childhood, frequently recalling experiences from when I was two and three. She had assumed that the memory was with me all that time and wondered why I never spoke about it with her. Of course, by that time I had become quite knowledgeable about such "visitors" and their flattering deceitful messages, and now had a much different view of the encounter. I was left to wonder why the man bothered to come to me with his deceptive message, only to fail in propagating the lie further. I felt the bizarre nature of the experience was surpassed by the peculiar loss of the memory, followed by its sudden recall many years later.

Without realizing that I may actually have been an experiencer of a visit from a non-human entity, I became curious as I looked into what was termed the UFO phenomenon and found a poll conducted by The Roper Organization. The poll was commissioned by Robert Bigelow, and the Bigelow Holding Company,[5] to survey American adults to determine the extent of their participation in the UFO phenomenon.[6] Its purpose was to alert the mental health profession that patients with claims of close encounters are not necessarily delusional. The results of the survey were published along with a plea to mental health professionals by John E. Mack, MD, Professor of Psychiatry at the Harvard Medical School, to treat patients claiming to have encountered unknown craft or beings, in a manner that seeks to discover if the experience actually occurred—and not just assume it did not.

The survey was conducted so precisely that the results were given a margin of error of only plus or minus 1.4 percent. The most pointed question asked if the respondent had seen a UAP. The affirmative response was a surprising 7 percent of all American adults. There are currently 209 million adults in America, so 7 percent represents 14.6 million. In surveys there is a segment of the adult population known as the Political Social Actives (PSAs), which is made up of those who participate at higher levels in the community—which would include many members of the Church. This PSA segment of society remains a constant 10 percent of the general population. What is interesting is that PSAs responded affirmatively to the survey questions almost 50 percent more often than the average American adult. To the above question regarding having seen a UFO, for instance, the PSA response was 10 percent. I found that eight percent of members of the Church I polled responded "Yes" to having seen a UFO.

---

5. Robert Bigelow (born May 12, 1945) is an American businessman and owner of the hotel chain Budget Suites of America and is the founder of Bigelow Aerospace, a NASA contractor. Bigelow is also the founder of The National Institute for Discovery Science (NIDS), a privately financed research organization based in Las Vegas, Nevada, which operated from 1995 to 2004 to study paranormal activity with scientific methods and instrumentation.
6. *Unusual Personal Experiences: An Analysis of the Data from Three National Surveys*. The Bigelow Holding Company, Nevada (1992).

MY INTRODUCTION TO THE UNKNOWN

The commissioners of the poll wanted to get an idea of the extent of the "alien abduction" phenomenon, where people believe they are taken by unknown beings against their will, and asked if the participant had experienced any the following, which are indicators (in the opinion of the commissioners) of a prior UFO or "visitor" abduction experience. Included are the questions and the responses, both the average and the PSA responses.

- Seeing a ghost. [Response: Average 11 percent, PSA 16 percent]
- Feeling as if you left your body. [Response: Average 14 percent, PSA 23 percent]
- Seeing a UFO. [Response: Average 7 percent, PSA 10 percent]
- Waking up paralyzed with a sense of a strange person or presence or something else in the room. [Response: Average 18 percent, PSA 28 percent]*
- Feeling that you were actually flying through the air although you didn't know why or how. [Response: Average 10 percent, PSA 18 percent]*
- Experiencing a period of time of an hour or more, in which you were apparently lost, but you could not remember why, or where you had been. [Response: Average 13 percent, PSA 17 percent]*
- Seeing unusual lights or balls of light in a room without knowing what was causing them, or where they came from. [Response: Average 8 percent, PSA 11 percent]*
- Finding puzzling scars on your body and neither you nor anyone else remembering how you received them or where you got them. [Response: Average 8 percent, PSA 9 percent]*
- Having seen, either as a child or an adult, a terrifying figure—which might have been a monster, a witch, a devil, or some other evil figure in your bedroom, closet, or somewhere else. [Response: Average 15 percent, PSA 19 percent]
- Having vivid dreams about UFOs. [Response: Average 7 percent, PSA 10 percent]

To the uninitiated, many of these questions may appear to be unrelated to the UAP phenomenon. What do bedroom visitations, unnoticed scars, and unusual lights in the house have to do with UAP? Are these not spiritual, medical, or psychological manifestations that should be dealt with in those terms? The commissioners of the survey concluded that, based on their inside knowledge of the UAP phenomenon, anyone who answered affirmatively to four out of the five questions followed by "*" was likely to have been abducted by aliens without his or her knowledge. Is this a credible conclusion for scientists and doctors to reach? You be the judge as you examine the materials included herein.

Based on the survey results, two percent of American adults answered affirmatively to four of the five key indicator questions, resulting in a likelihood that 4.1 million have likely been abducted. This is a staggering statistic. Is there really a large body of experts who believe that millions of American adults have been abducted and taken aboard UAP for examination and related procedures? Apparently so. What is so chilling, as we discuss below, is that many repeated "abduction" experiences begin in childhood, adding millions more to the total—just in America. In fact, the poll results appear to hold true globally, indicating that 7 percent of 5.8 billion (406 million) adults in the world have seen a UAP, and 2 percent have been abducted—that's 116 million adults—plus many children. If we break those statistics down by days in the average number of years that these events allegedly occur in a person's life, we discover UAP gridlock in our night skies, with more than 20,000 sightings nightly on average.

There is no demographic preference for who sees UAP and who does not. A Young Women president is just as likely to have a sighting over Orem, Utah, as an Australian aborigine in the bush or a Russian fisherman on a trawling ship in the North Atlantic. Many thousands of Americans have reported encountering UAP occupants. Thousands complain of being abducted, examined, and worse. The statistics are constant worldwide.

Interestingly, the survey commissioners were quite surprised by the 8 percent response to the question dealing with unusual lights inside the house. They are of the opinion that this occurrence is so uniquely associated with the UAP phenomenon that it is a clear indicator of UAP activity. However, anyone who researches spiritual experiences knows that such a phenomenon is clearly present in many spiritual encounters as well; with both good and evil entities. This illustrates a point that we examine in great depth herein—that UAP sightings, encounters with beings that claim to come from other planets, bedroom visitations, ghost encounters, fairy and dwarf meetings, poltergeist activities, and cryptid and demonic encounters all seem to be very closely related in ways that are quite nebulous to researchers. Even top scientific researchers like Professor J. Allen Hynek of Project Blue Book, Professor John E. Mack, M.D. of Harvard Medical School, and Dr. Jacques Vallée each came to the uneasy conclusion that the UAP/alien phenomena appear to be something different than mere extraterrestrial visitors from other planets—they seem to be of some sort of "interdimensional" or even "spiritual" origin. Of course, that was the theme of my first book as a result of my own research nearly thirty years ago.

Like other leading investigators of unusual phenomena, I didn't arrive at my conclusions easily, or early in the process. Through the years of pondering the UAP and "visitor" enigma and its implications, I, as all observers, had developed certain ephemeral viewpoints as I weighed new information gathered while reading gospel commentaries, while watching new and improved episodes of space and mystery programs, or while glancing discretely to the left in the supermarket checkout lines. In the same way most of us attempt to decipher events related to the Second Coming, I would take each new piece of UAP information, analyze it, and attempt to make it fit into an appropriate pigeonhole I had already created in a previous attempt. It would have been easy to dismiss the entire phenomenon as a large-scale hoax, a cultural craze, or a modern reflection of massive abnormal psychology. However, the possibility of human visitors from other planets was always very real, especially in light of our understanding that we are not Heavenly Father's only children in the universe. Therefore, I felt it was necessary to take people seriously when they said they had seen an unusual craft exhibiting seemingly impossible aerial acrobatics from an unmistakable range. Debunkers attempt to dismiss every sighting as a blimp, balloon, bird, airplane, star, or temperature inversion, but that is just desperate nonsense in many close-up sightings. If just one person in a hundred-year period sees just one real extra-human craft, then that makes the phenomenon real. When my missionary companion, bishop, or relative solemnly recounts a close-up sighting to me, I have no option other than to give the subject the serious consideration that person deserves.

I find that if I ask people about their personal experience with unidentified sightings or encounters, at the moment they understand it is safe to speak about it, most will tell me about a personal experience, or that of someone they are close to. For instance, in preparing for this publication I called a website hosting company to secure the domain UFODislosure.us so I could post US government UAP disclosure updates for the public. The tech on the phone asked if I was a legit UFO writer, and I explained my approach to the subject. He hesitated briefly and then said, "You know, I was out in the desert with my friends one night, and before we went to sleep, we saw some lights coming in low across the desert. It was weird, because they came so fast, and were in formation, like a triangle. As they got over us we could see that it was a triangle shaped craft of some kind, with three bright lights—one on each corner. It was really strange because it didn't make any sound. It stopped for a few seconds, then took off like a bullet, and was going so fast that it was out of sight within a second." This is typical of many UAP sightings—a black triangle with bright lights on each corner, that makes no sound and rockets away in a flash.

In addition, a couple of days ago as I attended a family hospice gathering for my passing mother, my brother-in-law, Phil, shared a sighting he had when he was around twelve. He said, "We lived in Wilsonville, Oregon, and had a grassy ditch at the edge of the yard, where I would sit, and lay back and watch the sky. I was laying there looking up one day when I saw a silver thing up in the sky. I assumed it was an airplane, or a helicopter, or something like that—but it flew across the sky pretty fast, then just stopped. I was curious, so I watched it and a few seconds later, I saw a second one do the same thing. Then a third, and so on. As the ninth silver thing flew to the formation, I saw they had made a perfect square in the sky. After a few seconds, the entire formation turned simultaneously, making it look like the square turned, then they all took off in formation. They flew straight up and were completely out of sight within a second or two."

The truth is that the unknown craft phenomenon, or UAP/UFO, is so common that it's getting difficult to find someone who hasn't seen one, or who doesn't personally know someone who has seen one. Over a million Church members have personally witnessed a UAP—8 percent of your ward members, on average. Many have been victims of abduction. Believe me, they have come to me for answers and help. If this shocks you, it shouldn't because the abduction phenomenon is prolific. When I polled 100 Church members twenty-nine years ago, 27 percent said they personally knew someone who had witnessed a UAP. I haven't taken a recent poll, but my gut feeling is that nearly thirty years later, that percentage has risen dramatically, and that many more people are more willing to discuss it now that the cultural stigma is dissipating.

There is much to be considered when attempting to understand and discern the UAP and "visitor" phenomena. We might even feel that the subject is unworthy of our attention because of its former prominence among the fringe element; the "crackpots" and "misfits" of society. The silence of the Lord on the subject might also persuade us to ignore whatever it is that others are saying they see in our skies. These feelings are no longer justified, in light of the astounding numbers of honest people who are claiming close encounters with UFOs/UAP, and recent government admissions that unknown craft are penetrating our restricted airspace and maneuvering in a seemingly impossible manner. This is especially true when we consider the tremendous impact the phenomenon is having on American and world cultures, religions, and politics. The effects of the UFO/UAP phenomenon are overwhelming and far reaching, even here in the safe haven of Church culture and life. We continue with the encounter experiences of two other groups who were, or are members of the Church.

TRAVIS WALTON

In the small town of Snowflake, Arizona, an early Church pioneer outpost, lives a community of Church members. One of them at that time, Travis Walton, has one of the most celebrated, credible tales of abduction in UAP history. Most UFO books and unsolved mystery television programs include Travis's experience in their roster of top encounters. The motion picture *Fire in the Sky* is based on Travis' ordeal, although only the portions that portray the experience of those on the ground remain true to the facts of the experience. I have spoken with many experts in the field, including physicist Stanton Friedman and investigator Ben Hansen, and they uniformly believe Travis' account of the experience—in no small measure because all of those involved, some active Church members, took repeated polygraph tests and were found to be truthful.

One evening Travis and a group of his workmates were traveling home in their pickup through the woods after a day at work. As they talked and laughed, they suddenly saw a bright light through the trees. They thought it might be an unreported forest fire, so they drove near it. As they approached, they saw that it was no fire. Travis was nearest the door, so he got out and had a look. He describes how he saw a bright craft hovering off the ground. It was not obscured nor hazy but had a "clear and distinct" form. Travis says it was so close he could have thrown a rock at it. It was the classic disc shape, was making a low rumble, and glowed a golden hue.

The thought occurred to Travis, foolishly in retrospect, that the thing "might take off" in a moment, so he moved in to get a "closer look." As he stepped forward, the low rumble suddenly got louder and the craft moved, startling Travis. He jumped forward and got behind a log. Everyone in the truck was yelling at him to come, so he stood to run back, now only around eight feet from the surface of the disc. Suddenly there was a bright flash and energy discharge, which knocked Travis to the ground. Travis' buddies in the pickup were already of the opinion that Travis should not have left them in the truck to wander near the strange hovering craft. Upon seeing these otherworldly hostilities and Travis' seemingly dead body lying motionless on the ground, they sped off in a panic.

Travis' best friend and future brother-in-law, Mike, was at the wheel. Within a quarter of a mile, Mike began to regain his thinking processes and remembered that Travis was lying alone in the dirt back there. He stopped the truck, and an argument about returning ensued. Soon, all were thinking clearly, and they returned to the scene. Travis was nowhere to be found, however. No sign of the strange craft could be detected either.

The frightened men all held hands as they warily searched the surrounding forest for Travis. They could find no sign of him. They decided to get help from the authorities and raced to the sheriff's office in town. The sheriff was summoned to the scene, and after a brief search, decided

MY INTRODUCTION TO THE UNKNOWN

to continue their man hunt in the morning. Already, however, his suspicions of foul play were growing—tales of UFO abduction were new to him too. Travis' mother was notified of his disappearance.

The next morning the sheriff's office and Travis' friends conducted a thorough search of the area, finding no clues. Travis' workmates recounted how they had seen the UFO and how Travis had approached it, only to be knocked to the ground by a brilliant flash. The sheriff developed serious doubts about the UFO story and began investigating Travis' disappearance as a homicide. Travis was dating Mike's sister at the time, and the sheriff suspected that Mike had objected, then killed him in a dispute, and the other men had helped bury Travis' body.

The group of men were questioned extensively over the next few days, and a polygraph expert was called in to check their stories. The polygraph expert had never before had so many prime witnesses to the same event. After subjecting all of the men to examinations, he concluded that they were absolutely telling the truth. So—where was Travis? Five days after his disappearance, Travis Walton walked out of the woods. He narrates what happened as the beam of light hit him in the woods: "When I felt the numbing shock, I blacked out. And the next thing I knew, I regained consciousness—not quickly, sort of gradually. My head wasn't real clear, I was in a lot of pain. I was laying on my back—I didn't know where I was. I remembered what had happened in the woods. As I was regaining consciousness I was trying to figure out where I was and what was going on. I thought maybe I was in a hospital or something—I had been hurt." As Travis looked around him, he discovered he was lying on a table in an examination-looking room, but that he was in no hospital—not one that accepts Blue Cross anyway. He saw two small gray humanoid beings at the edge of the table and pushed his weak arm against the one closest to him. It gave easily and tumbled back into the other one like a small child. Travis jumped off in a panic. He backed away from them as they stepped toward him.

Travis continues: "When I was standing in front of those things that were coming towards me—and they stopped there, and they stood there looking at me—these huge eyes, just seemed to look right through me. I didn't get any impression of emotion, it was very detached—sort of, a just observing sort of thing, but it seemed like they could see everything I was thinking of doing. It was very disturbing to me to feel so . . . exposed. And these huge eyes looked at me and . . . when they'd blink, and on an eye that big the eyelid just slid down and opened like a window opening and shutting—and it just had the strangest sort of feeling, and I just couldn't, I couldn't bear their gaze."

The two small gray beings walked toward Travis as he threatened them with a glass rod he found on a shelf behind him and shouted out threats and "Get back! Get back!" He saw a doorway on the other side of the Grays, and threatened them as he planned how to get around them and escape. They remained expressionless and unfazed, but walked right past him and out of the room. Travis took off, running wildly through the slippery, illuminated maze of corridors. He finally arrived in a room with a high-tech chair in the middle. He was alone, so he went over to look at the chair. He recounts: "There was a lever there, and when I moved that, the star pattern [that had appeared in front of him] appeared to move. That kind of disoriented me for a minute, because I felt like I was moving, kind of, for a second, because this was—to have everything suddenly shift like that. I figured I had better quit messing

Small Gray entities: bulbous head with large, almond shaped black eyes and a tiny nose and mouth. Courtesy of Ronald Kinsella.

with that. I had, by that time surmised, that I was in some sort of craft—I connected it to what had happened before, and figured I might crash this thing or something."

As Travis looked around the room and wondered what might happen next, a tall, young-looking human man with long hair entered the room. Travis explains: "This person was not like the humanoid creatures that I had seen earlier. This looked like a human being. It looked like a man, in a blue uniform. I went up to him, thinking that I was being rescued, that I was being saved—that this was a person. I started asking all kinds of questions. 'Where am I? Where are we? And who were those things that I saw? Talk to me!'"

The young human-looking man silently put his hand on Travis's shoulder and led him out of the room into the corridor and through another doorway. "When that door opened there was an inrushing of air, and it felt fresher and cooler than where I'd been. It must have been, like—the air I was in was real heavy, moist, stifling. He just pulled me quickly on—went through some doors, down a hallway to another room."

In the other room, Travis and the young human were met by two more humans, another young man and a female. They maneuvered Travis, who started protesting and fighting them, into an examination chair, something like a dental chair, and applied a "gas mask" device to his face. He lost consciousness at that point and next found himself waking in the forest as the craft flew away into the sky, five days after his abduction. He thought that only two hours had passed and was shocked to discover it had been five days. Travis has come to wonder if the three "humans" who came to deal with him after he fought off the gray beings might have been the Grays, applying a mental disguise presentation to satisfy him that he was among his own kind to render him more manageable.

Like his workmates, Travis was also subjected to a lie detector test concerning his disappearance and abduction, which he passed—nearly twenty of them as of this writing. Travis has suffered a great deal of frustration and pain as a result of his unusual encounter—not resulting so much from the trauma inflicted by his abductors, but from that inflicted by those who accused him of deceit. Everyone he meets fails to see him as a person now, he complains, but they see him as "that man," the "abductee." Travis laments, "Every contact I have with people is colored by and filtered through the distorting lens of something that just happened to me—years ago." In fact, this is the reason that most people do not report their encounters. Hopefully, people will begin to feel safer in this regard, because we all need to know what is really happening. There is a feeling among some analysts that Travis' case may be different from most, because those inside the craft may not have intended to take him. It is thought that his unexpected close approach to the craft may have inadvertently injured him, and those in the craft decided to bring him aboard to heal his wounds and then set him free.

HIGH STRANGENESS

Something that most UFO/UAP researchers are quite hesitant to report when discussing unknown craft in our skies is the "high-strangeness" aspect of many encounters. For instance, at the most basic level, a MUFON researcher may hear a witness say, "The craft floated through the trees then through the fence, and hovered over the field," and write, "The craft floated over the trees then over the fence, and hovered over the field." What's the difference? Reporter bias. Also, a desire to help the encounter seem believable—because it appears to be a real encounter, but the strange details could make it seem contrived. The reporter hears the report through a filter of what he assumes is possible, and probable. In fact, if asked to clarify, the witness will restate, "The craft went through the trees and the fence, like it was a ghost." In this same regard, many who claim to be abducted report that they are raised from their beds in the night, floated to the wall or ceiling, and then floated right through the barrier as though it were nothing but fog. In this regard, before we begin our assessment of government admissions that UAP are real and that they are as perplexed as anyone regarding what they are, let's examine the experience of members of the Church, Steve and Dawn Hess.

After the publication of my first book twenty-nine years ago, I received many inquiries from Church members and leaders asking for guidance with their paranormal encounter experiences. One such family, Steve and Dawn Hess, had been plagued by repeated UAP encounters, and their Relief Society president suggested that they come to ask me about my expertise. They visited with me in my office and related the following account to me, which I included in a follow-up book, *Alien Encounters: The Deception Menace*. In that book I titled their experience "The Mojave Triangle." A subsequent book was published by another author detailing their experience, and a television program dedicated to their encounter was produced for Paranormal Witness, titled "The Mojave Encounter," the twelfth episode of season 5, aired on October 19, 2016. Although I have no method of vouching for the reliability of any particular encounter account, I feel the Hesses' experience is appropriate for sharing herein, and include it because it is one of the most complete accounts of multiple abductions imbued with high strangeness among Church members that I have received. Warning: portions of their experience are quite terrifying, and I urge you to skip ahead a few paragraphs at a time if you encounter material that is too frightening for you. Please do this at all times while reading this book. I don't want to lose you along the way, but want you to arrive at the end with me; a fully informed reader, even if you skipped a few darker portions.

THE MOJAVE TRIANGLE

Steve and Dawn Hess lived a quiet, normal life in southern California, with their two-year-old, Steve Jr., and newborn girl, Bethany. Steve was a devoted husband and father, and a hard-working supervisor of a construction company. Dawn was a loving wife and mother, choosing to stay at home with the baby. The Hesses were well-educated, conservative people, Dawn springing from LDS Church roots.

Steve was the rugged type, a hometown football hero and avid deer hunter. Although Dawn was athletic, she had little interest in hunting and no interest in killing trophy-sized bucks in the Mojave Desert. However, in late October of 1989, Steve was able to persuade Dawn to go hunting with him for a few days by throwing in some sightseeing and entertainment along the way. She succumbed, and the children were left with their grandparents for the three-day hunting trip.

The first day of their excursion was spent driving and sightseeing, as promised, and they ended up pulling off the road for the first night. There, they slept in the back of the pickup, in the comfortable bed with all of the necessities, protected by the canopy shell. The next day was spent hunting and sightseeing, ambling toward Steve's favorite hunting spot. When they arrived at the BLM campsite, which had never been full in Steve's twenty-year recollection, they were astounded to learn that there was no room for them. Steve drove them out to a campsite in the desert where he and his family had camped many times, and they set up camp and cooked dinner.

Dawn was a little apprehensive about camping alone in the middle of the desert—more concerned about motorcycle gangs or psychotic killers than anything. Steve assured her that this place was safe—a lot safer than Los Angeles, anyway. They went about their business, preparing for the coming darkness, when Steve got a strange feeling, a feeling he had felt fourteen years earlier at Lake Mojave. He turned suddenly in the direction of the nearby mountain, combing its base visually to see who might be watching. There was no one. As he lifted his eyes, however, he saw something that had haunted him since his experience back in 1975. There, at Lake Mojave, he and his family had met his best friend's family for a camping trip. He and his buddy, Keith, had gone fishing in the lake at night, only to be terrorized and chased by a large light that came up over the horizon. Steve's only memories ended at the point where he had stopped to help Keith escape and had been trapped in a light falling on him from the dark sky. He found himself wandering into camp awhile later, terrified—a feeling that never completely went away in the intervening years.

As soon as Steve saw the light up behind the mountain, it fell below the ridge, as if to hide from him. This was unnerving to Steve. He attempted to conceal his fear, but Dawn noticed a change in him, exciting her own uneasiness. Steve engaged Dawn in conversations about the beautifully clear, starlit sky, and demonstrated how the desert was teeming with animal life by throwing a hunk of bread into the nearby brush and watching as a small herd of kangaroo rats pounced on it and carried it away in small pieces. The desert was filled with the chirping and cooing of its inhabitants. Because the stars were

MY INTRODUCTION TO THE UNKNOWN

so brilliant, Dawn induced Steve to point out the constellations to her. Steve named them one by one as Dawn tested his knowledge. At one point she asked about a particular cluster as she mentioned how it was the brightest in the sky. Steve was astounded as he turned to see the assembly of nine unfamiliar pinpoints of light, near the ridge where he had spotted the ominous light just moments earlier. The group of lights was very bright, radiating light, and was within a few hundred yards of them. Steve was panicking inwardly, as he made fumbling excuses about weather balloons to his questioning wife about why the stars had begun moving in unison across the sky. They watched in amazement, wondering about these brilliant objects, until Dawn announced that they were now blinking to one another as if in communication, and were definitely not stars or balloons. Because of world conditions at the time, the Hesses thought that this may have something to do with nearby military bases. Just as the nine flashing objects floated directly over the Hesses, they disappeared—in an instant they were just gone. Steve and Dawn rapidly searched the starry sky, finding the shining objects now to the west, and several thousand feet up, in the shape of the letter "M."

This was too unusual, even for unknown military maneuvers. Steve and Dawn looked at each other and began to discuss the implications of what had just occurred, when they both looked up at the same time. Hundreds of the flashing lights were now above them, communicating back and forth, blinking out what seemed to be secret messages. Now, the Hesses knew they were seeing something they weren't supposed to see. As they watched in unbelief, they were numbed as the objects began, one by one, to fall gracefully from the sky and land in the desert.

In terror, fearing a full-scale Russian invasion or something to the effect, they looked on as more of the orbs floated to the desert. Soon, the desert was filled with thousands of small white lights, moving toward the Hesses' campsite. Incomprehensibly, the sky was now completely black, devoid of any stars, and the desert background noises had ceased entirely. Steve ran to kick out the campfire and ordered Dawn into the back of the pickup. He followed her in, seizing his deer rifle in one hand and shotgun in the other. He loaded his rifles, put on his vest with plenty of ammunition, and waited for the fight to start.

As the thousands of lights fast approached, Steve took aim and was ready to shoot, taunting them with his screams to "come and get it." Dawn, however, was trying to calm him, already receiving telepathic messages that they must surrender or die. With Dawn's guidance, Steve soon heard a "cease and desist" message and felt the will to fight the attackers drain from him. Steve, perplexed by this new pacifism, turned to look out of the back of the canopy at Dawn's prompting. There, he saw two cylindrical forms, approximately three feet high and two feet in diameter, just materializing, but becoming only semisolid. There they oscillated between material and translucent, bluish-gray, making a noise like static electricity, and reeking of pungent sulphur.

Steve lost his balance, falling toward the objects. To his surprise, the nearest of the two floated toward him in uniform fashion, at the same speed and within the same distance. He sat back quickly and the hovering sentry moved away from him correspondingly. As Steve and Dawn looked out the back of their camper, their attention was drawn beyond the two sentries, and they saw that the thousands of lights that had fallen from the sky and raced across the desert had now stationed themselves around the campsite. As they surveyed the sea of glowing objects they knew they were in real trouble—each of them had a pair of red, glowing eyes, staring at the campers with malice.

Then, the small "creatures," translucent with manlike faces and monkey-like bodies, began to frolic around the campsite and surrounding desert, swinging through the mesquite trees and tumbling in the sagebrush. Their play was mocking and malicious—they seemed to be evil. As Steve and Dawn looked on in numbed awe, Dawn finally broke the silence, voicing her dread. "We're going to die."

The Hesses fought to retain control of their minds. It was obvious that the "voices" in their heads were exerting some kind of control over them, but they couldn't tell how much of what they were seeing was real or imagined. Steve told Dawn to pinch him, and they engaged in an ongoing reality test, asking each other questions about what they were seeing, hearing, and smelling. The reality check established that they were both perceiving the same things.

Steve and Dawn began, the best they could, to analyze what must be happening to them. They considered a military explanation, a psychological interpretation, and anything else they could think of. Nothing made sense. They had begun hearing one another's thoughts, as though tuned in to a central telepathy system. They noted the details of their experience. For example, these little malevolent creatures had to be weightless because as they frolicked through the branches of the mesquite tree, the limbs remained rigid—not even the thin branches bent as the creatures swung on them. Perhaps they were only psychic projections—downloaded theater.

Steve leaned out the back of the truck, shouting at the creatures. As he inclined toward the sentries, one came near him. He reached out his hand and touched it, only to receive a burning electrical shock. The dwarfish creatures appeared to become more excitedly malevolent as the Hesses' terror grew. The gremlins teased and taunted with evil delight as Steve and Dawn held each other in the back of their pickup.

Then, the terror was heightened as they watched a gigantic UAP descend to the earth, hovering about three hundred feet above them and filling the entire valley, blackening the sky beyond the mountain peaks. The craft was the classic disc shape, with a dome in the center on top, and flashing lights blinking in rhythms and codes around the perimeter. They watched in awe and horror as there suddenly appeared six miniature versions of the craft on its underside, and a huge cylindrical light beam shot out from its belly, "beaming" objects into and out of the main craft.

The beam was at least two hundred feet in diameter, and they saw what appeared to be forms in the shapes of living things—not the actual living things themselves—being beamed up and down in the light. The dark silhouettes of deer, cactus, donkeys, mice, trees, bushes, and cattle were floating up and down in the bizarre spectacle. Just then, a lighted form appeared on the underside of the craft. A yellow, red, and white triangle detached itself and floated to the desert floor, where it began what appeared to be a search of the area, one point down, meticulously combing the basin. The light emanating from the triangle would normally be too bright for human eyes to observe, yet Steve and Dawn looked directly at it, wondering how they could stand the brightness.

They then felt a rumbling within the earth beneath them. They concluded that the triangle must be acting like a drill of some kind, wondering why the triangle might be drilling in the desert so far beneath their campsite. They continued their reality testing, asking each other what they were perceiving. The smell of sulphur had by now become so overwhelming that their breathing was difficult, accentuated by the adrenaline pumping through their veins. As they held each other, contemplating the outlandish scene that had paraded before them for the past two hours, they anguished at what appeared next.

Steve recognized these creatures and knew they were the ones sending the telepathic messages. There were nine Gray beings, the standard short, spindly bodied type with their large, black, almond-shaped eyes wrapping around bulbous heads. Not much in the way of mouths, noses, or hair. These had an eerie glow to them. They encircled the camper and began their game of mental torture. Dawn suddenly "knew" that these were here to keep her and Steve prisoner, while other Grays picked up their children from Grandma's house. Dawn could hear the children screaming for help, pleading for their mother's intervention. Steve could feel the cold observation as the beings scanned his mind, observing him like a laboratory specimen—less than a living being.

Regaining a small degree of his former will to protect himself and family, Steve suddenly burst out with murderous threats against their captors, who sent him reeling with what felt like an "explosion" within his brain. Dawn, panicked, held him, and asked what had happened. He only got out half a sentence when the "experiences" began. Suddenly, full sensory visions, complete with all of the attendant feelings, filled Steve's head. Experiences from his life were relived in rapid succession: the praise and glory of the game winning touchdown; the first time he saw Dawn; hunting with friends; unwrapping Christmas presents—all with the sights, sounds, smells, and feelings of the real occasion. Then the pleasantness disappeared, and other sensations and emotions were explored. Steve lost all contact with Dawn and the world, and was completely controlled by the Grays while staring into each others' eyes. He was transported to scene after scene, each evoking strong emotions—love, hate, anger, contentment, humiliation, jealousy, pleasure, and pain. The Grays drew it all out of him with callous precision, coldly staring as they forced Steve through a lifetime of emotional highs and lows.

MY INTRODUCTION TO THE UNKNOWN

Then they made Steve relive the terror at Lake Mojave. They were the ones who had chased him unmercifully that night fourteen years before. They were telling him this—they wanted him to relive his horror and to know that it had been them. Steve began to come out of his trance now, but Dawn had already begun her mental roller coaster ride. Steve tried to help her fight them, but to no avail—she was already gone, reliving her emotional highs and lows, suffering for their pleasure.

Dawn received the same emotional treatment as Steve, climaxing with the birth of her first baby, Steve Jr. She relived the sheer agony and trauma of childbirth, and then was drawn into the hospital corridor with the sense that something was wrong with the baby, hearing an infant's crying at the other end of the unit. The cast of characters included Steve, their four parents, and some hospital personnel. The drama was executed with perfection by the players—the subtle, suggestive movements, slowly bred fear, then terror, culminating in finding Steve Jr., three years old, in the operating room, surrounded by masked surgeons. He called out to her for help, accusing her of abandoning him. Then she saw that something horrible was being done to him. His chest cavity was opened and clamps and IVs were hooked up to him, with blood spurting freely from his arteries. The caustic odor of sulphur[7] was heavy in the sterile room. She then saw that the surgeons were actually the Gray beings, and Steve Jr. cried out, "They've taken me. Used me for experiments."

This scene was accompanied by a deep, menacing sense of loss that took Dawn close to death. Steve and Dawn were being tortured, not only psychologically, but physically. Their body functions, especially their temperature and nervous systems, were fluctuating. The beings were experimenting. Breathing was labored; they were both struggling, trying to stay alive. Just as they both were slipping into unconsciousness, chests heaving trying to take in oxygen, a white fog rolled into the campsite from somewhere in the desert. It came to the back of

---

7. You may have read or heard many encounter experiences, where the heavy smell of sulphur is present. This caustic odor is related in many encounters, even dating back thousands of years to clearly demonic encounters.

the pickup and into the camper. It was freezing cold, but as it reached Steve and Dawn, it had an immediate effect on their body functions. It controlled their breathing, like a force on the outside of their chests. It calmed them, instantly, alleviating their high state of anxiety. They were spared, for now at least.

As the wintry haze receded, the Hesses were relieved of their torture. They came to their senses and began to discuss what was happening. They surveyed the activity outside, which had not changed; the triangle still made its unending search for something unknown, and the rumblings beneath them in the earth continued. The Grays stared with chilly indifference, and the gremlins scurried about in their raucous play. The Hesses discussed the possibilities: were they mining rare ores for their fuel or industrial needs, or did they have another mission? "Something to do with souls," Dawn intuited. She didn't know where the thought came from.

As they reasoned about their captors and their possible motives, Dawn was suddenly pulled again into another game of emotional roller coaster. This time they knew what was coming and fought to block the Grays out, but to no avail. Steve tried to help Dawn concentrate and block them, but the disconnected visions flowed; pride, love, terror, and humiliation kept coming. Then, the most repulsive of all memories—the stranger in the school yard, asking for help, telling young Dawn that her daddy had said it was alright. She followed him into the nearby wooded area where he attacked her. Every emotion—the pain, the trauma—it was all there. Only this time, as she came to, she realized that it was Steve's face on the rapist. She recoiled from him, just as the beings began to control his actions. A sneer and leer came over him as he made an inappropriate suggestion that this might be a good time to be intimate. Dawn, still reeling from the rape she had just suffered by a man with Steve's face, was astonished at the suggestion as she looked at the Grays just standing and observing blankly. Dawn was enraged at Steve's coarse insensitivity.

As Steve came to his senses, he found Dawn screaming at him. His apologies went unnoticed. Then, as Dawn was calmed by the vapors of the frosty mist, Steve began to recede into his next psychic whirlwind. He suddenly found himself in a beautiful Pacific Northwest forest early in the morning, wondering what he was doing there and having no recollection or intimation of his torment. He breathed in the nippy, fragrant air, feeling the sun's rays on his skin. His appetite controlled him; he had to find food, and answers.

Steve suddenly smelled a campfire and followed the alluring aroma through the trees and brush. Everything was exactly as one would expect. He felt very much at home in these surroundings. As he approached, the campfire smoke blended with the scent of cooking rabbit. He was ravenous and had to eat, no matter what. He neared the camp but was cautious—there was something abnormal about it. The fire was neatly laid with the roasting rabbit above it. But there was no other sign of anyone having been there—no sleeping bags or gear or even a footstep in the leaves and twigs. His voracity overcame his sense of propriety, and he took the rabbit and ate. The sensation of satisfaction of appetite was unparalleled. Steve tore at his feast until he heard a small crackle nearby in the forest. He tossed the remainder of his meal into the brush and headed through the trees, up to the ridge. He suddenly felt watched, as thoughts of hunters baiting their quarry swirled through his brain. Instinctive fear surged through him as the feeling of being hunted overtook him, but it was too late. At the same time that he heard the crack of a rifle he felt the searing rage of a bullet thundering through his left leg.

His entire body went numb as the bullet impacted him, spinning him to the ground. The pain and shock were real, the trauma exacting. He spontaneously jumped up and rambled helplessly through the brush. He was being hunted and had to escape. Questions plagued him as he focused all of his energies on surviving the hunt. The throbbing ache in his leg held him back, while his struggle for his life propelled him forward. He stopped and tore a strip of material from his shirt and applied a quick tourniquet to stop the deluge of blood from his wound.

As he raced off again, dragging his leg, Steve's hopes shattered as he heard the baying of dogs on his trail. His instinct drove him, and he headed for the small river. He splashed out into it and headed straight across to the bank. He made a few tracks and returned to the river, moving upstream about twenty yards, and went for a tree with adequate cover. As he climbed he heard the dogs arrive at the river. They searched for his scent, but had lost it. The hunters soon arrived and cheered the dogs on. The lead dog found his way to Steve's tree as a hunter took aim and shot. The bullet tore into Steve's right shoulder, shattering the bone and liquefying the flesh. He fell from the tree. The dogs rushed him, tearing his flesh. Steve's mind was fading, thinking thoughts of his wife and children—how much he would miss them. The hunters approached, one of them taking his hunting knife and slitting Steve from sternum to pelvic bone, letting his warm insides roll out over him. Steve faded completely as they began skinning him.

Steve came out of this horrendous vision/experience groggy and frightened. Dawn calmed him as much as she could. Five and a half hours had passed since the stars had begun to fall from the sky. Just as the two felt they could no longer take this torture, signs of relief came. First, the gremlins began to recede into the desert—first dozens, then scores at a time; then the Grays walked out of their sight. Steve and Dawn were jubilant there in the back of the pickup, thanking God for answering their many heartfelt prayers for them and their children. They were going to live!

This jubilation was quickly quenched, however, as the Grays returned to observe this manipulated ecstasy. The gnomes also returned, this time attacking the pickup camper, creating as much hellish terror as possible. This enraged Steve, and he reached for his shotgun, reviving his sense of safeguarding family. He was filled with fury as he vowed to blast them all. But then, the voice began working on him as his passion was drained by an unseen force. It assured him, "Don't do anything to hurt us. Put the gun down. You have no chance." And then, "In the end, we'll kill you if you try to harm us."

As Steve and Dawn sank in despair, more Grays arrived, watching the back of the pickup. A procession of dozens of them passed by, observing in frigid silence. The great column of light that had been beaming life forms up and down for several hours now neared the truck, and the rumbling in the earth intensified and began to shake the pickup as the beam approached. Steve and Dawn both felt at the same moment that the time had come for them to be taken aboard the craft hanging above them. As the beam neared the couple, the truck shook and rocked violently, tossing them about inside the camper, emptying the camping containers onto the Hesses. The stench of sulphur and burning metal permeated their lungs and stung their eyes. The gremlins taunted with delight, threatening and pressing their faces to the windows mockingly. The Grays watched, taking it all in. Panicking from their apprehension of what was to follow, Dawn gasped as one of the distant Grays lifted its arm, pointing one of its three fingers at her. A small light, the size of a used piece of blackboard chalk, came hurtling through the air, through the window, and into Dawn's abdomen. Dawn tried to reach inside her clothing to brush it off, but it wasn't there—it was inside her.

As Steve and Dawn dealt with this horror, their attention was again diverted to the column of light, which had engulfed them now. The stench, the violent shaking, the howling grinding of the noise beneath them were overwhelming as the two screamed with fear of being lifted up into the large "mother ship."

They suddenly felt an upward momentum and slight swaying, as though they were being elevated. But as they looked outside, everything seemed normal. The desert was still right there, and the mesquite tree and cactus and brush and rocks were all still there. Yet the sensations of rushing air and of being hurled through the atmosphere were present. Their senses told them that the "drilling" sound must have cut a great chunk of the earth right out from beneath them, and that they and their surroundings were being moved to some other place at high speed. Yet, looking out the windows, they could see the distant mountains and the desert floor leading to them without interruption. They were not moving, despite what their senses told them.

There was an inrushing of chilled air, and the noise, the sulphur and drilling all suddenly ceased. The UAP had disappeared, the Grays were all but gone, and the gremlins were retracting into the desert, then beaming up like stars falling upward. A point of light descended in the sky off to their left. As it approached, they could see that it was a person, a beautiful woman in a flowing, luminous white gown. If ever an angelic personage had appeared to mortals, this feminine, seraphic being met their every expectation of what it would be like.

She floated to within about thirty feet of the Hesses, hovering lithely above the ground, standing approximately eight feet tall. A soft, reassuring telepathic voice now permeated them: "It's all right. I'm here now to protect you. Be at peace. It's almost over." With that, the angelic being ascended slightly and disappeared in an instant as Steve and Dawn watched in astonishment.

This "angelic" visitation had changed everything. The aliens were nearly all gone now. Had Steve and Dawn been "chosen" for a special experience or a special purpose? Had they overcome a great test, to prove their worthiness? These questions ran through their minds as they suddenly noticed that the cold fog that had numbed their bodies all night had vanished. They suddenly had an overwhelming desire to use the bathroom. Some plastic containers would have to do. They weren't ready to exit the protective camper just yet.

Sleep was overtaking them hastily as they watched the last of the gremlins beam up to a central point of light that took on the shape of their absent moon. Steve and Dawn awoke about four hours later at 8:00 a.m., Steve guessed. His watch was not working. Dawn manned the truck's radio to see if there were any reports of large objects in the sky, while Steve searched for physical evidence of their visitors. Dawn was disappointed that there was no talk at all about a UFO invasion. Steve scoured the campsite and then the surrounding desert; not a single footprint or broken twig. There was no sign that anything had occurred at all.

Steve started up the pickup and they took off in search of witnesses. They came upon some elderly campers about six miles away, but they reported that they had gone to bed early and hadn't seen anything unusual. As the Hesses headed back toward the highway to find a phone to check and see if the children were all right, they watched in astonishment as the triangle, the illuminated "searcher" from the night before, came racing through the sky and followed them. They scrutinized it carefully as it flanked them while they sped toward the highway. Will this nightmare ever end? they wondered. A telephone call they placed from a desert cafe assured them that all was well with the children at Grandma's house.

The Hesses returned to their home and children and tried to live a normal life. However, they soon found that the nightmare was not over. In the months that followed, they were plagued with "Grays"

MY INTRODUCTION TO THE UNKNOWN

and other visitors in their home, who took them aboard alien craft and performed horrendous physical and reproductive experiments on them. Poltergeists and other paranormal phenomena afflicted them and their children in their home. They received "revelations" from the beings who had the apparent ability to monitor the Hesses continually. They described their abductions to what appeared to be a large craft, and answered my questions about the beings, the messages, and the precise details of the craft's interior and the "props" that filled the environment. For instance, in one "presentation," Dawn was handed a Styrofoam cup filled with something. I asked her if it felt like an actual Styrofoam cup in her hand. Did it have the same ridges and reliefs that a real Styrofoam cup has? The thick lip at the top? Did it give her that Styrofoam feel on her fingers? She replied yes to each question. I asked if she felt that the raised symbols and numbers from the manufacturer were imprinted on the bottom of the cup. She responded yes—if she had turned it over and looked at the bottom, it seemed so genuine that she would have been surprised if the identifying markings were absent. I asked for this level of detail, because I highly suspected that their "journeys" to the craft were psychic downloads—mere mental theater projected psychically by their abductors. After all, they had just described how the interior shapes and dimensions of the large room they were taken to kept shifting and changing in size and shape.

The beings were, Dawn learned, acting under the direction of the "One Supreme," whom the entities told her was God. In these subsequent encounters, the Hesses were terrorized, flattered, told their children would be killed, and told their children would be great world leaders. At one point they were assured that their little son would one day be called to be the prophet of the Church. The lies, deceit, manipulation, and mental and physical torture continued, only spread out over time.

The Hesses didn't know what to do about this new phenomenon in their life. They finally confided in their parents, who received the information with mixed reactions. They confided in a friend, who eventually put them in contact with trauma researchers and regressive hypnotists. Research was conducted and hypnosis sessions held. The Hesses came to believe, as a result of their sessions, that they had not slept for the last four hours in the back of their pickup, but were dragged kicking and screaming aboard the UFO and brutally examined and experimented upon.

The visitations and abuse continued for a few years. Steve eventually joined the Church, and together they sought spiritual guidance, having come to believe that the "beings" may not be extraterrestrial after all. As soon as spiritual protection was invoked through priesthood blessings, the encounters and paranormal activity ceased. That was approximately a year and a half before Steve and Dawn sought me out, and as of the time of our interview the abductions and hauntings had not returned.

As I mentioned earlier, I did not recall my small, wrinkled man visitation until a few years after my first book on the subject was published. As I listened to the Hesses' account of being told by the entities that their children would be world leaders, I knew of such deceitful messages to others but did not yet recall my own delivered message of grandeur.

ARE THESE UAP AND ENTITY ENCOUNTERS EXTRATERRESTRIAL?

At the time of my first publication, no other planets had actually been discovered by astronomers outside of our own solar system. Now, thousands have been identified, and many scientists postulate that there exist numerous planets circling myriad stars in our universe—that all stars have planets in orbit. Of these planets, some scientists estimate that a very low percentage (still, thousands to billions of planets in our galaxy, and trillions in the universe) are capable of sustaining life. Although it would be statistically nearly impossible for intelligent life to exist on such planets from an evolutionary viewpoint,[8] which is the main reason that most scientists have historically rejected the idea of intelligent life elsewhere in the universe, the scriptures inform us that many (innumerable) are populated with human and other life forms that have been placed there by God. Being armed with this knowledge, it would be easy for us to say "yes," we are most likely being visited by our brethren from one or more of these distant planets. That appears to be the case in the instance of the Udo Wartena encounter. There are, however, certain patterns to

---

8. Frank B. Salisbury, "UFO, APPENDIX," *Nature*, Oct. 1969, 2.

the forms of visitation, the forms of communication, and the content of such communication from the bulk of these UAP occupant encounters that give us great pause. We discuss these below.

Also, why is the government suddenly renaming UFOs and designating them UAP (unidentified aerial phenomena)? Is there a difference? There is. The U is still "unidentified," and A and F have similar meanings—but the difference between "object" and "phenomena" (plural) is revealing. An object is a solid thing. A phenomenon is a concept or occurrence—a much broader meaning than an object. Google Dictionary defines it as "a fact or situation that is observed to exist or happen, especially one whose cause or explanation is in question." The government has expanded the term to include questionable situations, events, and occurrences that aren't necessarily nuts-and-bolts objects. Again, I suspect that some top-level government and military leaders are aware of the bizarre nature of UAP occupants and their twisted, or at least amoral treatment of humans, and the anti-Christ messages they deliver during their grotesque pageants.

So, the question arises: Are UAP real objects? Does their presence represent a physical object, or an ephemeral phenomenon? Perhaps a mixture? Most scientists initially found it too difficult to accept the existence of UAP, in any form. Many, however, came to find the evidence too compelling to ignore, and began accepting the possibility of extraterrestrial life and its visitation to Earth. Famed physicist Dr. Michio Kaku recently said, "We are witnessing a tipping point. The burden of proof used to be on the believers to prove that UFOs are real. Now, the burden of proof has shifted to the government and the military to prove that they're not real."[9]

I watch Dr. Kaku as he reviews military UAP videos, and he is animated as they perform feats that are physically impossible for our own craft—especially as he watches them move from the air to the water and back to the air. "Look at this thing! It's traveling much faster than it should," Kaku exclaims. "How many aircraft do we know can dive into the ocean? But these craft effortlessly go back and forth between

---

9. "The Evidence is Overwhelming" segment on *Tucker Carlson Tonight*, Fox News, Sept. 22, 2019.

the water and the air. Our missiles cannot do that. The stresses would be enough to rip the metal apart." That was when the government issued its admissions that they have captured video and high-resolution multiple sensor tracking information that demonstrates unknown objects are flying circles around our fastest jets, and the highly trained pilots are reporting that "they aren't from here."

Many of these scientists, with no religious training or background, for the reasons discussed herein are beginning to rethink the "extraterrestrial visitors" assumption for many encounters. Now, having accepted the possibility of extraterrestrial life, they, like laymen, are finding great difficulty in ascertaining whether or not UAP are manifestations of extraterrestrial visitation, or something else. Professor Frank B. Salisbury, who studied the subject in depth and penned the foreword to my book, vacillated between nuts-and-bolts objects and dimensional/spiritual manifestations. I asked him about his stance shortly before his death, and he said his pendulum was swinging back toward nuts-and-bolts. However, many other top scientists and ufologists are scratching their heads and saying that the phenomenon appears to be interdimensional, or even spiritual in nature. What does that mean? Are they saying that demons are manifesting UAP and their occupants? Or are they intimating that they believe life has developed in other dimensions of existence, and it is highly intelligent and slips into our dimension thousands of times daily to conduct experiments on us and see the sites?

Though the Church at present has no official position stated on the UFO/UAP phenomena, we can survey the volumes of UAP literature, search the scriptures and the prophets, and attempt to understand the UAP phenomenon within the gospel framework. Taking certain gospel principles as true and universal, we have the advantage over most who try to make sense of UAP and their occupants. With the gospel as our guide, we can further analyze the UAP "message" to mankind, holding it up to the light of revealed truth and discerning its actual source.

To unravel the tangle of ufology (the study and body of UFO reports) and how it relates to information we receive through our study of the gospel, we survey the UFO/UAP literature and look closely at those who are experiencers or victims of close encounters with UAP and their occupants. We compare it with what the scriptures, prophets, and others have revealed about the existence and nature of life in our universe, and discover whether or not it enlightens us concerning the current UFO/UAP enigma. We also survey the history of UFO/UAP phenomena, in their various forms and manifestations, including accounts of Church members, at all levels. Finally, we analyze the "message" and other information we are receiving from UAP and related sources, and weigh in the balance the nature, origin, and character of these, our "space brothers."

The UFO/UAP phenomenon is real and widespread, and I can predict with certainty that it will continue to have far-reaching effects on society, nations, and religions in coming years. It is possible that Earth is periodically visited by interplanetary craft piloted either remotely or by extraterrestrial human occupants. However, many UAP sightings and "alien" encounters appear to correspond better to traditional supernatural or spiritual phenomena—often like that experienced by the first missionaries to England. In fact, it is often impossible to discern the difference between aliens and the evil spirits, poltergeists, cryptids, and related counterfeit angelic apparitions that are manifested with increasing frequency as we approach the final days of this dispensation of time. Because we know several of these paranormal phenomena to be satanic deceptive apparitions, it is quite possible that many UAP sightings and encounters have similar origins and purposes—although we should not leap to conclusions that all, or even most, fall into that broad category. The truth is that our observations and interactions with UAP are broad and confusing, and it's difficult to tell so early in the process if we are just too different from "them" to get a good read on what they are trying to communicate, or if they are the same beings that have attempted to undermine and destroy humanity since they were thrust down from the presence of the Father.

I attempt herein to document cases and testimonies that provide our database, and statements and conclusions of the world-class experts that have investigated them, who often reach conclusions similar to mine—to the extent I actually formulate conclusions. I invite you to analyze the data in a thoughtful, prayerful manner. Your ability to do so is at least as developed and legitimate as mine. Whether or not your conclusions are the same as mine, by reading these materials you will at least have received an updated education regarding phenomena that will take on greater prominence and significance in our very near future.

CHAPTER 4

Government Disclosure of UAP

When you have eliminated the impossible,
whatever remains,
however improbable,
must be the truth.

—*Sherlock Holmes (Sir Arthur Conan Doyle)*

The US government and its military leaders felt they had a vested interest in tamping down the public's belief that superior craft were invading American airspace in the 1950s and 60s. After all, if the military and government were powerless to keep unidentified craft from flying over our cities and most secret and sensitive military and defense installations, including nuclear and ICBM[1] launch sites, what good were they? The government had a strong interest in maintaining the *status quo* with a public that placed high value on traditional beliefs that held there were no beings smarter or more powerful than the American government. In response to the rising number of public UAP sightings, the government operated a series of programs that

---

1. Intercontinental ballistic missiles carry nuclear payloads to other continents and are extremely dangerous.

sought to debunk the very existence of UAP, ending the last of them, Project Blue Book, in 1969.

THE NEW YORK TIMES

That was what we were told anyway, and we believed it—until *The New York Times* published the now iconic story that revealed to the world that the government is tracking the UFO/UAP phenomenon very closely. Government disclosure began with Christopher Mellon, the Deputy Assistant Secretary of Defense for Intelligence for Presidents George W. Bush and Bill Clinton, and who served on the staff of the Senate Intelligence Committee, leaking the declassified "Tic Tac" and "Gimbal" videos to *The New York Times*. *The New York Times* published an article by Helene Cooper, Ralph Blumenthal, and Leslie Kean on December 17, 2017, revealing that the US government has an active UFO program and is spending millions to understand UAP. The article is titled "Glowing Auras and 'Black Money': The Pentagon's Mysterious U.F.O. Program," and begins, "WASHINGTON—In the $600 billion annual Defense Department budgets, the $22 million spent on the Advanced Aerospace Threat Identification Program was almost impossible to find. Which was how the Pentagon wanted it."

HARRY REID AND AATIP

In fact, Church member and US Senate Majority Leader Harry Reid had a great deal to do with focusing the government's attention on the problem of unidentified aircraft invading the nation's restricted airspace on a daily basis. In the 1990s[2] Reid became aware of the prolific nature of unidentified craft over American cities and sensitive military installations, and began to address the problem within the black budget programs of the military. He found tremendous resistance, however, and was dismayed by military policies that highly discouraged military pilots and others from reporting sightings and encounters with such unidentified craft. Those policies were well known to derail the careers of anyone

---

2. Yes, approximately twenty-nine years ago.

reporting an encounter or sighting incident. In 2007 Reid was able to obtain funding for the newly established Advanced Aerospace Threat Identification Program (AATIP), which began the arduous process of trying to reverse the policies of the Pentagon and other agencies that discouraged open reporting of UFO/UAP encounters.

Senator Reid says that he spoke with Senator John Glenn, who told him he thought that the federal government should be "looking seriously into UFOs and should be talking to military service members, particularly pilots, who had reported seeing aircraft they could not identify or explain." Reid enlisted the support of two other senators and top members of a defense spending subcommittee, Ted Stevens,[3] an Alaska Republican, and Daniel K. Inouye, a Hawaii Democrat, who immediately agreed to support the new program, and $22 million was set aside to support the efforts of AATIP.

The New York Times article explains:

> For years, the program investigated reports of unidentified flying objects, according to Defense Department officials, interviews with program participants and records obtained by The New York Times. It was run by a military intelligence official, Luis Elizondo, on the fifth floor of the Pentagon's C Ring, deep within the building's maze.
>
> The Defense Department has never before acknowledged the existence of the program, which it says it shut down in 2012. But its backers say that, while the Pentagon ended funding for the effort at that time, the program remains in existence. For the past five years, they say, officials with the program have continued to investigate episodes brought to them by service members, while also carrying out their other Defense Department duties.
>
> The shadowy program—parts of it remain classified—began in 2007, and initially it was largely funded at the request of Harry Reid, the Nevada Democrat who was the Senate majority leader

---

3. Senator Reid explained, "Ted Stevens said, 'I've been waiting to do this since I was in the Air Force,'" because Stevens had been a pilot in the Army's air force, flying transport missions over China during World War II. During the meeting, Reid said, "Mr. Stevens recounted being tailed by a strange aircraft with no known origin, which he said had followed his plane for miles."

at the time and who has long had an interest in space phenomena. Most of the money went to an aerospace research company run by a billionaire entrepreneur and longtime friend of Mr. Reid's, Robert Bigelow, who is currently working with NASA to produce expandable craft for humans to use in space.

On CBS's "60 Minutes" in May, Mr. Bigelow said he was "absolutely convinced" that aliens exist and that U.F.O.s have visited Earth.

The AATIP program began as part of the Defense Intelligence Agency (DIA), which Senator Reid says was extremely resistant to cooperation in the beginning. As AATIP began to collect data, however, it became apparent that there was a substantial phenomenon of unidentifiable[4] aircraft in our airspace, and that the superior maneuvering and other capabilities of the UAP as the Pentagon called them, posed a real and clear threat to America's military superiority in our own airspace.

The New York Times article further reveals:

> The money was used for management of the program, research and assessments of the threat posed by the objects. The funding went to Mr. Bigelow's company, Bigelow Aerospace, which hired subcontractors and solicited research for the program. Under Mr. Bigelow's direction, the company modified buildings in Las Vegas for the storage of metal alloys and other materials that Mr. Elizondo and program contractors said had been recovered from unidentified aerial phenomena. Researchers also studied people who said they had experienced physical effects from encounters with the objects and examined them for any physiological changes. In addition, researchers spoke to military service members who had reported sightings of strange aircraft.

The AATIP program collected video, audio recordings, radar and other high resolution multi-sensor data, and eyewitness accounts of

---

4. I use the designation "unidentifiable" for these craft because as of this writing, they are not only unidentified in the historical sense but because of their capabilities, they appear to be so far in advance of any technology that we possess to render them unidentifiable by any human equipment, means, or agency.

reported UAP incidents, including footage from a Navy F/A-18 Super Hornet showing "an aircraft surrounded by some kind of glowing aura traveling at high speed and rotating as it moves." The Navy pilots can be heard trying to make sense of what they are seeing. "There's a whole fleet of them," one exclaims.

When funding ended for AATIP, Director Elizondo submitted his resignation letter stating that there was a need for more serious attention to "the many accounts from the Navy and other services of unusual aerial systems interfering with military weapon platforms and displaying beyond-next-generation capabilities." He insisted that "there remains a vital need to ascertain capability and intent of these phenomena for the benefit of the armed forces and the nation." In the *NYT* interview, Mr. Elizondo said he and his government colleagues had determined that the phenomena they studied didn't seem to originate from any known nation. "That fact is not something any government or institution should classify in order to keep secret from the people," he said. Before Elizondo resigned, he was able to get three videos declassified, which Christopher Mellon later leaked to *The New York Times* for its groundbreaking story. Since leaving the Pentagon, Elizondo has been an outspoken proponent of studying the UAP[5] phenomenon in much greater detail and determining what they are, who is controlling them, and what their intentions are.

DEPARTMENT OF DEFENSE AUTHENTICATES THREE VIDEOS

As a result of the AATIP disclosures, the government declassified and released a few of the videos in which military aircraft encountered unidentifiable craft maneuvering in a seemingly impossible manner. Although the government possesses hundreds of such videos and photographs, many in very high definition, because these particular videos had been leaked and were circulating in the public domain (YouTube, websites), the appearance

---

5. UAP was adopted by AATIP in the place of the former term UFO and is proffered as the catch-all term for the "sightings/observations of unauthorized/unidentified aircraft/objects that have been observed entering/operating in the airspace of various military-controlled training ranges."

of transparency became advantageous, and the videos were authenticated and released. On April 27, 2020, the Department of Defense issued the following official statement vouching for the authenticity of the videos:

Immediate Release

Statement by the Department of Defense on the Release of Historical Navy Videos

April 27, 2020

The Department of Defense has authorized the release of three unclassified Navy videos, one taken in November 2004 and the other two in January 2015, which have been circulating in the public domain after unauthorized releases in 2007 and 2017. The US Navy previously acknowledged that these videos circulating in the public domain were indeed Navy videos. . . DOD is releasing the videos in order to clear up any misconceptions by the public on whether or not the footage that has been circulating was real, or whether or not there is more to the videos. The aerial phenomena observed in the videos remain characterized as "unidentified."

Because of the importance attributed to the encounters of the military personnel involved in the videos that were authenticated by the Pentagon, they have become the focus of proponents of UAP research and debunkers, who have grasped at any straw to attempt to explain them as mere nothingness. However, we must understand that the reason the Pentagon feels so adamantly that these videos represent actual encounters with true UAP is that their own pilots witnessed them from very observable distances, and they were recorded on a number of sophisticated aerial monitoring systems, including the latest generation of radar and FLIR technology. We will get into some of the specifics about the monitoring systems, but first, it bears attention that the eyewitnesses are the best trained, most knowledgeable experts on flight, flight systems, aircraft, and maneuverability in the world. These are the best of the best, the crème de la crème of the United States' military pilots, and the government has spent millions of dollars training each of these pilots to know and understand everything in the air around them. They were in the middle of live training sessions with all systems switched on and tightly focused when the encounters occurred. The Department of Defense authenticated the videos based on all of the supporting evidence in its possession.

Senator Harry Reid immediately tweeted: "@SenatorReid · Apr 27, 2020 I'm glad the Pentagon is finally releasing this footage, but it only scratches the surface of research and materials available. The US needs to take a serious, scientific look at this and any potential national security implications. The American people deserve to be informed."[6]

"FLIR1 Tic Tac" is from November 14, 2004, and "Gimbal" and "GoFast" are from January 21, 2015. Joseph Gradisher, official spokesperson for the Deputy Chief of Naval Operations for Information Warfare, clarified that these videos represent only "some of the UAP sightings" the Navy is investigating—a fraction. "Those three videos are just part of a larger effort by the US Navy to try and investigate a series of incursions into our training ranges by phenomena that we're calling unidentified aerial phenomena." Gradisher explained that the Navy is trying to eliminate the stigma of reporting UAP, which in the past pilots may have been disparaged—or ignored—or retaliated against for reporting. "We want to get beyond that stigma, and encourage our aviators to report anything that they're seeing out there," he said.

UAP TASK FORCE

We discuss the declassified and released Pentagon videos below, and the encounters they evidence, to demonstrate the true nature of the craft observed and recorded by our military. However, we note that soon after the Department of Defense (DOD) released their authentication of the above-mentioned videos, they also announced

---

6. Senator Harry Reid and your humble author agree on very little, especially in the political arena. He is extremely liberal, and I am a constitutional conservative, trained in constitutional law by Rex E. Lee, US Solicitor General in the Reagan administration, Founding Dean of the BYU J. Reuben Clark Law School, and President of BYU. Yet, Senator Reid and I agree completely that more study, more data, and heightened security are required as a result of what our finest pilots and others are witnessing in our airspace.

the establishment of a special UAP Task Force to study the phenomenon. The UAPTF, which essentially takes over where AATIP left off, is spearheaded by the US Navy, which is the branch of the military that has been most active in the release of UAP videos and tracking information. The US Air Force, on the other hand, has openly dragged its feet, and only grudgingly updated its policies.

Immediate Release

Establishment of Unidentified Aerial Phenomena Task Force

Aug. 14, 2020

On Aug. 4, 2020, Deputy Secretary of Defense David L. Norquist approved the establishment of an Unidentified Aerial Phenomena (UAP) Task Force (UAPTF). The Department of the Navy, under the cognizance of the Office of the Under Secretary of Defense for Intelligence and Security, will lead the UAPTF.

The Department of Defense established the UAPTF to improve its understanding of, and gain insight into, the nature and origins of UAP. The mission of the task force is to detect, analyze and catalog UAP that could potentially pose a threat to US national security.

As DOD has stated previously, the safety of our personnel and the security of our operations are of paramount concern. The Department of Defense and the military departments take any incursions by unauthorized aircraft into our training ranges or designated airspace very seriously and examine each report. This includes examinations of incursions that are initially reported as UAP when the observer cannot immediately identify what he or she is observing.

The UAPTF has as its first concern the establishment of a process to "standardize collection and reporting" methods for incidents involving UAP, something that has made UAP research nearly impossible due to the lack of reported data. In that regard, the DOD has suddenly shifted its policies concerning military personnel reporting unexplained phenomena, setting up internal systems and new guidelines that promote such reporting, and legitimizing the experiences of its personnel—

hoping to remove the stigma formerly associated with reporting. The Navy established its new standardized reporting system in March 2019, and the Air Force adopted a similar mechanism in November 2020. The UAPTF is specifically tasked "to improve its understanding of, and gain insight into, the nature and origins of UAP."

THE JUNE 25, 2021, SENATE INTELLIGENCE REPORT

Also noteworthy in this flurry of government admissions about the existence of UAP is Senate Intelligence Committee Chair Marco Rubio, who has been growing increasingly concerned about UAP invading restricted airspace, especially around highly sensitive nuclear, military, and defense installations. Senator Rubio placed a requirement in the COVID law as part of the Intelligence Authorization Act, signed into law at the very end of President Trump's presidency in 2020, that all US intelligence agencies deliver a report on UAP to Congress within 180 days, no later than June 25, 2021. The "unclassified" report to be released to the public, ostensibly compiled by the director of national intelligence and the secretary of defense, was intended to make public what the Pentagon knew about unidentified flying objects and data analyzed from such encounters. The report was actually compiled by a couple of government staff employees in the department with a $0.00 budget for the project, and whose security clearances were insufficient to view any materials related to UAP. They were given no dedicated time to compile and write the report—but were obliged to do so in addition to their normal jobs. They also had to prepare the classified version of the report for the US Senate Intelligence committee. The unclassified report was published on June 25, 2021, and it was only six pages in length, plus a cover page and two pages of appendix notes. Titled "Preliminary Assessment: Unidentified Aerial Phenomena," the report begins:

> This preliminary report is provided by the Office of the Director of National Intelligence (ODNI) in response to the provision in Senate Report 116–233, accompanying the Intelligence Authorization Act (IAA) for Fiscal Year 2021, that the DNI, in consultation with the Secretary of Defense (SECDEF), is to submit an

intelligence assessment of the threat posed by unidentified aerial phenomena (UAP) and the progress the Department of Defense Unidentified Aerial Phenomena Task Force (UAPTF) has made in understanding this threat.

This report provides an overview for policymakers of the challenges associated with characterizing the potential threat posed by UAP while also providing a means to develop relevant processes, policies, technologies, and training for the US military and other US Government (USG) personnel if and when they encounter UAP, so as to enhance the Intelligence Community's (IC) ability to understand the threat.

The gist of the short report is that due to the stigma that until recently had been associated with reporting encounters with and sightings of UAP, not enough data had been collected to reach any conclusions, but that the UAP Task Force had established encounter and sighting reporting and data collections systems, and would be gathering and analyzing data in a broad, uniform manner from that point on. It reported that it studied 144 recent reports of UAP that originated from USG sources. Of these, it states, 80 reports involved observation with multiple sensor systems,[7] like those discussed below. Eleven of the cases involved a "near miss" between the UAP and military aircraft, resulting in the Executive Summary conclusion: "UAP clearly pose a safety of flight issue and may pose a challenge to US national security." The report specified that the UAP exercise "signature management," which means they actively attempt to cloak any electromagnetic signals that usually emanate from a normal aircraft and reduce our ability to detect them with radar or other sensors. Of the 144 cases, they were able to resolve only one to any degree of satisfaction. The rest remain in the UAP category based on data collected from eyewitnesses and multiple sensor data gathered and analyzed. The report came to no final conclusion about what the UAP were and who controlled them, based on the lack of data beyond the eyewitnesses and sensor data, though they confirmed they were intact recordings of unexplained/

---

7. The importance of multiple sensors is that it eliminates the possibility of a malfunctioning or misread single sensor.

unexplainable actual physical objects, and not false readings, and had been detected by different types of highly sophisticated military sensors simultaneously, in addition to trained pilot visual observation.

The report failed to discuss any matters prior to the 2004 "Tic Tac" encounter, including Area 51, S4, Groom Lake, Roswell, and other highly publicized government and military involvement in UAP cases in the past seventy-five years. There were no glaring admissions of captured extraterrestrial spacecraft, collected metamaterials from UAP, or other headline grabbing disclosures. Although most interested observers expected this first official report to be a very tiny first step in the direction of disclosure of decades-long government involvement in collecting data and materials related to various UAP phenomena—the report did admit that the UAP considered in the report appeared to be far beyond current US military capabilities. In the section titled "And a Handful of UAP Appear to Demonstrate Advanced Technology," the report explains, "Some UAP appeared to remain stationary in winds aloft, move against the wind [ruling out balloons], maneuver abruptly, or move at considerable speed, without discernible means of propulsion. In a small number of cases, military aircraft systems processed radio frequency (RF) energy associated with UAP sightings." The phrase "maneuver abruptly, or move at considerable speed, without discernible means of propulsion" is a blockbuster admission that the UAP in the 143 unresolved reports are unlike any technology known to the US government—or any other government on Earth. We discuss a few of such UAP cases below, and like the UAPTF, no one is specifically saying that the UAP are technology from other planets. However, we are wondering where they are from, and who builds and controls them. If not the US, then who? China? Russia? US Intelligence says it is not us, or them. Are they extraterrestrial? There is no direct proof of that, either. One thing my Intelligence associates tell me is that in a number of UAP encounter cases, the UAP in question actively jammed the radar systems of our own aircraft. That is not a passive jam, but active jamming, which is a specific act of war.

The UAPTF created five categories that they feel all UAP will eventually fit into, stating, "If and when individual UAP incidents are resolved they will fall into one of five potential explanatory categories: airborne clutter; natural atmospheric phenomena; USG or industry developmental programs; foreign adversary systems; and a catchall 'other' bin." Of course, the "catchall" bin called "other" is where 143 of the 144 UAP reports ended up in this first report to the Senate Intelligence Committee. Of course, the report was unclassified, as ordered by the law, but a classified version of the report has also been provided to the Senate Intelligence committee members. My intelligence community associates relate that the classified report is much longer and is accompanied by several photographs and videos that the DOD has not made public.

Senator Marco Rubio, the head of the Senate Intelligence Committee who demanded the report to congress, told *60 Minutes* that unidentified aerial phenomena detected by our military are "not ours," and he says he's concerned they might represent a "foreign" surveillance threat. Subject matter insiders understand that Senator Rubio, like others, well knows that these UAP are not Russian or Chinese, but in order to publicly broach the subject in a manner that doesn't invoke the stigma of "little green men," he must frame the discussion as a national security concern to the government. "We certainly want to make sure that it's not a foreign adversary capability, meaning . . . the Russians, or the Chinese . . . have developed some technology. . . It's a huge counterintelligence threat if that's what it is. We want to take that seriously." He was asked why setting up a UAP reporting system and analyzing the data retrieved from observations and encounters was so important to America's intelligence community, and he answered, "I want this to be taken seriously, and I want a process to take it seriously. . . Until we get some answers. Maybe it has a very simple answer. Maybe it doesn't." There it is.

Although the June 25 report to Congress lacked very much new usable information about the nature and origin of UAP, seeing that the public was already in possession of much of the same data, it was transformational in a way, because it took interest in UAP out of the fringe realm of pop culture and put it squarely into the official policy and security interests of the US government, causing a 180-degree turnaround in how federal agencies and the military will approach the phenomenon. Under the laws, the stigma of UAP encounters has been officially ended.

From the government's view, as long as UAP remain unidentified, as the report acknowledges, they represent a national security threat to the United States. Any object that can fly into our restricted airspace with impunity, including over our defense and nuclear facilities, when we have no idea what it is, how it works, what its purpose is or who created and sent it, constitutes a serious potential threat to our security. As Christopher Mellon explains, "We know we're vulnerable. We don't know what their intent is. We have some idea of their capability. That is deeply concerning. Threat is a function of intent and capability."

Commenting on the Report the day it came out, Christopher K. Mellon tweeted: "@ChrisKMellon · Key takeaways of the #UAP #UFO report reading between the lines: 1) It isn't us; 2) We don't understand the revolutionary technology we are observing in some cases and; 3) We don't think it is Russia or China. Time to get to work!"

"60 MINUTES"

In anticipation of the release of the UAPTF report to congress, CBS aired a special "60 Minutes" UAP report on May 16, 2021, which began, "We have tackled many strange stories on 60 Minutes, but perhaps none like this. It's the story of the US government's grudging acknowledgment of Unidentified Aerial Phenomena, UAP, more commonly known as UFOs. After decades of public denial, the Pentagon now admits there's something out there, and the US Senate wants to know what it is."

The host immediately asks former Director of AATIP, Luis Elizondo,[8] "So what you're telling me is that UFOs—Unidentified Flying Objects—are real."

Elizondo responds, "Bill, I think we're beyond that already. The government has stated on the record that they're real. I'm not telling

---

8. Strangely, the Pentagon has made public statements denying that Luis Elizondo ever served in any such capacity. Christopher Mellon, the Deputy Assistant Secretary of Defense for Intelligence, is very clear that he knew Luis Elizondo when he held that position. Senator Harry Reid was instrumental in creating AATIP and interacted with its leadership often. He said of the DOD's attempt to discredit Elizondo, "You may disagree with him, but you shouldn't try to damage his career by saying he wasn't there. He was there."

you that. The United States government is telling you that." Elizondo continues, "What I'm telling you is that it's real. The question is what is it? What are its intentions? What are its capabilities? Imagine a technology that can do 600 to 700 G-forces, that can fly at 13,000 miles per hour, that can evade radar, and that can fly through air, water and possibly space, and has no obvious signs of propulsion, no wings, no control surfaces, and yet can still defy the natural effects of earth's gravity. That's precisely what we're seeing."

The program shows short clips from some of the videos that we examine below, and the host says, "The Pentagon admits that it doesn't know what this is . . . or this . . . or this."

Next, *60 Minutes* interviews former Navy F/A-18 Super Hornet pilot Lieutenant Ryan Graves, who says that whatever it is out there, is "a security risk." He reports that his squadron began seeing UAP hovering over restricted airspace southeast of Virginia Beach in 2014, when they received updated radar systems in the jets that also made it possible for them to zero in on the UAP targets with infrared targeting cameras. The pilots were able to get close enough to many of the UAP, some taking out their smartphones and snapping photos through cockpit windows, which have been authenticated by the DOD. We consider the three photos together below.

Lt. Graves says that pilots training off the East Coast see UAP like this all the time. "Every day, for at least a couple of years." When asked if he and his fellow pilots are alarmed by the presence of these unknown objects, he says, "I'm worried, frankly. If these were tactical jets from another country that were hanging out there, it would be a massive issue. But because they look slightly different, we aren't willing to actually look at the problem in the face. We're happy to just ignore the fact that these are out there watching us every day."

In fact, the government's official position was to just ignore it—until the videos began to surface on YouTube and elsewhere, demanding that someone begin taking UAP seriously.

When questioned about his part in getting the declassified Navy UAP videos into the public forum, Chris Mellon told "60 Minutes" that in his official positions with the government he had access to all of the top-secret programs, and he said, "It's not us. That's the one thing we know."

Similarly, other news organizations have been taking the UAP threat very seriously for some time. Tucker Carlson of Fox News has been reporting on the UAP developments since 2017, culminating in his recent lead into the story: "We've spent some time reporting on this story—we should have spent a lot more time, because this could be the most consequential thing to happen to this country, to this world, maybe ever." Another Fox News headline read, "UFO Reality No Longer a Question." Church member Glenn Beck ran with a story in June 2021 titled, "How are These UFO Confirmations by the Pentagon NOT Front-page News?" Within the discussion between Glenn and his associates were questions about the religious implications of such a story. In the few weeks since that story, the confirmations have indeed become front-page news.

USS NIMITZ FLIR1 "TIC TAC" ENCOUNTER

The three declassified and authenticated Pentagon UAP videos we discuss herein are selected visual recordings of cockpit instrumentation displays from United States Navy fighter jets based aboard aircraft carriers USS *Nimitz* and USS *Theodore Roosevelt* in 2004, 2014 and 2015, with some additional footage taken by other Navy personnel in 2019.

On November 14, 2004, the USS *Nimitz* Strike Group was on a training mission in the Pacific Ocean just 100 miles southwest of San Diego. Two Navy pilots were in the air during the training exercise flying their F/A-18 Super Hornet Navy jets—Commander Dave Fravor, a graduate of the TOPGUN Naval Flight School and the F/A-18 Black Aces Squadron Commander on the USS *Nimitz*, and on his wing was Lieutenant Commander Alex Dietrich.

The USS *Princeton* was nearby and had been recently outfitted with an advanced new radar system. Its operators had been tracking highly anomalous objects for days,[9] and now detected "multiple anomalous aerial vehicles" over the horizon, in a V formation, one of which they reported

---

9. All told, radar operators with the Princeton spent about two weeks attempting to figure out what the objects were, a process that included having the ship's radar system shut down and recalibrated to make sure that the mysterious radar returns were not false positives, or "ghost tracks."

had just descended from "above 80,000 feet" in 0.78 seconds—a speed of not less than 55,000 mph—without creating a sonic boom.[10] US Navy Chief Master-at-Arms Sean Cahill (now retired), was an eyewitness to the Nimitz Tic Tac UAP event, and saw it from the USS *Princeton*. He said,

> I helped coordinate ships' movements over a period of days with Sr. Chief Kevin Day, down in the Combat Information Center [CIC]. He had been picking up anomalous contacts on the Aegis Radar System that were coming in at suborbital altitudes, then going down to 80,000 feet,[11] and then, what was spectacular was that they would immediately translate down to sea-level. Then there were groups of them proceeding in a southerly direction against the wind. This was so strange and worrisome to Kevin that he began a series of diagnostics. He and a radar tech named Kevin Voorhees both rebooted the system numerous times, double-checked everything and triple-checked, and finally Kevin went to our Captain and said, 'Sir, I'm pretty sure that we have real contacts—these are not ghosts in the system based on the upgrade.' . . . We have zero craft in our arsenal that can do that. Kevin sent a sortie of F-18s out to where the radar was picking them up—the captain ordered it.

Pilots Fravor and Dietrich were in their F/A-18 Super Hornet Navy jets, each with a WSO (weapon systems officer—affectionately, Wizzo) in the seat behind them, and were ordered to investigate the craft that had dropped in so fast. The jets were flying close to each other, and Fravor and Dietrich both could see water on the surface of the ocean being agitated by something large just under the surface. Around the surface of the roiling water were "Tic Tac shaped objects, matte white in color, darting around instantaneously like ping pong balls." Fravor and Dietrich could clearly see that the object in the roiling water was about the size of a Boeing 737 commercial airliner, which is over 100 feet long with a little wider wingspan. They immediately began talking about what might be bubbling up

---

10. All of the tracking data from the various systems confirm the rapid acceleration and extreme velocity of the UAP.
11. This is an impossible accomplishment for any known earth-based technology because de-orbiting a craft requires several specific maneuvers, and we have none that could just halt re-entry at 80,000 feet, then proceed to sea-level in less than a second.

white water like that, because the sophisticated systems on the ships were detecting no vessels or submarines in the water.

As they looked they suddenly saw a smaller object just above the agitated whitewater that they immediately thought looked similar to a giant "white Tic Tac" candy—like a cylinder with rounded ends. They estimated that the object was around 40 feet long, and it appeared to be about 50 feet above the water. The white object looked like a flying propane tank and had no wings and no other flight control surfaces. It had no apparent means of propulsion, like a jet engine or propeller, and there were no exhaust plumes around it. It was perfectly round and smooth, with the exception of two small protrusions that stuck out a couple of feet and bent at a right angle, reminding them of small antennae or other sensor instruments. Fravor describes the movement of the object as somewhat erratic, moving in all directions, while remaining in the same relative north-south configuration.[12] Dietrich said it reminded her of dropping a phone in the kitchen and watching it bounce around "with no predictable trajectory."

Fravor agreed, saying it reminded him at the time of a ping pong ball bouncing around randomly in an enclosed area.

Simulation of "Tic Tac" shaped UAP near USS Nimitz Strike Group.

---

12. Picture a chalkboard eraser in your hand on the chalkboard, and holding it in the same position in your hand, you move it up, down, right and left, and in several directions quickly while keeping the eraser pointed upward.

GOVERNMENT DISCLOSURE OF UAP

As Dietrich circled above, Fravor spiraled downward in a tight circle and went in for a closer look at the Tic Tac object. As he moved closer, he noticed the object suddenly turn for the first time, and begin mirroring his own movements, spiraling upward on the opposite side of his circle. As he met the object in the middle, it suddenly disappeared. Fravor said, "It sped off—it just disappeared. We have nothing that goes that fast; and just starts climbing at will. Then it was just gone." He was astounded at how rapidly it moved, then suddenly zipped out of visual range so fast it was hard to see it leave.

When asked about their brief encounter with the UAP on "60 Minutes," Dietrich replied, "Your mind tries to make sense of it—like maybe it was a helicopter or a drone—but when it just disappeared, it was just gone. It was unidentified, and that's why it was so unsettling to us—because we weren't expecting it, and because we couldn't classify it." She added, "I felt the vulnerability of not having anything to defend ourselves."

The host asked, "You're seeing something that defies explanation," and Dietrich and Fravor replied, "Yes. Very much." The WSOs in the back seats both watched the UAP as well, and the four of them were able to watch the UAP for a full five minutes before it shot off. Fravor told ABC News that he didn't know what the Tic Tac was, but that "it was really impressive, really fast, and I would like to fly it."

Seconds later, the USS *Princeton* reacquired the target with its advanced radar system, locating the Tic Tac sixty miles away, in the "safe zone"—the area designated as the place where pilots could take their planes in the middle of the exercise for a brief time out if they needed it. The two inexplicable things about this are 1) no one but the pilots were told where the safe zone was—they were told verbally before they got into their jets,[13] and 2) traveling sixty miles in such a short time from a dead stop requires a phenomenal take-off—like a bullet from a rifle—and a high rate of speed. The UAP object made no sonic boom as it shot sixty miles in mere seconds.

---

13. By going immediately to the safe zone, the operators of the UAP were sending an obvious message to the US Navy; that they know everything—even secrets whispered into ears back on the ship.

A short time later, Chad Underwood, on another flight crew under Fravor's command, acquired the object and quickly locked onto it with their F/A-18 Super Hornet Raytheon Advanced Targeting Forward-Looking Infrared (ATFLIR) Pod, the most advanced sensors and powerful tracking systems on the market. The display is pictured here, populated with the sensor array information as it existed at the beginning of the 1.25 minute video. Commander Underwood explains that he got a radar lock on the object but was quickly "actively" jammed by the UAP.

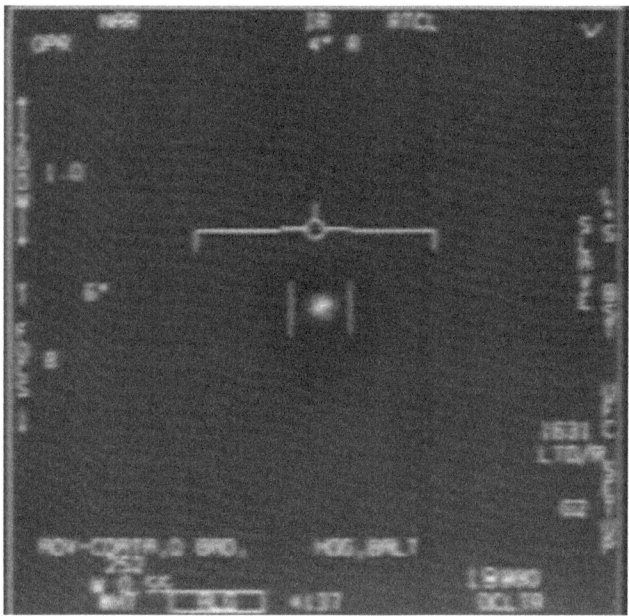

Raytheon AN-ASQ228 ATFLIR pod display information.

Starting Information on the Display

- Sensor is in Infrared Mode
- Sensor then switches to TV (Visual) Mode
- Sensor Azimuth is Aimed 4º Right of Aircraft Axis
- Sensor is Aimed 6º Above Aircraft Axis
- Sensor Zoom is at 1.0, Switched to 2.0 (Alternates)
- F/A-18 Calibrated Airspeed (252 KTS) Mach Number (0.55)

- "HOT" Display Designator: Hot Items are White, Cold are Black (Alternates)
- F/A-18 Altitude: 19,950 FT

In the released 1:15 video of the ATFLIR screen, the WSO followed the UAP with precision, alternating the tracking systems and ATFLIR Pod display at times to get the best information about the unidentified object they were tracking. The object being watched and tracked is warmer than the background and is clearly oblong in shape on the display. The WSO gets a good lock on the object, then it breaks the lock, and is quickly recaptured. After a minute and fifteen seconds, the object suddenly shot off with rapid acceleration, moving off the left of the screen with high velocity—too high for the sensors to track. Below is a screenshot of the Tic Tac object as the WSO doubled in on the zoom and switched from Infrared Mode to TV Mode.

NOTE: I have uploaded each of the discussed videos and photographs to the website UFOdisclosure.us where you can see them.

The FLIR1 video authenticated and released by the DOD is just over a minute long. In November 2019, *Popular Mechanics* interviewed several Nimitz witnesses who said they saw a longer, better quality video of the encounter than the one released to the public. One witness, for example, said he "definitely saw video that was roughly 8 to 10 minutes long and a lot more clear." Because that video was never leaked, the government has kept it classified.

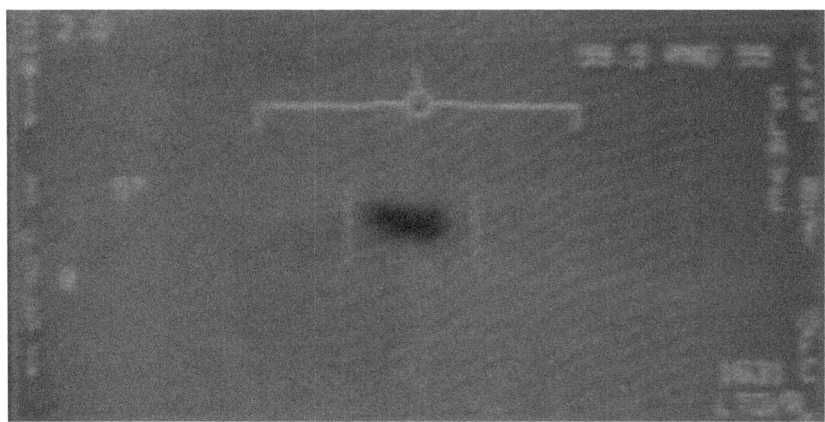

Closeup of ATFLIR Display as WSO zooms to 2.0 and switches to TV Mode.

Christopher Mellon was interviewed by "60 Minutes" and asked about his thoughts on the origin of the object in the Tic Tac video. He said of the object's acceleration and extreme velocity and deceleration, "There's nothing we can build that would be strong enough to endure that amount of force and acceleration." In fact, every government official who has commented on the Tic Tac and related UAP videos has agreed—"it's not one of ours."

Two computer and data communications specialists, one on the USS *Nimitz* and one on the USS *Princeton*, report that men who represented themselves to be US Air Force officers boarded their respective ships with helicopters within a couple of hours of the Tic Tac encounter, and demanded all of the hard drives that contained the data of the encounter. The Navy captains of the ships ordered the data specialists to hand over all of the backup hardware, which is extremely unusual. Observers speculate that there are three possibilities for the USAF to show up so quickly after the encounter to confiscate all of the high-resolution multi-sensor data evidencing the encounter:

1. The Air Force is extremely interested to know if the UAP are the technology of Russia or China;
2. The Air Force is extremely interested to know if the UAP are the technology of off-world civilizations; or
3. The Air Force has developed its own extremely sophisticated technology and is testing it against the best resources of the US Navy.

Of those possibilities the most comforting would be the last, because it would be so much safer than 1 or 2. However, government and military insiders keep telling us that the technology is not ours, and that its far too sophisticated to belong to any of the earth's superpowers.

USS ROOSEVELT "GIMBAL" NAVY VIDEO

During 2014–2015, fighter pilots associated with the USS *Theodore Roosevelt* Carrier Strike Group were training off the East Coast when they recorded the Gimbal and GoFast videos.

Gimbal is an official thirty-four-second US Navy video of a 2015 encounter with a UAP, captured by a US Navy F/A-18 Super Hornet from the nuclear aircraft carrier USS *Theodore Roosevelt*, off the eastern seaboard, near the Florida coast. Like the FLIR1 Tic Tac video above, the F/A-18 was using the Raytheon AN/ASQ-228 Advanced Targeting Forward-Looking Infrared (ATFLIR) pod. The ATFLIR contains the most advanced sensors and powerful tracking lasers available and must be operated by a fully trained WSO. The ATFLIR has high resolution and can locate and designate targets exceeding 40 nautical miles from the sensor.

The strange objects, one of them like a spinning top moving against the wind, appeared almost daily from the summer of 2014 to March 2015, high in the skies over the East Coast in restricted military training airspace. Navy pilots, such as Lieutenant Ryan Graves, reported to their superiors that they had been seeing the objects "every day, for at least a couple of years," and that they were flying without refueling for twelve hours at a time, and had no visible engine or infrared exhaust plumes, or wings and flight surfaces.

Lieutenant Graves explains that he and Lieutenant Danny Accoin, another Super Hornet pilot, were part of a squadron, the VFA-11 Red Rippers out of Naval Air Station Oceana, Virginia, and they were training for a deployment to the Persian Gulf. They were practicing diving from high altitudes and testing new radar systems recently installed in the jets. They were concerned about UAP that began showing up on their onboard sensors, which were mimicking their movements, and sometimes coming dangerously close to their jets. They couldn't see them visually, until 2014 when a fellow pilot reported that he had seen the UAP and almost hit it. He said it was "like a sphere encasing a dark cube. The corners of the cube each touched the inside of the sphere." The pilots were spooked by the presence of the UAP in their training airspace because the videos they were taking showed objects accelerating to hypersonic[14] speeds, making sudden stops and instantaneous turns, which they knew were beyond the physical limits of a human crew. In other words, the acceleration and rapid stops and instant changes in direction would kill a human and tear an aircraft to pieces.

---

14. Hypersonic means faster than the speed of sound. Sound travels at approximately 767 mph, depending on the temperature and conditions—the colder the air, the slower the speed of sound.

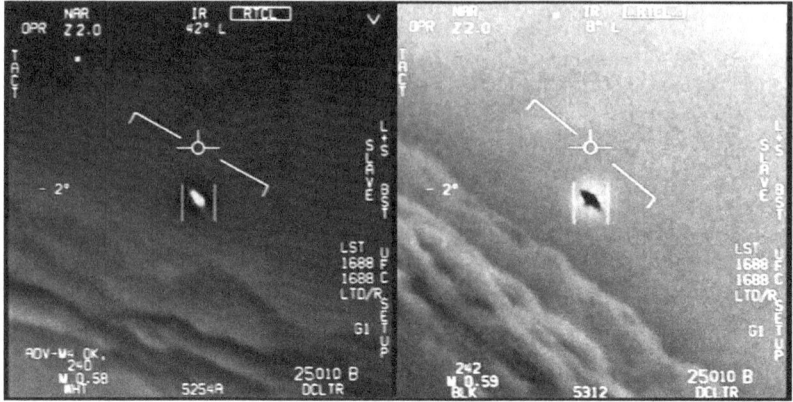

Raytheon AN-ASQ228 ATFLIR pod display information.
Left is starting screen. Right is after rotation.

Starting Information on the display:

- Sensor is in Infrared Mode
- Sensor then switches to TV (Visual) Mode
- Sensor Azimuth is Aimed 54° Left of Aircraft Axis
- Sensor is Aimed 2° Below Aircraft Axis
- F/A-18 is in a 20° Left Turn
- Sensor Zoom is at 1.0, Switched to 2.0
- F/A-18 Calibrated Airspeed (238 KTS) Mach Number (0.58)
- "HOT" Display Designator: Hot Items are White, Cold are Black (Alternates)
- F/A-18 Altitude: 25,010 FT

The thirty-four-second Gimbal video shows a spinning, elongated craft, likely a "disc," traveling against the fast wind, from right to left on the sensor screen. The pilots and WSOs are seeing a "fleet" of the smaller objects just off camera,[15] and radio transmissions convey the following conversations about the one UAP object that is centered in the sensor, while they observe several of the objects on their advanced radar systems.

---

15. The sensor has a very narrow focus and locks on to the target, excluding a very wide field of vision.

0:02—Radio transmission: "It's a %*@$# drone."

0:05—Radio: "There's a whole fleet of them. Look on the ASA [radar display]." The first person responds, "My gosh!"

0:11—Radio: "They're all going against the wind. The wind is 120 knots [138 mph] out of the west."

The speed and altitude of the UAP is unusual for any drone-type aircraft. On that information alone, the likelihood of an entire fleet of drones capable of operating under these conditions is highly improbable, requiring resources only a few nations could afford.

During this conversation the sensor is switched from "white-hot" to "black-hot," rendering a much clearer image. The pilots and WSOs can now see that the UAP looks like a distorted oval with small protrusions from the top and bottom. The object's opaque aura is now also very distinct, revealing a "cool" glow that extends about a body thickness around the entire object. They can also see that there are no observable wings, flight surfaces, propulsion devices or exhaust plume.

0:15—Radio: "Look at that thing, dude."

0:24—The UAP makes two quick adjustments, then rotates.

0:25—Radio: "That's not [unintelligible], is it?"

At **0:27** the object begins a series of distinct rotations and changes orientation by almost 100 degrees. Its orientation is now perpendicular to the horizontal plane despite the headwinds. This maneuver is executed in a manner that is inconsistent with current principles of aerodynamics, and possibly indicative of a vacuum environment. As the video concludes, the object's orientation and performance seem to defy current principles of physics to include atmospheric resistance and normal aerodynamic forces. During the orientation change, it also slows to a near stop, but does not change altitude.

0:28—Radio: "Look at that thing!"

0:30—Radio: "It's rotated."

This last portion of the video is extraordinary for three reasons. First, the UAP rotates in a manner that exposes its flat, broad underside to the headwinds in front of it, without changing its resistance to the high winds or its velocity. Second, in that configuration, it matches the description of Robert Lazar as he explained how the "Sport Model" UFO craft in government possession at S4 near Groom Lake functioned. He made drawings and built a model of the craft he claimed to work on, and explained how it flew through air and space, specifically indicating that it had to orient itself belly-first toward its high velocity flight path. We discuss his claims about how the technology functions and how he came to be associated with the project below. For now, it is fascinating that a UAP that appears to be shaped like the Lazar Sport Model rotated to fly in the same configuration that he described, when the high winds would have rendered it unmanageable for a regular military aircraft. Also important, as demonstrated on the black-hot screen, is the white glow or "halo" around the disc. At a time when every propulsion expert would say that the area surrounding the object should be dark, to register some amount of heat from the propulsion system, the immediate area around the object is white, or cold. In other words, there appears to be a field propulsion halo or bubble surrounding the object, indicating that it could well be utilizing an electro-magnetic, highly magnetic or antigravity propulsion field. This would represent a quantum leap in propulsion technology.

The Super Hornet pilots are highly trained observers and skilled at scrutinizing their targets to ascertain "friend or foe" status. They are specifically trained to look for discreet changes in shape, size, position, flight attitude (angles), and speed to determine the nature of the threat. They are highly skilled at discerning nuanced details that few people would normally recognize, which is why they break "character" in the radio transmissions—they are clearly seeing something they can't explain.

There is no known technology that enables a craft to fly in this manner, remain in the airspace for twelve hours without refueling, rotate so its broad bottom surface bucks the high velocity winds without any change in its air speed, and generate a cold field of any type around the craft while in flight. These highly unusual characteristics, coupled with its lack of wings and flight surfaces and visible means of propulsion, are the reason the DOD admits it is not technology of the United States.

GOFAST NAVY VIDEO

The "GoFast" video was captured around the same time as the above Gimbal video by fighter pilots associated with the USS *Theodore Roosevelt* Carrier Strike Group, who were training off the East Coast.

GoFast is an official thirty-four-second US Navy video of a 2015 encounter with a UAP, captured by a US Navy F/A-18 Super Hornet from the nuclear aircraft carrier USS *Theodore Roosevelt*, off the eastern seaboard, near the Florida coast. Like the FLIR1 Tic Tac and Gimbal videos above, the F/A-18 was using the Raytheon AN/ASQ-228 Advanced Targeting Forward-Looking Infrared (ATFLIR) pod. The ATFLIR contains the most advanced sensors and powerful tracking lasers available.

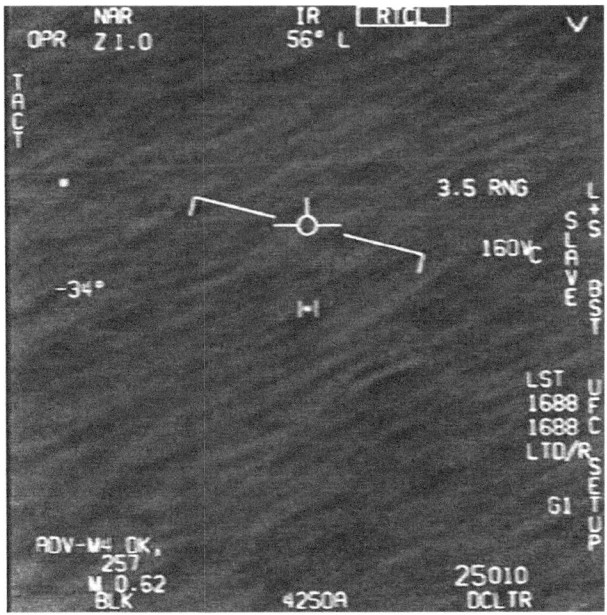

Raytheon AN-ASQ228 ATFLIR pod display information

Starting Information on the Display

- Sensor is in Infrared Mode
- Sensor Azimuth is Aimed 35º Left of Aircraft Axis
- Sensor is Aimed 22º Below Aircraft Axis
- F/A-18 is in a 5º Right Turn
- 4.1 NM Slant from Target to Aircraft
- Sensor Zoom is at 1.0
- F/A-18 Calibrated Airspeed (252 KTS) Mach Number (0.61)
- "HOT" Display Designator: Hot Items are White, Cold are Black
- F/A-18 Altitude: 25,000 FT

The twelve- to eighteen-foot long smooth, rounded UAP object was spotted by US Navy F/A-18 Super Hornet pilots as it zipped along just above the ocean below at around 220 mph in a lateral controlled flight. The water surface temperature is about 62.6º F. We know from the "White-Hot" setting of the sensor that the UAP object is much colder than the water with no exhaust plume, because it is much lighter in color. The WSO makes a few attempts to manually track the object, but it is too small, and too fast, so he engages the autotrack tracking system, and successfully captures it in the "trap box" shown in the center of the sensor screen.

In radio transmission recordings we hear someone exclaim, "Whoa! Got it!" and laughing.

The pilot doesn't recognize the object and asks, "What the #*$% is that thing?"

Someone asks the WSO, "Did you box a moving target?"

The WSO responds, "No. It's in autotrack."

The pilot says, "Oh, my gosh. Dude."

Someone says, "Wow. What is that thing, man?"

Another person says, "Look at that flying!" He laughs.

The unidentified object appears as a small, white, smooth oval moving at high speed from the top right to lower left of the screen. Like the FLIR1 Tic Tac and Gimbal UAP, the GoFast object has no obvious wings or tail, which would be visible at this range. There is no exhaust plume from the object, and no observable means of propulsion.

ADDITIONAL DOD VIDEOS

Following the authentication and release of the above three videos by the DOD, additional military videos have recently come to the public's attention. These are authenticated photos and videos from actual military encounters with UAP, presented in high-level briefings to educate military intelligence officers about the nature of the UAP, and how they are presenting themselves in military exercise conditions. The intelligence briefing contained an estimated ten videos (FLIR and HUD), plus another ten to twelve photos documenting the details of some of the UAP.

These are images and videos shot by our US military during a variety of UAP encounters. Some of them represent incursions by Advanced Transmedium Vehicles (ATV) of "unknown origin." These UAP are observed and recorded interacting with and observing our Navy's warships in a restricted training airspace. The night vision and FLIR technologies are integrated into some of the most sophisticated weapons systems on the planet.

JULY 2019 USS RUSSELL "PYRAMID" SHAPED UAP

This UAP encounter series occurred during July of 2019, involving Strike Group 9, within the Warning areas off of San Diego, close to where the FLIR1 Tic Tac video was shot. Navy personnel onboard the USS *Russell* observed and recorded "a swarm" of "pyramid" shaped UAP craft just 700 feet off the deck of the Navy destroyer using a night vision video recording device.

The original night vision video is in green, and the pulsating triangular objects flying over the ships are bright white and lit up. The pipe-looking object in the lower right corner of the still shot is part of the ship, with the UAP in the background at approximately 700 feet.

In April 2021, Pentagon spokesperson Sue Gough confirmed that publicly available footage of what appeared to be an unidentified triangular object in the sky had been taken by Navy personnel aboard the USS *Russell* in 2019. The Pentagon also confirmed photos of objects

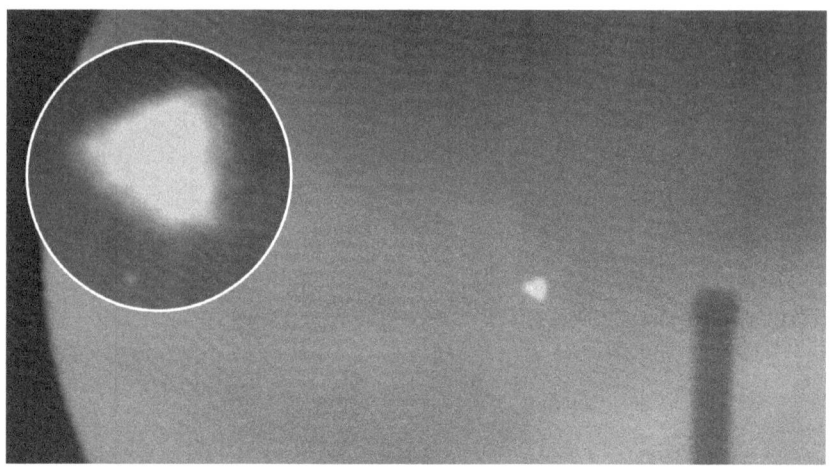

Still image from night vision video recorded by the Navy showing pyramid-shaped UAP flying above the USS Russell. Magnified UAP added into the round inset.

described as "sphere," "acorn"[16] and "metallic blimp." The following month, Gough further confirmed a second video had been recorded by Navy personnel and is under review by the UAP Task Force. The video, recorded on July 15, 2019, aboard the USS *Omaha*, purportedly shows a spherical object flying over the ocean as seen through an infrared camera at night, moving rapidly across the screen before stopping and easing down into the water.

JULY 2019 USS OMAHA "SPLASH" UAP

On July 15, 2019, the US Navy photographed and videotaped "spherical" shaped UAP and advanced "transmedium"[17] vehicles near

---

16. We discussed above the "acorn" shaped Die Glocke and a similarly configured object that purportedly crashed in the woods outside of Kecksburg, Pennsylvania on December 9, 1965. Although the acorn shaped UAP currently in question may not be exactly acorn shaped, the fact that it is described that way by observers could mean the Kecksburg crashed UAP may have been similarly designated, for similar reasons.
17. Transmedium indicates that the craft is able to fly or move through more than one medium—such as air, space, water, and so on.

the USS *Omaha*, an Independence-class littoral combat ship of the United States Navy. The video was shot from a sensor screen in the Combat Information Center of the USS *Omaha*, about 125 miles off the coast of San Diego, presumably by one of the sensor operators with his personal smartphone camera. Radar data indicated that the group was being swarmed by several UAP, up to fourteen at one count, and the radar screen video has been widely published as well.

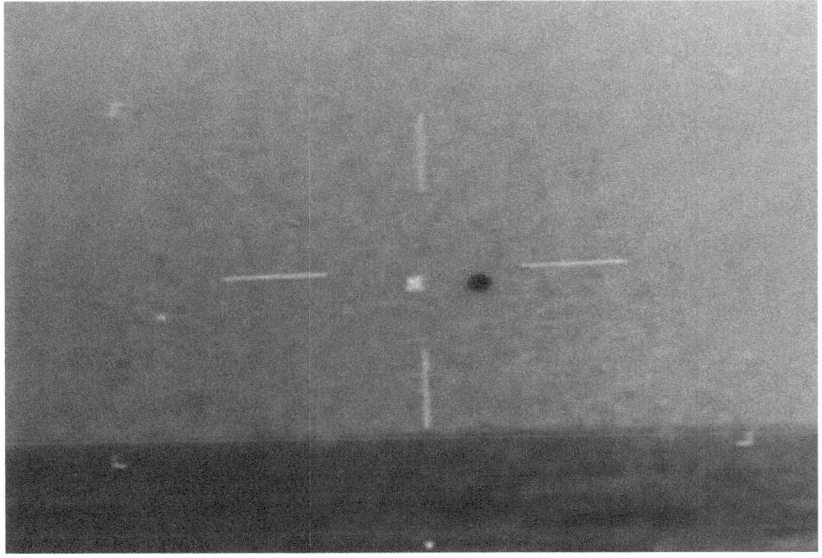

USS Omaha Navy images showing trans-medium Sphere travel from low orbit, to the air, to underwater.

Several of these spherical objects had been warming the ships in the group all day, one having followed beside one of the ships for over an hour and was recorded on thermal imaging. Between 9:00 p.m. and 11:00 p.m. a number of the spherical UAP objects were flying above the vessels, in various formations, as though they were inviting the Navy to film and video them, even allowing military aircraft to approach them during filming. A video was shot by a visual intelligence officer who went up to the deck to document the event. That video was released on the evening of June 29, 2021, by Jeremy Corbell and George Knapp, a filmmaker and broadcast journalist, respectively, who have worked tirelessly to get UAP videos and other information into the public domain.

In the sixty–second video this particular UAP dropped quickly to just above the surface of the water and hovered, making movements to the right, and the screen moves to stay with the object.

At the 25-second mark of the video we hear an operator calling for "possibility to launch helo, ASAP."

The UAP slowly begins descending toward the water, and the operators discuss what is going on.

At the 45-second mark an observer says, "Whoa, it's getting close."

At the 51-second mark we hear an operator say, "We have 31–knots sustained winds topside—gusts of 40 . . ."

At that point we see the UAP disappear into the ocean and at the 57-second mark an observer says, "What was," as another says, "Splash. Splash. Mark bearing and range."

The Navy immediately dispatched helicopters and a submarine to search for the object or wreckage, but was unable to locate anything.

THREE UAP PHOTOS FROM FA-18 COCKPIT

When the DOD was authenticating the above videos, it also confirmed the authenticity of three photographs titled "sphere," "acorn," and "metallic blimp," mentioned above, which were taken by an FA-18 pilot and WSO on March 4, 2019. The UAP event series took place in the W-72 warning area off the coast of Oceana Naval Air Station.

The intelligence briefing clarified that the WSO captured the three different craft during the same sortie, with the same cell phone. This helps demonstrate the extent of the UAP activities in these highly restricted military training zones. The skies are swarming with these

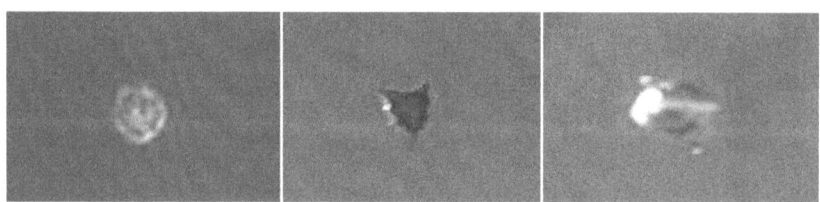

Three UAP photographed by military pilots with smartphone camera.

unidentified craft, in all their varieties and capabilities. As Navy pilot Lt. Graves has stated on a number of occasions, military pilots have been seeing and dodging these unknown objects in restricted airspace "every day for years."

AGUADILLA HOMELAND SECURITY VIDEO

A very interesting video comes from the Aguadilla Airport in northern Puerto Rico, occurring on the evening of April 26, 2013, at approximately 9:20. The video was taken by a Homeland Security camera operator onboard a government airplane. He attempted to get Homeland Security to analyze the video, but they told him at the time that the federal government wasn't interested in UAP. He then took it to Air Force Intelligence, but they likewise told him that the military has no interest in UAP. The pilot then felt free to take the video to a scientific organization, specifying he didn't want any "UFO people" in the group due to the stigma associated with UFO believers. A team of analysts working with the Scientific Coalition for UAP Studies (SCU), a private group of scientists, military analysts, and investigators, analyzed the video for two consecutive years and finally produced a very long report scrutinizing the incident—all 7,027 individual frames of the 3:54 video, along with all of the other available thermal, visual, sensor, weather, and flight data in the region. The team tested a similar WeScam Model L3 camera, which was the camera that captured the video, to test hypothetical objects under similar conditions.

As the Homeland Security flight was cleared to take off from the airport, radar picked up several objects in the area and out over the water beginning to swarm. The plane lifted off the runway and turned out over the ocean and saw a red light in its flight path and asked the tower what the object was. No one new—it just suddenly appeared, so the flight circled around it to see what it was, and the light turned off. That made the authorities onboard wonder if drug smugglers were behind the mysterious lights, and the pilot instructed the thermal camera operator in the government plane to turn on the camera and start recording as the plane came around to its point of origin. The camera operator located an object flying through the area at approximately 85 mph and began to track it manually. Below is a screenshot of the object. The thermal camera makes the pitch-black darkness look light, and the UAP object looks like a black dot to the upper right of the targeting box in the center of the screen.

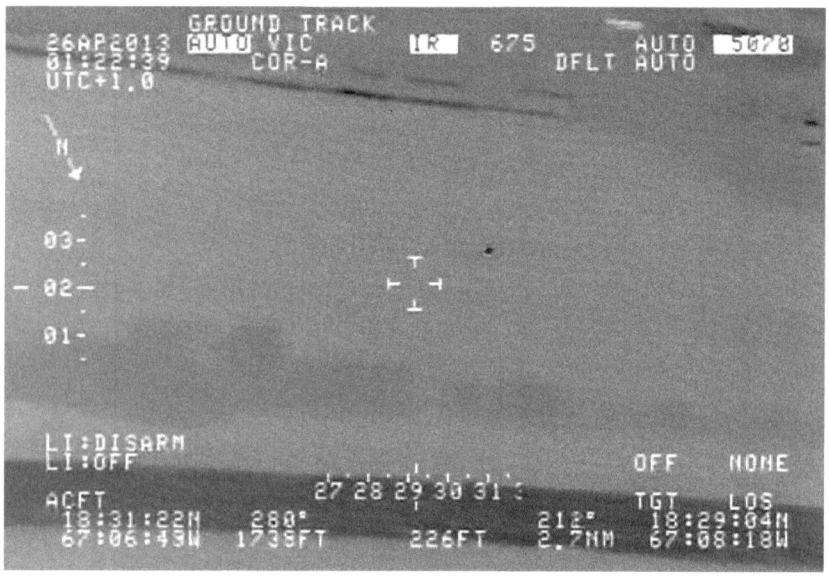

Aguadilla Puerto Rico UAP Object. Thermal Camera Screenshot.

The Homeland Security plane followed the flightpath of the UAP, which took it in a full circle around the airport again, causing the control tower to instruct a waiting FedEx plane to hold on the tarmac. The UAP headed over the airport runways, then over a supermarket and lowered its elevation as it zipped across a neighborhood. At that point the object approached the water and submerged itself going around 109 mph without making a splash, but it can be tracked on the video by the small expansion wake it creates from just below the surface. The object continues to travel underwater at 85 mph for a few seconds. As it comes out of the water the thermal image shows that the object remains the same temperature—which is hot. After it flies above the water for a few seconds the object splits into two separate objects, which fly parallel to each other several feet apart, above the surface of the water for several more seconds. After a few more seconds one object lowers itself into the water and continues under the surface, while the companion object continues above the water. After a few more seconds the remaining object begins to slow its speed, then lowers its altitude until it too travels under the surface of the water. Besides those on board, ground and air control witnessed the object, as well as other flight professionals in the area.

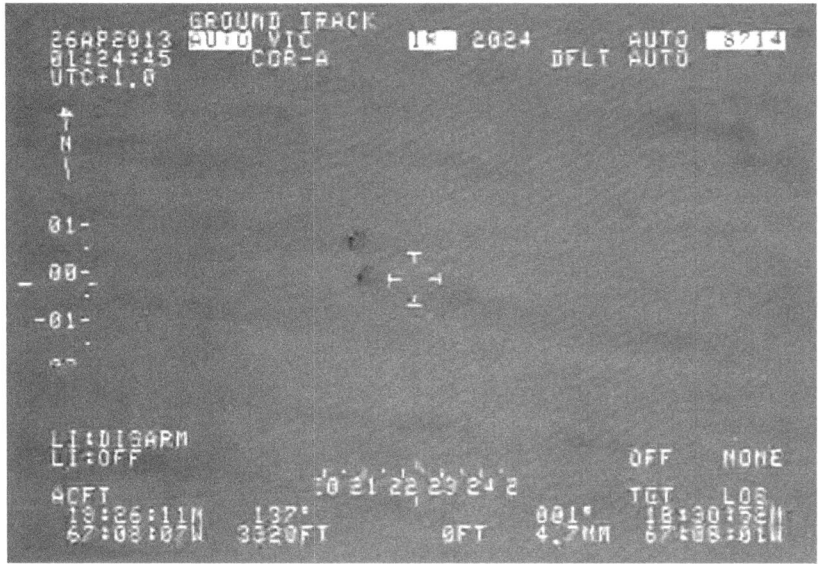

Aguadilla UAP Object Split into 2 Objects. Thermal Camera Screenshot.

Debunkers have tried to suggest that the object was a balloon or Chinese lantern. Of course, no balloon or lantern is capable of entering the water and traveling submerged at 85 mph, then exiting the water, and splitting in two, only to continue its flight path. The velocities involved are not that high. A military drone may be able to perform some of the feats witnessed in the video, but no drone can enter, exit the water, split into two, exit the water, and continue on its flight path. The SCU team performed a thorough investigation and counted pixels in many of the video frames to ascertain levels and sizes, determining that the UAP object was approximately four feet in diameter.

ATTEMPTS TO DEBUNK THE DOD-AUTHENTICATED VIDEOS

All of the videos that were first declassified then released and authenticated by the Pentagon are said by the Pentagon to be 1) not ours and 2) unidentified. Many debunkers have made desperate attempts to throw mud at the wall to see what might stick, in a frantic attempt to prove that the pilots didn't see what they saw, and the extremely sophisticated sensors and digital cameras didn't see what they recorded. They dust off and parade around all of their tired old excuses for what everyone clearly saw and recorded—it was a planet, a bird, a plane, a balloon, a temperature inversion, a kid with a new Christmas drone, and so on. They even attempted to invent new ways for the RAYTHEON AN-ASQ228 ATFLIR to malfunction, or to create visual artifacts—the kind that had never existed before in these sensors, which cost several million dollars each. Navy ATFLIR expert John Ehrhart looked into the debunkers' assertions and clarified that there was absolutely nothing in their arguments that even made sense. He explained, for instance, "Nothing inside the ATFLIR system is or could cause the rotational flux of the target that is at a higher rate than the background. There's no way the optics are causing that rotation."

Likewise, other attempts to debunk what the DOD has grudgingly admitted is "unknown" to the US government and military, fall far short of providing any usable information. The debunkers employ silly straw man tactics to try to undermine the government's admissions. First, the government has not come forth voluntarily or frivolously, to admit that it dropped the ball technologically, or in keeping up on its intelligence duties by allowing another nation to get a 1,000–year jump on it. The last thing the federal government has wanted to admit is that it is not the strongest or smartest person in the neighborhood. Indeed, it has done everything in its power since the late 1940s to dispel any and all notions that any nation or people have any advantage over the American military.

To the extent we believe UAP have been in our airspace since the 1940s or earlier, the federal government has categorically denied that it is true, and went to extraordinary lengths to tell its citizens, "Nothing to see here." Therefore, now that the Pentagon admits that UAP, as recorded in various videos, do not belong to America, and many spokesmen go as far as to say they don't belong to other superpowers, it is pointless to say that the government is simply mistaken—the billions of dollars it spends on pilots, personnel, and equipment to identify flying threats is entirely valueless. Perhaps the government is lying, in an effort to scare foreign governments into thinking it is more powerful than it is. Sure—they could hire Industrial Light & Magic to manufacture the videos. If that far flung theory were true, however, it wouldn't make the debunker theories any more valid. It would simply raise very serious questions about the competency of those running the Pentagon.

The main debunker theory about the recent UAP videos released by the DOD is that they are merely drones of the US military, or of Russia or China. The argument falls flat, however, in light of the fact that these same types of craft have been witnessed and recorded for seven decades—all the way back to when the state-of-the-art technology consisted of an internal combustion engine turning a propeller. Even the most ardent skeptic could never assume that the Chinese or Russians of 1948 possessed the type of technology exhibited by UAP at that time.

PRESIDENTIAL STATEMENTS ABOUT UAP

Donald Trump

On June 19, 2020, Donald Trump Jr. interviewed his father, President Donald Trump, for a Father's Day video event called "Triggered." Donald Jr. asked, "Before you leave office, will you let us know if there's aliens? Because this is the only thing I want to know. I want to know what's going on." He mentioned Roswell[18] and said, "We really want to know what's going on there."

President Trump smiled and said, "There are millions and millions of people that want to go to it, that want to see it. I won't talk to

---

18. In 1947, a rancher discovered unidentifiable debris in his sheep pasture near Corona, New Mexico, around 60 miles outside of Roswell. Air Force officials first confirmed that it was a crashed alien ship, but the next day reversed themselves and claimed it was nothing more than a crashed weather balloon. We discuss Roswell below.

you about what I know about it, but it's very interesting. But Roswell's a very interesting place—and a lot of people would really like to know what's going on."

Donald Jr., then asked, "So, you're saying you may declassify it?"

President Trump replied, "Well, I'll have to think about that one. All right?"

It is very interesting to me that most of the recent government disclosure activity has occurred under the Trump administration. It's almost as if the president, a clear populist, was seriously contemplating disclosing what the government knows about the phenomenon, which is a clear indication that there is something to disclose, but for reasons that are unclear, did not do so before leaving office. It was also President Trump who established the US Space Force (USSF), the newest branch of the armed forces, on December 20, 2019. Trump explained, "Space is going to be the future, both in terms of defense and offense . . . we're now the leader on space," as he was presented with the official flag of the newly created military branch.

Also, almost inexplicably, in his recent book and in media interviews in December 2020, former Israeli Security Chief, Haim Eshed, says extraterrestrials do exist, and President Trump knows all about it. Eshed's assertions are outlined in detail in *The Universe Beyond the Horizon—Conversations with Professor Haim Eshed by Hagar Yanai*, published in November 2020. Before going into any additional details about what Eshed has "revealed," let's have a quick look at his credentials:

Smithsonian National Air and Space Museum Wall of Honor:

- Professor of aeronautics and astronautics
- Veteran pilot and flight instructor
- Member of the American Institute of Aeronautics and Astronautics
- Co-founder of the Israel Space Agency and Space Research Institute in the TECHNION-Israel Institute of Technology.

We also know this about Director Eshed:

- Award: Israel Defense Prize
- Rank: Brigadier General
- Service: Military Intelligence Directorate

Dr. Eshed, for all intents and purposes, is the perfect state official to disclose what is occurring in the UAP phenomenon. For decades he was the ultimate leading expert on space, national security, and all matters dealing with international relations in the arena of space exploration. Professor Eshed, former head of Israel's Defense Ministry's Space Directorate, told Israel's Yediot Aharonot newspaper in an interview in Hebrew, published in English by the *Jerusalem Post* a few days later, that President Trump was aware of the extraterrestrials' existence and had been "on the verge of revealing" information about humanity's interactions with them for the past few decades, but was asked to delay his decision in order to prevent "mass hysteria." Dr. Eshed explained, "They [extraterrestrials] have been waiting until today for humanity to develop and reach a stage where we will understand, in general, what space and spaceships are."

Although Professor Eshed's statements are shocking to the world and governments around the world have been scrambling since his book was published to find ways of explaining his revelation, and no one is really quite sure how to approach the issues he has revealed, he says he is only speaking out now because attitudes have changed and people seemed more receptive to his information. "If I had come up with what I'm saying today five years ago, I would have been hospitalized," he admitted to *Yediot*. "Today, they're already talking differently. I have nothing to lose. I've received my degrees and awards, and I am respected in universities abroad."

Our takeaway from Dr. Eshed's revelations is that he, like President Trump, felt pressure to keep what he has discovered from the public. But he, unlike President Trump, and other world leaders, is now old, has received all of the accolades he cares to receive, and feels he has nothing to lose by revealing what he knows.

We note that President Trump did not reveal "what he knows about it" before leaving office. Of course, the circumstances of his leaving office were somewhat chaotic, and his intent to return is undetermined as of this writing, so we aren't entirely surprised that he has not yet said anything further on the matter.

I, for one, am very interested in Professor Eshed's explanation about the key information that humans lack before being introduced into the "galactic federation" of planets and beings—a general understanding of the nature of "space and spaceships." From a gospel view, the true nature of creation and the function of the universe is key to understanding the forms of life that occupy it and the laws by which that life interacts and proliferates. Until we truly understand the underlying matrix that creates, binds, and governs the entire universal fabric and the bodies and spaces between, we will not be in a position to reach out beyond our tiny island in the middle of nowhere and visit those who God tells us are very much like us.

Barack Hussein Obama, Jr.

I have a working theory that the embedded career professionals in the federal government who know something about the true nature of UAP share parts of that information with Republican presidents, but not with Democrats. We will see some anecdotal evidence of this hypothesis as we take a quick glimpse at what each recent president has revealed. From President Trump's statements, we get the feeling that he knew something but may not have known a lot—unless we accept Professor Eshed's statements as true. President Obama reveals that he asked about UAP when he first got into office. In an appearance on "The Late Late Show" Obama said in a light tone, "The truth is that when I came into office, I asked, right, I was like, 'Alright, is there the lab somewhere where we're keeping the alien specimens and spaceship?' And you know, they did a little bit of research and the answer was no." Then he stopped laughing and said, "What is true, and I'm actually being serious here, is that there are, there's footage and records of objects in the skies, that we don't know exactly what they are. We can't explain how they moved, their trajectory. They did not have an easily explainable pattern. And so, you know, I think that people still take seriously trying to investigate and figure out what that is." From this, it appears that President Obama had seen some of the videos considered by the UAPTF and discussed in the Report to congress, but that was all he was told.

Former CIA Director John Brennan, who served under Obama for four years, revealed what he thinks about the UAP videos and the general subject of UAP. "I've seen some of those videos from Navy pilots, and I must tell you that they are quite eyebrow-raising when you look at them," Brennan said in the interview in George Mason University's Mercatus Center. "You try to ensure that you have as much data as possible in terms of visuals and also different types of maybe technical collection of sensors that you have at the time," he explained. "You really have to approach it with an open mind, but get as much data as possible and get as much expertise as possible brought to bear." Asked what he felt the UAP videos and encounters mean, he replied, "I think some of the phenomena we're going to be seeing continues to be unexplained, and might, in fact, be some type of phenomenon that is the result of something that we don't yet understand and that could involve some type of activity that some might say constitutes a different form of life."

This is a very interesting answer because Director Brennan, who knows everything there is to know about American and foreign weapons technology, said nothing about our technology or the technology of another superpower. He referred instead to "a different form of life," in direct connection with what we are seeing in the UAP videos. Also interesting is his lack of specificity with regard to what form of life that might be. No one appears to be willing to say "extraterrestrial" any longer. Indeed, from what I have been hearing for the past few decades, few are convinced that the UAP and their creators are actually extraterrestrial. But, if not from "out there," then where? We discuss the possibilities below.

George W. Bush

President Bush never spoke about his knowledge of UAP publicly. However, on August 8, 2019, on the Fox News show *The Five*, Dana Perino, regular co-host and former Press Secretary to Bush, made an interesting comment on Bush's knowledge on the subject. She first remarked on Bernie Sanders' promise to reveal all he could learn about UAP if he were to be elected president. "He probably won't [reveal UFO information], because the CIA will stop him." That in itself was quite interesting—to learn that a very close associate of a president of the United States believes that any attempt by a sitting president to reveal UAP information will result in him being stopped by the CIA. Does this mean that the CIA has more power than the US president? How would the CIA "stop" the president? Her admission also makes us reevaluate the far-flung conspiracy theories about the assassination of the "space president," John F. Kennedy. When her fellow co-hosts asked her about what she may have learned about UFOs from her former boss, President George W. Bush, she admitted, "I asked him, and he wouldn't tell me." We note that Bush did not say, "No, there's no such thing." He instead told her that he simply *wouldn't* tell her.

Bill Clinton

President Clinton spoke about UFOs and UAP after his presidency and revealed the following: "First thing I did is send people to Area 51 to see if there were any aliens there," he told late night host Jimmy Kimmel. Also, "I did attempt to find out if there were any secret government documents that reveal things, and if there were, they were concealed from me too. I wouldn't be the first president that underlings have lied to and that the career bureaucrats have waited out. But there may be some career person sitting around somewhere hiding these dark secrets even from elected presidents. If so, they successfully eluded me—and I'm almost embarrassed to tell you that I did try to find out."[19]

John Podesta, who served as White House Chief of Staff to President Bill Clinton from 1998 to 2001, counselor to President Obama

---

19. *Jimmy Kimmel Live!*, Jackhole Industries/ABC, April 2, 2014.

from 2014 to 2015, and campaign adviser to Hillary Clinton, very actively attempted to get to the bottom of the UAP question but was stymied at every turn. The career bureaucrats referred to by President Clinton simply outwaited all of them, it seems. Hillary Clinton took Podesta's advice and promised to be more transparent about UAP if she were to be elected to the presidency, but that never occurred. In a June 25, 2014, email disclosed by WikiLeaks, the late NASA astronaut Dr. Edgar Mitchell[20] requested "a conversation with you [Podesta] and President Obama regarding the next steps in extraterrestrial disclosure for the benefit of our country and our planet." We don't know if that meeting happened, but the email dump revealed a follow-up email on April 30, 2015, where the former astronaut requested an "ASAP" Skype talk with Podesta to discuss "the difference between celestials in our own solar system and their restraint by those from the nonviolent contiguous universe." The details of these communications are unclear, and there is no record if the meeting was held. When penning the foreword to the 2011 book by Leslie Kean, one of the journalists who wrote the now famous *New York Times* article about UAP, titled "UFOs: Generals, Pilots, and Government Officials Go on the Record," he wrote, "It's time to find out what the truth really is that's out there. The American people—and people around the world—want to know, and they can handle the truth."

Ronald Reagan

President Reagan publicly discussed his 1974 encounter with a UAP, describing it as possessing abilities and technology far in advance of anything on Earth. While serving as governor of California, Reagan was in an airplane during his first well documented encounter, and he pointed the UAP out to the pilot, Bill Paynter, and asked him to follow it. The pilot was shocked and tried to follow, but

---

20. Edgar Dean Mitchell, PhD, was a United States Navy officer and aviator, test pilot, aeronautical engineer, and NASA astronaut. As the Lunar Module Pilot of Apollo 14, he spent nine hours working on the lunar surface in the Fra Mauro Highlands region, making him the sixth person to walk on the Moon. He was a proponent of learning more about UAP, and became quite active in the UAP research community.

the erratic zig-zag pattern was impossible to duplicate. They soon lost the UAP. Paynter explained, "It appeared to be several hundred yards away. It was a fairly steady light until it began to accelerate. Then it appeared to elongate. Then the light took off. It went up at a 45–degree angle, at a high rate of speed. Everyone on the plane was surprised. . . . The UFO went from a normal cruise speed to a fantastic speed instantly. If you give an airplane power, it will accelerate—but not like a hot rod, and that's what this was like." The following week Governor Reagan recounted the sighting to Norman C. Miller, Washington Bureau Chief, for the *Wall Street Journal*: "We followed it for several minutes," Reagan recounted. "It was a bright white light. We followed it to Bakersfield, and all of a sudden to our utter amazement it went straight up into the heavens."[21]

Actress Lucille Ball shared a story about a second encounter that Ronald Reagan and his wife Nancy purportedly had while they were driving on Mulholland Drive on their way to a party at the home of actor Steve Allen. According to Ball and Allen, the Reagans arrived over an hour late and reported that a UAP had landed near their vehicle. Reagan claimed a ladder appeared and an alien climbed out of the craft. The alien told him to quit his acting work and go into politics. Of course, we receive this account from unreliable sources, but other guests at the Allen party confirmed that the Reagans were very late to the party and were quite shaken. When he became president, President Reagan remained silent on the subject, although he spoke privately with at least a few world leaders about the possibility of banding together if it became necessary to fight an alien invasion.

Reagan recounted his UAP experience to Soviet leader Gorbachev, during a meeting of the then two-most-powerful men on Earth. According to *The Herald*, "At a private meeting between them in 1985 at the Geneva Summit, Reagan asked Gorbachev: 'What would you do if the United States were suddenly attacked by someone from outer space? Would you help us?'"

"No doubt about it," Gorbachev answered.

---

21. "Ronald Reagan Sees a UFO," HowStuffWorks, Editors of Publications International, Ltd.

"We too," said Reagan. On September 21, 1987, President Reagan gave an address to the United Nations General Assembly. In the speech Reagan asked rhetorical questions and commented about the nations and cultures of the world uniting in common efforts to live in peace and avoid wars and bloodshed. "Cannot swords be turned to plowshares? Can we and all nations not live in peace? In our obsession with antagonisms of the moment, we often forget how much unites all the members of humanity," he said. "Perhaps we need some outside, universal threat to make us recognize this common bond. I occasionally think how quickly our differences worldwide would vanish if we were facing an alien threat from outside this world. And yet, I ask you, is not an alien force already among us? What could be more alien to the universal aspirations of our peoples than war and the threat of war?"

I tend to think that President Reagan, a Hollywood professional for many years, was actually recalling an episode of *The Outer Limits* television show from September 30, 1963. In that episode, which I'm sad to say I am old enough that I watched on the original broadcast date, titled "The Architects of Fear," a group of scientists wishing to avoid imminent nuclear conflict and annihilation concocted a scheme to surgically alter one of their number, and pretend that the earth is being invaded by hostile aliens. The purpose for their ruse was—you guessed it, to unite the world against a common enemy and come out on the other side as peaceful friends.

Jimmy Carter

President Carter reported seeing a UAP while at Leary, Georgia, in 1969. He recounted the sighting a number of times, including on *Larry King Live*. He says, "I was outside a school lunchroom one night right before sundown. It was getting dark, and we were getting ready to eat supper. And I and about 25 men were standing around and all of a sudden in the western sky we saw a strange light coming toward us; a round light. It got closer and closer and right above the pine trees it stopped and then it began to change colors from blue, to red, to white. Then it stayed there for a while. We were all aghast. We didn't know what it was. And then it just disappeared into the west. That was the end of it."

Carter reported the encounter at the time and spoke openly about it whenever asked about it. He never made any references to government UFO or UAP knowledge during or after his presidency. However, attorney Daniel Sheehan reports that President Carter demanded that his CIA Director, George H. W. Bush, prepare a complete report for him on UAP and occupants, and was flatly told the subject was above the president's security clearance, and he lacked the "need to know."

Carter then asked Marcia Smith, Director of the Science and Technology Division of the Congressional Research Service, for a classified report on UAP and the potential existence of extraterrestrial life. As part of her research, Smith contacted Daniel Sheehan, General Counsel for the National Jesuit Office and Social Ministry Office, and asked for access to Vatican archives that would shed light on what the Vatican had learned about the subject over the past 2,000 years. Sheehan contacted the Vatican and informed them that the new US president had made the request, and they were all surprised and disappointed when the Vatican likewise replied it was above Carter's pay grade.

Gerald R. Ford

President Ford was a leading voice of the people as a congressman from Michigan and didn't appreciate the treatment that his citizens received at the hands of Project Blue Book when investigating UFO reports. He sent letters to congressional committees and spoke in public, calling for a serious government study on the UAP phenomenon. In a letter of demand sent March 28, 1966, Ford said,

> The Air Force sent a consultant, astrophysicist Dr. J. Allen Hynek of Northwestern University, to Michigan to investigate the various reports; and he dismissed all of them as the 'product of college-student pranks or swamp gas or an impression created by the rising crescent moon and the planet Venus.' I do not agree that all of these reports can be or should be so easily explained away.
>
> Because I think there may be substance to some of these reports and because I believe the American people are entitled to a more thorough explanation than has been given them by the Air Force to date, I am proposing that either the Science and

Astronautics Committee or the Armed Services Committee of the House schedule hearings on the subject of UFO's and invite testimony from both the executive branch of the government and some of the persons who claim to have seen UFO's.

I have just today received a number of telegrams urging a congressional investigation of UFO's. One is from retired Air Force Col. Harold R. Brown, Ardmore, Tennessee, who says, "I have seen UFO. Will be available to testify."

Are we to assume that everyone who says he has seen UFO's is an unreliable witness? A UPI story out of Ann Arbor, Michigan, dated March 21, 1966, states that "at least 40 persons, including 12 policemen, said today that they saw a strange flying object guarded by four sisterships land in a swamp near here Sunday night."

In the firm belief that the American public deserves a better explanation than that thus far given by the Air Force, I strongly recommend that there be a committee investigation of the UFO phenomena.

I think we owe it to the people to establish credibility regarding UFO's and to produce the greatest possible enlightenment on this subject.

In fact, a lot of talk came and went, and when Gerald Ford eventually became the president, he never spoke of the subject again.

Presidents before Gerald Ford may or may not have known about government involvement in UAP. Richard Nixon may have been extremely interested in the subject, and legend says that he took actor Jackie Gleason, a huge UFO buff, to an Air Force base in Florida and showed him the bodies of aliens in a warehouse basement. The story is not documented in any trustworthy source, so we can't afford it any credibility. Likewise, many have come forward with stories of President Dwight Eisenhower making secret deals with aliens, only to back out of them when he witnessed the incredible abilities of their spacecraft firsthand. Again, these accounts lack credible sources, so we won't afford them serious consideration here.

Additionally, there are hundreds of books that discuss many pages of secret government documents that have surfaced over the past seventy-five years. These documents purport to demonstrate government knowledge of "extraterrestrial" craft and visitors. For our purposes, the sources of these documents are unreliable. I, with my trusty computer and printer or second-hand-store typewriter, am capable of hoaxing such documents, so why couldn't someone else? Those documents fail to meet a minimal level of evidence in my opinion, and certainly fail to rise to the level of proof. Unfortunately, this may be the very fact that has delayed the government's need to disclose its knowledge of UAP these many decades—the fact that documentary evidence is not really "proof," absent verifiable supporting evidence of their authenticity.

In truth, officials in governments all around the world, from presidents and kings all the way down to their security details, have witnessed UAP in our skies, and some have witnessed them in Intelligence audio, visual, and sensor data recordings. Most of those government leaders have been very slow to publicly share the details of their knowledge, whether it is firsthand or acquired from intelligence sources. The recent spate of US government admissions are accompanied by open admissions of the existence of UAP by other governments from around the world as well. Several agencies and governments from Europe and South America have released many of their UAP related files, and have allowed officials to speak openly about governmental knowledge of such matters.

All of this, however, only answers the first question: Are there UAP in our skies and waters? The answer is yes. It does not answer any of the follow-up questions, however. What are they? Whose are they? Why are they here? We attempt to look into the answers to these questions, and others, in the following chapters.

For further updates on matters we have discussed herein, or to share your personal experiences with the unknown, please visit the website we have set up at UFOdisclosure.us

CHAPTER 5

Latter-day Prophets Speak about Extraterrestrial Life

AN INFINITE NUMBER OF EARTHS IN THE SCRIPTURES

Before we can intelligently discuss the existence and nature of life elsewhere in our universe, we are wise to first seek enlightenment from the Lord on the subject. When we gain a knowledge of what He has revealed on the treatise, we can then apply our acquired insights to attempt to fill any gaps left by the scanty information gained from this primary source of revelation—the prophets and the standard works of The Church of Jesus Christ of Latter-day Saints. The standard works are surprisingly clear, yet concise, in answering the question, does life exist on planets other than Earth? The universe is immense and filled with kingdoms, as latter-day revelation informs us: "And there are many kingdoms; for there is no space in which there is no kingdom; and there is no kingdom in which there is no space, either a greater or a lesser kingdom" (D&C 88:37). The use of the term *kingdom* is very general in this context and appears to convey less information about actual kingdoms than the true nature of space and various means of existing within that space. To the extent we understand the creation wrought by our Father in Heaven, we know that His creation is one large body of "substance" and that space is not empty, but every bit of it is filled with light and matter (wave, particle and wave/particle) that voluntarily obey the voice of their Creator.

We used to think of space as a vast empty nothingness, devoid of all matter and energy—the icy cold vacuum of space. In the past decades we have come to better understand the true nature of the universe; that it is better seen as a vast something—perhaps better pictured as a giant sea filled with a continuous three-dimensional substance, like water, or a thin web of element, consisting of waves and particles. The words *expanse* and *firmament* come to mind as we contemplate the universe filled with substance. You may recall from chapter 1 the discussion of the expanse: "And the Gods also said: Let there be an expanse in the midst of the waters, and it shall divide the waters from the waters.[1] And the Gods ordered the expanse, so that it divided the waters which were under the expanse from the waters which were above the expanse; and it was so, even as they ordered. And the Gods called the expanse, Heaven" (Abraham 4:6-8). The word chosen in Genesis is *firmament*. Joseph Smith used the word *firmament* when interpreting Facsimile No. 2 from the Book of Abraham: "Fig. 4. Answers to the Hebrew word Raukeeyang, signifying expanse, or the firmament of the heavens; also a numerical figure, in Egyptian signifying one thousand; answering to the measuring of the time of Oliblish, which is equal with Kolob in its revolution and in its measuring of time." And similarly, in his interpretation of Facsimile No. 1, the prophet rendered it thus: "Fig. 12. Raukeeyang, signifying expanse, or the firmament over our heads; but in this case, in relation to this subject, the Egyptians meant it to signify Shaumau, to be high, or the heavens, answering to the Hebrew word, Shaumahyeem."

---

1. I used to sit in priesthood meetings where we would try to skip over this part, visualizing the creation of the earth with rocks and water. This description was difficult to envisage. I have come to think of water as hydrogen, which is the most abundant element in the universe, we are told. With this in mind, it makes much better sense.

What the Prophet understood by "expanse" and "firmament" was that what was termed the Aether in his day was not emptiness, but was a "solid" universal construct. Indeed, there is no space wherein there is no element governed very directly by God through the mediumship of the Light of Christ. Unified Theory? String Theory? Yes—the entire universe is a wonderful, beautiful, glorious expression and extension of our Heavenly Father, Who "comprehends" and governs every minute particle and wave of existence through this emanating light.

MODERN PROPHETS SPEAK WITH AUTHORITY

Before initiating a discussion of what latter-day prophets have said concerning the multiplicity of worlds and their respective natures and inhabitants, it may be necessary to provide a reasonable basis for some to believe that these men possessed abundant personal knowledge of such matters. It also may be prudent to establish a reliable reporting system, in order to properly authenticate any purported statements by latter-day prophets. Therefore, I shall endeavor to use only properly reported statements herein, or note unauthenticated reports.

It must be remembered that all scientific knowledge ultimately comes from God, as was taught by Joseph Smith: "The learning of the Egyptians, and their knowledge of astronomy was no doubt taught them by Abraham and Joseph, as their records testify, who received it from the Lord."[2]

President Spencer W. Kimball further taught that sometimes God's technological gifts to mankind remain inferior to revelation when man is seeking higher knowledge of God's creative works: "Astronomers have developed powerful telescopes through which they have seen much, but prophets and seers have had clearer vision at greater distances with precision instruments such as the Liahona and the Urim and Thummim, which have far exceeded the most advanced radar, radio, television, or telescope equipment."[3] In all cases, the reader is free to discern the authoritative value of each statement concerning

---

2. *Teachings*, 251.
3. *The Teachings of Spencer W. Kimball*, 445.

the stars and planets, their natures, their inhabitants, and travel and communication between them.

JOSEPH SMITH UNDERSTOOD EXTRATERRESTRIAL LIFE

Joseph Smith, the Prophet of the latter-day restoration, was, in my mind, as qualified as any prophet to speak on topics concerning the cosmos and its inhabitants. As with all prophets claiming any insight into the nature of the planets and the inhabitants thereof, Joseph Smith had to acquire his information through revelation. He was allowed to look into the eternities on various occasions, viewing and discerning the creations of God, as in the vision of the eternities recorded in Doctrine and Covenants 76. In performing the work of translating the Book of Abraham, and in similar pursuits, Joseph Smith gained the very same understanding of the universe held by Father Abraham, as recorded by Joseph in his journal: "October 1.—This afternoon I labored on the Egyptian alphabet, in company with Brothers Oliver Cowdery and W. W. Phelps, and during the research, the principles of astronomy as understood by Father Abraham and the ancients unfolded to our understanding, the particulars of which will appear hereafter."[4] Despite this promise, little else was offered on the subject by Joseph in the *History of the Church*. William W. Phelps did refer to these "records found in the catacombs of Egypt." However, in passing on some information he claimed to have originated with Joseph concerning the age of what he termed "this system." He said that "eternity . . . has been going on in this system, almost two thousand five hundred and fifty five millions [2,555,000,000] of years."[5] Whether "this system" refers to our solar system, galaxy, one of the higher orders of systems comprising our universe, the universe itself, or Heavenly Father's eternal kingdom, we have no answer. I infer that it refers to God's kingdom/universe, based on the use of the term "eternity." What is unique about the statement is that in Joseph Smith's day, no one spoke of the age of

---

4. *History of the Church, 2:286.*
5. *Times and Seasons,* V, January 1, 1845, 758.

the universe in terms of billions of years. Now, scientists guess, based on their perceived status of an oscillating universe theory, that its age could be in the range of 2.5 billion years. Recent guesses augment this figure to 10 to 15 billion years.

Like Abraham, Joseph had complete access to and training in the use of the Urim and Thummim. It should be remembered that during Joseph's annual visits to the place where the golden plates were buried, he was taught by the angel Moroni. These instructional encounters included, along with explanations of the scriptures and gospel doctrines, training in the use of the Urim and Thummim. Joseph's Urim and Thummim was the very same possessed by the brother of Jared (see D&C 17:1), and he also possessed the "seer stone," which he used as a Urim and Thummim.[6] Besides its use as a translating device, the Urim and Thummim was used to see things from God's vantage point. Joseph later explained what one sees in a Urim and Thummim as he described the future state of this earth and its celestial inhabitants (see D&C 130:6–10).

Therefore, a Urim and Thummim is a device used by its operator to see all things past, present, and future of a lower or higher order, if the operator is so authorized.[7] Abraham explained that it was through the use of the Urim and Thummim that he was able to discern the nature of the cosmos (see Abraham 3:1) Joseph Smith not only translated[8] the Book of Abraham, but he also rendered interpretations of Facsimiles 1 through 3, No. 2 of which contained explanations of Abraham, chapter 3, as cited above. Based on the foregoing, it cannot be doubted that Joseph Smith possessed superior knowledge concerning the cosmos. It is possible, in fact, that he knew as much as, or more than, any other prophet on Earth.

---

6. Joseph retained the seer stone throughout his life. As of the time of President Joseph Fielding Smith, the seer stone was still in the possession of the Church (see *Doctrines of Salvation*, Vol. 3, 225).
7. "And the things are called interpreters, and no man can look in them except he be commanded, lest he should look for that he ought not and he should perish. And whosoever is commanded to look in them, the same is called seer" (Mosiah 8:13).
8. Rather than translate, Joseph received direct revelation containing the original content of the Book of Abraham, using the Egyptian text as a mere focal point for the exercise.

We cannot assume that Joseph considered the topic of the cosmos inappropriate for discussion and instruction among the brethren of the early restoration, inasmuch as he taught it to them himself: "I also gave some instructions in the mysteries of the kingdom of God; such as the history of the planets, Abraham's writings upon the planetary systems, etc."[9] Joseph said, speaking of William McLellin, Brigham Young, and Jared Carter, "I exhibited and explained the Egyptian records to them, and explained many of the things concerning the dealing of God with the ancients, and the formation of the planetary systems."[10] Commenting on this quote by Joseph Smith, President Joseph Fielding Smith added: "There is a prevalent notion in the world today that before the time of Columbus, Galileo, and Copernicus, all ancient people believed that the earth was flat and the center of the universe. From the writings of the Scriptures, and more especially those which have come to us in this dispensation, we know that the ancient peoples, when they were guided by the Spirit of the Lord, had the true conception of the universe. . . . We learn from the Book of Mormon (Helaman 12:13-15) that the Nephites understood the nature of the planets. It was not until apostasy and rebellion against the things of God that the true knowledge of the universe, as well as the knowledge of other truths, became lost among men."[11]

Interestingly, I have a very close friend, a brother in the gospel, who served a Spanish-speaking mission to lands south of the US, where it is thought that some of those featured in the Book of Mormon may have dwelled. As he discussed these matters with a local man, after he returned to the mission for a visit, the man informed him that he believed him and offered to take him to a secret archeological site that the government was keeping under wraps. My friend was excited to see the site. On the appointed morning, he rode a long distance in a windowless panel van and was blindfolded for the last several minutes of the trip. The blindfold was removed after they walked for a short distance, and he found himself in an underground cave system. He

---

9. *Teachings*, 118.
10. *History of the Church*, 2:334.
11. *Teachings*, 118, footnote 2.

was led to a wall where he found depicted a view of the earth as if from space, and the continents were portrayed with accurate dimensions and shapes. He was shocked and asked for confirmation that the depiction was real. Yes, he was assured, it was at least thousands of years old. Although I can't personally vouch for the accuracy of the carbon dating employed or the veracity of my friend's guide, I don't doubt the purported existence of such an ancient depiction, understanding that the ancients were well aware of the true nature of the cosmos.

Not only did Joseph Smith teach that there exist millions of worlds that are inhabited by beings, just like those that dwell on Earth, but he also taught that unusual animals inhabit those planets: "I suppose John saw beings [in heaven] of a thousand forms, that had been saved from ten thousand times ten thousand [100,000,000] earths like this,—strange beasts of which we have no conception: all might be seen in heaven."[12]

BRIGHAM YOUNG ALSO KNEW OF LIFE ON OTHER PLANETS

President Brigham Young was also quite clear in speaking of the existence of millions of life-sustaining earths like our own. He taught, "There is a Power that has organized all things from the crude matter that floats in the immensity of space. He has given form, motion and life to this material world. . . . He is the Father of all, is above all, through all, and in you all, he knoweth all things pertaining to this earth, and he knows all things pertaining to millions of earths like this."[13]

President Young further explained, "God has been creating worlds like ours for a very long time. . . . There never has been a time when there have not been worlds like this. There is an eternity of matter, and it is all acted upon and filled with a portion of divinity. . . . Eternity is without bounds, and is filled with matter; and there is no such place as empty space. And matter is capacitated to receive intelligence."[14] He explained that knowledge and intelligence, coupled with element, "enthroned in glory" become

---

12. *Teaching,* 291.
13. *Discourses of Brigham Young,* 11:120; 11:41.
14. Ibid., 7:2.

angels, or gods that can control the elements of the universe and even command the creation of worlds.[15] This is what you and I are created for.[16]

JOSEPH FIELDING SMITH TAUGHT OF EXTRATERRESTRIAL LIFE

President Joseph Fielding Smith likewise taught that Heavenly Father has countless planets inhabited by His offspring. He said, "The Lord declared to Moses that his great work and glory is 'to bring to pass the immortality and eternal life of man.' For this purpose earths have been made and are now being built; and the Lord's purpose is to provide for his children immortality and eternal life, not only on this earth, but on the countless earths throughout the universe. . . . The Lord has said: 'And as one earth shall pass away, and the heavens thereof even so shall another come; and there is no end to my works, neither to my words.'" He also clarified, "Other earths, no doubt, are being prepared as habitations for terrestrial and telestial beings, for there must be places prepared for those who fail to obtain celestial glory,[17] who receive immortality but not eternal life."[18]

This last statement demonstrates a heretofore undiscussed principle—

---

15. This statement does not necessarily indicate that the divine extinguishing of planets actually occurs (although we have no direct revelation concerning the lives or cycles of stars), but only that Gods have such power. The quote should be considered in light of the statement by President Joseph Fielding Smith quoted in chapter 2. This teaching is supported by Orson Pratt in *Journal of Discourses*, 19:290.
16. Ibid., 3:356.
17. President Smith, as well as other prophets, made clear that the planets created for probationary life, like Earth, will be eventually inherited only by those who obtain celestial glory: "MANY CELESTIAL EARTHS. This earth on which we dwell, like many that have gone before, is destined to become a celestial sphere and the righteous shall inherit it forever" (*Doctrines of Salvation*, vol. 2, 26).
18. *Doctrines of Salvation*, vol. 1, 72–74.

that there exist billions[19] of planets in our universe peopled by those who have been born on other worlds, who have died and been resurrected, and having failed to obtain a celestial glory, were assigned to a specially prepared planet of a terrestrial or telestial nature to serve as their eternal inheritance. The existence of such planets raises many questions regarding the spirits of such planets, their death and resurrection, and interplanetary contact of the inhabitants of those worlds with other worlds.

SPENCER W. KIMBALL TAUGHT OF EXTRATERRESTRIAL LIFE

Speaking of the time when righteous priesthood holders will have obtained the creative powers of Godhood, President Spencer Kimball offered some enlightening comments about life on other worlds that may help answer some of the questions raised above. "We take one element, and we transform it and organize it into another. . . . There are in the universe numerous bits or quantities of materials—gases and other elements—which brought together in the proper way can create an earth and can eventually produce fruit trees, grain fields, and forests. . . . The time will come when we will not only create with our wives the mortal tabernacles which our earthly children occupy, but we will be able to expand our efforts and extend them and go out into the great eternities."[20]

In responding to some of the questions raised above, President Kimball asked and answered the following: "Is man earthbound? Largely so, and temporarily so, yet Enoch and his people were translated from earth, and the living Christ and angels commuted. Is there interplanetary conversation? Certainly. Man may speak to God and receive answers from him. Is there association of interplanetary beings? There is no question. Are planets out in space inhabited by intelligent creatures? Without

---

19. The number of such terrestrial and telestial planets would necessarily be twice the number of "probationary state" planets, because each probationary planet becomes the celestial abode of its righteous inhabitants, leaving the necessity of two new planets for those who inherit the other two levels of glory.
20. *The Teachings of Spencer W. Kimball*, 53.

doubt. Will radioed messages ever come between planets across limitless space? Certainly, for there have already been coming for six thousand years, properly decoded, interpreted, and publicized messages of utmost importance to the inhabitants of this earth. Dreams and open vision, like perfected television programs, have come repeatedly."[21] Not only does President Kimball confirm the existence of life on other planets but also the existence of interplanetary travel and communication—at some level.

WHO MINISTERS TO THIS EARTH?

If we consider interplanetary exchange in a strictly angelic sense, the question, "From how many planets could Earth be visited?" becomes a narrow one because of the following scripture: "In answer to the question—Is not the reckoning of God's time, angel's time, prophet's time, and man's time, according to the planet on which they reside? I answer, Yes. But there are no angels who minister to this earth but those who do belong or have belonged to it" (D&C 130:4–7). Only those angels who have been, or will be born on this earth can perform angelic ministrations here. Because this angelic class of beings resides on God's celestial planet,[22] we know that most angelic ministrations are limited to visitors from that planet. Certain translated beings, however, as already discussed, minister to this Earth "angelically," who probably do not reside on God's celestial planet. The citizens of Zion most likely live on a terrestrial planet near God's celestial planet. Other translated beings such as Moses, Elijah, John, Alma the Younger, the Three Nephite apostles, possibly Melchizedek and his city of Salem,[23] and other individually translated persons who at times minister to this Earth, may dwell on planets other than Zion's terrestrial abode—we

---

21. Ibid., 445.
22. None of this indicates, however, that angels that belong to other worlds do not simultaneously reside on God's celestial planet. In fact, we must assume that such is the case in light of Joseph Smith's teaching that God's throne is surrounded by "sanctified beings from worlds that have been" (*Mormon Doctrine*, 65–66).
23. Inspired Version, Genesis 14:32-34.

do not know where they are.[24] All of this merely tells us that the Earth has interaction with at least two other planets—possibly more. This principle is limited to ecclesiastical exchanges, however. The scriptures cast little light on our greater question of whether "exploratory" exchange between probationary planets like Earth is allowed, and if so, whether Earth is a participant therein. None of this addresses the issue of the existence of the Watchers. Although we don't know for sure if such angelic or translated beings actually existed, especially in the context of early instructors to Adam and his children, the ancient texts are adamant that such was the case. If so, then who are they? What are they? Are they still among us? Do they still come to visit and help? How do they travel? Where do they reside? We include these Watchers in our discussion shortly.

If we are seeking to establish a pattern or to extrapolate a rule from what we have learned so far, there are certain principles that come to mind. We have little indication from the scriptures whether or not the rule that "Earth's only ministers are from Earth" applies to angels who minister to other planets. It is possible that angels from other planets are assigned to minister to planets other than their own. We have the teaching of Joseph Smith that translated beings who are pursuing a course of advancement have as their terrestrial habitation "a place prepared for such characters [that] He held in reserve to be ministering angels unto many planets."[25] This could indicate that individual translated beings minister to many planets, or that the group of beings ministers to many planets, but each individual is sent only to his home planet. If the former is true, which is quite possible from the text of the statement, this is a strong indication that there exists a distinct rule among other planets regarding interplanetary ministration. The egocentric thought that this earth may be different than other worlds, and that a separate set of rules may apply, is further supported by Earth's uniqueness due to the personal (temporal) and sacrificial

---

24. Although the scriptures are not specific concerning the whereabouts of these translated persons and groups, there are indications that all translated beings are with Zion.
25. *Teachings,* 170.

presence of the universal Savior. This uniqueness, however, leads us only to an indication of "quarantine" of this Earth that does not exist among other worlds. If there exists such a limitation at the angelic ministration level, there could well exist the same limitation at the temporal social/exploration level as well. Of course, we don't know—but attempt to discern the truth of the matter through reasoning and whatever inspiration the Lord provides on the matter.

ETERNAL PRINCIPLES ARE UNIVERSAL

Presiding Bishop Orson F. Whitney once delivered an address to the Saints in which he illustrated that our own Earth is just like the multitude of other probationary planets in our universe. He explained,

> The earth upon which we dwell is only one among the many creations of God. The stars that glitter in the heavens at night and give light unto the earth are His creations, redeemed worlds, perhaps, or worlds that are passing through the course of their redemption, being saved, purified, glorified and exalted by obedience to the principles of truth which we are now struggling to obey. Thus is the work of our Father made perpetual, and as fast as one world and its inhabitants are disposed of, He will roll another into existence, He will create another earth, He will people it with His offspring, the offspring of the Gods in eternity, and they will pass through probations such as we are now passing through, that they may prove their integrity by their works. . . . A man must obey the same principles now that were obeyed two thousand years ago, or six thousand years ago, or millions of ages ago, in order to attain the presence of His Father and God.[26]

This statement emphasizes that all of the planets and their inhabitants are governed by the same set of laws and eternal principles. We shall see in later chapters that this is an important principle to keep in mind while attempting to determine the nature and origin of phenomena related to UAP and their purported occupants—because they often seem to be totally outside of this plan. Orson Pratt likewise

---

26. *Journal of Discourses*, 26:195–96.

spoke of the "sameness" of the "worlds without number" referred to in the scriptures:

> Notwithstanding the unnumbered worlds which have been created, out of each one of these creations the Lord had taken Zion (in other words a people called Zion) to his own bosom. What does this signify? Are we not to understand that all these creations were fallen worlds? . . . I mention these things to show that we have, in the revelations that God has given, many indications, that there are worlds beside our own that are fallen; also that we may see that the Lord has one grand method, for the salvation of the righteous of all worlds—that Zion is selected and taken from all of them . . . and for that reason the Lord withdraws his presence from them, and visits them in their hour, and time, and season, and then withdraws from them, leaving them to ponder in their hearts the commandments given them.[27]

If we entertained the thought that perhaps some or many of God's "worlds without number" are significantly different from our own experience, and the laws and designed system within which we operate and through which we pass, these teachings tend to negate such a possibility. The prophets indicate that there is substantial uniformity for all the worlds.

In a discourse given on March 14, 1875, Orson Pratt continues his thoughts on the subject. "He [Christ] withdraws. What for? To fulfill other purposes; for he has other worlds or creations and other sons and daughters, perhaps just as good as those dwelling on this planet, and they, as well as we, will be visited, and they will be made glad with the countenance of their Lord. Thus he will go, in the time and in the season thereof, from kingdom to kingdom or from world to world, causing the pure in heart, the Zion that is taken from these creations, to rejoice in his presence. . . . It matters not how far in space these creations may be located from any special celestial kingdom where the Lord our God shall dwell, they will be able to see him at all times."[28]

Elder Pratt raises an interesting issue in this passage. He reveals

---

27. Ibid., 19:293.
28. Ibid., 17:332.

that the veil that separates us from God will be withdrawn after the resurrection, and we will constantly be in His holy presence and continually see Him before us—no matter where we are located physically in the universe. If ever principles of quantum mechanics and the ever-present condition of the Unified Field and Quantum Field/String Field Theory facilitated by the eternally emanating Light of Christ from the presence and person of God were elucidated in plain, gospel terms, this is it. Elder Pratt continues, "He does not mean that the Lord God is right within a few rods of every individual; this would be an impossibility, so far as the person is concerned; but he means that there is a channel of communication, the privilege of beholding Zion, however great the distance; and the privilege of enjoying faculties and powers like this is confined to those high and exalted beings who occupy the celestial world. All who are made like him will, in due time, be able to see, to understand and to converse with each other though millions and millions of miles apart."[29]

SEEING THE LIGHT

Concerning the question of whether or not many of the twinkling celestial bodies in our night skies are celestialized planets, as suggested above by Bishop Whitney, and enhancing his teachings concerning the physical relationships between the creations of God scattered throughout the universe, the ever-prolific Orson Pratt described the future state of our planet and then conjectured concerning the ability to see, or communicate with a celestial planet: "And the earth will at that time have no more need of the light of a luminary like our sun, or any artificial light, for it will be a globe of light."[30] In this same vein, Orson Pratt gave a great deal of thought to the problems of interstellar communication as they relate to the inhabitants of celestialized planets, and speculated that there are methods of instant communication between worlds, not restricted by the speed of light.[31]

---

29. Ibid., 17:332–333.
30. Ibid., 19:290–292.
31. Ibid.

Although these mental exercises may appear to be little more than old-fashioned attempts to reconcile religion and nineteenth-century science, the point is well taken that we have little knowledge concerning Heavenly Father's methods of universal travel and communication. Certainly, the universal, omnipresent matrix of the Light of Christ puts all things in immediate "connection" with God, regardless of distance. The subject becomes prominent as we discuss below, in that UAP occupants' claims regarding similar subjects are recently deemed worthy of scientific consideration and research. Is there travel faster than the speed of light? Is there communication faster than the speed of light? Professor Einstein said no, but quantum theory and the Einstein-Rosen Bridge/Wormhole theory connecting different locations of the universe through a quantum shortcut (portal) may actually steer our thinking in different directions—directions that reveal just how correct Orson Pratt was. He applied somewhat similar thinking to the problem of interplanetary communication between probationary planets as well, positing, "What a happy state and condition, not only to study these things pertaining to this little world we inhabit, but to extend our researches to our neighboring worlds, learning the laws, institutions, and governments of the peoples that inhabit them, also their history, and everything pertaining to them, and then extending our researches still further."[32] I think he would have enjoyed the *Star Trek* lifestyle.

EXTRATERRESTRIALS AMONG MEN ANCIENTLY?

Many have adopted the theory that extraterrestrials visited the earth anciently, built the megalithic structures around the world, and genetically altered pre-humans to develop into the humans that are now present on the earth, and are in fact, the gods worshipped and written of anciently—including the God of our own Hebrew and Christian religions. As I watch television shows about ancient civilizations and their astounding accomplishments, I always cringe as the narrator delivers the opinions of "ancient astronaut theorists," who invariably dress and groom themselves in a manner to attract attention from across any sized room. These

---

32. Ibid., 292.

ancient astronaut theorists attribute every mark in the soil and scratch in stone to ancient man's desire to memorialize the arrival of, and interaction with, extraterrestrials. They ascribe every human accomplishment to these ancient visitors. They also attribute every interaction with angels and God as dealings with extraterrestrial visitors.

The premier champion of this "angels=aliens" theory is the ever-prolific Erich von Däniken (net worth, $30 million), best known for his original book and the motion picture based thereon, *Chariots of the Gods*. In his book, *Signs of the Gods*, von Däniken, as in his other dozen or so books on the subject, pursues his extraterrestrial deity through any scripture or other written record that makes any mention of flight, fire, light, cloud, transportation, vision, visitation, markings on the ground, art, religion, legend, or miraculous occurrence. Personally, I find his leaps to conclusions to detract greatly from the few times that his research turns up something useful. He has a following, however, led by an army of ancient astronaut theorists who have co-opted programming and overrun television networks that purport to focus on travel, discovery and history.

When von Däniken speaks of the giants of the Old Testament, he asserts they are the same that appear throughout mythology as cyclops and similar creatures, and "must," therefore, be the very beings responsible for the famous "ruts" and megalithic temples of Malta. He claims that they flattened various stone and plains surfaces around the world anciently, because their interstellar spaceships require runways, landing strips, and launch pads. This is how von Däniken reasons, anyway. In support of his theories, von Däniken cites The Book of Enoch, wherein God chastises the angels: "'Why have you done like the children of earth and begot giant sons?' In chapter 18 of The Book of the Secrets of Enoch,[33] Enoch speaks of the "Grigori," a race of soldiers with human appearance held at bay in the fifth heaven, being of gigantic size, whose faces were withered and melancholy and whose mouths were silenced. Enoch is told that three of these followers of Satanail, the one who rebelled, broke through to the Earth and "saw the daughters of men how good they are, and took to themselves wives, and befouled the earth

---

33. *The Apocrypha and Pseudepigrapha of the Old Testament in English*, R. H. Charles, D.Litt. , D.D. , Ed. (Oxford at the Clarendon Press: 1913, Vol. II).

with their deeds, who in all times of their age made lawlessness and mixing, and giants are born and marvelous big men and great enmity" (verses 1–6). In fact, there is quite a lot of discussion in various ancient documents about the Watchers and their offspring, and it is a discussion worth pursuing when considering the types of beings that may exist in, or have access to, our world. But to automatically ascribe extraterrestrial origins to anything we don't fully understand is intellectually lazy—and as I said, it has become pervasive.

Von Däniken further cites in support of his "angels=aliens impregnated Earth women" theory, chapter 100 of Kebra Nagast, which he claims to be an ancient Ethiopian writing, which says: "But every daughter of Cain with whom the angels had consorted became pregnant, but could not give birth and died. And of the fruits of their wombs some died, and others came forth; they split their mother's womb and came out of the navel. When they were older and grew up, they became giants."[34] My main issue with von Däniken and his progeny is that whatever truth may be reflected in these ancient uncanonized texts, they say nothing of extraterrestrials. They say angels and sons of God. Von Däniken has supplanted angels and sons of God with extraterrestrials, without any basis.

Perhaps God did assign Watchers to assist our first parents in learning the arts of life—building shelters and then structures, hunting food and planting crops, compounding healing herbs, weaving cloth, smelting and fashioning metals, and so on. Perhaps they did assist Noah in preparing for the demise of all life on the planet. But no information is afforded us in any of the ancient texts about the origin of these Watchers, except to say they were angels sent by God. The Books of Enoch speaks a great deal about the Watchers, and the fall of 200 of them, and the evils committed by the fallen ones. To the extent they were real beings as represented in those writings, they were very active in the early development of humanity—for good and for evil. If they existed at all, they were related in some way to angels, and as we have seen, angels are the children of God, in the varied stages of their eternal lives, sent to humanity to deliver a message or to lend

---

34. *Signs of the Gods*, 117.

assistance in some authorized manner. If there truly were Watchers assigned to the earth in the very beginning, the only real question is, what type of children of God were they? Or, more specifically, where were they in their eternal course at the time they were assigned to be Watchers? Were they pre-existent spirits? Apparently not, because the ancient texts reveal that those who rebelled were able to impregnate the human wives they took. Were they mortals, perhaps from another world? Were they resurrected men from another world? We have read a number of passages from scripture, and the prophets indicate that the only angels who minister to men and women on this planet are those who are of this planet—so that tends to eliminate those possibilities, unless a Watcher is a special class of translated being that is permitted to assist on new worlds, regardless of his own origin.

There are some indications that Lameck, a prophet, knew of the Watchers and had some knowledge of their ability to impregnate women. This information comes to us from uncanonized sources, so this is only speculation, although we do find the mention of Watchers in the context of angels in the scriptures.

Indeed, the prophet Daniel uses the term *watcher* in the same phrase as angel and holy one: "I saw in the visions of my head upon my bed, and, behold, a watcher and an holy one came down from heaven; . . . This matter is by the decree of the watchers, and the demand by the word of the holy ones: to the intent that the living may know that the most High ruleth in the kingdom of men, and giveth it to whomsoever he will, and setteth up over it the basest of men. . . . And whereas the king saw a watcher and an holy one coming down from heaven, and saying, Hew the tree down, and destroy it" (Daniel 4:13, 17, 23).

In Hugh Nibley's wonderful thirteen-part article published in *The Ensign,* titled "A Strange Thing in the Land: The Return of the Book of Enoch," Part 13, he presents an astonishing link between the Joseph Smith revelation providing content from the original five-part Book of Enoch, which is currently in the Book of Moses in the Pearl of Great Price, and the Dead Sea Scroll Book of Enoch.[35] In the Joseph Smith revelation, as

---

35. J. T. Milik and M. Black, eds., *The Books of Enoch, Aramaic Fragments of Qumran Cave 4* (Oxford: Clarenden Press, 1976).

Enoch was sent to the land of Mahujah to call the people to repentance, he was questioned directly by someone named Mahijah, thus providing him with an opportunity to teach the people and call them to repentance. Nibley explains, "What always impressed me as the oddest detail of the Joseph Smith account of Enoch was the appearance out of the blue of the name of the only non-biblical individual named in the whole book—Mahijah. (Moses 6:40.)" This is because in the Dead Sea Scrolls Book of Enoch, Mahijah is the name given for one of the Watchers—or a giant son of a Watcher. The fact is remarkable, because the Joseph Smith revelation version matches the Dead Sea Scroll version in a manner that is impossible to be a coincidence, thus proving to the world the revelatory authenticity of the Prophet Joseph Smith. It is also significant because it informs us that the Mahijah of Moses 6:40 was likely a Watcher, or the giant son of a Watcher, thus evidencing[36] the existence of the Watchers.

Also significant is the tie-in to beings who present themselves as Watchers. As we learn in our discussions below about victims of nightmarish "extraterrestrial" abductions, some of the abductors identify themselves as the "Watchers"—who claim to have watched over mankind and assisted humanity "since the beginning."

A UNIVERSAL HIERARCHY OF NOBILITY

After confirming many of the teachings already discussed concerning the plentiful existence of human life on millions of Earthlike planets, Elder B. H. Roberts additionally spoke of the "noble ones" that stand at the head of each of these world families, and their mutual association in the eternities. He provides some insight into the rise of noble ones on each of the Father's planets, saying, "The noble and great ones are

---

36. As discussed briefly above, evidence and proof are two different qualities of supportive information that demonstrates the truth of a matter asserted. Evidence exists in a full array of supportive information, from weak to strong. Proof, however, is very strong supportive evidence of the truth of an asserted matter, which is difficult to overcome. In this context, I am not saying that this constitutes proof of the existence of Watchers—I am saying it is evidence, which I feel is fairly substantial in supporting the truth of the matter asserted.

made rulers then; and doubtless the principle here operating in respect of those intelligences appointed to our earth, operates in all worlds and world systems. Some of the 'good and the noble and the great ones' stand at the head of worlds and world groups, forming grand presidencies, in order and gradation, based upon their power and their appointment, which in turn depend upon their character, their nobility, greatness, and their worthiness, measured by their capacity to serve. . . . These are the 'rulers' in the universe, the Divine Beings who make up David's 'congregation of the mighty.'"[37] The interesting point is that these spiritual nobility appear to belong to a grand governing counsel with communication between planets—not unlike Professor Haim Eshed's "galactic federation of planets." However, the implication is that such a grand counsel exists between celestialized worlds. One wonders if there is such a counsel for mortal planets—perhaps giving rise to certain rules and regulations, such as "We are not permitted to interfere," as told to Udo Wartena. The question naturally arises: Permitted by whom?

As we have considered many of the teachings of latter-day Church leaders on the subject of God's children strewn throughout the cosmos, we find little usable information about issues of interplanetary visitation and communication, which are subjects of great importance in light of the UAP/UFO phenomena. As of the time of this writing there are no official, definitive declarations or policy statements from Church leadership concerning these questions, so we employ our own best information gathering and reasoning abilities to measure the claims being made by many against the staff of already revealed truth.

---

37. *History of the Church*, 2:394–397.

CHAPTER 6

Scriptural Spacecraft?

JOSEPH SMITH VISITED BY UAP?

It is surprising how many ufologists point to the events of the Restoration as evidence of early extraterrestrial contact with humans on Earth. They are fascinated with scriptures like the following, and I have even watched UFO encounter programs featuring this experience as evidence of extraterrestrial visitation to Earth in the form of angelic beings:

> I saw a pillar of light exactly over my head, above the brightness of the sun, which descended gradually until it fell upon me. It no sooner appeared than I found myself delivered from the enemy which held me bound. When the light rested upon me I saw two Personages, whose brightness and glory defy all description, standing above me in the air. (Joseph Smith—History 1:16–17)

> While I was thus in the act of calling upon God, I discovered a light appearing in my room, which continued to increase until the room was lighter than at noonday, when immediately a personage appeared at my bedside, standing in the air, for his feet did not touch the floor. . . . Not only was his robe exceedingly white, but his whole person was glorious beyond description,

and his countenance truly like lightning. The room was exceedingly light, but not so very bright as immediately around his person . . . After this communication, I saw the light in the room begin to gather immediately around the person of him who had been speaking to me, and it continued to do so until the room was again left dark, except just around him; when, instantly I saw, as it were, a conduit open right up into heaven, and he ascended till he entirely disappeared, and the room was left as it had been before this heavenly light had made its appearance. (*Ibid.* 1:30–43)

While Church members do not link the angelic visits that heralded the gospel's restoration with UAP, the similarities between Moroni's visit and *Star Trek* special effects are regarded as noteworthy by many ufologists. Other aspects of Joseph's experiences intrigue UFO researchers as well. The methods of God, Jesus, and Moroni appearing to the boy Joseph Smith in a beam of light has been used as evidence in some UFO books and documentaries to prove that Joseph was contacted by extraterrestrials—because only they would appear in conduits of light, according to the producers.

Keep in mind the many religious parallels to UAP sightings and other close encounters as we survey close encounters documented in the literature. The similarities between many UAP encounters and many spiritual apparitions (good and evil) are marked, giving rise to many feeling that religious encounters were actually extraterrestrial encounters, while many, like me, feel that many UAP encounters are actually spiritual encounters—but not from God or His holy messengers.

WHO BELIEVES THAT ANGELS PILOT UAP?

Our Heavenly Father is omniscient and omnipotent. Why would He, or His angels, need a pressurized metal casing with an antigravity drive to travel through the vast reaches of space? Did He and His Beloved Son step out of a craft in the Sacred Grove? Did the angel Moroni show up in Joseph Smith's backyard in a spaceship? No. Moroni appeared in a constricted beam of very bright light coming down through the roof of Joseph's bedroom. In the old *Star Trek V* movie, a powerful being has convinced a band of true believers that he is God and demands a spaceship to take him to a distant planet. I concur with the question raised by the legendary Captain James T. Kirk: "Excuse me, I'd just like to ask a question—What does God need with a star ship?"

When I conducted a poll of Church members and asked if they believe that God or His angels travel to Earth in craft, only two percent responded yes. In contrast, some other sectors of society are quick to believe that UAP in our earthly skies are piloted by divine messengers. Anyone involved with the occult, from astrology to spirit mediums, reincarnation, the power of crystals, and transcendental meditation to dial-a-psychic readings is a statistically good candidate to believe that UAP are piloted by ministering spiritual beings.[1] Many liberal Christian churches have surprisingly high percentages of membership that likewise accept this belief. These two categories already put us into the many tens of millions of believers just in America—non-Christian populations are much more open to these extraterrestrial spiritism philosophies. Most disturbingly, however, many average people with transitory Christian beliefs who are moderately exposed to UAP literature and other media accounts are beginning to take on composite spiritual beliefs about UAP and their purported occupants. Erich von Däniken and his ancient-alien promoters have sold many millions of books, and their movies and television programs have been viewed by hundreds of millions. The fact is that although it is possible that many UAP have spiritual origins, we have every indication that they are not piloted by ministering angels sent from the presence of God.

UAP IN THE BIBLE

Thousands of books and television programs tout man's "alien" origins and claim that the Bible is laden with tales of UAP visitations to Earth. These writers cite scriptures, generally from the Old Testament, that refer to flying and flaming chariots and other objects as evidence of divine dependence on mechanical vehicles for mobility not

---

1. The occult aspects of UAP are discussed in greater depth below.

only between planets but also on the Earth's surface. Herein is a summary of the arguments that are typically presented with reference to the Bible.

Chariots of Fire

The assumption of the prophet Elijah is frequently cited and held to be especially descriptive of an ancient flying metal chariot: "And it came to pass, as they still went on, and talked, that, behold, there appeared a chariot of fire, and horses of fire, and parted them both asunder; and Elijah went up by a whirlwind into heaven. And Elisha saw it, and he cried, My father, my father, the chariot of Israel, and the horsemen thereof " (2 Kings 2:11–12). Interestingly, the Church version of the Bible cross-references this passage to Abraham 2:7 and Ezekiel 1:4. Abraham 2:7 reads: "For I am the Lord thy God; I dwell in heaven; the earth is my footstool; I stretch my hand over the sea, and it obeys my voice; I cause the wind and the fire to be my chariot; I say to the mountains—Depart hence—and behold, they are taken away in an instant, suddenly." The Church annotators cross-reference Abraham 2:7 with 2 Kings 2:11, the assumption of Elijah, and to Isaiah 66:15, which says, "For, behold, the Lord will come with fire, and with his chariots like a whirlwind, to render his anger with fury, and his rebuke with flames of fire."

Although we can somewhat easily interpret God's elemental chariots as being merely descriptive of His comings and goings as being with power and celebration, the chariot of fire that took Elijah into heaven may have a more functional character. A look at the sight beheld and described by Elisha includes "horses of fire" complete with "horsemen." UAP theorists say that these are mere descriptions of mechanical apparatus that propelled the craft, but it could well be that Elisha was shown a vision that accompanied Elijah's assumption, for the purpose of imbuing the occasion with power and authority—which has been the result. There are those who are always quick to explain away ancient reports by "interpreting" them into something they're not, saying that the report is phrased in the terms and understanding of the time. Of course, the ancients usually lacked the language and understanding, technological or religious, to convey a description of what they actually saw in terms that we can comprehend with clarity. Even if true, however, this is not a license to interpret every flying object in vision or miracle as having a UAP origin—which has become the practice of these "angels=aliens" protagonists. "Horses" just may mean "horses."

The Camp of Israel Led by a UAP

Another proffered evidence of the Biblical UAP phenomenon is the pillar that accompanied Israel on its exodus from Egypt, across Sinai, to the promised land. "And the Lord went before them by day in a pillar of a cloud, to lead them the way; and by night in a pillar of fire, to give them light; to go by day and night" (Exodus 13:21–22). "And the angel of God, which went before the camp of Israel, removed and went behind them; and the pillar of the cloud went from before their face, and stood behind them: And it came between the camp of the Egyptians and the camp of Israel; and it was a cloud and darkness to them, but it gave light by night to these: so that the one came not near the other all the night. . . And it came to pass, that in the morning watch the Lord looked unto the host of the Egyptians through the pillar of fire and of the cloud, and troubled the host of the Egyptians, And took off their chariot wheels, that they drave them heavily" (Exodus 14:19–25).

These verses inform us of some interesting characteristics of this pillar. First, we are told that the Lord went before Israel in the pillar. We can understand this to mean that He led them by the means of the pillar. However, we are next told that "the angel of God, which went before the camp of Israel, removed and went behind them." This gives us a more focused view of the nature of the pillar, that it was an angelic presence. UFO theorists conjecture that the pillar was possibly UFO exhaust, as evidenced by its dark cloudiness at times, and light at others. Therefore, they conclude that the "angel of God" was in a craft or device that exhausted a misty substance that could be lit up or left dark. Protagonists further claim that the "east wind" that blew and parted the sea and dried its floor in a single night was an antigravity field generated by the craft. This antigravity theory, they say, is supported by the fact that the Lord was able to remotely take "off their chariot wheels." And finally, because the Lord "looked unto the host of the Egyptians through the pillar of fire and of the cloud" as he troubled them with these difficulties, they surmise the pillar was more of a device than a presence. Candidly, most UAP reports say they are rarely accompanied by sound or exhaust plumes. We don't know if the Lord sent a flying device or an angel, or a mist, or employed antigravity fields from a machine to remove the wheels of chariots—He could have done any of these if He chose to. He likely sent a real angelic personage to accomplish all of them. Notwithstanding, it wouldn't make Him an alien if He utilized devices, and it wouldn't make the cloud a UFO.

God's Use of Devices

Does God use "devices" to carry out His divine purposes? Hugh Nibley says yes. Referring to Joseph's Smith's use of the Urim and Thummim and the seer stone to translate the Book of Mormon, Brother Nibley describes how Joseph would translate for hours, never opening the plates: "'I frequently wrote day after day:' E. W. Tullidge recalls, 'often sitting at the table close by him, he sitting with his face buried in his hat, with a stone in it, and dictating hour after hour with nothing between us. . . . He used neither manuscript nor book to read from . . . the plates often lay on the table without any attempt at concealment, wrapped in a small linen tablecloth.' David Whitmer confirms this: 'He did not use the plates in the translation, but would hold the interpreters to his eyes . . . and before his eyes would appear what seemed to be a parchment, on which would appear the characters of the plates . . . and immediately below would appear the translation in English.'"[2]

Why God utilizes physical "gadgets," as Brother Nibley terms them, is not apparent. He evidently reserves invisible miracles for occasions when He warrants it understood that a miracle is occurring. Otherwise, God provides an Ark of the Covenant, a serpentine staff, a Urim and Thummim, a spherical compass, or a luminous set of stones to act as a medium through which the benefit is conferred on man. We

---

2. *The Message of the Joseph Smith Papyri, an Egyptian Endowment*, 51.

note that in each case where a gadget is supplied, it is for the use of the mortal—not God or an angel. An angel may appear wielding a sword, but he doesn't need it to dispatch evil. God may sit on a throne, but He doesn't require a gold chair to relax.

We are left with the question then, does this mean that God might employ the use of flying machines to transport Himself and His servants? The obvious response is, He could if He so chose—but He does not need to use such devices, in the same way He does not need an Ark of the Covenant to speak to the prophet, or a Urim and Thummim to show a vision of other worlds, or a latter-day temple to meet with His people. One thing we can be sure of, to this extent—this is an option that God could exercise if it pleased Him. It does not account for the millions of UAP sightings that are reported in these latter times. Those beings are nothing like God or angels.

The Wheels of Ezekiel

The most vivid of all Biblical descriptions of flying "vehicles" is that of the prophet Ezekiel. With a little imagination, we can appreciate why Biblical UAP adherents believe that Ezekiel saw a genuine UAP. "And I looked, and, behold, a whirlwind came out of the north, a great cloud, and a fire infolding itself, and a brightness was about it, and out of the midst thereof as the colour of amber, out of the midst of the fire. Also out of the midst thereof came the likeness of four living creatures. And this was their appearance; they had the likeness of a man" (Ezekiel 1:4–28). Following a long and detailed description of the object, Ezekiel continues his narrative in chapter 10, describing its takeoff:

> And the sound of the cherubims' wings was heard even to the outer court, as the voice of the Almighty God when he speaketh. And it came to pass, that when he had commanded the man clothed with linen, saying, Take fire from between the wheels, from between the cherubims; then he went in, and stood beside the wheels. And one cherub stretched forth his hand from between the cherubims unto the fire that was between the cherubims, and took thereof, and put it into the hands of him that was clothed with linen: who took it, and went out. . . And as for their appearances, they four had one likeness, as if a wheel had been in the midst of a wheel. . . And their

whole body, and their backs, and their hands, and their wings, and the wheels, were full of eyes round about, even the wheels that they four had. . . And the cherubims were lifted up. This is the living creature that I saw by the river of Chebar. And when the cherubims went, the wheels went by them: and when the cherubims lifted up their wings to mount up from the earth, the same wheels also turned not from beside them. . . . And the cherubims lifted up their wings, and mounted up from the earth in my sight: when they went out, the wheels also were beside them, and every one stood at the door of the east gate of the Lord's house; and the glory of the God of Israel was over them above. (Ezekiel 10)

Many UAP books attempt to show a "UFO/history/religion" connection from Ezekiel's vision. They further generally offer an artist's conception of the "craft" described in great detail in the scripture. NASA Saturn V engineer Josef F. Blumrich attempted in 1968 to debunk the theory that "Ezekiel's wheel" was a flying craft. He published a book in 1973 entitled *The Spaceships of Ezekiel*, in which he described how his debunking effort became a successful design venture. He writes, "Seldom has a total defeat been so rewarding, so fascinating, and so delightful!" His design is simple, resembling a domed upside-down loudspeaker with four vertical landing gear adorned with propellers. Although this type of undertaking might be enjoyable to an engineer, it is incongruous that beings that are capable of intergalactic flight would zip around in Earth's atmosphere in a propeller-driven craft that gets extra lift from those blazing rocket boosters (I see fire mentioned ten times). I assume that whatever presentation was made by the Lord to the people of Israel to assure them that Ezekiel's assumption was cloaked in glorious pomp and circumstance, no propellers, rocket boosters, or spacecraft were necessary.

Having said that, this is a description of the "translation" of the prophet, not unlike the translation of many thousands of others. We understand that the actual, physical location of Zion was taken off-planet with the people of that marvelous city. So, we must ask ourselves if it was accomplished in more of a miraculous instantaneous manner, or if there was some sort of mother ship involved in the extraction of the entire city from the surface and transportation to its final destination. Personally, I'm

SCRIPTURAL SPACECRAFT?

hostile to the idea that God sent spaceships to collect the prophets and others, but we know it's possible. However, God's choices and methods have nothing to do with His necessity of traveling in a spaceship if He desires to visit one of His worlds without number, or His need to send an intergalactic taxi to collect Ezekiel. He doesn't need propellers, and He doesn't need rockets. If He did employ godly technologies, as a matter of course, they wouldn't be the hodgepodge of faces and fire and wheels and animals described in Ezekiel. Whatever the people of Israel saw, it was to communicate a message to them—one that was impactful in their language and understanding. If you or I were to witness Ezekiel being taken up, we would probably use an entirely different vocabulary to describe it.

As a footnote to Ezekiel's experience, Ezekiel reports that he encountered an oddly colored man in connection with this craft: "And he brought me thither, and, behold, there was a man, whose appearance was like the appearance of brass, with a line of flax in his hand, and a measuring reed; and he stood in the gate" (Ezekiel 40:3; cross-referenced from Ezekiel 1:7) (color of craft's feet). The "flax" or "measuring reed" in the fellow's hand is a point of interest to UAP investigators. UAP occupants are sometimes said to carry rods in their hands. Of course, these were tools and emblems of principality at the time of Ezekiel, so I assume there was more of an interpretive value to the props than literal tools being employed to perform a task.

Biblical UAP proponents cite many more examples of flying UAP in the skies above the people of Israel from the Bible—generally, anything that flies, floats (clouds), or shines is proffered as evidence for their theory. Whatever presentations God sends His people to illustrate His message is often in the spoken or visual language of that particular people. For us to look back thousands of years in time and attempt to foist our own cultural expectations on a vision or visitation that was tailored to them is pointless. However, to the extent God or angels appear to have employed the device of a chariot, or a cloud, or a flying wheel to convey a message, we concede that that was the method used. We just don't see any evidence in all of these references that God or angels must utilize spacecraft to get from one place to another. In fact, we see God and His Son arriving and leaving, flying from the earth accompanied by angels—all without a craft of any kind.

In the book of Acts we read, "And when he had spoken these things, while they beheld, he was taken up; and a cloud received him out of their sight. And while they looked steadfastly toward heaven as he went up, behold, two men stood by them in white apparel; Which also said, Ye men of Galilee, why stand ye gazing up into heaven? this same Jesus, which is taken up from you into heaven, shall so come in like manner as ye have seen him go into heaven" (Acts 1:9–11). In the Book of Mormon we learn, "And it came to pass, as they understood they cast their eyes up again towards heaven; and behold, they saw a Man descending out of heaven; and he was clothed in a white robe; and he came down and stood in the midst of them; and the eyes of the whole multitude were turned upon him, and they durst not open their mouths, even one to another, and wist not what it meant, for they thought it was an angel that had appeared unto them" (3 Nephi 11:8–10) "And while they were overshadowed he departed from them, and ascended into heaven. And the disciples saw and did bear record that he ascended again into heaven" (3 Nephi 18:39).

Again, we know that there is a message in each instance of arriving and leaving. Does Jesus need to come down from the sky and land among His people in a miraculous way? In Luke, the resurrected Lord suddenly stood in their midst in the upper room. "And as they thus spake, Jesus himself stood in the midst of them, and saith unto them, Peace be unto you" (24:36). There was no craft and no display. There was no message in the manner of His appearance. He was just there.

Enoch's Escort

In the beginning of the uncanonized *The Book of the Secrets of Enoch*, the 365–year-old prophet recounts an unusual event that gave rise to an intriguing encounter:

> And when I was asleep, great distress came up into my heart, and I was weeping with my eyes in sleep, and I could not understand what this distress was, or what would happen to me. And there appeared to me two men, exceeding big, so that I never saw such on earth; their faces were shining like the sun, their eyes too were like a burning light, and from their lips was fire coming forth with clothing and singing of various kinds in appearance purple, their wings were

brighter than gold, their hands whiter than snow. They were standing at the head of my couch and began to call me by my name. And I arose from my sleep and saw clearly those two men standing in front of me. And I saluted them and was seized with fear and the appearance of my face was changed from terror, and those men said to me: "Have courage, Enoch, do not fear; the eternal God sent us to thee, and lo! thou shalt to-day ascend with us into heaven, and thou shalt tell thy sons and all thy household all that they shall do without thee on earth in thy house, and let no one seek thee till the Lord return thee to them. . . . It came to pass, when Enoch had told his sons, that the angels took him on to their wings and bore him up on to the first heaven and placed him on the clouds. And there I looked, and again I looked higher, and saw the ether, and they placed me on the first heaven and showed me a very great Sea, greater than the earthly sea. They brought before my face the elders and rulers of the stellar orders, and showed me two hundred angels, who rule the stars and their services to the heavens, and fly with their wings and come round all those who sail. (chapters 1, 3, and 4)

Later chapters relate how Enoch was shown the workings of the planets and stars and the myriad angels assigned to oversee those functions. The most interesting aspect of these accounts is the description concerning the appearance of the angels and their mode of transportation. The assertion that the angels possessed "wings" that enabled them to fly from one heaven to another is most fascinating in light of our knowledge that angels do not have wings—not as part of their anatomy, anyway. Could this indicate that they used something with wings for transportation as some would have us believe? Functionally, wings are not necessary for flight—not interstellar flight, anyway—not for God, not for angels, or for UAP. Therefore, Joseph Smith's explanation of such symbolic representations to the ancients seems more likely an explanation: "Q. What are we to understand by the eyes and wings, which the beasts had? A. Their eyes are a representation of light and knowledge; and their wings are a representation of power, to move, to act, etc." (D&C 77:4).

I tend to agree with the Prophet, which, of course, is always a wise course. I believe that all of these eyes, wings, faces, wheels, fire, beasts, and birds are all just representations of ideas and concepts that the vision or visitation is intended to convey to the viewer. In fact, if this were a discussion on prophetic language, we would see that many of the items and animals used in the presentations carry meanings that are intrinsic to those items—bats, eagles, cattle, dogs, babies, virgins, candles, lamps, curtains, swine—each has a meaning to the people of the Lord, and they reacted to those things differently than we do, based on their attitudes about them, which were usually derived from Leviticus and other pronouncements of the Lord.

UAP in Egyptian Religious Texts

In drawing parallels between the ancient gospel and other religions of antiquity, Hugh Nibley makes reference to interplanetary visitations by beings from other worlds who commute for purposes related to man's spiritual welfare:

> The founding and building of the Egyptian temple and the establishing of its rites is always done, according to Mrs. Reymond's study, by beings who sail from other worlds, and, when their work is done, "the Shebtiw seem to have sailed away again" (E. Reymond, *Mythical Origin*, 27). Some such space travel (often indicated in the Coptic Gnostic writings) is indicated in C. T. 162 (II, 03f): "He takes the ship of 1000 cubits from end to end, and he sails in it to the stairway of fire." All of which most cogently brings to mind Joseph Smith's interpretation of the ship-figure (fig. 4) in Facsimile II of the Book of Abraham: . . . a numerical figure in Egyptian signifying one thousand; answering to the measuring of time . . . "Very common are references to the dead King's being hauled by cables to heaven or rowed thither by crews of the Unwearied or the Imperishable Ones (*i.e.*, unsetting stars). The sky ship can make the trip both ways: 'I go down among the weak ones (hasw, uninitiated) . . . I have seized on to the cable of the Hnt-mn-it.f; I row in my seat in the divine ship. I have gone down upon my throne in the divine ship. I control, none being near my throne in the divine ship; I am in control, not being without a boat, my throne being in the divine ship at Heliopolis" (C. T. 151, II, 257).[3]

---

3. *The Message of the Joseph Smith Papyri, an Egyptian Endowment*, 138.

SCRIPTURAL SPACECRAFT?

Facsimile No. 2, Figure 4.

Brother Nibley adds to this colorful description of ancient space travel: "It is in the solar ship that the initiate joins his father on the horizon. One steps into the Sun-ship just as it reaches that place where the sky touches the earth at the horizon as the water meets the land at the sacred wharf of the pyramid or temple. It is a ship that carries one in a state of effortless suspension through the void between the worlds."[4]

Remembering that all of this describes the transporting of the dead king's soul to his eternal resting place, much like our own celestial kingdom, the resemblance to reports by abductees of the "state of effortless suspension through the void between the worlds" is remarkable. Perhaps they have a common origin, as we discuss below. One last interesting aspect discussed by Brother Nibley is the purported means of propulsion of these great Solar Barks: "As the ship moves on, we remember that after all it is the Solar-bark, a Skyship, 'Moving in Light' (Thausing, Gr. Th., p. 9)."[5]

In UAP literature there are a few accounts of UAP occupants describing the propulsion system of their ship to their guest. One such description was that of Udo Wartena, above, whose hosts explained the mechanics of their craft to him and then revealed to him that they focused on a distant star and used its energy to draw them through space at speeds greater than the speed of light. He then adds, "My host specifically mentioned 'skipping upon the light waves.'" The similarity

---

4. Ibid., 135
5. Ibid., 236.

between "skipping upon the light waves" and "moving in light" from the above citation is an interesting parallel. Of course, the Egyptians learned about the cosmos from the prophets Abraham and Joseph, who well understood the fundamental functions of light in the creation and governance of the universe and its elements. Although Egyptians building solar barks to transport them to their ultimate kingdom in the afterlife is more akin to boys building rocket ships in the backyard from scraps of lumber, the principles of being transported to celestial glory by magnificent light waves are certainly in keeping with eternal truths.

Again, according to the uncanonized ancient writings dealing with matters that occurred before the Flood, Satan and the fallen Watchers meted out destructive technologies to the people of Cain for over 1,000 years before the Flood finally wiped them all out. We may or may not accept these accounts as accurate, but the implication is that God caused Noah and his sons, and their wives, to covenant with Him that all knowledge of the technologies and practices that had led to the earth's destruction must be left behind in the floodwaters. They would be hidden from their children, forever, to prevent a repeat of the utter destruction of humanity and life that had been the result of Satan's "flood" of evil, whoredoms, sorceries, incest, cannibalism, theft, murder, war, and secret combinations. All of the technologies were to be left behind, and Noah and his family were to reenter the telestial, dry earth as if none of it had ever happened, weaving simple clothing, tending domestic animals, reading by oil lamplight, and planting crops by the new seasons.

Facsimile No. 2, Figure 3.

SCRIPTURAL SPACECRAFT?

As a postscript to Egyptian religious accounts of space travel, it is noteworthy that in Facsimile 2, Figure 3, of the book of Abraham, there is a figure sitting on a throne, riding in a thousand-cubit Solar Bark, which Joseph Smith describes in his interpretation: "Fig. 3. Is made to represent God, sitting upon his throne, clothed with power and authority; with a crown of eternal light upon his head; representing also the grand Key-words of the Holy Priesthood, as revealed to Adam in the Garden of Eden, as also to Seth, Noah, Melchizedek, Abraham, and all to whom the Priesthood was revealed." The solar bark "craft" that is propelled through the cosmos on light waves, expanded and inflated by 1,000 as it begets time in its wake, is much more than wishful thinking. Gospel initiates are endowed with the gift of the grand key words of the holy priesthood, and employ them to pass through the dimensional portals from one sphere of existence to another, passing by the sentinels who are posted to guard the way.

Egyptian hieroglyph carving from the Temple of
Seti I at Abydos. Some see a helicopter, ship, airplane, etc.

Additionally, there are several depictions of mechanical-looking devices and modern-looking craft, and people and other humanoids seemingly wearing "astronaut" garb and other specialized equipment in the writings and pictographs of the Egyptians and other ancient cultures. There are advanced mathematical and astronomical insights embedded in the structures of the ancients, as well as tales of interstellar dogfights in the skies above ancient cities. Ancient alien theory adherents point to these as proof positive that extraterrestrials must have visited the earth anciently and instructed humans in mathematics, astronomy,

The "Dendera Light" relief in the Temple of Hathor, Dendera, Egypt. Cord leads to large bulb device that produces a ray?

astrophysics, chemistry, metallurgy, and so forth. Of course, there are other sources for such knowledge.

For instance, the Great Pyramid is an architectural marvel, with high level mathematics and ultra-modern construction techniques employed to build it. What documentaries never mention is that the nomadic Bedouins introduced the structure to the first Europeans to visit the Holy Land as The Pillar of Enoch, explaining that it had been built by that ancient prophet and his people before the Great Flood. When asked about the other pyramids around Egypt, they said these were made by the Egyptians and Pharaohs who tried to mimic the grandeur of the society that had existed under Enoch. Could there be any truth in those assertions?

> Now this king of Egypt was a descendant from the loins of Ham, and was a partaker of the blood of the Canaanites by birth. From this descent sprang all the Egyptians, and thus the blood of the Canaanites was preserved in the land. The land of Egypt being first discovered by a woman, who was the daughter of Ham, and the daughter of Egyptus, which in the Chaldean signifies Egypt, which signifies that which is forbidden; When this woman discovered the land it was under water, who afterward settled her sons in it; and thus, from Ham, sprang that race which preserved the curse in the land. Now the first government of Egypt was established by Pharaoh, the eldest son of Egyptus, the daughter of Ham, and it was after the manner of the government of Ham, which was patriarchal. Pharaoh, being a righteous man, established his kingdom and judged his people

wisely and justly all his days, seeking earnestly to imitate that order established by the fathers in the first generations, in the days of the first patriarchal reign, even in the reign of Adam, and also of Noah, his father, who blessed him with the blessings of the earth, and with the blessings of wisdom, but cursed him as pertaining to the Priesthood. Now, Pharaoh being of that lineage by which he could not have the right of Priesthood, notwithstanding the Pharaohs would fain claim it from Noah, through Ham, therefore my father was led away by their idolatry. (Abraham 1:21–27)

Other ancient architectural marvels boast precisely carved stones, with perfectly flat surfaces, and inside right-angles and converging corners and drilled holes that have no variance in the surface flatness, angle or dimension. Some show signs of machine tooling, as well as precision polishing, to within microns of perfection. These construction wonders often display ancient knowledge of advanced mathematics, including pi and the golden mean. Some incorporate advanced understanding of the cosmos, including varying levels of precision of the solar year.

In short, it's true that ancient humans enjoyed an advanced level of technical and scientific sophistication that we have only recently begun to recapture. The question remains, what was the source of that knowledge, and why was it all lost for a time? Ancient astronaut adherents claim, with no compelling evidence, that the only possible source of such knowledge is visiting extraterrestrials. Or, they say it was the result of secret knowledge imparted by the fallen Watchers—whom they insist were extraterrestrials.

I tend to think that much of the technology and knowledge we find is left over from civilizations that flourished before the Great Flood. I also tend to think that after the Flood, when humanity finally reentered the earth's surface and began to build from scratch, that there were millennia of non-interference, followed by natural technical, mathematical, and philosophical advances, based on inspiration and clear human reasoning. There has been a flourish of scientific and engineering breakthroughs in the past 200 years, and we appear to be on an exponential trajectory into future developments.

Puma Punku, a large temple complex near Tiwanaku, Bolivia, is part of the larger archaeological site Tiahuanacu. Thousands of heavy, hard stones are machined and surfaced to modern machining specs and interlock with precision.

It doesn't appear that Satan has been allowed to share scientific knowledge with humans[6] to the same degree he did before the Flood, but he does seem to be actively steering technology and its uses in destructive directions.

---

6. However, many have said that the Nazis were in active alliance with spiritual or demonic powers, which provided them with many advanced technologies. These theories are compelling, but evidence is scant. The Nazi Vril Society cult "wonder women" were very active in medium contact with "alien" benefactors whom the Nazis claimed assisted them in developing advanced weapons, including Die Glocke and other antigravity and super-explosive devices. Theorists contend that an Allied Forces delay of just two additional weeks would have allowed the Nazis to complete some of their weapons technologies, resulting in an entirely different outcome of World War II.

CHAPTER 7

UAP in the Sky

Reports of unidentified flying objects of one kind or another in our skies have persisted for thousands of years. Not unexpectedly, observers of these phenomena have generally recounted what they observed in the descriptive language of the culture, religion, technology, and scientific understanding of the era. Although this in itself is not surprising, the details of such narratives create something of a yardstick by which the veracity or origin of the account may be measured. With some exceptions, the same yardsticks can be employed to examine modern UAP accounts as well. Here, we survey a brief history of UAP sightings in their various forms, just hitting the highlights to get an idea of how we got to the point we currently find ourselves.

ANCIENT UAP REPORTS

From the time man learned to write down on parchment or clay tablets the important details of his day, brief accounts of mysterious flying vessels have been inserted between other affairs of state. As discussed above, many believe that various accounts in the Bible have such origins. In ancient China a legend of humanoid visitors in "flying carts" with gilded wings found its genesis, and the tale has been passed on for centuries. In Rome, "flying shields," sometimes accompanied by spurting fire, were widely reported. Written in the Sanskrit *Drona*

Parva text are accounts of a superhuman race conducting aerial dogfights in flying vessels called "vimana." One translation renders specifics of an air battle thus: a "blazing missile possessed of the radiance of smokeless fire was discharged."

Two of the most famous remote reports of flying vessels are those that occurred in the skies over Nuremberg, Germany, and Basel, Switzerland, in 1561 and 1566, respectively. During these spectacular displays, thousands of local citizens were treated to a spectacle of several large discs, spheres, and tubes that appeared in the skies and "danced" or weaved themselves about in something described as an aerial ballet. When finished, these objects suddenly resolved themselves into fiery red spheres and disappeared. Numerous historical reports like these have come to light in recent years. We hear of very similar craft performing in analogous fashion today.

Famed UAP investigator and author Dr. Jacques Vallee has documented many similarities and parallels between the medieval "fairy faith" and modern accounts of UAP sightings, encounters, and abductions. The medieval peasantry were so overwhelmed by their encounters with small humanoids who whisked them away, generally into underground complexes, and performed physical examinations, as well as reproductive experimentations, that they revered these "fairies" as a supernatural force to be reckoned with. One village documented how one of its prominent midwives was somewhat politely abducted and taken to an underground area where a small humanoid giving birth needed assistance. When the ordeal was over, the midwife was thanked and returned to her village to tell the tale. Accounts like these are disturbingly similar to modern abduction accounts, as outlined in the following chapters.

UAP REPORTS IN RECENT HISTORY

The current era of UAP sightings actually began in the late nineteenth century—around the period of the great airships. With popularized reports of high-tech flying machines hitting the public press, stories of flying machine sightings proliferated into an American avocation. Although many such accounts were accurate reports of prototype gas-filled balloon craft flying overhead, making mysterious noises and sporting eerie, colored lights, others were preposterous, and obvious fabrications intended to attract attention to the reporters. First, newspaper reporters were known to fabricate such tales to boost circulation. Then telegraph operators did it for the pure pleasure of telling the tales.

With the advent of giant airships developed by industrialists bent on assisting with skirmishes in Cuba and elsewhere around the world, tales of peculiar night encounters with futuristic voyagers abounded. Although it is true that a handful of experimental airships nocturnally[1] crisscrossed the United States at speeds of twenty to thirty miles per hour, tales of ultramodern craft moving at 200 miles per hour (or much faster) surfaced sporadically. These accounts gave rise to reports of people witnessing hieroglyph-speckled crafts piloted by superhuman beings clad in space-type uniforms. Many reports, made by credible citizens of the period, were very similar to UFO/UAP accounts of today—with rapid movements and departures, and emanating light beams that probed and lifted.

CULTURAL UAP EXPECTATIONS

As of 1900, physical descriptions of these mysterious, advanced craft were often limited to airships of the period—the dirigible kind, with fewer of the flying saucer and extraterrestrial thus far. This "airship" portion of UAP history illustrates a disturbingly consistent phenomenon that has perplexed researchers for decades. From the late nineteenth century through the present, the UAP phenomenon, although consistent in other respects, has manifested itself in the technological and cultural (including science-fictional) trappings and expectations of the era. Many of the reports of the 1940s and 1950s were more modernistic than those of the twentieth century, but not as sleek and futuristic as many current craft. Although mentioned briefly above, this phenomenon warrants a separate discussion here.

---

1. Experimental flights of these craft were conducted at night because hot air balloons fly better in cold weather; and supposedly, to protect pending patents.

As noted and discussed by Dr. Salisbury in *The Utah UFO Display*, UAP appear to people of different cultures, beliefs, and experiences, in manners seemingly diverse than those of dissimilar backgrounds. For example, the encounters at Fatima, Portugal, discussed later in this work, were "packaged" specifically for rural Portuguese Catholics of the early twentieth century. Other encounters in South America appear to be tailored to Catholics of that region. There is a slight difference in belief, and therefore, cultural expectation. The astute reader may say, "But the Fatima and other 'Madonna' sightings appear more like spiritual manifestations of some kind rather than a UFO experience." This observation is one that should be kept in mind as all UAP sightings are analyzed. Author Brad Steiger has observed, "A historical survey reveals that reports of strange objects in the skies are laced through documents of the ancient and recent past. Interestingly, the records seem to indicate the UAP have adapted themselves to the cultural milieu and the technologic capacities of the observers."[2] As stated frequently herein, many UAP researchers are turning from their "nuts-and-bolts extraterrestrial vehicle" explanations of UAP origins to more metaphysical interpretations. The line between "nuts-and-bolts" and "spiritual" becomes quite hazy as the overall UAP occurrence is examined.

The "tailoring" of these divergent manifestations becomes somewhat apparent in the following chapters. The differences are not limited to those of perception, either. The craft, the humanoids, and the "UAP message" and its means of deliverance are manifested in a diverse, yet somewhat predictable fashion. This is why Dr. Salisbury employs the word "display" in his title—to illustrate the "theatrical" aspects of the encounters. As we begin our survey of modern UAP accounts, I invite you to note this pattern, as well as others that you detect, and to discern for yourself the paradigm of the UAP encounter.

UAP in the Twentieth Century

The first half of the twentieth century saw the rapid escalation of reports of UAP, but again, the accounts were initially limited to airships

---

2. *The UFO Abductors*, 212.

and later, airplane-like craft and rockets. However, by now, popular literature had become overrun with Jules Verne and H. G. Wells "wannabees," and science fiction paperbacks became an American staple. Popular writers and radio programs weaved tales of air and space travel that captured the imagination of most of America, and then the world. Stories of close encounters with aliens from Mars, Venus, Jupiter, and even the Moon became common. Dime novel and mystery magazine publishers did all they could to promote their science fiction bonanza by creating eyewitness accounts of exotic interplanetary rockets manned by inhuman aliens; bug-eyed, gill-breathing monsters, whose designs were generally imperialistic and methods cruel.

As the skies began to fill up with shiny airplanes, test rockets, and other experimental craft, and as the minds of the public became habituated to the idea of interplanetary space travel, reports of weird flying machines abounded around the world. These accounts were often, but not always, the creations of unscrupulous reporters and publishers wishing to boost careers and increase circulation. By the time H. G. Wells' 1898 book *War of the Worlds* hit the radio airwaves, the public was willing to believe. Other UAP sighting narratives made by average citizens of the time were somewhat less sensational and often mistaken, yet reported by believable townsmen who lent credibility to the UAP "industry."

PUBLIC UAP REPORTS BY CREDIBLE WITNESSES

During World War II pilots and crewmen reported seeing small globes following them as they flew in formation. These "foo fighters" (also known as "Kraut Balls"), as the allied airmen came to call them, were thought by both sides to be the secret weapon of the other. Fliers complained of being followed by one to ten of these red, orange, or clear spheres, believing them to be the result of superior German technology. Allied pilots soon learned, however, that the spheres were harmless. Former B-17 bomber pilot Charles Odom told the *Houston Post* that the foo fighters "looked like crystal balls, clear, about the size of basketballs" and that they would advance to within about 100 yards of the flight formation and "would seem to become magnetized to our formation and fly alongside. . . . After awhile, they would peel off like a plane and leave."³ These observations were so widespread that most World War II fliers reportedly experienced them. Subsequent to World War II, many pilots continue to report the presence of these luminous, enigmatic spheres. This is especially true in aerial combat situations, such as in Korea and Vietnam.

When astronaut Gordon Cooper was training as a pilot over Germany in 1951, he and his squadron of fighter jets chased a large formation of UAP. He explained what it was like:

> Unlike fighters they would almost stop their forward velocity, and change 90°, sometimes in their flight path. Within the next two to three days we had practically all the fighters we could muster on the base up climbing as high as they would climb, with guys with binoculars with them still trying to spot these strange devices flying overhead. We never could get close enough to really pin them down. They were round in shape, and very metallic looking. They would come over and do the same maneuvers that we made, except that one of them would just go zip—and you just can't do that in a fighter.⁴

THE MODERN ERA OF UAP

The current era of UAP was ushered in on June 24, 1947, when Kenneth Arnold, a respected Boise, Idaho, pilot was flying over Washington state and keeping his eyes peeled for a reported aircraft in distress. As he watched the skyline carefully, he observed what he described as "nine peculiar aircraft" flying in formation and maneuvering at approximately 1,700 mph, a speed unattainable in 1947. He described the discs as shiny, with the sun glinting off of them. He described their movement to be like saucers skipping on water. Arnold was a sober professional and experienced aircraft observer. His mission that day was to locate a downed C-46 Marine transport plane. He was watching very carefully when the nine metallic "discs" came into view.

---

3. Raymond Fowler, *The Watchers*, 70.
4. OMNI interview of Astronaut Gordon Cooper, March 1980.

UAP IN THE SKY

Pilot Kenneth Arnold presents an artist's rendering of one of nine discs he saw near Mt. Rainer.

Although his report was covered heavily by the national press and media, Arnold rejected the publicity that came his way as a result of what he saw on that clear summer day. He had assumed that the unidentifiable aircraft belonged to the US military and fully expected a reasonable explanation of why disc-shaped craft without tails and propellers were flying at phenomenal speeds near Mt. Rainier, Washington, just as soon as he contacted the general manager of central aircraft at the Yakima Airport. The general manager was slightly dubious of Arnold's report, however, which set Arnold on a path leading to Military Intelligence to learn if unmanned guided missiles were being fired in the region. There was none.

In the next hours and days, hundreds of reports flooded the air traffic airwaves and the media that others had seen clusters of Arnold's shiny flying "saucers." This proliferation of flying saucer reports caused Arnold to later write: "From then on, if I was to go by the number of reports that came in of other sightings, of which I kept a close track, I thought it wouldn't be long before there would be one of these things in every garage. In order to stop what I thought was a lot of foolishness, and since I couldn't get any work done, I went out to the airport, cranked up my plane, and flew home to Boise."[5]

---

5. Kenneth Arnold, with Raymond Palmer, *The Coming of the Saucers* (1952).

Arnold attempted a few times to investigate what he considered to be credible UAP sightings. However, when he learned that sensationalist publishers were using his name to promote their books and magazines, he gave it up.

Arnold's sighting and report of 1947 remains a credible UAP sighting. The public believed his report. The press believed him. Even Military Intelligence accepted Arnold's story as completely true, without concluding the origin of the discs. Even then, however, UAP debunkers were on the scene attempting to prove that Arnold had witnessed nothing more than natural phenomena that only appeared like flying "saucers skipping over the water" at 1,700 mph.

The decade of the 1950s saw the shift of science fiction from paperbacks and magazines to the silver screen. Flying saucers and their alien pilots were now being imprinted onto the psyches of industrialized nations in panoramic technicolor. As hundreds of thousands, and even millions, of theater goers were deluged with the extraterrestrial phenomenon, the numbers of reported sightings escalated proportionately. UAP protagonists claim that the proliferation of sightings was not the result of public "over eagerness" to see UAP, but of more eyes watching the sky.

By the 1960s counterfeit UAP were being mass-produced by any teenager with a dry-cleaning bag, balsa wood, and a candle.[6] High-altitude weather balloons and meteorological phenomena produced reflected atmospheric flashes that caused even the best trained pilots to believe that they were witnessing a true-to-life UAP. Many UAP sightings were retrospectively learned to be mere test flights of conventional aircraft outfitted with special lights or other test gear. UAP debunkers, such as Philip Klass, began to denounce all UAP sightings, incredulous that such things were even possible. Their attitude was that because it was "impossible," any report of one *must* be

---

6. It is interesting how many of these inexpensive lighted hot-air balloons have appeared on the front pages of newspapers with headlines announcing the arrival of UFOs to the local community. The balloons provide impressive night sky effects, including high-speed formation maneuvering, and have fooled thousands of observers.

a mistake or a fraud. The government and military soon began to debunk the UAP phenomenon, persecuting any military or airliner personnel who reported seeing one. Under the weight of the social stigma created by these campaigns, the public became incredulous about those claiming to see UAP.

THE CONTROVERSY OVER UAP EVIDENCE

With the affluence and technological advancements of the 1950s came the availability of inexpensive, good quality photographic equipment. UAP reports began to be accompanied by photographs of flying saucers. Expert analysis revealed no evidence of counterfeiting in many of these photographs, though others were obvious fakes. It did not take long for people to learn that a snapshot of a Buick hubcap flying through the air, or a double exposure of eerie lights in the night sky could bring instant national fame, and sometimes fortune. While most of the genuine, at least unmanufactured photographs reveal mere obscure shapes and smudges in speckled skies, a few, still frequently reprinted in UFO books, present clear images of saucer or disc-shaped objects in clear skies.

UAP PHOTOGRAPHS
Trent Photos

One such set of photographs were taken in McMinnville, Oregon, on May 11, 1950, by farmer Paul Trent. Evelyn Trent saw the craft over their farm and told Paul, who ran and got their camera. He was able to snap two photos before it sped away. Evelyn described its rapid departure, saying, "It just came up like that, and tipped [showing with her hands that it appeared to turn on edge], and shhwwuupp, I mean, it really went. It went fast. I've never seen anything go so fast in my life as that thing went." This photograph shows a clear image of an up-side-down-plate-looking craft, with a small, pointed dome in the middle of the top. The photograph is one of the few ever to pass the scrutiny of the famed Condon Committee, an investigative committee well-known for its unkind treatment of UAP witnesses. The Condon

Trent photos from McMinnville, Oregon. Second photo is placed in the inset.

Committee concluded, "The simplest, most direct interpretation of the photographs confirms precisely what the witnesses say they saw."

Modern photographic analysis confirms that the Trent photographs are authentic. The two photographs were recently subjected to thorough computer enhancement scrutiny. The results prove that (1) the photographs contain no wires to hang a UAP model—a favorite debunker claim; (2) the UAP is an actual three-dimensional image, not flat or superimposed; (3) the UAP was at least one kilometer away; and (4) the UAP is twenty to thirty meters (60–90 feet) in diameter.

Tremonton, Utah, Film

One of the most fascinating early UAP photographic windfalls occurred in Northern Utah on July 2, 1952. Navy Warrant Officer Delbert Newhouse and his wife were driving near Tremonton when she spotted flashes in the clear day sky. Delbert explained, "They were like two saucers, one inverted over the other. They seemed to be made of some kind of polished metal. When I first saw the objects, they were almost overhead. By time I had the camera ready to go they had moved to a considerably greater distance."

Delbert, a US Navy military aerial observation photographer, happened to have his military 16mm high-quality movie camera in the trunk of the car. When he realized that he was observing something very rare in 1952 aviation, he rushed to the trunk for his camera and photographed a cluster of shiny round discs flying in formation through the summer sky. Government Intelligence analyzed the film for thousands of hours and finally pronounced it to be authentic. But the military was already debunking UAP, so they said it looked like a flock of birds—perhaps seagulls, because they are white. No one took the Seagull story seriously, because the Navy's own data demonstrated that the reflective nature of the objects was too radiant for seagulls, or any other bird.

The 1960s and 1970s produced a flood of UAP sightings and other close encounters, together with prolific evidence of UAP existence. Hundreds of clear photographs were published depicting clear shapes of advanced flying machines. Educators, policemen, ministers, engineers, and civic leaders reported seeing discs, saucers, cylinders, and other strange flying objects. People above reproach, former skeptics, were now confirming what they had seriously doubted only a moment before becoming witnesses themselves. Airline pilots dodged flying discs buzzing around the 350 mph passenger planes as if they were standing still. Radar centers tracked bogeys on their screens traveling at thousands of miles per hour. Reconnaissance jets were scrambled around the globe only to be chased back to base or to see metallic discs disappear into high altitudes in a flash.

JAL FLIGHT 1628 SIGHTING

On November 17, 1986, the Japanese crew of Japan Airlines Flight 1628 was flying over eastern Alaska after sunset, heading west toward Japan in their Boeing 747 cargo freighter. Captain Kenju Terauchi, a former fighter pilot with more than 10,000 hours in the air, and the other two members of his flight crew had set the plane on autopilot and were cruising at 565 mph at an altitude of 35,000 feet. As they cruised over the remote region, they suddenly saw two unknown craft coming from below and taking positions as if to escort the cargo plane. The captain assumed they were military jets until they abruptly zipped directly in front of the cargo plane and took a stacked position just in front of them. Captain Terauchi described their move as a disregard for inertia, saying, "The thing was flying as if there was no such thing as gravity. It sped up, then stopped, then flew at our speed, in our direction, so that to us it appeared to be standing still. The next instant it changed course. . . . In other words, the flying object had overcome gravity." They could now see the objects better and described them as rectangular looking, but felt they were actually upright cylinders, like a soda can. As the two objects made this "reverse thrust" move, the captain said it caused a bright flare for a few seconds, to the extent that he could feel the warmth of their glows through the cockpit glass.

The crew notified Air Traffic Control of what had happened, and asked if they were seeing the traffic on radar. ATC could not see the objects just ahead of them. After a couple of minutes the two objects took a side-by-side configuration and led the cargo jet on its course for the next ten minutes. The two objects suddenly disappeared from view, but the crew could now make out a round glow in the distance in front of them. They set their onboard radar on the object and were picking up a return. They started to feel heavy turbulence, which continued throughout the ordeal. The captain informed ATC about the new object in the distance and asked if they were picking it up on radar. They were not, but Elmendorf's NORAD Regional Operations Control Center (ROCC), directly in their flight path, reported a "surge primary return" shortly thereafter. As JAL 1628 got closer to Fairbanks, the city lights were bright enough that the crew could begin to make out the craft just ahead. They were astounded to see a very large round object, with something around the midsection that made the craft look like the planet Saturn, close up, and Captain Terauchi reported that it was four times the size of an aircraft carrier.

ATC asked Captain Terauchi if he felt they required a military escort at that point, and he recalled a few of the military pilots who had died in UAP confrontations, and declined the offer. The JAL flight proceeded toward Japan for several minutes, and then the large craft suddenly disappeared. A day later at FAA headquarters, they briefed Vice Admiral Donald Engen about the JAL encounter. He watched the video and asked them not to talk to anybody until they were told it was all right, but to prepare a full presentation of the data for a group of government officials the next day. The meeting was attended by three members each of the CIA, FBI, and the president's Scientific

UAP IN THE SKY

Captain Terauchi of JAL 1628 displays a hand-drawn depiction of the large UAP.

Study Team, among others. After the presentation, all present were instructed that the event was considered top secret and that their meeting "never took place." The intelligence officials took possession of all the presented data. They failed to ask those present if that constituted all of the data. John Callahan, Senior FAA Official, had the original video, the pilot's report, and the FAA's report back in his office, which were later utilized at a massive press conference exposing the incident and cover-up. Captain Terauchi spoke to the press about his experience and was immediately transferred to a desk job, where he remained for years until he was finally reinstated to his pilot's position.

THE GULF BREEZE UAP

In some cases, UAP have frequented certain locations for weeks, or even months, allowing the local citizens to see them many times. In one such case, citizens were able to move in with sophisticated photographic equipment to record their presence. This is the case of the Gulf Breeze, Florida, sightings. There, in late 1987, Ed and Frances Walters, local prominent business people, as well as many others, reported numerous sightings of flying vehicles. Ed and Frances armed themselves with a Polaroid camera (it is difficult to fake Polaroid photographs), a video camera, and even a sealed four lens 3-D camera supplied by MUFON UAP investigators. In the book *The Gulf Breeze Sightings*, the entire UAP experience between November 1987 and May 1988 is set out in detail, accompanied by more than twenty of the most impressive UAP photographs in existence. During the six-month sighting period, 135 of the local citizens of Gulf Breeze confirmed having seen the same flying vehicles photographed by the Walterses and published in the local newspapers. Experts from Jet Propulsion Laboratories[7] and NASA examined the photographs and a video tape for nearly a year, concluding that they were unable to find any indication of counterfeiting in the photographs, the video tape, or in the person of Ed Walters, the primary photographer. Psychologists, UAP-sighting investigators, and polygraph experts fully examined Ed and Frances Walters, and concluded that there exists a low likelihood of a hoax on their part.[8]

Experts with the Mutual UFO Network (MUFON), an organization holding itself out to investigate and document reported UAP sightings, agree that the Walters case is the best documented American case to date. I have interviewed many of the investigators in the Gulf Breeze study, and all of those interviewed assert that they absolutely believe that the sightings occurred and that the Walterses were not perpetrating a hoax. In my interview with Duane Cook, the editor of the *Gulf Breeze Sentinel*, Duane revealed that he was quite skeptical of running the story at first, although he had the photographs and initial

---

7. Among these is Dr. Bruce Maccabee, an optical physicist employed by the US Navy, then Jet Propulsion Laboratories. Dr. Maccabee was engaged to study the Trent photos, the Newhouse film footage, as well as the Gulf Breeze photos, and is considered to be the gold standard in validating or debunking aerial photographs.
8. All of this is not to say that the Walterses were not inundated with debunking efforts to assassinate their characters. Approximately two years after their UAP sightings stopped, debunkers planted a model of one of the UFOs in the Walterses' former house, and found a young man who would testify that he was in on the entire hoax. He could not withstand the scrutiny, however, and finally confessed that he had been put up to the debunking effort.

analyses of them in hand. The turning point for him was when he decided to ask his parents' advice, who were visiting from out of town. He expected their usual conservative arched eyebrow at the thought of publishing such nonsense, when instead he was met with, "That's the thing we saw on our way into town the other night!" They had observed the same UAP as they were driving to Cook's house, but did not know what it was, and decided not to say anything about it. Of course, Cook ran the story.

The Gulf Breeze sightings produced more than sixty photographs of the UAP,[9] forty-one of which were taken by the Walterses, none of which was ever claimed to show evidence of counterfeiting by photographic analysis experts. Because of the well-documented nature of the Gulf Breeze sightings, I refer to that case in this chapter and those below as a benchmark of what appears to be occurring in contemporary UAP sightings and encounters. However, I do not attempt in this section to analyze the true nature or origin of the UAP referred to—I simply present the documented facts as they have been reported. Other cases are used as benchmarks of the "abduction" phenomenon, discussed below.

MALMSTROM NUCLEAR MISSILE SITE

In March 1967, First Lieutenant Robert Salas was stationed at the Malmstrom Air Force Base Nuclear Missile Site in Montana, assigned to the 490th Minute Man Missile Squadron. His principal duty was to monitor and ensure the readiness and security of the 10 Minute Man underground nuclear missiles under their command, and to launch the missiles if ordered to by the Pentagon. Each of the missiles was 100 times more powerful than the atomic bomb that leveled Hiroshima. On the night of March 24, he was the Deputy Combat Missile Crew Commander, and he received a call from the Flight Security Controller (FSC) who was the ranking person in charge of security topside. The

---

9. Not all of the UAP were exactly alike. There does seem to be similarity between them, however, as between a particular manufacturer's line of automobiles.

FSC reported that the security team had been observing strange lights just above the facility, and they were making highly unusual maneuvers. He said he didn't think they were normal aircraft, because they made no sound and were making high velocity starts and stops, and sharp midair directional changes. Lieutenant Salas wasn't sure what to make of the call but told the FSC to let him know if anything else happened. Within a couple of minutes the phone rang again and he picked it up, only to hear the FSC screaming that he was looking out the front window facing the front gate. "There's a large . . . glowing, pulsating red oval shaped object hovering over the front gate! It's about 30 to 40 feet in diameter." He told Salas that he had his men outside with their weapons drawn watching the object. Salas asked him if the object had structure to it, and the FSC said it was hard to tell because of the bright glow of the light emanating from it. "Do you have any direction for me?" he asked the lieutenant. Salas told him not to let anything inside the perimeter, at which point he heard the FSC shout, "One of my men is hurt," and the line went dead.

Salas's commander had been resting while Salas was on duty, but Salas ran in and woke him, telling him what was happening. Just then the alarms and indicators at the commander's console began to go off, and the missiles began to go offline, one at a time. Lieutenant Salas and Commander Meiwald jumped to the console and immediately began going through the checklist. It was extremely unusual and unlikely that one Minute Man missile would go offline—but by now all ten had gone down. The solid row of ten red fault indicators they were looking at was unprecedented in Air Force history. The missiles were disabled and could not be launched if they received the LAUNCH order from the Pentagon. Some of them had security violation lights going off as well, and this suddenly had the appearance of a wide scale Soviet attack, disabling all of the American nuclear missiles just before a Soviet nuclear strike. Lieutenant Meiwald queried the system and received a "guidance and control system failure" code on the faults. Lieutenant Meiwald grabbed the phone and called the Wing and Squadron Command posts, and repeated to Lieutenant Salas, "The same thing just happened at another site." Indeed, ten more Minuteman missiles had just been disabled at another site. Salas phoned the FSC and told him to get over to the disabled launch silos and check them personally. He replied that the object had just flown off, but within a moment he got word from the security team that a similar object had just come overhead near one of the launch facilities. That object took off at high velocity and the teams stood guard the remainder of their duty shift, as the tech team attempted to bring the missiles back online.

Throughout the region and for several nights all of the teams were on high alert, and some reported seeing UAP and receiving self-defense instructions from their commands in the event they encountered one. Airman First-Class Patrick McDonough was present when a craft came down over a missile launch facility and hovered just 300 feet above them. He describes it in an affidavit: "It was disc-shaped and its diameter appeared to be around 30–50 feet. It appeared to have dim lights outlining the disc and a white light emanating from the center. It stayed there approximately 20–30 seconds and, from a dead stop, sped off to the East at a tremendous speed. There was no noise or wind."

RENDLESHAM FOREST INCIDENT

There are two Royal Air Force bases, called Bentwaters and Woodbridge, on the east coast of England. Bentwaters is to the north of Woodbridge, and between them lies the thick forest called Rendlesham. Even though the bases are RAF, they are actually operated by the United States Air Force as US nuclear bases to reach targets in and near eastern Europe. On the night of December 26, 1980, base guards and security personnel spotted bright lights in the Rendlesham Forest and feared that an aircraft had gone down and needed assistance. Security teams rushed into the forest to rescue survivors and put out the fires, but as they got near the source of the lights, they spotted a landed UAP craft sitting in a small clearing on the forest floor. It was a fairly small, triangular shaped craft, with a raised triangular dome in the center. They could see that some of the tree branches had been broken off as the craft had landed. Two airmen moved forward toward the landed craft, AFC John Burroughs and Staff Sergeant Jim Penniston. As the two men approached, the craft began to quietly ascend vertically until it reached the treetops. Then it suddenly accelerated away at an incredible speed. Penniston had been trained as a specialist in aircraft recognition and he said, "That's no aircraft."

In an interview, Sgt. Penniston recounted: "I could see a dome of light over the forest. And then I could see multiple-colored lights inside the forest . . . and what appeared in the forest floor in front of me was a triangular craft. I wasn't sure if I was going to survive because my movements were labored up to that point. I was feeling like I was walking through a pool of water. I was struggling to get close to it. When I got within ten feet of it, all that dissipated. There was like a—I call it a sphere of influence around it, around the immediate craft itself. As I got closer to the craft, the fabric of the craft where the colors were running through—it finally just dissipated and stopped—and all that was left was a black, opaque craft, which was shiny in nature. I would describe it as looking like black glass. It was obvious it was not a U.S. Air Force craft."

Sergeant Penniston continues, "It was still well-lit underneath, and I didn't need a flashlight or nothing like that. It didn't have, seams. It didn't have rivets, or stuff like that. I was looking for things like an aircraft would have—like landing gear, it didn't have landing gear. And as I walked around it I was looking for crew compartments, I was looking for flaps, intakes, exhaust . . . it was void of all those things. I came around on the far side of it and then I could see there was writing on the side of the craft itself. When I got to the part where I could see

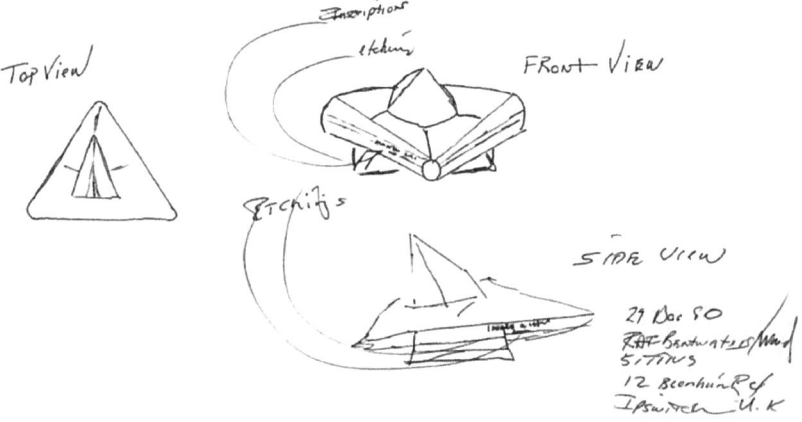

Drawing by Sgt. Penniston of triangular UAP on Rendlesham Forest floor.

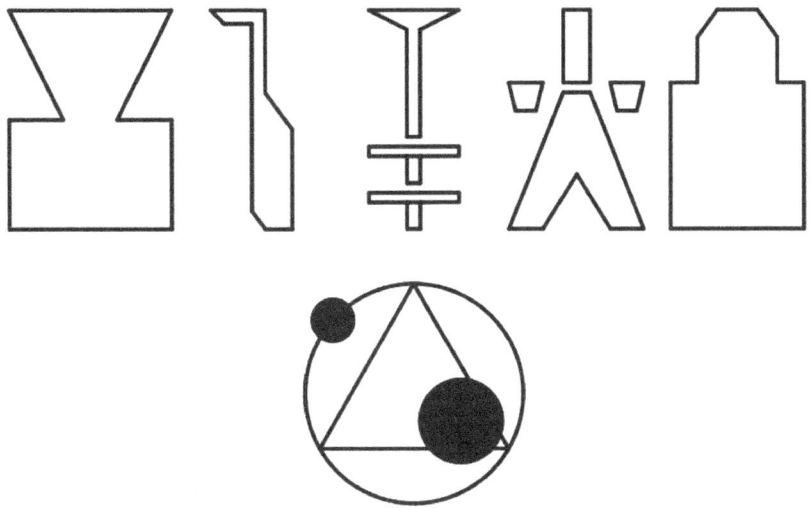

Drawing of glyphs seen on side of triangular craft by Sgt. Penniston.

the writing, there was like glyphs. It wasn't any writing that I've seen before. They stretched about three feet wide, and they were about five to six inches high."

"So I was touching the glyphs, and they went from the smooth fabric of the craft to, touching the glyph, they were like going from smooth black glass to sandpaper. That's what it felt like—like they were etched in there. And then when I touched the top, triangular one, there was a blast of white light—I mean, I was blinded . . . and stunned. All I could see was white light, but during that, that's when I saw, like digital stuff—like ones and zeros. I didn't know if it was from the light, I didn't know what it was from."

That night Sergeant Penniston noticed that he could visualize the ones and zeros in his mind's eye, and no matter what he did, he couldn't get rid of it. He started to write them all down: 1,0,0,1,1,1,0,1,0,0. The more he wrote them and got them out of his system, the less anxiety he felt, and the better he began to feel. He got them all written in his notebook, and the anxiety disappeared. He put his notebook away and never revisited the notes— until more than thirty years later when he accidentally came across his notebook and opened it to show someone the glyphs as he had written them down, and the interviewer saw the ones and zeros and asked about them. "Oh—that's the download I got when I touched the glyphs on the side of the craft," he replied.

Sergeant Penniston wrote out his statement to the OSI base command office. All of the detail was included in four legal-sized pages, but they typed up a simple, generic report that left out most of the UAP information and told him he had to sign it. He was ordered by men in civilian suits, "This is an official investigation now, and this is the cover story you're going to tell anyone who asks you about it." They told him, "If you do this, it all goes away." Penniston said that he really just wanted it to all go away. "I wanted to keep my career intact—because only whackos talked about UFOs. It's the end of your career."

Two nights after the initial sighting of the triangular UAP, there was a Christmas party and the doors suddenly burst open. A young officer rushed to the base commander and his deputy commander, Lieutenant Colonel Charles Halt, and said, "Sir—it's back!" The Commander looked at Halt, and Halt, who had heard the rumors about the supposed UAP two nights earlier, was only agitated by such nonsense. Halt told the commander to just remain at the party and enjoy the festivities, while he put a team together to go out and debunk this "UFO nonsense" once and for all. Halt was a very by-the-book officer, and he was meticulous at documenting everything he did. He carried a portable cassette recorder on him at all times, and took it with him out into Rendlesham Forest to make a permanent record of how he would disprove the foolishness that had occupied too much precious military time already.

Lieutenant Colonel Halt and his team arrived in the forest where the lights had been two nights earlier. Looking over the site, he was surprised to see landing gear indentations in the frozen ground. He realized it must have required tons of weight to make those impressions. He observed burn marks on the trees—the side facing the landing gear indentations. They checked for radiation and got higher readings than at surrounding areas. Halt had the team check for radiation everywhere in the area, and they found the readings higher where the landing gear had touched down, and on the sides of the trees facing where the craft had landed. Halt said, "I was very puzzled about this, but I assumed there must be some kind of explanation." At that point they suddenly noticed strange reddish-orange lights—an object coming in their direction. "It was glowing, and oval in shape—sort of like a large basketball or beach ball. It has a dark center and it's moving," Halt recalled. We hear from his own recorder:

> Sgt. Nevilles: Watch it throw the hell off my flashlight there. There it is!
> Lt. Col. Halt: I see it too. What is it?
> Sgt. Nevilles: We don't know, Sir.
> Lt. Col. Halt: Yeah, it's a strange, small red light. Looks to be out maybe a quarter to half a mile—maybe farther out. I'm gonna switch off. [Comes back on] The light is gone now. It was approximately 120 degrees from the site. Is it back again?
> Sgt. Nevilles: Yes, Sir.
> Lt. Col. Halt: Everything else is just deathly calm. There's no doubt about it, there's some kind of strange, flashing red light ahead.
> Sgt. Nevilles: Yeah—It's yellow.
> Lt. Col. Halt: I saw a yellow tinge in it too. Weird. It appears to be making a little bit this way? It's brighter than it has been . . . it's coming this way. It is definitely coming this way. Pieces of it are shooting off. There is no doubt about it—this is weird!

Halt shared in an interview, "We're looking at the thing, and we're probably about 200 to 300 yards away. It looks like an eye winking at you. It's still moving from side to side . . . and when we put the starscope on it, it sort of has a hollow center, a dark center, it's like a pupil of an eye looking at you, winking. And the flash is so bright to the starscope that it almost burns your eye." Lieutenant Colonel Halt recalled, "We see it in the forest. It moves through the trees—avoiding trees—it doesn't touch any of the trees, bobbing up and down, moving through the trees. So I said, 'Let's try to approach it.' So we tried to approach it, and it recedes. It goes back out into the farmer's field." From his recording: "The ones to the north are moving. One's moving away from us. It's moving out fast. There's one on the right heading out too." Someone says something in the background, and Halt replies, "Yeah, they're both heading north." Then Halt said, "Here he comes from the south. He's coming toward us now!" Halt recalled, "We stopped at the edge of the forest and watched it. And I can see the glow from it on the farmer's house, which is on the far side of the field. All the windows reflected it. It was so bright it looked like the house was on fire."

Halt speaks into his recorder, "Now we're observing what appears to be a beam coming down to the ground. This is unreal." Halt recalls, "The object's dripping or shedding some kind of material like molten metal, or some kind of sparks or something. Then it silently explodes like fireworks into multiple white objects—then they disappear." Halt says, "We were in shock. I'm thinking the whole time, I wish I hadn't gotten involved in this. Nobody's going to believe what we're telling them. I'm thinking ball lightning—all kinds of explanations—but nothing fits."

In an interview Halt admits, "I have no idea what it was. It was under intelligent control." Asked what made him think it was under intelligent control, he responded, "Because it moved through the forest avoiding the trees, and when we tried to approach it, it moved away from us." Asked, "Are we alone, Colonel?" He replied, "Definitely not."

When Sergeant Penniston rediscovered his ones and zeros around 2010, the interviewer wondered if it might not be a binary code of some kind, something like the hexadecimal[10] binary language we utilize to store all data on computers in its most basic machine language form. He took copies of the pages and took them to a computer programmer, who ran the binary code through his system and got back an interesting translation: "EXPLORATION OF HUMANITY. CONTINUOUS FOR PLANETARY ADVANCE. EYES OF OUR EYES. ORIGIN YEAR 8100."

---

10. In my early career I learned computer programming, and in those days you had to learn hexadecimal base 16 language to program in Assembler language. In that binary language, each group of 16 digits, ones and zeros, is a data point—a number or letter or symbol in English. Of course, if you were to write the code in any other language, or based on any other system—say, base 15 or base 17, then the binary code is just gibberish to the decoder.

Following that, there was a list of what observers believe are longitudinal and latitudinal global coordinates, which happen to match some of the more important historically interesting and "sacred" locations on the planet, like the Great Pyramid at Giza, Egypt, the Nazca Lines in Peru, the Temple of Apollo in Greece, and similar sites of profound human interest in millennia past. Interestingly, one of the coordinates is to a location where a fabled Celtic island called Hy-Brasil was shown off the coast of Ireland in some ancient maps, but is not actually located there. It is sometimes referred to as the Celtic Atlantis.

Of course, the "coincidence" that the ones and zeros just happen to line up in a familiar binary code base that is interpretable into the English language letters and numbers is beyond credulity. Not that it is a false interpretation, or that Sergeant Penniston or the computer programmer are perpetrating some sort of hoax. It is just obvious that someone or something has planted a message, highly complex in its own right, even without the aspect of a psychic download from touching the mysterious craft. Then, the message refers to places of historical and religious significance—following the interpretation method of the familiar binary code—from the memory of a soldier who received it psychically. It is a step too far. Who is behind it?

When Sergeant Penniston is asked what he thinks about the interpretation of his binary message, he says, "I never thought it was extraterrestrial. I still don't. We believe—based on the evidence—that it's an interdimensional-type craft. It seems to clearly be us from the future." This last bit of speculation is what Penniston and many teams of investigators have concluded after eleven years of seeking answers.

Interestingly, theoretical physicist and well-known author on time travel physics, Professor Ronald Mallet, University of Connecticut, has made headlines lately with his theory that messages can be sent forward or backward in time utilizing—you guessed it—"a series of zeros and ones in a binary code." He says, "I showed that a string of subatomic particles, or neutrons, could be arranged so that some point up, while others point down, representing zeros and ones.

These zeros and ones can then encode a binary message, which could be sent into the past or the future."[11]

By way of follow-up to the incidents in Rendlesham Forest, the US Veterans Administration granted benefits to AFC John Burroughs for radiation exposure he suffered from the UAP in the woods that night. In addition to UAP triggering various US military nuclear crises as outlined in these accounts, reporter George Knapp was able to comb through records just after the collapse of the USSR and discovered a similar pattern of UAP flying over Soviet nuclear missile sites, and likewise interfering in their operation, and in one case, taking nuclear missiles to a "launch" status.

NASA ASTRONOMER SIGHTING

Marian Rudnyk is an astronomer and planetary scientist schooled in planetary geology. He began work at NASA's Jet Propulsion Laboratory (JPL) as a planetary photogeologist, where he performed planetary mapping studies of features like ice fractures on Jupiter's moon Europa and lava flows on Mars. He later worked as a NASA astronomer at Palomar Observatory as an asteroid hunter. During his career he made numerous named discoveries, his first being Asteroid 4601 Ludkewycz. He moved on to managing JPL's Planetary Image Facility and was on the imaging-science flight teams for such missions as Magellan at Venus and Voyager 2 at Neptune. He was no friend of "UFO nuts" and was dismissive of anyone who claimed that UAP exist.

All that changed on the afternoon of January 1, 2017, as he was eating at a McDonald's in Monrovia, California. It was daytime, a cloudy day, and he wondered what the four craft were that came from the upper cloud deck and continued to descend as they moved toward Rudnyk and his mother, who were enjoying lunch. At first he assumed they were specialty craft coming in for the New Year's celebrations, but as he watched them, it became fairly clear that they were disc shaped. He couldn't believe what he was seeing, so he stood from his table and

---

11. Maurizio Di Paolo Emilio, "Ronald Mallett's Conception of Time in Physics," *EE Times Europe*, May 26, 2021.

ran outside to get a better look. The four discs were getting closer and were quite clear to the eye. They were identical to one other, with four dark triangular panels on the underside, each something like a small pizza wedge. They were flying in formation, but one appeared to be having trouble staying in the formation, and as they got closer Marian could see that it had "dark splotches" on the underside, as though it had been damaged. He thought that it must have been hit by lightning, or fired upon by our military. He watched for another moment as the other three discs adjusted their formation to include the wounded disc, bringing the entire team closer to the ground. Marian was astonished, and the thought went through his mind, "It's real! It's all true! The UFO nuts are right!"

As the wounded disc continued to struggle and sink, the other three dropped down and tried to recreate the diamond formation around it, attempting to assist it. Marian was fascinated to see the noiseless craft maneuvering, unaffected by the gusting winds and each surrounded by an aura or what Marian thought of as "ionization glows," and suddenly thought, "Oh no—what am I doing? I've got my digital camera here with me!" He grabbed his camera and pulled it up and snapped a shot of the four discs. However, the camera behaved differently than it had ever done before and went through a cycling pattern that continued for the next ten seconds. When it was finally ready for another shot, Marian calculated how long it would take them to reach the closest location near him and decided to try to shoot in video mode until then. He hurriedly switched to video mode and hit the record button. He immediately saw the autofocus going crazy in the camera, as multiple autofocus squares appeared in the viewfinder and danced around on the screen's image, obscuring it from his view. A streetlight pole came into the video as Marian recorded the four discs crossing the sky, complicating the focusing issue even more. He had shot thirty-four seconds of video already, so he decided to switch back to photo mode, shooting three additional photos of the four craft.

He noticed that the wounded disc was beginning to recover at this point, and the diamond formation tightened as the discs began to climb rapidly. The thought occurred to him that he was a NASA astronomer, and he'd just shot some pretty good photos and a fairly long video of these four discs—who would never have come down so close if not for the damage done to the fourth disc. What he could really use to fully document the sighting was a second eyewitness. He thought about his mother, but she was nearly eighty and wouldn't be able to get outside in time before they were gone. He took a last look and turned quickly to look through the front window of the restaurant, trying to see if he could get the attention of one of the employees inside. He couldn't catch their eye, so he turned back toward the discs, only to find they were already gone.

When Marian's employers discovered he had witnessed and photographed the event, he was immediately contacted by the US Air Force Space Command, who asked him to show them the photos over his computer. He did so, and the commander said, "Yep—that sucker's real, all right." Space Command immediately demanded that Marian turn over all copies of the photos and video, and that he wipe them out of all of his storage and never reveal any of it to anyone. Just around that time he was contacted by science powerhouse UAP investigators, nuclear physicist Stanton Friedman and Dr. Bob Wood, and sent them original digital versions of the disc photos and video. Space Command was furious when they learned of it and made Marian Rudnyk's life a living nightmare for the next few years. Navy FA-18s and several other military aircraft were immediately sent to scour the hills around Monrovia, and Marian has been buzzed by the aircraft frequently, had his electronics and social media accounts disrupted, and has been followed by "MIB" military types who have threatened him in the presence of others at times.[12]

UAP DESIGN

Most reported UAP appear to be the classic round "two plates pressed together" saucer or disc type. In recent decades, the triangular model with a large light at each corner is ubiquitous. Tubes and spheres are frequently seen as well—and give the impression of being

---

12. *INTERSECT: A Former NASA Astronomer Breaks His Silence About UFOs*, 2019.

unmanned drones of some kind. Most that are seen in our skies are thirty to sixty feet across on average. Some are reported to be as large as aircraft carriers, or even bigger.

General Gulf Breeze UAP design appeared to be more functional than aesthetic—used car models have better aesthetics than do some UAP. Besides the basic rounded and contoured shape of the main body, the Gulf Breeze UAP have what appears to be diamond and square-shaped "portals" that encircle the entire craft. The diamond-shaped portals are reported to radiate with bright light at times, while the square shapes appear completely dark. The portals are reported by some to be unequally spaced around the craft. The main body varies in reported color, "gray/blue to a rich orange-brown," sometimes changing color while being observed. Nearly all of the Gulf Breeze UAP had a large bright light in the center on top,[13] and a "power ring" looking light on the bottom. Ed Walters recounts that the power ring was generally "bright white with a darker orange core."

The power ring seems to be of importance to the mobility of the UAP, although this is merely an observation. For instance, often times the power ring would become very bright just before the UAP flashed away, or "winked out."[14] During normal operation[15] the inside of the power ring is described as a "twisting, throbbing mass of . . . silent energy storm." The photographs and video taken of the power ring support this description. In the Walters photograph #19, wherein the UAP is approximately ten feet above the road, the bright light of the power ring is reflected off the road. Ed Walters owns the copyrights to those photographs, but you can see them at History.com. Photographic

---

13. This feature is nearly universal in UAP reports.
14. Observers, including Ed and Frances Walters, reported that when the UAP left in a hurry, they did so in such a manner that left the observer wondering if the craft had dashed away at incomprehensible speeds, or if it had just "disappeared." Some of the photographs show streaking as if the UAP had moved quickly. However, the 1 minute 38 second video tape shows only that the UAP was there in one frame, and gone in the next, indicating that it had instantly disappeared. Again, this characteristic is very common.
15. Normal operation of the UAP was to hover or move slowly from place to place, bobbing and weaving as they went. Less frequently, the UAP could move great or short distances in a flash.

analysis reveals that the light source was very bright, but experts were puzzled by the phenomenon that the light appeared to be confined to a specific area and did not light up more of the road and surroundings. Many UAP encounter accounts report a light that does not spread out and reflect like natural light. A final interesting feature of the power ring is that it appears to be the source of a blue beam reported by the Walterses and other observers.

THE BLUE BEAM

Ed Walters's first reported encounter with one of the UAP was accompanied by his being trapped in such a blue beam. After describing how the UAP, appearing like it was "right out of a Spielberg movie that had somehow escaped from the film studio," just floated into his neighborhood, over his neighbors' houses,[16] Ed Walters says he dashed for his polaroid camera that he uses in his construction business. He recounts: "It glided along without a whisper of sound.[17] There was no hum, no wind, not a single disturbance to the air, trees, or houses as it passed over them.[18] While rocking back and forth, it did not seem to spin, so I never saw all sides, only what was in the photographs."[19]

After Walters took several photographs, the UAP moved directly over him. He explains what happened when he looked up into the power ring:

> Bang! Something hit me. All over my body. I tried to lift my arms to point the camera. I couldn't move them. They were blue. I was blue. Everything was blue. I was in a blue light beam. The blue

---

16. After the *Gulf Breeze Sentinel* had published Walters's photographs of this UAP, witnesses came forward with testimony that they had also seen the UAP that evening near the Walterses' home.
17. In all of the reports of these Gulf Breeze UAP, the observers are unanimous that none of the UAP made an audible sound.
18. This lack of disturbance of the air is likewise significant, because many reports indicate that a UAP would flash a quarter mile in a second, just over the observer, then back to the original position in a like amount of time, with no wind, sound, or sonic boom. Again, this is a very common feature in UAP sightings.
19. *The Gulf Breeze Sightings*, 28.

beam had hit me like compression. It was pressing me firmly, just enough to stop me from moving. I screamed, with my mouth frozen half open, but the sound was hollow. Dead, like a vacuum. I couldn't even move my eyes or eyelids. I thought I was dying. I was trying to breathe, there was air, each breath shallow. . . . The best I can tell, this all took less than twenty seconds. Then my feet lifted off the ground. I screamed. A voice groaned in my head. 'We will not harm you.' I screamed again. The deep, computerlike voice said, "Calm down." But it was in my head, not my ears. I screamed, as well as I could, 'Put me down!' A few seconds passed as I slowly rose away from the pavement. A dream? Hell no! This was real. The feeling of helplessness was the worst. No control, just a piercing smell, a little scent of ammonia mixed with heavy cinnamon that scorched, then stuck to the back of my throat. My heart was pumping so hard I could feel its throb as it thumped against my unmoving chest. I could feel the thumping vibration pass down my legs. The voice groaned, "S-t-o-p i-t." I screamed, "Screw you!" All this happened fast. Now I was about two feet above the street. I panted for air, but the smell stung my lungs. My brain started to black out, so I screamed, 'Aagghh!' The scream was black and dull, just outside my mouth. Almost the way you feel if you dive to the bottom of a swimming pool with the pressure holding everything, even your own voice, close to you. The voice came back, but now it seemed to be female. An easy hum filled my head. Suddenly, from within my head, came the sharp vision of a dog. Then another and another. I was confused. What are these dogs? Rapid visions, one after another, on and on. It seemed that I could almost see words beneath the dog visions. Something was flashing dog pictures in my head just as if they were turning the pages of a book.[20] The hum continued. I had the sensation I was four feet above the ground. Wham! I hit

---

20. In a later encounter, Ed Walters reports that the UAP attempted to distract him with flashed pictures of naked women. Although this, in itself, could tend to detract from the credibility of a UAP sighting, in this case, it lends some credence. Ed reports that the UAP flashed indiscriminate pictures at him; naked women that are not generally thought of as "attractive." Apparently, the UAP was not aware of certain aspects of Earth culture and male preferences. Ed was not distracted.

the pavement hard and fell forward on my knees. The blue light was gone. The hum was still in my head, but it quickly decreased and was gone, like the hum of a speeding car as it races by. I collapsed onto my chest into the middle of the road, filling my lungs with real air. My stomach turned and I choked, trying not to throw up.[21]

Ed Walters says that as he rolled to his back he saw a small airplane entering the area's airspace, and assumed that the plane scared the UAP away in the nick of time.[22]

If not for the photographs that Ed was able to take during this sighting, he says it would be an encounter that he would never have reported—understandably. If not for the photographs being determined to be authentic by leading photographic experts, the Ed Walters story would be difficult to accept as authentic. Although thousands claim to see UAP, Ed Walters's account is pivotal because of the photographs. There exists so little credible, tangible evidence of UAP encounters generally that Ed Walters's bonanza of photographic confirmation renders it a good case for analysis. The UAP returned many times and made many attempts to abduct Walters. Investigators feel, after subsequent events, that Ed Walters had closer ties with these UAP than he realized, or remembered, and there was a specific purpose for their repeated attempts to pick him up.

The blue beam described by Ed Walters was repeatedly seen by six Gulf Breeze residents in all,[23] and was photographed from a distance and up close by Walters. We learn of other properties and functions of the blue beam in similar encounters had by Ed and Frances Walters. On one occasion, Ed recounts he was scurrying out the back door to get a photograph of a UAP he spied behind his house when a blue beam flashed down at him and hit him on the leg. Rather than just having the effect of rendering Ed's leg useless or paralyzed, the beam

---

21. *The Gulf Breeze Sightings*, 29–30.
22. As observed below, UAP pilots may be surprised by unnoticed traffic entering their field of control. If this occurred here, it could be the reason the UAP abandoned its design to abduct Ed Walters.
23. Interestingly, some reported the blue beam being "shot" into the water in the Gulf of Mexico.

effectively froze the leg in its three-dimensional position. Ed's momentum carried him forward, with his leg "pinned" where it was, slightly injuring him as he hyperextended the knee. Ed, with the assistance of Frances, was barely able to pull himself free of the blue beam. However, on another occasion when Frances dodged a blue beam that was near her, she reports, "Leaves and bits of gravel swirled around and within the beam."[24] Besides attempting to elevate Ed Walters with the blue beam, the pilots of the UAP evidently use the blue beam as a transportation device to exit and enter the UAP.

TELEPATHIC COMMUNICATION

Telepathic communication between "others" and humans is frequently reported. The implication is that these entities are so advanced that not only do they communicate telepathically with one another, but they are also able to read our minds and speak directly to us, mind-to-mind. What do we learn from this purported ability? Is it the product of an elevated or advanced mind—perhaps an ability that awaits all evolving lifeforms given enough time? Is it a technological ability—perhaps an implanted device that allows the creatures to "broadcast" and receive brainwaves? Or, is it a spiritual ability—like a communication from an angel or unembodied spirit, whom we know has no physical mouth to communicate. In fact, we know that the small Grays, and larger Grays, as well as Reptilians and Insectoids, and some abducting humans, all appear to communicate with their earthly victims telepathically. In fact, it appears that all of the entity races (dozens are identified), except for humans, are telepathic. Does that tell us that there is really just one type of being behind the abduction phenomenon and it masquerades as many types? I suspect it may. Many investigators and analysts suspect that abductions and other encounters are occurring on a psychic or otherwise purely mental level, and that if the person were observed during an "abduction" episode, we would see him or her in a trance or sleeping state. Even in that scenario, which appears more likely than physical abductions, the sights,

---

24. *The Gulf Breeze Sightings*, 179.

sounds, feelings, and communication being received would still be on that telepathic level—downloaded psychically to the victim. We know that Steve and Dawn Hess were receiving these types of psychic or telepathic downloads. Although they did their best to block them, they discovered that there was nothing they could do to resist the beings.

Another aspect of the telepathic capabilities of the beings is their ability to influence the thinking of humans, without the human realizing it. In fact, many people who recount horrific abuse at the hands of their captors later report, "But I think the beings are just trying to help us." The conclusion flies in the face of every fact related by the victim, yet the victim seems to be invested in the abduction activities of the beings at some level. Is this a form of Stockholm syndrome, where a hostage begins to sympathize with her captors and becomes empathetic to the cause, if not the means employed to attain it? Or, is it the result of telepathically implanted suggestions that the experience is actually "good"? Researchers tell us they have "proof" that human-alien hybrids are circulating in society and that they possess the gift of telepathy. If true, could this be problematic? I could certainly see how. Persuasion through lies is a favorite tool of Satan. Imagine if there were a small army of hybrids walking among us, mixing in at work and in government, psychically implanting ideas in people's minds—ideas that support the cause of the beings but are detrimental to humans. This is precisely what some are reporting. Is there a way to block psychic downloads or telepathic implants from these beings, whoever or whatever they are? Pardon me while I look for the tinfoil hat emoji on my keyboard. In fact, there are those who claim that the same type of Faraday cage headgear worn by high tension wire workers to protect them from electromagnetic brain damage does, in fact, protect one from telepathic entities. I would love to see proof of that. Or, there are some who report that blasting loud, raucous music during an abduction often thwarts the entities.

An important aspect of Ed Walters's UAP encounters is the telepathic communication between the UAP and him. During many attempts to pick him up, he heard voices coaxing him into the open. The voice would assure him that he was in no danger and that he should go with them. Not only did Ed Walters hear the computerlike and female voices in his head, but he also heard, or overheard, human voices speaking in Spanish and sometimes in other languages that he did not recognize, as well as ambient sounds like doors, clanks, bumps, and compressed air releases. All of this latter communication resembled inadvertently overhearing conversations, as if something had gone awry with the UAP's communications systems, into which Ed Walters had evidently been plugged in some way. Is telepathy a function of a device on the UAP then? Or is it theater?

GOVERNMENT COVER-UP—MEN IN BLACK

Stories of government cover-up abound with almost every UAP report that surfaces. By some reports, the government is as in the dark as anyone concerning UAP, and by others, the governments of the world are active participants in a massive cover-up. In nearly every UAP sighting in which evidence of the sighting is claimed to exist, government "men in black" (MIB) are reported to appear at the witnesses' doors demanding the evidence and threatening witnesses in the event they divulge any information regarding their sighting. If such evidence is turned over to these men in black, it is never seen again. Many UAP witnesses also claim that their houses and cars are buzzed by enigmatic helicopters following their sightings. When I first reported on the MIB twenty-nine years ago, most people had never heard of them. Of course, a movie of the same name was released in 1997, informing the world of the phenomenon—sort of.

Even more interesting are the "spooky" aspects of MIB. For example, witnesses claim to see a UAP on their way home from shopping, and when they arrive at their house (within five minutes), MIBs are already waiting for them, making demands and threats. These MIBs are often seen driving showroom quality cars that are twenty or thirty years old. Further reports claim that witnesses have attempted to follow MIBs in their unique automobiles, only to come to the end of a cul-de-sac or other dead end road and find no sign of the MIB or their car. Some investigators feel that the MIB and unusual cars and helicopters are so enigmatic that they may actually be connected with the UAP instead of the government.

On May 15, 2009, Sheraton Hotel employees say these two men, caught on hotel surveillance video, approached them and warned them against revealing details of their UAP sighting.

The general manager and another employee of the Sheraton Hotel on the Canadian side of Niagara Falls witnessed a black triangle-shaped UAP fly slowly and silently over the hotel on the night of October 14, 2008. They described the craft as approximately 240 feet long, with three white lights on all three sides, and a pulsing red light in the middle. They watched it for ten minutes as it quietly and slowly flew east to west over Niagara's Horseshoe Falls toward their hotel, about 500 feet above the ground. The craft was emitting a bright white beam light into the water below, and as they watched in awe, the light beam suddenly shifted its aim at them. They were startled and ran inside the hotel. One week later, the hotel manager went out to the parking lot around 1:00 a.m. and witnessed an identical UAP flying in the same direction, but much higher. Seven months later, on May 15, 2009, the two strange men caught on the hotel's surveillance video system entered the hotel and went straight to the general manager's office and told him never to discuss the sighting he had experienced. As seen in the surveillance video, the two men were dressed in black suits and overcoats, and wore black fedoras—which would have been perfectly normal fifty years earlier.

Raymond Fowler, noted researcher and author, relates a cross-country ski outing with his daughter during which they both saw a man dressed in black, standing under a tree in the distance. Fowler recounts that he had a slightly uneasy feeling about the man, possibly because the man was in an area surrounded for miles by deep snow, dressed in city clothing. They watched the man periodically as they neared the tree. As they approached, their attention was momentarily diverted. When they looked back to the tree, the man was no longer there. They skied quickly over to the tree, only to find it surrounded by deep snow—and no footprints. These are only a few of thousands of such reports from around the country.

UAP AROUND ENERGY INSTALLATIONS

Although less documented than some citizen sightings, many energy installations have at times been the object of government concern with military reports of UAP in the vicinity. The Kuwaiti oil field installations were at one time the object of multiple UAP sightings, causing the Kuwaiti government distress about its precious resource. Often, high voltage power stations or transmission lines have been the location of UAP sightings. Ufologists proffer guesses at why UAP pilots might be interested in such low-tech power supplies, but nothing substantive has yet come to the fore. Some UAP debunkers feel that high voltage power supplies may actually be the sources of some UAP sightings. They theorize that certain "fireball" sightings may actually be energy flashes that emanate from high voltage sources in a manner not yet identified by electrical science. Others have hypothesized that UAP gather needed energy resources from these power stations.

FROM HARDWARE TO SOFT SIGHTINGS

Many ufologists are turning from "nuts-and-bolts" theories of UAP origins to decidedly more metaphysical explanations. Aside from the many paranormal explanations that we discuss below, some theorize that UAP are physical manifestations of electromagnetic phenomena created by stress fracturing of the Earth's crust, much as the lights that reportedly accompany or precurse an earthquake. Some studies indicate that there may exist a correlation between seismic activity and UAP sightings. Other studies even suggest a relationship between the phenomenon and the observer, where the observed light responds to the thoughts and emotions of the observer. It's very strange, but many experiments have produced affirmative results.

These electromagnetic fields, whatever their source, theoretically generate perceptual and reasoning difficulties in persons exposed to them, trigger irrational perceptions of the lights. Supposedly, one's shaded comprehension of the nature of the light being observed is generated by one's own cultural expectation of what enigma or mystical manifestation is occurring. For instance, protagonists claim that certain British haunts, well known for their UAP sightings, were formerly well known for their spook lights, spirits, demons, and Madonna sightings. They speculate that two persons with quite diverse backgrounds viewing the same phenomenon at the same time may perceive something altogether different.

SPHERICAL PROBES

The subject of purported instances of brightly lit spheres or other reports of traveling lights takes on new perspective with certain UAP reports recounting encounters with "probes" that have the appearance of floating spheres of light, just larger than basketballs, or smaller. Many of the UAP sightings reported on television programs and elsewhere are accompanied by other spherical lights that probe the area, and then return to the UAP before it leaves the vicinity. One such report is documented by Budd Hopkins in his book *Intruders: The Incredible Visitations at Copley Woods*.[25] Intruders tells of the encounters of a young mother, called Kathie Davis for the purposes of the book, who later revealed that she was actually Debbie Jordan-Kauble, who was plagued by repeated visitations by UAP. Although her encounters fit more properly into the chapters below, the spherical light probe is of interest.

---

25. A Motion picture made for television based on *Intruders* was released in mid-1992. The television movie was a dramatization of the kinds of events in the book, in which component characters of abductees and investigators were created to experience the UAP/abduction phenomenon.

Earlier in the evening, Kathie's mother reported seeing the light through the kitchen window, near the hummingbird feeder in the back yard. Significantly, within a couple of days, the shrubbery in the immediate vicinity had withered. Upon investigating the floating lights, Kathie, during hypnotic regression, said she became semi-conscious and her will was taken over by an external force. She was led to the back yard where a white sphere of light "looked at her" at eye level, then moved slowly downward. Suddenly, the sphere entered her, causing her much pain and flooding her body with light. She felt as if a bolt of lightning had hit her in the chest, then flowed throughout her body.[26] She was unable to see most of the time because she was flooded with the light, as if lit up internally. She knew that these "globes" were connected with UAP because she saw them detach themselves from the outside of a UAP and float around "exploring."[27]

I've listened to Debbie recount her experiences a number of times, and although I feel she is being abused by evil beings and has not sought the proper type of help, she is a down-to-earth, Midwestern woman who works hard and cares about her family, and appears to be relating her experiences in a truthful manner. We examine her ongoing encounters in greater depth later in this book.

These spheres of light are ubiquitous in UAP accounts, and some speculate that they appear spherical and semisolid because they are actually probes of various shapes, which rotate at a high speed, giving them that appearance.

---

26. *Intruders*, 43.
27. Betty Luca reports several encounters with such probes also as documented in *The Watchers: The Secret Design Behind UFO Abductions*, (Raymond E. Fowler, New York: Bantam Books, 1990.

CHAPTER 8

Saucers on the Ground

LONNIE ZAMORA SOCORRO, NM ENCOUNTER

On April 24, 1964, at approximately 5:45 p.m., Police Sergeant Lonnie Zamora was pursuing a car south of Socorro, New Mexico, when he saw a cloud of smoke over the hill, about a half mile away. Zamora called the radio dispatcher, Nep Lopez, and reported a possible motor vehicle accident. Or perhaps the old dynamite shack had exploded, and Zamora said he was pulling off of the speeding car to go investigate. Zamora pulled his car into the area and said, "By the time I got there I could see this big white object sitting in the arroyo."[1] He immediately observed a shiny object "to south about 150 to 200 yards," and rolled his patrol car closer, to within fifty feet of the object. At first he tried to make sense of what he was seeing and thought that perhaps it was an overturned white car, with the top facing him. He tried to use the radio to tell the dispatcher what he had found, but his radio was dead. He saw two small men, the size of children standing in white overalls next to the vehicle, "walking around the craft." He wondered if they might be in danger near the vehicle. Officer Zamora

---

1. An arroyo is a gully formed by fast-flowing water in an arid region, found chiefly in the southwestern United States.

focused on the vehicle and could now see that it was round, like an oval, "like aluminum—it was whitish against the mesa background, but not chrome," he said. One of the small men was standing in front of the other one and turned to look straight at Zamora. The they both moved quickly toward the craft and walked up inside and "started their motor—or whatever it was." Within a moment Zamora heard a roar from the direction of the craft and saw a "big blast of fire right under it. I could see it, and could feel that heat," he reported. "It took them a little while to get airborne, and they got up about 20 or 30 feet, and they stayed there a little while, and then it was just as quiet as it could be, and then it just flew away."

Zamora cued his radio and found that it was working again. He asked Lopez to look out the station window to see if he could see a round, balloon-shaped object flying through the sky. Lopez said he couldn't see it through his window, and Zamora asked him to call State Police Sergeant Chavez and ask him to meet Zamora at his location. When Chavez arrived, Zamora led him to examine some burning brush where the craft had been. There were four distinct areas where the landing gear had been on the ground, and they found two sets of small footprints, about four inches long, within the perimeter. When other police officers arrived, they saw patches of smoldering grass and brush. The state police informed the Air Force of the sighting made by a very reliable police officer, and the US Air Force, and the FBI and other government agencies came to the site to investigate, as did Dr. J. Allen Hynek and other investigators from the Air Force's Project Blue Book. Until this time, Dr. Hynek had been a skeptic—a debunker of UAP cases he was assigned to. Seeing how honest and sincere Sergeant Zamora was, and how shaken he was, Dr. Hynek had to admit that this was a true case of an unidentified flying craft. This case changed his outlook. He no longer felt that because it is impossible, it didn't happen. He began to approach his work with an open mind, and soon found that he believed the earth was being visited by craft of unknown origin.

LANDING SITES

With the increasing frequency of UAP sightings pouring into local police stations, newspaper offices, newsrooms, and then on the internet over the past decades, we would be surprised if no account ever reported that a UAP had landed on the earth. Science fiction literature and motion pictures provided an incessant parade of such landings, the public assumed that was the purpose of alien visitation, if such existed. It was not long before witnesses around the globe began reporting that UAP had been seen on the ground.

By the 1960s UAP protagonists had organized themselves into research and investigation teams, pouring over photographs and interviewing witnesses in search of credible evidence that UAP exist. With incoming reports of UAP landings, researchers and teams scrambled to landing sites to investigate and gather data. Government investigators had also been assigned to look into the phenomenon—because if new or unknown technology did exist, terrestrial or otherwise, it was a basic function of government intelligence to seek it out.

With these massive investigations being conducted by forensic scientists and other skilled observers, we would expect a great deal of evidence to be produced at UAP landing sites. Had murders occurred at the sites, incredible amounts of microscopic and other evidence of the presence of certain persons and equipment would easily have been produced and analyzed. However, the data have been scant and inconclusive. Again, as with photographs and other evidence of UAP, landing sites sometimes have been counterfeited by publicity seekers and overzealous "believers." These practices have strained public and professional faith in ufology, casting dark shadows over the authenticity of all alleged landing sites. However, in addition to the eyewitness accounts of actual UAP landings, some residual evidence exists.

Most alleged landing sites are made up of some sort of circular pattern etched or charred in the vegetation, or of evidence of landing gear, generally three in number, having left their mark. The circular patterns are often composed of flattened grass or other vegetation that is often dead or dying.[2] There are occasionally reported residual signs of a chemical or a radioactive substance, and some circular patterns glow in the dark for a few days before fading. An anomalous landing site existed during the Gulf Breeze sightings. A report of an analysis of the site made by Max E. Griggs of the University of Florida is reprinted on pages 343–44 of the Walters book. The analysis consists of testing for several possible causes for the presence of the dead grass within the circular pattern, which happened to be the approximate size of the reported UAP. The experts tested for chemical agents, signs of lightning strike, fungal, bacterial, viral, pathogen, disease, insect infestation, and nutrient deficiency, all to no avail. The report concluded that although no cause was found, "evidence supports either the influence of short-lived toxic chemical or exposure of the grass to an energy source capable of killing it. Either of these would have required mechanical precision to do what was observed on the field."

A similar landing site is described in the Kathie Davis[3] case in *Intruders*. Budd Hopkins provides a series of photographs of the site ranging from six weeks following the UAP landing to one year after. A copy of the "Physical Laboratory Report" is reproduced therein, revealing that grass and soil within a couple of inches of the landing site UAP pattern are normal, while samples taken from within the pattern are discolored and quite dense. To duplicate the coloring and texture of the site samples, adjacent samples had to be heated to 800 degrees Fahrenheit for six hours. This procedure alone could not duplicate the density of the site samples, however. It is no surprise

---

2. However, there do exist the much debated circular and other rather complex patterns found in crop fields throughout the world. Other than the surgical precision of the swirling pattern of the trodden vegetation, no harm is usually done to the plants. British authorities have conducted tireless research to discover the source of these precise patterns. Some indications are that they are not man made—while some people claim that they, indeed, have created the patterns as a hoax.
3. Again, Kathie Davis is a pseudonym for Debbie Jordan-Kauble, but because Kathie Davis was used in the book, we will continue to address her as Kathie Davis herein.

that the photographs reveal a distinct decline in vegetation within the landing site pattern, given the changed condition of the soil.

CRASH AND RETRIEVAL COVER-UPS

One frequent excuse by UAP enthusiasts for the absence of landing site evidence is removal of UAP traces by government cover-up teams. Not only do UAP protagonists claim that government teams move in on landing sites quickly and remove all residual signs of UAP visitations, but persistent rumors circulate throughout ufology that governments of the world have recovered at least one crashed UAP and have sequestered it. A number of books, and even a motion picture or two, have represented that military bases in the southwestern United States and elsewhere around the globe are collection sites for such finds. AATIP Director Luis Elizondo and Senator Harry Reid have indicated that the US government possesses "metamaterials" collected from UAP and that they are waiting to see if anyone who is now in charge of such specimens, perhaps the UAP Task Force, has tested the materials and determined their properties. Those materials were not mentioned in the recently released report to Congress.

"Crash and retrieval" stories date back to the 1884 American West. The tales are similar no matter where or when they supposedly occurred. The common scenario is this: There was a crash of a UAP; someone arrived on the scene to find wreckage, and often, dead or dying alien bodies; the government threatened the local citizenry not to reveal what had happened; and government personnel transported the booty to a local air base hanger. Once safely sequestered, no civilian, military, or governmental person ever reveals any portion of the story, except an occasional unnamed mole, whose story can never be checked. These crash and retrieval stories persist, even though little evidence of them finds its way to the public.

These reports are difficult to accept at first glance. The notion that our government, or most other governments for that matter, is capable of keeping such events from the public strains our collective perception of governmental capabilities. Our government is totally incapable of keeping its own political leaders from revealing our nation's uppermost military secrets to the world press on the capitol steps. A successful seven-decade government cover-up of captured UAP seems unlikely under these circumstances, although some argue that many leaks and whistleblower disclosures have actually occurred, exposing the entire program. It is evident from our current state of technology that no technological quantum leaps have occurred as a result of discovered alien propulsion systems or other advanced devices. We still burn fossil fuels in internal combustion engines that are reminiscent of century-old prototypes, and we clumsily blast payloads into Earth's orbit and beyond with rockets, not unlike those used in China centuries ago. All of this while every politician on the planet would give anything for a non-polluting energy and transportation source. The story is the same in all scientific disciplines—metallurgy, chemistry, and even astronomy—slow, steady-as-she-goes progress despite desperate need of quick applications of superior technology. Recent developments in microprocessor technology is one of the few real accomplishments, leading to data processing power and global networking on an unprecedented scale. It's very doubtful, however, that computers and the Internet would be the only byproducts of a back-engineered alien craft.

The absence of evident technological exploitation of downed UAP does not necessarily debunk the possibility of the existence of government-held alien spacecraft. It is possible that such advanced technology is either too sophisticated to be copied with today's state-of-the-art science and equipment or too damaged to be of any substantial use. A third possibility is echoed by many who claim that the US government actually possesses superior technology that it hides from the public—a clandestine government agency with secret technology. If that were true, as is believed by millions of Americans, it would mean the government is hoarding technologies for secret military use, to the exclusion and detriment of its citizens. Although such technologies as appear to be observed in UAP would have significant military applications, they would also have numerous and far-reaching domestic benefits—pollution free energy and transportation, off-world mining and other resource availability, inexpensive food production and resource management, and environmental rescue.

Of course, as we've discussed briefly, the government to first develop any of these technologies by back-engineering metamaterials and antigravity systems would suddenly become the undisputed leader of the world, and would have the means to reshape the world and its societies in its own likeness—in any manner it desires. America could spread democracy and individual liberty to the entire world, and the prosperity and high living standards that naturally follow. It could easily and simply overrule the despots who trample the rights of their own citizens. If communist China or Russia were to suddenly possess such advanced technologies, however, their imperialistic appetites would be unstoppable, and there wouldn't even be a peep of resistance. The technology is simply too far advanced to be resisted by any current defense systems possessed by any nation. Again, the fact that China and Russia are still struggling to get on top in terms of military strength and political clout, stealing current technologies from other nations and struggling to secure the energy they require to operate and expand is very strong evidence that neither of them is in possession of any extremely advanced or extraterrestrial technologies. To an extent, the same can be said of America. Most of its resources are devoted to areas that would be transformed by such technology, and the power-hungry in our government and military simply do not appear to have the long-term self-restraint to sit on that much advanced technology and game-changing power for decades.

THE ROSWELL CRASH

Notwithstanding the argument that there doesn't appear to be a flood of advanced technology flowing from secret government labs, there are those who are adamant that the American military, as well as other nations, has retrieved crashed extraterrestrial craft. The best documented crash and retrieval case perhaps is the 1947 "Roswell UAP crash" incident, which was actually located about sixty miles away in Corona, New Mexico.[4] Just before 10:00 p.m. on July 2, locals sighted what they reported as a large glowing object

---

4. *See Crash at Corona: US Military Retrieval and Cover-up of a UFO* by Stanton T. Friedman and Don Berliner (1992); Charles Berlitz and William L. Moore, *The Roswell Incident* (New York: Grosset and Dunlap, 1980).

flying at high speeds. Later, during a thunderstorm, rancher Mac Brazel heard a thunderous explosion that was much louder than the thunderclaps of the storm. The next morning he found unusual debris strewn across the desert grazing areas that he described as very thin, pliable, and extremely strong. He said that he was able to crumple the metal into a ball, but when he released it, it would spring back into its original shape. Other reports relate that he also found a downed saucer.

Brazel had to drive to Roswell a few days later, and when he told some friends there what he had found, they convinced him to report it to the military. He agreed and called the sheriff and Army Intelligence from the Roswell Army Air Field, the home of the world's only nuclear airwing, including the Enola Gay, the B-29 that had dropped the first atomic bomb on Hiroshima, Japan. The Army dispatched Chief Intelligence Officer Major Jesse A. Marcel with another officer, and they found a field of debris strewn across an area the size of "a dozen football fields." Major Marcell later explained on camera, "There was so much of it. It was scattered over such a vast area. We found a piece of metal about a foot and a half to two feet wide, and about two or three feet long. It felt like you had nothing in your hands. It wasn't any thicker than the foil out of a pack of cigarettes. The thing that got me was that you couldn't even bend it, you couldn't dent it, and the sledgehammer would bounce off of it."

Roswell crashed disc. Illustration courtesy of Ronald Kinsella.

Marcell got around sixty troops to the crash site and collected all of the materials and took them to the base. He was ordered to immediately transport all of it to the Fort Worth Army Air Field. Lieutenant Warren Haught made a statement to the press at that time, telling the *Roswell Daily Record*, "The many rumors regarding the flying disc became a reality yesterday when the intelligence office of the 509th Bomb Group of the Eighth Air Force, Roswell Army Air Field, was fortunate enough to gain possession of a disc through the cooperation of one of the local ranchers and the sheriff's office of Chaves County." That was it—the official statement of the US Army. He plainly said the Army had retrieved an actual "flying disc" from the Corona ranch.

When Major Marcell arrived at the Fort Worth Army Air Field with the debris, he says he was met by Brigadier General Roger M. Ramey, who told him that the matter was spiraling out of control, and that Marcell was ordered to keep silent about the disc and debris because the story was becoming a media frenzy. Marcell says he was ordered to arrange some foil sheets with various broken pieces of wood and rubber from a torn up old weather balloon and pose with them for the press. He explains, "All I could do was keep my mouth shut. General Ramey was the one who told the newspaper what it was, and to forget about it—it was nothing more than a weather observation balloon. Of course, we both knew differently."

Roswell Daily Record Newspaper dated July 8, 1947.

SAUCERS ON THE GROUND

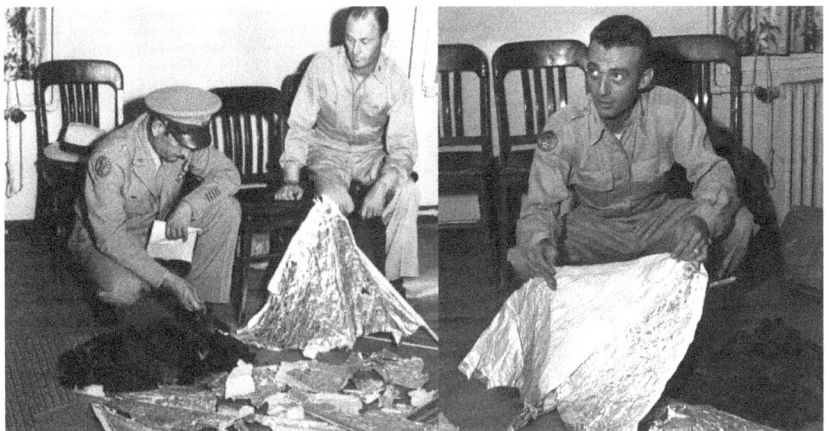

Left: Brigadier General Roger M. Ramey, Commanding General of 8th Air Force, and Colonel Thomas J. Dubose, inspect broken weather balloon debris. Right: Major Jesse A. Marcel.

Because the airbase was inundated with inquiries about the disc for the next several days, Brigadier General Roger Ramey made a public radio announcement that the whole affair had been a misunderstanding, and repeated that the wreckage they recovered was merely a downed weather balloon.

Col. Thomas Dubose, 8th Air Force Chief of Staff, pictured on the left with General Ramey, later described on camera how he was ordered to lie about the true nature of the recovered debris. He says he was told, "This was the highest priority you could exhibit, and you will say nothing. 'More than Top Secret,' as he said. 'Beyond that. This is the story we're going to tell the public.' It was a cover story—the balloon part of it. In order that we don't have any more inquiries about what we picked up on the desert."

Author Whitley Strieber documents subsequent attempts to publicize a government cover-up of the Roswell incident:

> Major Marcel had in 1979 contributed a videotaped statement to a documentary entitled Flying Saucers are Real. In his statement, the major was absolutely unequivocal. "One thing I was certain of,' he said, 'being familiar with all air activities, was that it was not a weather balloon, not an aircraft, or a missile. . . . A lot of the little members had little symbols which we were calling

hieroglyphics because they couldn't be read. . . . It [the metal] was not any thicker than the tinfoil in a pack of cigarettes, yet when I tried to bend it, it would not bend . . ." Major Marcel added, "The reason that this story has remained hidden from the public for over thirty years is that General Rainey released a cover story at that point." (The General claimed that the debris had been identified as coming from a crashed weather balloon.) The Major's statement was made after he had retired from the air force with an honorable discharge a few years before he died."[5]

Unsolved mystery types of television programs have attempted to document these cases, as well as some others. Again, some evidence of a crash and retrieval exists, but nothing conclusive has yet been produced. Few doubt that something was recovered in the Southwest—but what it was, we do not know, and we don't know if any advanced technologies have been reaped from those retrieved materials. Major Jesse Marcel concludes, "Being in the Intelligence Office, I was familiar with just about all materials used in aircraft and air travel. This was nothing like that. It was not anything from this earth. That, I'm quite sure of."

Lieutenant Colonel Philip J. Corso released a book in 1997 titled *The Day After Roswell*. In the book he alleges that he was heavily involved in the research of extraterrestrial artifacts and technology recovered from the 1947 Roswell Incident. Lieutenant Corso contends that a covert government team was assembled under the leadership of Admiral Roscoe H. Hillenkoetter, the first director of Central Intelligence, and was tasked to collect all information on off-planet technology. Lieutenant Corso claimed that studying the technologies and reverse engineering the artifacts to the extent possible indirectly led to the development and parsing of accelerated particle beam devices, fiber optics, lasers, integrated circuit chips, and Kevlar material. He maintained that part of his assignment was to secretly distribute the technology to various government and military contractors, and that the Reagan administration's Strategic Defense Initiative (SDI), or "Star

---

5. Whitley Strieber, *Transformation: The Breakthrough*, New York: Beechtree Books/William Morrow, 1988.

Wars" as the media derided, was intended to achieve the destructive capacity of electronic guidance systems against incoming enemy warheads, and the ability to disable hostile spacecraft, including those of extraterrestrial origin. Corso was invited to share his top-secret information on Art Bell's "Coast to Coast AM" national nightly radio program, and was found dead of a heart attack within the year.

AREA 51 AND ROBERT LAZAR

In the early 1990s we began to hear reports of UAP-style US military craft floating and darting silently in the Nevada desert north of Las Vegas. Although these accounts were unconfirmed initially, ufologists were buzzing with reports that the US government, at least the Air Force, had not only retrieved crashed UAP and possibly their occupants, but had also entered into a secret "treaty" with aliens providing that in exchange for returning the materials and bodies to the aliens, and for looking the other way in human abduction cases, the extraterrestrials would supply the US military with advanced technologies—technologies that were now being utilized by the Air Force, and kept under wraps.

Although the sources of these kinds of reports were unconfirmed, at least early on, one government employee stepped forward with a very detailed account of his employment at what is known as S4. Area S4 is a highly secured area about fifteen miles south of Area 51, a government research base where high-tech weaponry is developed. All of this is located about 125 miles north of Las Vegas, in the middle of the vast desert. Robert Lazar claimed that he was one of many physicists employed to "back-engineer" (sometimes called reverse-engineer) alien craft in the possession of the US government. Reverse-engineering is the process whereby an engineer will dissect an already existing product or technology and attempt to copy it—to reproduce it. Lazar says that Area S4 contained nine secluded hangars in the side of a mountain, protected by ground-to-air anti-aircraft missiles. He claimed that the hangars contained at least nine alien "discs."

Lazar describes one disc on which he worked, which he saw fully functional in flight, and in which he spent time while it was energized.

He describes this particular model as being about sixteen feet in height and about forty feet in diameter, containing three interior levels. The bottom level contains the propulsion system, which consists of "three gravity amplifiers and amplifier guides," which are used to "amplify and focus the Gravity A wave" generated in the "reactor." The small reactor is located in the center of the middle level, and acts as a particle accelerator which bombards element 115 with protons, turning it into element 116. The resulting element 116 has a half-life of a fraction of a second. When the element 116 immediately breaks down, it releases antimatter, the heat from which is generated into electricity. The deteriorating element 116 also releases the gravity A wave, which is amplified and utilized by the gravity amplifiers.

The middle level area of the reactor also serves as the control center, having seats that are adapted to a person the size of a child. Lazar claims: "The walls of the center level are all divided into archways. At one point in time when the disc was energized, one of the archways became transparent and you could see the area outside of it just as if the archway was a window. After the panel had been transparent for a while, a form of writing, which was unlike any alphabetic, scientific, or mathematical symbols I have ever seen, began to appear on the transparent archway." Lazar continues: "I was never given access to the upper level of the disc, so I can't enlighten you as to what the porthole areas are—other than I can assure you that they are not portholes."

The gravity amplifiers create (access and amplify) an intense gravity field around the discs, which in turn creates a space-time distortion around them. These space-time distortions enable the controller to coordinate warps in the fabric of space-time, distorting it to a point that distant coordinates in the linear space-time continuum are brought together like folds in a cloth. When the target location is warped to within close proximity of the disc, the gravity field is decreased, space-time is released and allowed to return to its natural form, and the leap is made. Thus, incomprehensible distances are traveled, not in a straight line, but in a "shortcut" leap, like a secret passageway shortcut between two points through a space-time portal that opens and closes.

Lazar explains that when the disc is in close proximity to a planet, which radiates its own longer gravity B waves, the gravitational field around the disc can be amplified to the point that the space-time distortion is so intense that the disc appears to fade from view. In this phase, all an observer can see is the sky surrounding the craft.

Lazar claims that three projects were being conducted while he was at Area S4. His was the gravity propulsion project. The second project was called "Project Sidekick," which "dealt with a beam weapon that had a neutron source and was focused by a gravity lens." The third, called "Project Looking Glass," dealt with the physics of seeing back through time. Lazar says that he learned of the other projects, and the general background of the isolated effort as part of his indoctrination. Therein, he would be taken into a room with a small table and chair and given a stack of briefings to read. The briefings contained information "relating to aliens and alien technology." The aliens purportedly came here from the Zeta Reticuli 1 and 2 star systems. They come from the fourth planet out from star number 2 (binary star system). The beings are described as the small Gray variety—those encountered by many humans, including Ed Walters and others discussed herein.

Lazar says he was given limited access to the technology and was able to see it work. He was told to put his hands on an antigravity device if he could and found it to be impossible. His flesh and bone hands were repelled like a magnet is repelled by the like pole of another magnet. He struggled to place his hands on it but just could not. He finds this experience to be as compelling as it is unique. Other demonstrations of the technologies convinced him that whatever the source, the US government was in possession of technologies at least hundreds of years ahead of anything he had ever seen or read about.

Lazar could not tell from the year-dating system in the briefings when the beings first arrived, but they had been visiting Earth for a long time. They had presented photographic evidence of their visits that they contended was over ten thousand years old. Technology and information exchanges continued in Nevada until 1979, they said, when some kind of rift developed between the aliens and the government. The beings left, leaving their high-tech equipment behind. This is when the back-engineering program began. According to the documents Lazar was shown, the aliens will return at the date "1623," although we don't know when that is because we don't understand the dating system. Lazar was told he was hired in 1988 to replace one of several engineers killed while opening an antimatter reactor.

According to the briefings Lazar read, the alien beings shared information with our government concerning their ability to remotely anesthetize the human brain and body. This can only be done when the brain is in a relaxed mode—in or around sleep. Any stimulants like loud noise or stimulant drugs render the process ineffective. In the briefings, the beings credit themselves with genetically manipulating our species from lower animals, and refer to us as "containers," although Lazar has no idea "what we're containers of."

All of this information shared by Bob Lazar was difficult to verify. He first appeared on an interview in 1989 with television investigative reporter George Knapp on Las Vegas TV station KLAS. During that broadcast he used a pseudonym with his face hidden to tell his story about reverse-engineering UAP at S4. He explained that the engineering facility was adjacent to Papoose Lake, which is located south of the main Area 51 facility at Groom Lake. The site consisted of concealed aircraft hangars built into a mountainside, he said. Lazar explained that his job was to help with the reverse-engineering of one of nine flying saucers. The story Lazar shared was incredible, and went as viral as a story could go before the internet. It finally seemed that a genuine whistleblower had stepped out of the shadows and was sharing secret information the government had possessed all along.

Lazar's story became difficult to accept because when local television reporter George Knapp investigated his claimed credentials, he could not obtain verification from the institutions Lazar named. Lazar claims he earned a master's degree in physics from the Massachusetts Institute of Technology (MIT) and a master's degree in electronic technology from California Institute of Technology (CalTech). He also claims that he worked at Los Alamos National Laboratory as an engineer and was employed by the US Department of Naval Intelligence before being hired at Area 51. Upon checking with the universities to verify the degrees, each reported that there were no records of Lazar attending either MIT or CalTech. His employment with the US Department of Naval Intelligence and Los Alamos National Laboratory were likewise reported as unverified. Things seemed suddenly bleak for investigative reporter George Knapp, who had put Lazar on the air and was now fielding calls of interest from the networks.

George Knapp told Bob Lazar that no one at any of the institutions on his resume knew who he was or had any record of him being there. Lazar was perplexed and told Knapp that he felt the government was probably making good on their promise to destroy the reputation of anyone who divulged any information about their work. Knapp was skeptical but willing to dig deeper. Lazar gave him the names of fellow students at the universities, and Knapp interviewed them and confirmed that they had gone to those universities with Lazar. Lazar dug through his personal papers and was delighted to find an old employee telephone directory from Los Alamos National Laboratory. He opened it to the page containing names beginning with L, and there he was—"Lazar, Robert."

1982 Employee Directory from Los Alamos National Laboratory with Robert Lazar's name and phone number included.

Upon further investigation, investigative journalist George Knapp found a 1982 newspaper article in the *Los Alamos Monitor*, in which Lazar was on the cover and was identified as an engineer at Los Alamos National Laboratory. Upon confirming that Lazar had actually been employed at Los Alamos National Laboratory, Knapp went back to the personnel director who had denied it, and confronted him with the evidence. The personnel director suddenly refused to speak with Knapp further and cut off all communication with him. Upon further investigation, Knapp confirmed nearly every aspect of Lazar's history, and as of today strongly believes his entire report of what he experienced at Area 51.

Furthermore, a physicist, Dr. Robert Krangle, who has all of the correct educational and employment credentials, has come forward and confirmed that he worked at Los Alamos National laboratory with Bob Lazar in the 1980s. Krangle says: "He was a physicist. Which, I am a physicist. We kind of recognize each other, you know it's the classic pocket condom with all of the proper different colored pens, so he fit that mold. If nobody would have told me, one look, he is a physicist. You know, he is properly dressed in geekdom." Not only did he look the part, but Krangle says he attended security meetings with Robert Lazar. He explained that in these meetings, "They give you the usual briefing asking you not to talk about what you are doing or seeing." Krangle also says he understood why Lazar's employers were so upset with him. "I understand how Los Alamos would blackball him. He committed professional suicide," Krangle explained. "He broke from the fold and talked about it. Within that security community. It is that mentality: 'Don't talk about what you do.'" Of course, we must ask, if Bob Lazar actually worked at Los Alamos, why are his government employers lying about it? The answer seems clear: they are upset that he is divulging information about top-secret projects he worked on, not at Los Alamos, but at S4 at Area 51. There is no other reasonable explanation for creating and continuing the lie in the face of clear evidence to the contrary.

Despite all of the attention focused on Area 51 by Bob Lazar, the federal government continued to deny its very existence for many years. Under the Clinton administration, a federal lawsuit by employees who

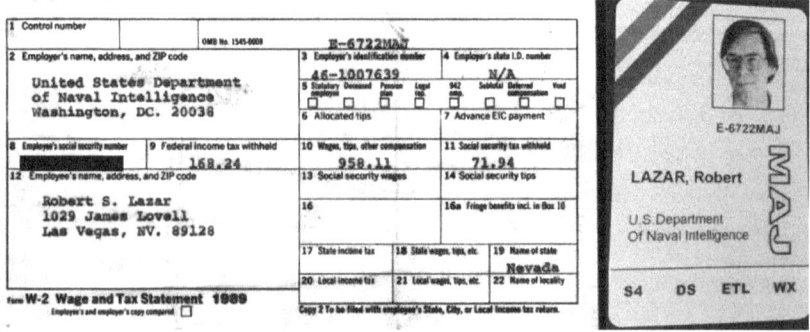

Robert Lazar, pictured with a copy of his W-2 employment tax record.

were injured by exposure to hazardous materials at Area 51 was allowed by the federal courts, and claims for injuries were paid, while the government continued its story that no such facility existed. The cat was out of the bag by that point, and insiders reported that all of the projects of "high value" at Area 51 and S4 were shipped out to other bases in Utah and Colorado. Thereafter, the federal government finally admitted the existence of Area 51. Dugway Proving Ground in Utah is now thought to be the new Area 51, dubbed Area 52.

With the advent of satellite-based earth imagery, generally available to the public through the internet, photographs of the entire region of Groom Lake and Area 51 are easily obtained with the click of a button on any computer screen. It is quite easy to see the specialized three-mile long runways and many large aircraft hangars and other buildings and facilities at the location that the federal government swore for decades didn't exist.

Satellite photo taken over AREA 51, Groom Lake, Nevada.

As a researcher and analyst, I have been asked my opinion about Bob Lazar's "story" many times. I recently watched a Netflix special on the subject titled *Bob Lazar: Area 51 & Flying Saucers*. My feeling remains the same as it always has been—that Bob Lazar appears to believe his experience and realizes that it appears "fantastic" to the rest of the world. He appears to comprehend that his story is difficult to accept, and admits that if he hadn't experienced it himself, he would be as skeptical as anyone. I tend to accept his innocence and earnest sharing of his experience. Of course, that doesn't prove that what was presented to him was the truth. Indeed, at some level, Bob Lazar, and the public at large, could be the victims of a government disinformation campaign. He understands that. There are many who report that the government actively seeks to diffuse the UAP phenomenon by throwing red herrings out for public consumption. Bob Lazar himself has many unanswered questions about the experience and the methods involved in presenting the information to him. Perhaps it was all true. I suspect that the real truth may lie somewhere between the truth and the lie of the experience. Not Lazar's lie—at least I don't think so. Perhaps a military propaganda general took the truth to his grave. However, if much of what Lazar experienced at S4 was legitimate, like witnessing the "Sport Model" fly using antigravity technology, then we have to consider the possibility that our government actually possesses the technology, and is hoarding it, without sharing it with its own citizens to relieve poverty, clean up the environment, and allow us to explore beyond our current boundaries.

MORE GOVERNMENT COVER-UPS

As discussed above, many believe that the US and other governments have been covering up the existence of UAP, and only grudgingly admitted that certain videos contain genuine images of vehicles of unknown origin. In the midst of these government admissions, the US military maintains that those videos were only declassified and authenticated because they had been circulated so widely over the internet, and had made the government look like liars on the subject. Go figure. Their position is that the videos should have remained classified and kept from the public. What does that tell us about the government's attitude and intent toward its citizens and transparency?

Why do these world governments cover up the existence of UAP? Some believe it is done to spare their citizens the psychological trauma of learning that we are not alone in the universe. This can hardly be a valid excuse among the industrialized nations, seeing that most of their citizens already believe in the probable existence of extraterrestrial life in some form or another. Even the Vatican, which famously used to burn heretics at the stake for saying that the earth orbits the sun, has begun to prepare its Catholic Church members for a revelation that extraterrestrial life exists.

Other UAP protagonists proffer the "warm-up" theory—that governments and institutions are collectively allowing the people of the earth to slowly get used to the idea that alien life may exist, and then they will one day tell us all about it—when they believe we are ready. Others propose that the extraterrestrials themselves are conducting a warm-up campaign, slowly making their presence known and building up to a worldwide announcement.

A DOCUMENTARY SMOKING GUN

UAP protagonists point often to documents unearthed pursuant to the Freedom of Information Act that reveal a keen government interest in UAP. These documents, however, rarely contain "smoking gun" admissions of knowledge or conspiracy. If, as is claimed by protagonists, the American government regards UAP to be such a high-level security classification, it is not surprising that no conclusive evidence exists in the released documents. The government has the option of retaining those documents it feels are still important to national security.

As we discussed briefly before, many official-looking documents have surfaced in past decades which appear to "prove" that the US government has clandestine projects that monitor UAP activities, including the abducting and testing of humans, as well as reverse engineering extraterrestrial technologies. Although I personally feel that these documents are easily manufactured so they fail to rise to the level of evidence sufficient for my acceptance, in light of recent grudging government admissions that AATIP and other programs were busily monitoring UAP and collecting related materials and data, we must assume that at least some of those earlier documents and their assertions could be authentic. We just don't know which ones. There is a trove of explicit documents that name names and provide details of activities, and if true, our government really has been aware of, and even complicit in extraterrestrial undertakings on earth.

Probably the best evidence of these is the General Nathan F. Twining memo. General Twining was Chairman of the Joint Chiefs of Staff, Department of Defense, and Senior Military Adviser to the President, the National Security Council, and the Secretary of Defense. He was diverted to Roswell during the incident there, and within a few weeks of the Kenneth Arnold sighting and Roswell, issued a memorandum dated September 23, 1947, which explained to his superiors:

SUBJECT: AMC Opinion Concerning "Flying Discs"

. . .

2. It is the opinion that:
   a. The phenomenon is something real and not visionary or fictitious.
   b. There are objects probably approximating the shape of a disc, of such appreciable size as to appear to be as large as man-made aircraft.
   d. The reported operating characteristics such as extreme rates of climb, maneuverability (particularly in roll), and motion which must be considered evasive when sighted or contacted by friendly aircraft and radar, lend belief to the possibility that some of the objects are controlled either manually, automatically or remotely.
   e. The apparent common description is as follows:
      (1) Metallic or light reflecting surface.
      (2) Absence of trail, except in a few instances where the object apparently was operating under high performance conditions.
      (3) Circular or elliptical in shape, flat on bottom and domed on top.
      (4) Several reports of well kept formation flights varying from three to nine objects.
      (5) Normally no associated sound, except in three instances a substantial rumbling roar was noted.
      (6) Level flight speeds normally above 300 knots are estimated.

Nick Pope, British Ministry of Defence, was responsible for investigating UAP phenomena in the UK to determine if they had any defense significance. Pope has become an advocate of government disclosure of UAP, although he adheres strictly to his security clearance oath. Pope informs us regularly that governments of the world are fully aware of UAP, but most of them have little understanding of what they actually are, and who builds and controls them.

GOVERNMENT DISINFORMATION?

Famous author Whitley Strieber relates that a noted documentary filmmaker approached him, having heard about his personal experiences with "visitors" much like those discussed in subsequent chapters, and wanted to compare notes. The filmmaker, who requested anonymity, reported the following. In the early eighties he had a very unusual encounter with a man who identified himself as a member of the Air Force. Their meeting was held at an Air Force base in connection with the documentary the filmmaker was preparing. He was allowed to read a briefing paper concerning crashed discs and retrieval of bodies of nonhuman beings. The filmmaker was specifically informed that he was being shown this paper at the direction of superior officers. The typed pages he had read were titled "Briefing Paper for the President of the United States." There was no specific president mentioned, and he didn't remember a specific date. He was not allowed to take notes on the spot, but he recorded his recollections later in detail. The controversial document surfaced in 1987, and the filmmaker's memory proved to be accurate.

The paper described a series of crashed UFO discs at Aztec and Roswell, New Mexico, at Kingman, Arizona, and a crash in Mexico. Nonhuman bodies had allegedly been taken from the craft and had been examined in laboratories. The creatures were described as about four feet tall, gray skinned, hairless, and having large heads compared to their smaller, thin bodies. Their faces were flat without ears or nose, and had a slit for a mouth. They had large eyes. Because of their skin color they were referred to as "Grays."

The paper also described direct contact between government officials and a survivor of one of these crashes. This being was called Ebe, an acronym for "extraterrestrial biological entity." The officials were told that the gray beings had carried out a long-term intervention in human affairs, manipulating mankind's biological, socio-cultural, and religious evolution. The being had eventually died of unknown causes. The paper outlined the government's efforts since the 1940s to ascertain the origin, nature, and motives of the beings, and, presumably, to gain some sort of control over the situation, or at least some insight into it.

The agent told the filmmaker that he was being shown the document and given the information because the government intended to release to him several thousand feet of film taken between 1947 and 1964 showing crashed discs and extraterrestrial bodies as historic footage to be placed in his documentary.

He never received the footage. Had he been shown a real document, or was he the victim of some sort of complicated disinformation scheme? When the promised footage didn't materialize, the company he was working for became disillusioned and dropped its plans for the documentary, which he believes was the real outcome desired by the Air Force.[6]

Whitley Strieber implies that the entire scenario was a government setup designed to raise the production company's expectations about the proposed documentary, in the hope the company would lose its interest in the entire subject when the promised blockbuster materials were not forthcoming. When the briefing document surfaced, it was analyzed by experts who pronounced it authentic—as to its origin but not its content.

Why would the government show such a paper to the filmmaker? The reason proffered by Strieber appears valid, assuming that the paper's contents were manufactured—which assumption I believe to be a safe one. The second question is more interesting. Why was the Air Force so interested in debunking the UAP phenomenon? Observers assume that it has been a matter of pride due to the Air Force's lack of ability to control our airspace—its primary justification for existence. Others believe that the "alien alliance" treaty motivates the

---

6. *Transformation*, 116.

government to cover up alien existence in this manner. In light of these facts, one wonders if the Canadian government was not also a pawn in a disinformation campaign in the above-cited Wilbert B. Smith document. We could ask the same question about Robert Lazar. Reports abound of such disinformation campaigns.

IF THERE IS A COVER-UP, WHY SETI?

Not everyone believes that the US government is involved in cover-ups or secret alien alliances. The fact is that the government has conducted a massive public effort to detect the presence of life *elsewhere* in the universe. When the SETI project was operating at the Aimes Hershey Research Center in Mountain View, California, it was headed by Dr. John Billingham, who said, "There is no doubt in our minds that intelligent life, far more advanced and complex than our own, is widespread in outer space. The United States wants to be the first nation to make contact. When we make contact it will be the biggest breakthrough in the history of mankind. These advanced civilizations could help us conquer problems like disease, pollution, food and energy shortages and natural disasters."[7]

The late Dr. Frank Drake, the pioneer of SETI, believed that 10,000 advanced civilizations could exist just in our own Milky Way Galaxy. But that number has been greatly increased in light of the discovery of thousands of planets already in our own galactic neighborhood, and the likelihood that approximately 100 billion stars in our single galaxy each have an earth-like planet in orbit.[8] Drake spoke of the investments and upgrades to the program and related that the true goal was to "answer age-old philosophical questions about ourselves—Where did we come from? Are we unique? What does it mean to be human?" He believed that we will eventually detect the broadcast signals of extraterrestrials—which, he said, "will profoundly change the world."

President Jimmy Carter, who himself claimed to be a witness of a

---

7. *UFO: End-Time Delusion*, 103.
8. This is an estimate, based on averages detected so far.

UAP and who asserted a belief in the extraterrestrial theory of UAP origins, was a major supporter of the SETI program and was responsible for much of its funding in the late 1970s. *UFO Magazine*[9] quoted from President Carter's speech to the NICAP (National Investigative Committee on Aerial Phenomena) describing his sighting: "Carter said that his sighting took place around 7:15 P.M. one October night in 1969. The UFO was a sharply outlined, luminous globe 'about the same size as the moon, maybe a little smaller.'"

These attitudes and statements make us think that not everyone is "in" on the cover-up, if one exists. Candidate Carter promised to reveal all government information on UAP if elected. President Carter revealed nothing but diverted many dollars to alien detection equipment. Apparently, no alien had yet been detected as far as he was aware.

INVISIBLE UAP

It is assumed that many more landings occur than are observed or reported. As in the case of the Gulf Breeze sightings, it is possible that some UAP possess the power to "cloak" themselves from human eyes and come and go unnoticed. During Ed Walters's ninth sighting, he reports: "Tonight was one of those 'no hum' visits. It was 8:00 P.M., and, as I said, I was peacefully writing in my log when I noticed an easy shadowy movement slide slow from the back of the high school gym along the dark grass field, closer and closer toward my back fence. The grassy field was dark green, and the textured shadow changed it to a fuzzy orange. It was clear to me now that the UFO could conceal itself from sight. The glow was there, but there was nothing above it. I had a clear view from the ground to sky and could see no craft."[10]

In an instant the UAP was suddenly there. As Frances Walters volunteered to telephone the police, the UAP disappeared. A moment later "the UFO popped back into view at about the same place it had left." One of the times a UAP seemed to disappear, a landing site was

---

9. M. J. Ernst, "President Carter Launches New UFO Study to Probe Air Force Coverup," April 1978, 30.
10. *The Gulf Breeze Sightings*, 112–13.

found the next day. The resulting ring of dead grass is the same discussed elsewhere herein.

The Navy pilots associated with the declassified and authenticated Navy UAP videos discussed above report that they were oblivious to the presence of the UAP until they received radar and other sensor upgrades a few years ago, and then started detecting them frequently on those systems—but were still unable to get a visual lock on them. Months after it was obvious the FA-18s were detecting their presence, the UAP were suddenly visually visible to the pilots. The implication is that many UAP possess cloaking devices that make them visually invisible to human eyes. Many UAP enthusiasts report that with the advent of upgraded civilian night vision equipment, they are frequently able to watch darting lights in the night skies that move and behave like classic UAP. Wilbur Allen, PhD, has developed a unique night vision camera set-up involving high-sensitivity infrared and an inverted telescope, which allows him to capture aerial objects and anomalies that are otherwise invisible to the eye, in very high-resolution color video.

Although many thousands of UAP have been reported to have been seen on the ground, most of the sightings are either identical to visual contact with airborne craft, uneventful except for the sighting itself, or they fit in the following type of encounter—that of a very personal kind. As we begin to consider encounters with entities and beings that don't appear to be from Earth, let us keep in mind what the Lord has disclosed about the forms of life in the universe, and the nature of the message being delivered by these entities.

CHAPTER 9

"Extraterrestrial" Visitors

As we begin to explore encounters with beings of unknown origin, let me say that history is replete with such encounters. We look at the historic origins below, but those that present themselves currently are of greater interest, because the manner of their appearance, actions, and "message" to humanity become of paramount importance in our examination of the phenomenon, ancient and modern. Two warnings are in order. Again, if you come upon material that is too dark for you, please skip ahead—a paragraph or a chapter—and just read the conclusion of that section. I don't want you to drop out and miss out on the discussion of what it may be that so many of us are encountering. Second, we all understand that not every person who comes forward with an account of an encounter with the unknown is accurately conveying the information. I believe that many are accurately recounting their true experiences. However, some may be conveying "imagined" or made up stories. A few may have mental disorders. However, if just one account is accurate, and I believe a high percentage of those shared herein are, we must take these phenomena quite seriously, and deal with them as a society, and as a people.

ZIMBABWE ARIEL SCHOOL ENCOUNTER

Around noon on Friday, September 16, 1994, teachers and school officials at the Ariel School in Ruwa, Zimbabwe, were in a

"EXTRATERRESTRIAL" VISITORS

weekly staff meeting. They sent the sixty-two young students, five to twelve years of age, black and white, out for an extended recess. Ruwa is a small farming community, somewhat isolated, and most of the children had never heard of aliens or UFOs. Some of the children noticed shiny discs zipping silently overhead against the blue sky and saw one descend close by, near a wooded area. Some noticed something glinting in the nearby gum trees, stopped to get a better look, and saw something that "looked like a round silver disc in the trees."

The children walked to the edge of the playground but dared not go beyond the logs placed on the ground as a boundary—it was a strict rule of the school. Near the disc the children saw a very small man, around three feet tall. He was very skinny with a "scrawny neck" and was wearing a tight, shiny "black and silver suit." They describe the small beings as having large heads and "huge, slanted black eyes." One of the beings was standing next to the disc, and another was moving around on top of it—but the children were spellbound because of the way they seemed to disappear and reappear in different spots around the landed disc.

Some of the children ran across the recess yard to tell their recess supervisor, Mrs. Kirkman, what they were seeing. Others remained at the edge of the schoolyard as one of the small beings approached a group of them. Several ran off, but a few of the older children remained. They said the being came within three feet of them, and was around the height of a sixth grader. One girl reported, "It felt scary when he was looking at us. Scary, because I've never seen a person who looked like that before." The children were mesmerized by the being's large, black eyes. They became entranced, and their minds were filled with thoughts and visions of how technology is destroying the earth. "They want people to know that we are actually making harm on this world, and mustn't get too technological," one student said. "We must look after the planet, or all the trees will just go down and there will be no air and people will be dying."

When interviewed as adults, one of the children said, "I was completely engulfed in those eyes. I had no idea of the passing of time. It was just mesmerizing." Another explained, "There was no

All of the children of the Ruwa school were asked to draw what they saw. Most looked much like these.

talking, just all images in the head. Telepathic communication." Another said, "They were trying to communicate. Trying to tell us something. Something about the environment." Explaining how she was receiving the telepathic messages, a girl said, "I kept getting these thoughts and ideas in my mind of technology. Technology is not helping. It is bad." Another explained, "We are going down the wrong path and we have to start recognizing that what we are doing is detrimental. Start making changes. They were reaching out to us. It's as though they wanted us to go with them. At that moment is when I just kind of snapped right out of the trance." The children one by one broke off contact with the being, and one said, "As soon as I broke contact, all of those feelings were gone. The technology, the bad, the horribleness that was happening and going around my body at the time stopped."

As the children were telling their teachers what they'd seen and experienced, calls were coming in to police and news stations from around the region reporting shiny craft flying around without a sound. One gathering of fourteen adults called to report how a silent "large glowing object" had come up over a hill near them, and before their eyes "split into two glowing orange balls."

Colin Mackie, the headmaster of the school, said of the experience: "I feel sure that the children feel that they saw something. We asked them to draw pictures of what they saw on Friday, and after looking at those, I definitely feel that they did see something." In fact, all of the children recounted the very same experience in interviews, and all drew very similar pictures of what they had witnessed. Famed

Harvard Professor of Psychiatry, Dr. John Mack, flew into Zimbabwe to question the children within two days of the event. He talked with all of the children, and his conclusion was that whatever they saw, it was a real event.

THE NATURE OF UAP "OCCUPANTS"

As we enter the world of sightings of and encounters with UAP occupants, we quickly perceive that this is the "Twilight Zone" of ufology. With the advent of direct contact with extraterrestrials, or whatever UAP occupants are, no clear answers present themselves concerning alien visitations to Earth—rather, the confusion intensifies. The answers we do begin to formulate leave us quite uncomfortable. Descriptions of the physical makeup of these extraterrestrial visitors vary widely. Accounts of such beings range from human-looking blonde-haired, blue-eyed men and women, to hulking lizard men, to tiny fur-clad gnomes.

Some UAP proponents have attempted to categorize aliens into four or five basic groups, cataloging a total of fifty-seven or so individual species. While some believe that the wide variety of alien forms is the result of our being visited by beings from different planets, others believe that we are visited by extraterrestrial humans, who in turn bring an entourage of "assistants"—robots or biomechanical creations to collect specimens, monsters to scare the earthling natives away while they perform their tasks, and lesser life forms to perform dangerous or mundane tasks. Other aspects of the natures and origins of the occupants of UAP (spiritual, metaphysical, electromagnetic, and psychic) are discussed below. Interestingly, proponents of human/alien theories often believe that much of the visitation is by humans or humanoids from this planet. More paranormal theories exist, postulating that UAP and their occupants are from parallel worlds that exist on other planes, much like we view the existence of the spirit world. Two major Earth/UAP theories are dominant, and we examine those first.

THE SUBTERRANEAN CIVILIZATIONS THEORY

The first theory is that human civilizations live in little-known subterranean regions of the earth. These earthlings enjoy the benefits of monitoring us without being observed by us. They have all of our technology, plus that of ancient advanced civilizations, plus some of their own. These types of lost civilizations used to be very prominent in cultural beliefs, but with the advent of technology and satellites that can photograph and constantly monitor the entire globe with infrared and other sensors, they have fallen out of favor.[1] Perhaps related to this theory is one that is taking on greater prominence in serious UAP thought centers—that the UAP are created and controlled by someone or "something" that has been here longer than we have—or at least, in parallel with humanity. As strange as this sounds, the very bizarre nature of communications that contactees receive from these beings indicate that whoever is making the contact is not from out there, but right here. Whether that indicates that ancient Earth civilizations have separated themselves from us and developed separately or not, we can only speculate. Major figures in the research, including Dr. Jacques Vallee, Dr. John Mack, and many others have begun to suspect that whoever or whatever it is that is behind the UAP, and especially behind the abduction and contact phenomena, is something local—possibly interdimensional. What does interdimensional mean? It could mean any number of things, including beings that have been created at differing vibrational or resonance rates than we have, and with whom

---

1. There have always been rumors that the Prophet Joseph Smith said the lost ten tribes of Israel live in the north countries, perhaps in a hidden or underground land. Most Church members of his day report that he said he believed that many of those who were lost and led away into the north countries were actually taken off-world, as were the people of Enoch's Zion, and Melchizedek's Salem. They will return from the north countries at some point, but we don't know if they are there now, or will be taken there to be delivered back to Earth. "And they who are in the north countries shall come in remembrance before the Lord; and their prophets shall hear his voice, and shall no longer stay themselves; and they shall smite the rocks, and the ice shall flow down at their presence. And an highway shall be cast up in the midst of the great deep" (D&C 133:26–27).

we don't interact under most natural circumstances. It could mean beings who have elevated their vibrational rates (as asserted by nearly all contactees and those who assertively attempt to contact the other beings), either through their own biological/spiritual efforts or through technology. It could mean those who have not received bodies and hate humanity with an unmatched passion.

Notwithstanding modern satellites and other monitoring abilities, many tell us of underground UAP basses and ancient but futuristic facilities recently uncovered in Antarctica and elsewhere. It is clear that many UAP are being seen entering and exiting our oceans, and many observers are certain that they have large bases, and possibly cities in facilities hidden far from human view under the water. Such underwater "hotspots" are thought to be just off our western coastline, south of San Diego where the Tic Tac UAP was encountered, and off the eastern coastline near the Oceana Naval Base, for instance. Many other regions are being watched closely, and there is a general observation that UAP are entering and exiting our oceans across the globe.

As for subterranean civilizations, there are people who profess to be members or former members of these civilizations—especially New Age occult disciples who are awash in a sea of false Eastern religious beliefs that they attempt to meld into modern philosophy and spiritualism. I listened to a local radio talk show several years ago, and the host conducted a telephone interview with a young woman who called herself Sharula Dux, who claims to be approximately 280 years old and a former resident of an underground city, Telos, in the Mt. Shasta area of northern California. She said that this city possesses, among other things, a high priest, for whom Sharula acts as a spiritual channeler to the surface world.

Sharula maintains that there exist more than 150 such subterranean cities around the world, which possess superior technology and whose citizens live to extreme ages. The longevity is attributed to their toxin- and radiation-free environment and certain "word of wisdom" lifestyles. Interestingly, accounts from extraterrestrial contactees also tell us that UAP occupants live to ages in the 1,000–year range. It is fascinating that both Betty Luca (an abductee discussed below) and Ed

Walters, as well as others including some Church member abductees, indicate that they were taken under the water to subterranean complexes when abducted by UAP occupants.

THE RETURNING EARTHLING THEORY

The second theory explains that somewhere in Earth's history a human civilization possessing extraordinary technology left this planet and visits it from time to time. Accounts relate that these former earthlings have either moved to another planet,[2] or developed the ability of intergalactic travel hyper-light speeds, causing their relatively short travels in space to translate into thousands of years to us. A subclass of this theory is that UAP are piloted by our own descendants who have mastered the science of time travel and have returned to help us. Indeed, on many occasions the UAP occupants have made this very claim.

THE EXTRATERRESTRIAL HUMAN THEORY

Having touched upon the human/extraterrestrial theories which hold that unknown earthlings are actually responsible for UAP, and reserving the "gnome and fairy" theories for later, the bulk of extraterrestrial personage encounters recount that human-like[3] persons are visiting our planet. We were introduced to some very normal-looking humans that invited Brother Udo Wartena aboard their craft and spent two hours entertaining him in a courteous manner. There are also hundreds of published accounts of encounters with human-looking visitors, some with minor differences than us. A major group is called the Nordics. The bulk of contemporary narratives, however,

---

2. Theories that we have descended from a race of humans from a fabled extra planet of our solar system are proffered by some. The theory purports that our earthling forefathers returned to that home planet but continue to visit us on Earth.
3. The term "human-like" is used broadly here. As pointed out above, humans on this Earth vary widely in size, color, characteristics, and appearance. If humans from other parts of the universe are actually visiting us, we could expect a reasonable amount of similarity or diversity without stretching the bounds of our understanding of the nature of humanity or "created in the image of God."

claim that short humanoids known as "small Grays" led by larger versions of those are manning the UAP.

SMALL GRAYS

Many people recounting UAP occupant encounters describe the beings as standing three-and-one-half to five feet tall, having gray colored, hairless skin, proportional gangly arms and legs, diminutive mouths and noses, no ears, and very large dark or black almond-shaped eyes set in a bulbous head with a pointy chin. These are the type of aliens described by Travis Walton and depicted in chapter 3, above. They are also those seen by Ed Walters, as well as most abductees, discussed below. Many abductees retrospectively "remember" the Grays after "hypnotic retrieval" sessions with psychologists or others. Sometimes the small Grays are accompanied, if not led by taller human-looking beings, taller Grays, or Insectoids or Reptilians.

During my mission in Italy, a wave of sightings occurred in that country. The effect was so alarming that the Italian Parliament debated the subject. One such case had occurred on July 4, 1978, when Italian Navy personnel ascended Mt. Etna and sighted "three red pulsating UFOs, one of which landed." They described it as being a "domed disc about 12 meters [40 feet] in diameter with red and yellow body lights." They then observed "two tall, golden-haired, white-robed beings accompanied by three or four shorter beings wearing helmets and spacesuits." During the inquiry, the military personnel said they "felt a compulsion" to climb the slopes.[4] The phenomenon of tall humans accompanied by small humanoids is common in reported observations of UAP occupants. Also common is telepathic suggestion to rendezvous at a predetermined place. Many report seeing taller Grays or humans working side-by-side with small Grays, and the smaller creatures appear to be somewhat robotic and surf-like; drones, who perform the mundane work for the taller creatures. Some abductees

---

4. It is noteworthy that many UAP sightings occur around active volcanoes around the world, and many have been captured on video and photographs in Mexico and Central America entering the volcanoes.

have even reported seeing pressure suits hanging inside pressure-lock doorways as they enter the craft, some in full human size, and some in small Gray size, hanging side-by-side.

Ed Walters experienced at least two occasions when he saw the small Grays up close, in full consciousness. On the first occasion, he was in bed when he heard his dog bark in an unusual manner. He recounts:

> The pistol in one hand, the camera in the other, I walked over to the French doors. . . . On the other side of the glass was a small creature. Big black eyes stared into mine. Just inches separated us. I screamed and fell backward onto the floor as my feet got crossed. My head and shoulders hit the closet door. The creature just stood there, staring in at me. It was maybe four feet tall. A dark, grayish-black, box-like thing hid most of its body. The 'helmet' over its head had a clear insert that revealed its eyes, really big eyes that covered the top half of its head. It grasped a glowing silver rod in its right hand. . . . I still had the pistol in my hand, so I quickly raised it and pointed it at the creature. I wasn't going to shoot unless it tried to get through the door."[5]

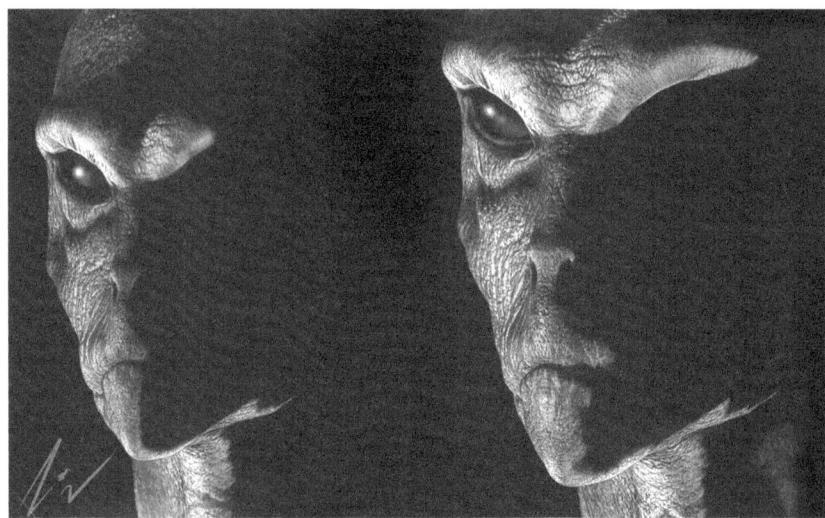

Small Grays, courtesy of Ronald Kinsella.

---

5. *The Gulf Breeze Sightings*, Ed Walters.

Walters decided to attempt a capture of this small Gray and ran out the back door only to be attacked by the blue beam. It is interesting that Walters recounts that this being wore shielding only in the front. As the creature walked away, its back was unshielded. The entire encounter was an apparent attempt to get Walters out into the open to abduct him with the blue beam. From this we surmise that the creature felt no need to protect itself in the back because it knew that Walters would be "beamed up" if he pursued the creature. Walters saw the blue beam shoot down from the UAP just a few minutes after its failed attempt to capture him, and took a photograph of it. Walters speculates that the creature was beamed up in the blue beam.

The use of the blue beam as a transportation device gives rise to Walters's second conscious encounter with the UAP occupants. Walters narrates that one evening while driving his pickup through a remote area to a construction site, the following happened:

> I pressed the gas pedal and rounded a curve. Everything turned bright white. The hood reflected a brilliant flash. Some of the "light" came through the windshield hit my arms. I yelled, "What the hell!?" . . . Within seconds, I realized I couldn't feel my arms. . . . The truck swerved from side to side and was almost out of control because I couldn't watch the road curves and watch my hands control the steering wheel at the same time. From overhead, and coming from behind, the UFO passed straight down the road in front of me. . . . I hit the brakes hard and came to a stop about 200 feet from the UFO . . . I panicked, afraid the white flash could hit me in the truck cab. Out of the truck and onto the ground I pushed myself in a gasping rush. . . I was halfway under the truck when it hit again. Flash! My legs stung and went numb from the knees down. I dug into the grass with my elbows and finally managed to make it to where my head was below the oil pan . . . A blue beam flashed from the UFO to the road. Five times it shot down. Each blue beam deposited a creature on the road close to the UFO. . . . Finally all five began to move in lock-step toward me. Each one had a silver rod. They moved the rods up and down in their right hands as they marched down the middle of the road.

With this, Ed Walters decided to get into his pickup and flee, which he did, with great difficulty. These silver rods are apparently the same as that carried by the single small Gray on the night it attempted to lure Walters out of the house. Apparently, such a glowing silver rod is a technical device used by these beings as a stun gun, communicator, or some other environmental control device. Also, his description of the five beings being transported to the road, one at a time, then walking together in lockstep, really causes us to wonder about the true nature of the creatures. There are those who have speculated that the small Grays are robotic servants of the larger Grays or other taller UAP occupants, which come in several forms. Some have said that dead Gray bodies appear to be semi-tissue, semi-robotic, or bio-mechanical. They appear to be in nonverbal communication with one another, and abducted and other victims relate that they hear the Gray beings speaking to them telepathically, often sending communications of "Don't be afraid, everything is fine." Although the encounters with the Grays are often quite uniform in nature, I find it interesting that the beings are reported to arrive in a wide variety of craft—not uniform. Although some seem to have authority, most appear to be drones, doing the hard work for others.

THE EPHEMERAL NATURE OF UAP OCCUPANTS

Descriptions of "aliens," or whatever the beings are that occupy UAP, range more widely than those offered above. "Moth-men" who fly without fluttering their wings have been reported around the world. Tiny two-foot-tall men with long white beards, or even giants, are commonly described. Ape-men, Reptilians, Insectoid Praying Mantises, and others are frequently reported. Many ufologists suggest that UAP occupants are ephemeral in nature, able to change their size, shape, and appearance at will. Some contactees report that the beings are self-described as being able to change their appearance. These facts raise many important questions for Latter-day Saints and for anyone else who is interested in the spiritual or demonic aspects of these phenomena.

Kathie Davis describes a childhood experience in which after seeing a flash of bright light and hearing a loud noise, she wandered to a "house" with the door open, although there was snow on the ground. Inside, she met a little boy who took her into his "playroom," where a small mechanical device surreptitiously cut her leg while the boy distracted her. Upon taking the blood sample, she recounts that the boy metamorphosed into a small, large-headed, gray-skinned person.[6]

PREDATOR CLOAKING TECHNOLOGY

I'm not sure anyone has discussed this phenomenon in our context before, but I was recently listening to Dr. Bruce Maccabee, the optical physicist employed by the US Navy and Jet Propulsion Laboratories to digitally analyze photographs, film, and videos to determine their authenticity, as he spoke of an incident at his own house. I also heard of a similar experience on Skinwalker Ranch, so I analyzed the two incidents and share them here. We begin with the events at Skinwalker Ranch in the Uintah Basin of eastern Utah.

Colonel John B. Alexander, PhD, is a NIDS[7] Science Advisory Board member and a noted researcher and author. We discuss the NIDS work at the Skinwalker Ranch in greater depth below. I was watching an exchange between Alexander and the current science team members featured on *The Secret of Skinwalker Ranch*, in the season 2, episode 3 installment titled "Laser Focused," and was interested as they were discussing the possibility that there is a junction of dimensional portals on the land and nearby properties. At that point Dr. Alexander recounts, "One of our guys talked about having an experience out at the old homestead area, that was again, very high strangeness, high credibility—and this was at night, and there seemed to be something moving across the trees, where you get a distortion, but it's not clear, just that something might be there."

At that point Dr. Travis Taylor shared a similar experience and said, "That's interesting. We saw something that we described after the

---

6. *Intruders*, 203–04.
7. Aerospace billionaire Robert Bigelow purchased the Sherman ranch and set up a team of scientists operating as the National Institute for Discovery Science (NIDSci), who studied the purported paranormal phenomena on the ranch for nearly two decades.

fact as looking like a 'Predator.'[8] It was there one second, and then it was just gone."

Dr. Alexander continued, "Yes, we had those kinds of experiences. Some of our people were out late at night, in the winter, and they looked up and there was something up in the trees. It looked like it was above one of the cattle. One of our guys had a rifle with him, and shot it. Whatever it was fell out of the tree, and disappeared totally. We went out the next day, and there was some snow on the ground, and the one thing we found was this track that looked like a gigantic raptor—three pronged, like out of Jurassic Park raptor print. We could not find any other tracks whatsoever."

Jan Maccabee is the wife of Dr. Bruce Maccabee. They live in Lima, Ohio, and have family in town as well. Jan is a hunter and an archer. She hunts trophy bucks in Ohio, and they have some of the largest trophy bucks in the state right on their property. They call a patch of trees on their land The 15 Acre Woods. On August 29, 2010, the second day of hunting season, Jan was in her tree stand in The 15 Acre Woods, about fourteen feet off the ground. She could hear the high school marching band over at the Shawnee High School fields. She could see everything in the woods below from her stand, and the birds and crickets and other normal sounds filled the air and all was quite natural. She took a couple of photos of herself with her Blackberry phone, with the high-resolution setting. At 6:20 p.m. the woods went suddenly quiet. "Dead quiet," she says. "No birds. No crickets. No nothing. It was great weather that night, perfect for hunting, and the sun was still up."

Jan wondered what happened to all of the regular little critters that chirp and peep, and why it had become suddenly silent. She next thought there was something wrong with her eye, and started wiping

---

8. *Predator* is a 1987 movie, the first installment in the *Predator* franchise. It stars Arnold Schwarzenegger as the leader of an elite paramilitary rescue team on a mission to save hostages in guerrilla-held territory in a Central American rainforest, who encounter the deadly Predator, a technologically advanced extraterrestrial who stalks and hunts them down. The Predator has a cloaking device that makes him virtually invisible, with the exception of a shimmering distortion of the regular scene behind him as he moves.

it, because some of the foliage around a tree about twenty feet across from her started to get a distorted look. She looked straight ahead, at eye level, and wondered, "What is this thing in the trees? It looked like a large thing of saran wrap, and I was fourteen feet up in the tree, and this was at the same level I was, and it hung quite a ways down." Jan Maccabee watched as a large portion of foliage around the tree seemed to distort in a wavy manner, thinking how it reminded her of the alien hunter cloaking device in the movie Predator.

"It didn't really scare me at that time, until the distortion looked like an arm reaching over to another tree, and it reached over about twelve or fourteen feet." Whatever was in the tree was very large, and when it reached for the other tree, its reach was at least twelve to fourteen feet. "Then, it all moved over to that other tree, like a big blob sucked over to it. The whole thing was at the other tree now." She had a feeling. "Something ain't right here." She was able to see the visual distortion for ten or eleven seconds from start to end. Then it settled in its new position in the second tree, and the distortion ended. She didn't see it move out of that second tree, and she never saw it move again. Although she doesn't recall pulling out her Blackberry and taking a photo, because she is the wife of Dr. Bruce Maccabee, she naturally got her phone out and took a photo. He has always told her, "If you see anything weird, get a picture." She took the photo of where the distorted blob had moved, then put her Blackberry back in her pocket.

Jan would normally have climbed out of the tree stand and run back to the house to tell her husband what she had just seen in the woods, she explained. But uncharacteristically, that didn't occur to her, and she remained up there for a while, about a half hour until sundown. In the meantime she pulled out her Blackberry and snapped a couple of photos of herself sitting in the tree stand. As it became dark, she climbed down the ladder and walked back to the house.

Dr. and Mrs. Maccabee had a dinner guest that evening, and it didn't occur to Jan to tell her husband about her experience the entire evening. Dr. Maccabee says, "And after dinner cleanup and a movie, the guests were about to leave when I checked my Facebook messages and saw one from Jan's nephew, a high school student." Her nephew, Matthew, related that there had been "a sighting" by a number of students and faculty at the high school during band practice out on the field just before dark. He knew that Dr. Maccabee is often hired to analyze photos of UAP and other anomalies, and thought he might be interested to learn that a large craft had appeared over their field while they all stopped to look at it. The practice field is only about a half mile from Jan's tree stand, as the crow flies, and Matthew reported that it showed up shortly after the time of Jan's sighting in the trees. Jan suddenly thought and said, "Wow—maybe that had something to do with what I saw in the woods." Her husband asked her what she was talking about, and she told him what she had witnessed.

Matthew explained that there were around thirty or forty kids marching on the field, practicing songs. It was band camp, which takes place in late August, just before school begins. "We were rehearsing out there, normally, about six or seven o'clock, during our normal routine. All of a sudden there was this bright white light in the sky that came out of nowhere. And we all just kind of stopped and looked at it. The light was above the tree line, close enough that it could catch your attention, and it was like it shouldn't have been there. It was too low to be there. The light was candle orange, and as far as I could tell, it had no definable edges to it. It was huge, and bright, and just kind of waxing and waning until it zapped out. Our band director never stops for anything, but he stopped and turned around and looked at it. It moved sideways, then in a matter of five seconds or so it disappeared, after getting smaller every second. Before I had time to even think about what I was seeing, it was gone." Matthew told his uncle that about five minutes later it reappeared, and this time it was amber in color. As the kids compared notes on what they had seen, some of the older ones said the same thing had happened a year before, and they actually stopped rehearsal because of it.

Dr. Maccabee inspected Jan's Blackberry and the photos she took—of course. He explains that something very odd happened to the camera, but he doesn't know what it was. She had first taken a couple of pictures of herself before the event. She also took photos of herself after the event. They were all in the camera's normal high resolution mode of 1200 x 1600 pixels. But the one photo that she took of the event was very strange. First, the resolution of that digital photograph had changed for that one picture. It went down to a resolution of 400 x 528. It's important to understand that it is possible to manually change the BlackBerry camera resolutions to 1200 x 1600, or 768 x 1024, or 480 x 640. There is no way, however, to change it to 400 x 528. Someone would actually have to rewire the phone physically or change the software to get that 400 x 528 resolution of photo. "But even changing the software would not change the number of pixels along the edge of the sensor." Dr. Maccabee then inspected and analyzed the photograph itself, and says that although it is well focused on the trees, there is so much digital interference in the image that it makes the picture unviewable. We looked at the photo, and although it has a few leaves and forest looking things at the edge of a couple of corners, for the most part it looks like a waterfall of light streaks covering most of the image. Dr. Maccabee has inspected the digital data in the photograph with the metadata and says that nothing about it makes any sense. Jan has never been back to the tree stand to hunt. She reports that there is too much of a weird, haunting feeling associated with the incident.

Although we can begin making a composite perceptual sketch of the nature of UAP occupants from the tidbits of information we gain from alleged observers, it is not until we commence an analysis of abduction reports that we gain any understanding of their purposes for visiting the Earth as claimed. The "space brother" preachings of the 1960s begin to pale in comparison as we compile the data that are streaming into investigation centers in connection with abductions, and the story they reveal is quite unsettling.

CHAPTER 10

"Extraterrestrial" Abductors

Interactions with beings of unknown origin have been reported throughout human history. As we read fairy tales and myths of non-humans kidnapping humans, a smile forms because we innately "know" that such things never really happened. However, modern tales of seeing and interacting with beings that are different from us have taken on an unsettling patina as we hear from large numbers of people making the claim—many of them from our own wards and stakes. We review and analyze these phenomena so we can better understand what our friends and neighbors are experiencing, and attempt to understand it from within the gospel paradigm so we can better deal with it in those terms. If the details of these encounters begin to bother you, please skip ahead—it's better if at least one of us is sleeping well at night.

MISSING TIME

Encounters are not always what they appear to be. Many report seeing a light in the sky, only to notice later that their clothes or bodies have been soiled or harmed in some manner. In past decades many people have come forward telling of perplexing experiences wherein they have seen a UAP, then have gone about their business without apparent interruption, only to find that an hour or two of time has escaped them, and no memory of the "missing time" can be recalled. The continuum of the passing of time seems completely uninterrupted to these witnesses, at first at least—yet there exist inescapable signs that something unremembered has occurred to them. This phenomenon is reported throughout the world, as well as by Church members. The Roper Organization poll cited above reflects that up to 13 percent of American Adults have experienced such a missing time episode.

JUDI MOUDY

Judi Moudy was the legal assistant of my former missionary companion, Stan Harter, who generously shared his own UAP experience with us. As I read through his account of his experience and discussed the details of it with him on the telephone, he related that his assistant came to speak with him of her own encounter, as she was preparing his dictated statement. He told me that he was quite impressed with her experience, as well as with her personally. He related that he had known Judi for a long while, trusted her completely, and knew that she was "incapable of lying." Judi tells of her encounter quite openly. Because it is so representative of so many "abduction" or missing time cases, and because Stan Harter has vouched for Judi's honesty, and specifically in the matter of this experience, we consider it first.

> I was fifteen years old at the time and had two friends spending the night. Rhonda, Julie, and I decided to sleep in my parents' travel trailer which was parked in the back yard. Our home was located on the last street in a subdivision and was adjacent to a large alfalfa field. It was about 11:00 p.m. The adjacent town is Midwest City, where Tinker Air Force Base (home of the AWACS) is located, and my house is in the flight path of the east-west runway. Thus, I grew up with sonic booms, loud planes flying overhead and strange lights in the sky at night.
>
> When Rhonda saw lights in the northern sky moving erratically, I told her it was probably just a plane coming in for a landing. All of a sudden the lights began moving toward us at a very high rate of speed. I had never seen a plane do this before. The lights kept coming toward us, getting bigger and brighter, until it was right over the field across the street. It was

just breathtaking. Prior to this time, the crickets were chirping and dogs were barking. When the craft hovered over the field, all noises ceased.

The craft was cigar-shaped with lights around the top, bottom and center. The lights in the center actually looked like portholes as the light in this area was coming out of the holes inside the craft as if they were windows. The craft paused for about one minute, then slowly moved to the right to the far end of the field, then went straight down. Julie, the most adventurous of us three, took off running across the street to see where it landed. Rhonda and I followed, but when we got to the yard across the street we saw bright blue beams of light shooting through the alfalfa and coming straight at us. It was a very strange light—we could see the beginning of it, then it was as if someone turned off the source, and the beam separated itself and kept coming at us as if sections of pipe were being shot out. The beams were short at first, then kept getting longer and longer. Another strange thing was that there was a chain link fence at the corner of the yard across from us. When the beams became long enough to reach the fence, the light would go over the fence! Just past this fence was the concrete street. When the beam of light hit the concrete, it disintegrated into steam!

We kept watching the beams of light for some time. Suddenly we all became VERY sleepy. I looked at my watch and told Rhonda and Julie it was 12:30 and that we should get to bed because we had to get up at 6:00 a.m. for early morning marching band practice. The next thing I remember, we were back in my front yard walking toward the trailer. We were completely exhausted and went inside to go to bed. When we turned on the lights, we noticed that we each had dirt on our arms and legs. Earlier in the evening, Rhonda had given herself a manicure complete with bright red nail polish. She now had mud under her nails! I turned and looked at the clock; it was 3:00 a.m. We couldn't understand what had happened. It seemed like I had just mentioned that it was 12:30.

When we awoke the next morning, Rhonda and Julie had terrible rashes on their arms and stomachs. I didn't have a rash, but I developed a SEVERE headache which lasted for several days. We discovered that each of us had an identical inch-long cut on the outside of our index finger on our left hands.

We walked over to the field where it had been to see if there was any evidence of its presence. As we walked out through the field, the alfalfa was about neck high. Then we came upon an area where the alfalfa had been "burned" in the form of a triangle with three large circles at the ends [corners]. The alfalfa in the center looked similar to singed hair.[1]

Judi's experience is much like those of many thousands of others. What happened during the missing two and one half hours? How did the girls become so dirty? What are the identical cuts from? These demand explanation. No explanation can be had absent the restoration of the girls' memories. However, others with similar experiences have remembered, or subsequently recalled, what happened to them.

At the time I was researching my first book, I was especially impressed by accounts coming out of Belgium and other areas concerning triangular black UAP. Thousands of official reports were made to the Belgian government, including many from government employees. These craft appear to be cigar-shaped when seen from the side, with a row of lights or lighted windows around the perimeter, as reported by Judi. When seen from below, however, witnesses report that the craft are actually triangular, having rounded, convex edges all around. The design is much the same as if one bent a pipe into a triangle and covered the inside hollow section with a covering, top and bottom. The Belgium triangle UAP reportedly had white glowing lights on the underside of the three corners. Thousands around the world have observed these triangular UAP.

THE BETTY AND BARNEY HILL ABDUCTION

One of the most famous UAP abduction cases, and the earliest to be widely reported, is that of Betty and Barney Hill. Their experience, as told in John Fuller's *The Interrupted Journey* (1966) and a series of *Look* magazine articles, typifies many contemporary abduction stories.

---

1. Letter to Author, dated May 12, 1992.

The Hills were reportedly driving late at night in the fall of 1961. As they made their tedious journey through the White Mountains from Montreal to their home in Exeter, New Hampshire, they spotted a bright light in the night sky that began to follow them. Barney stopped the car to get a better look at the object, when they noticed that it was a craft with windows, through which the Hills could see occupants. When the Hills saw this, they jumped back into their car and drove home, arriving two hours later than they thought it should be.

Within a week or so the Hills started suffering from recurring nightmares wherein they were forcibly abducted and taken aboard a UAP. Their captors were small Grays, with the exception of a taller leader and "doctor." This doctor is so described because his function was to perform certain physical examinations on the Hills. Betty was examined almost exclusively for her reproductive organs. She describes under hypnosis an examination technique that was completely unfamiliar to her or anyone else at the time: "The examiner has a long needle. . . . He said he wants to put it in my navel, it's just a simple test. . . . And I'm telling him, 'It's hurting, it's hurting, take it out.' And the leader comes over and he puts his hand, rubs his hand in front of my eyes, and he says it will be all right. I won't feel it. . . . He said it was a pregnancy test. I said, 'That was no pregnancy test here.'"[2]

Many years later our own technology developed the correlating procedure of laparoscopy to perform in vitro examinations. In fact, laparoscopy was later applied to treat infertility by placing sperm and oocytes directly into an infertile woman's fallopian tubes for in vivo fertilization. Barney Hill was similarly subjected to examination of his genitals, reporting that a circular instrument had been placed over the groin area, later resulting in the appearance of a circle of warts at the site of the instrument.

---

2. Raymond E. Fowler, *The Watchers: The Secret Design Behind UFO Abduction*, New York: Ban Books, 1990. Raymond Fowler cites the Betty Hill examination to compare with that of the subject of his book, Betty Andreasson Luca: "Oh! And he's going to put that in my navel! Ohhhh! Feel's like he's going around my stuff inside—feeling it—with that needle." Like Betty Hill, Betty Luca also received the benefit of the abductor putting his hand on her head to relieve her pain.

Other than their recurring dreams, the Hills had no conscious memory of the abduction. A few years later they sought psychiatric assistance, not understanding the reasons underlying stress they were experiencing in their lives and marriage. It was while under psychiatric hypnosis that the Hills independently recalled their harrowing experience of abduction and physical examination. While under hypnosis Betty was able to recall and draw a star chart she had observed on the UAP. Some feel that the chart she drew is extraordinary because it matches perfectly with faraway star systems. Critics feel that the chart is insignificant because of the high probability of matching any given star pattern with a true charting, given the large number of stars in our universe.

ONBOARD MEDICAL EXAMINATIONS

The disturbing pattern of UAP abductions that appear to be inundating investigators are those in which abductees report being taken aboard UAP and given medical examinations. Often, as with Betty and Barney Hill, these reported examinations are centered in human reproductivity. Stories abound that human semen and egg samples are collected during these abductions. Men claim that they are forced or enticed to breed with a female alien or human/alien hybrid. Generally, however, sperm samples are taken mechanically. Women further claim to be artificially impregnated with alien semen.

Many reports are surfacing that offspring of these human/alien reproductive experiments exist. Accounts are becoming more common that women who were in their first trimester of pregnancy are suddenly finding themselves no longer pregnant. Medical experts reportedly confirm that a *bona fide* pregnancy existed, and was then non-existent, leaving no trace that a pregnancy ever existed or that an abortion occurred. As much as this all sounds like fodder for selling supermarket tabloids, many ufologists are buying into the phenomenon. They report that upon the application of hypnotic retrieval to such a person, memories of multiple UAP abductions surface. In the first instance, generally in childhood, abducted youth are subjected to the taking of tissue samples. Later, as young adults, those who pass genetic muster are abducted for the taking of sperm[3] and ova. Sometimes, the abducted women are impregnated, generally artificially, and later the developing fetus is removed from the womb and a special therapy is applied to remove signs of pregnancy. Researcher and author Budd Hopkins documents in *Intruders* how multigenerational abductions have created experimentational bloodlines, evidently of high value to the abductors.

SYNCHRONOUS SPECTERS

The physical makeup of the "aliens," entities, or beings is also of great interest from a satanic-origin viewpoint. We have many testimonies, for instance, that the small Gray variety often float along without touching the ground, or that they walk and otherwise move in unison. The floating is easily explained in terms of spiritual manifestations. It could be explained technologically also—if they have personal antigravity devices. The aspect of moving and walking in "lockstep" unison is somewhat more intriguing. If we were looking at the problem from an extraterrestrial visitor theory viewpoint, we would think that the small Grays are in some kind of controlled telepathic communication. That is the initial appearance, anyway. However, why would spiritual beings walk and act in unison?

One aspect of demonic entities that comes to mind is that if a scene is being generated by just one of these beings, the movement portions of the manifestations may require more brainpower, or whatever the source of their manifestation abilities, than the being possesses. When Betty Luca was asked to observe a particular scene as an observer, the scene slowed to half speed, apparently due to the

---

3. Two of the men that Budd Hopkins worked with expressed that they had received vasectomies, due to an overwhelming, innate drive to do so. The one reports that he was later abducted for the purpose of mating with a hybrid woman (*Intruders*, 138–40). He recounts (through tears of humiliation) that after the perfunctory sexual encounter (unemotional for her, traumatic for him), he was nearly thrown out of the UAP for his misdeed. He received an unequivocal telepathic message that his captors were not amused.

"double processing" of the images. Assuming that she was being directly "fed" the images she was experiencing under hypnosis, a subject discussed below, this could explain the phenomenon. As any computer animator can attest, the more movement that is generated in an image, the more work and power that is required. Although we are not on well-trodden ground when discussing these aspects of demonic abilities, we can safely assume that when presenting any manifestation, demonic forces are taxed in the process—the more glorious or complicated, the more taxing. Also, the colder the area seems to get.

ANTONIO VILLAS-BOAS

Before the medical examination/reproductive experimentation aspects of the UAP abduction phenomenon were widely reported, a young Brazilian student, Antonio Villas-Boas, sheepishly reported a "rape" in 1957. Antonio was helping out on his father's farm, plowing a field by night, when an egg-shaped UAP landed within fifty feet of his tractor. The tractor turned off by itself as three or four short uniform-and-helmet-clad creatures exited the craft and came toward him. Antonio attempted to escape, but the creatures dragged him into the UAP. They took blood samples and removed Antonio's clothing. After rubbing his body with a clear liquid, the creatures put Antonio into a room by himself aboard the UAP. The room soon began to fill with a smoke, which made Antonio nauseous. A small, blonde, naked female "woman" entered the room, and after some prodding, was able to lower Antonio's defenses, and sexual intercourse ensued—twice. Following intercourse, Antonio recounts that the woman pointed to her abdomen and then to the stars. Investigators felt that her mute message indicated that a child would be born from their encounter.

HUMAN ACCOMPLICES

Kathie Davis reported an eerie encounter at a mountain cabin that she and others had with three young men who were plainly unconventional. This encounter was accompanied by a UAP sighting,[4] and missing time for all involved, including the adult cabin owners. They all relate that the "leader" of the three did all of the talking and was very interested in Kathie (not a good-looking young woman). The behavior of the three male visitors was quite suspect. For instance, they mentioned that they were together because they played in a band. When asked what kind of music the band played, they first asked what kind of music those present preferred and then responded that it was the kind of music they played. This sort of seeking out appropriate responses to questions was prevalent during the encounter.

As Budd Hopkins questioned those present about the incident, they all reported that they had absolutely no recollection regarding the appearance of the two taller, quiet young men. They all, however, remembered every detail about the leader. After giving individual descriptions of the leader, Hopkins remarked to each that his or her characterization sounded like a description of Kathie, to which they each agreed there did exist a strong family resemblance. In light of the leader's unusual interest in Kathie's life and background, and the multigenerational genetic and reproductive research apparently occurring in the "Davis" family, Hopkins's implication was that this young man was an unknown brother of Kathie's, retained by the aliens after conception, performing reconnaissance missions for the UAP occupants. The concept of human agents of UAP occupants is not at all new,[5] and we see many accounts where humans are on the craft assisting the beings.

---

4. This UAP sighting is noteworthy in that Kathie Davis describes the UAP in terms of seeing "four lights descending, spinning like pinwheels." Other than reports of the main body of a UAP slowly turning on its axis, few accounts mention "spinning." This "spinning like pinwheels" description is the closest account I have located to the "Wheels of Ezekiel" UAP theory proffered by those of the "biblical UAP" bent.
5. See generally, Jim and Coral Lorenzea, *Abducted,* Berkley Publishing Corporation; e.g., "The Walton Affair," 80–86.

INCIDENT AT DEVIL'S DEN

Terry Lovelace is a sixty-four–year-old lawyer and former assistant attorney general. He served in the Air Force from 1973 to 1979, was trained as a medic and EMT, and worked as a first responder at the emergency room of Whiteman Air Force Base Hospital. After military service he completed a bachelor's degree in psychology, *cum laude*, and earned a juris doctor from Western Michigan and was admitted to the bar the same year. He worked as a felony prosecutor, was quite interested in health care law, is a member of the American College of Health Care Executives, and was certified as a healthcare risk manager. While an Assistant Attorney General for the US Territory of American Samoa, he was General Counsel for LBJ Tropical Medical Center. In his recently published book, *Incident at Devil's Den* (Terry Lovelace, Esq., 2018), Terry shares the startling events that unfolded during a simple weekend getaway.

In 1977, Terry was a twenty-two–year-old staff sergeant, and he and his best friend and work colleague, Toby, got a sudden idea that they would enjoy going on a two-night camping trip to an Arkansas state park known as Devil's Den. They were both city boys and had never been camping, but it suddenly seemed like a good idea. They bought some inexpensive camping gear, and Toby seemed to intuit where they should camp. They passed the picnic and camping facilities, and went high up past the chain that blocked access to the dirt roads to the high plateau. They set up camp at the edge of a beautiful meadow, charred some hot dogs, and talked around their campfire for a while, watching the spectacular vista of stars. Around 10:00 p.m. the usual forest sounds of crickets and tree frogs fell quiet, and Terry suddenly got an eerie feeling—like he was no longer in the forest but in a 3D projected image of the forest, like a hologram. Nothing moved. There were no sounds.

Terry was unnerved by the sudden stillness, but Toby assured him they had simply spooked the frogs and crickets, and the sounds would quickly return. Just then Toby asked, "Hey, were those lights there before?" Terry looked and saw three bright lights in a triangle formation, just above the distant horizon. They debated what the lights might be for the next fifteen minutes. Then they noticed the three lights turned, maintaining their triangular formation, and rose high above the horizon, and began moving in their direction. A calmness suddenly replaced Terry's apprehension, and as the large, black triangular craft became more visible to them, his tranquility strangely turned to apathy. The large craft stopped when it got close and hovered around 3,000 feet over them. They could see it was large enough that it could fill the meadow if it were to land there. A six-inch white beam of light suddenly came from the craft and landed in the middle of their campfire, where it remained for a minute. Then it just as abruptly stopped, like it had been switched off. Next, they watched as a tiny pencil-sized column of purple-blue light began appearing and disappearing, several times a second, darting and dancing all over everything in the campsite, including the tents, the car, and the men. Terry was nonchalant and thought, "Oh, this is checking us out." The dancing light disappeared after a minute. Then the two men were left in dead silence, looking at the campfire. Toby said, "Well, I guess the show's over."

Terry was overcome with the desire to sleep, and the two men stood, picked up their air mattresses, and walked to their respective tents and threw them in, and climbed in and lay on them, without removing clothes or even boots—with the giant black triangle hovering overhead. Terry fell asleep instantly. He consciously remembered nothing, until he awoke four hours later to bright lights shining through the canvas of his tent. He was groggy and confused, wondering where the bright flashing colored lights were coming from. He recalled that they were camping and assumed that a park ranger must have found them, and the lights above the cab of his truck were flashing. He also felt a loud droning noise, as though a large piece of industrial machinery was whirring nearby. Terry tried to get to his hands and knees and was surprised how much pain he felt. Through the open front of his tent he saw Toby on his knees looking out of his small tent. As the lights flashed, Terry could see tears streaming down Toby's face. The reality of that fact suddenly struck him, and he began to panic, wondering what could be so frightening to make his manly colleague cry like that. He became terrified, wondering what could have happened to Toby, and wondering why he was feeling so bewildered. Terry tried to sit up.

As he did, he noticed his boots were unlaced, and he could feel that his socks were twisted, making his feet uncomfortable—something a military man would never allow to happen.

As he looked out of the front of his tent Terry could see "children" walking in a bright light out in the meadow. "What are those little kids doing here?" he asked Toby, who was peering out of his tent just across from Terry. He saw around fifteen of them, paired in twos and threes, walking into a bright light. And that's when he noticed the triangular craft was now hanging low over them—no more than thirty feet above, and it filled the entire meadow. The "children" walked with a distinctive gait, as if they had sore feet, and as they entered the thirty-foot diameter column of bright white light they seemed to dissolve, and were gone.

"Those ain't no little kids," Toby said, looking over at Terry. "Don't you remember? They took us. And they hurt us."

In that moment a flood of horrific memories rushed into Terry's mind, and he began to recall bits and pieces of the past four hours. Terror filled him as Toby just sobbed, as they watched the last of the creatures dissolve into the beam of light. Then the light was switched off and disappeared as the deep rumble of the droning sound stopped.

Terry had a memory. He was standing in a line, next to Toby, holding his clothes and boots, unable to move anything but his eyes. The craft looked as large as a Walmart and five stories tall from the outside, but in his memory, it looked twice as big from the inside. Everything was either white or stainless steel, and was lit everywhere with extremely bright white light emanating from the walls and ceilings.

As they watched the large black triangle, it began to float quickly upward like a hot air balloon. It made no sound, and they felt no moving air. As it rose higher, it moved faster until it was just a tiny white dot among the stars. Then it disappeared. Terry and Toby looked at each other, and their strength gave out. They each collapsed to the floor of their tents, rolling onto their backs. They both wanted to get away as fast as they could, but the thought of leaving the protective cover of the tents' canvas was unbearable.

They remained huddled in their tents for the next thirty minutes as Terry dealt with the incoming flood of memories. He was standing in the line, naked, holding his clothes, and he heard a woman scream. Toby wasn't next to him. There were small Grays hurrying around the craft, and abducted human men, women, and children stood huddled in lines holding their clothes and shoes, awaiting their turn. He heard Toby scream from somewhere on the craft, and he strained to move his eyes to look around, knowing it would soon be his turn. He saw humans, young, strong, good-looking people, who were dressed in flight suits with matching emblems, and wearing what appeared to be military-issue boots. They were obviously members of the crew, and busied themselves performing tasks. Terry was amazed to think that actual humans would be part of the ship's crew and would assist in the cruelty that was going on around him. There were five young men and one woman, and they seemed to purposefully avoid looking directly at him or any of the captives.

Terry noticed that a tall being with chalky pink skin seemed to be in charge of the area where he was being held. He strained to look sideways to get a better look at the being. The creature happened to be glancing in Terry's direction, and their eyes suddenly locked. "He was inside my head," Terry said. "He knew me—he knew my wife—he knew my secrets. He instantly knew everything about me. All I got back from those eyes was just raw intellect—not an ounce of empathy, mercy or anything remotely human." That momentary exchange with the tall being provided substance for Terry's nightmares for the next forty years.

Some of the beings moved Terry to an automated walkway, which drew him down a corridor, where he strained to see what seemed like aquariums, some empty, and some small ones filled with pink fluid and what at first looked like puppies with folds of skin. He arrived at the examination room, and the small Grays maneuvered him onto a stainless-steel examination table. He was still frozen stiff, unable to move, but he could tell they were doing something to his lower back. From the corner of his eye he could see that the being who was examining him was a tall insectoid—a praying mantis, with a triangular-shaped head. Whatever they were doing to him was causing him excruciating pain, and he attempted to scream, filling his lungs with air and pushing it out. But he couldn't hear anything. He was panicked and trying to scream, and the creature finally turned his triangular head toward him. Terry suddenly heard in his head with crystal clarity, "Why are you screaming? Stop screaming. You know we don't hurt you. You know we always take you back. Now stop screaming." At that point the creature tapped Terry on the forehead, and everything went black—until Terry revived in his tent.

As Terry contemplated the implications of that last statement, he realized that this was not an isolated incident. Indeed, over the next few months he would begin to remember other abduction experiences.

Toby suggested it was probably safe to make a run for their car and get out of there. They grabbed only a few belongings—wallet, flashlight—and bolted for the car. They were both in horrific pain, had an insatiable thirst, and were frightened beyond anything they had ever known. It was nearly an hour before they came to an open country convenience store, where they put their heads under the grimy faucet in the restroom and drank their fill. Terry looked in the mirror and saw that he was red—badly burned. He ached all over. In fact, every inch of his body was badly burned, as if overexposed to a welder's arc. As they exited the restroom the elderly attendant looked at them and remarked, "Ain't none of my business, but what you fellers been into?" It was actually a welcome relief to the men—the first empathy they had received since their ordeal began.

They raced back to the base and went to the hospital where they worked. They were immediately checked in by their friends and colleagues, who could see they had been through a horrible ordeal, and were soon visited by the hospital commander, then US Air Force Office of Special Investigations (OSI) officers, who drilled and grilled them. They were put into separate rooms and the base commander came in and ordered Terry that he was to have no contact with Toby of any kind—ever. Strangely, Terry had already lost his normal desire to spend time with his long-time best friend. They were subjected to threats, interrogations, and hypnotic sessions fueled by sodium amytal, where the doctor dug deep to get the memories, then tried to suppress them. Terry resisted and kept the memories, misleading his superiors about forgetting it all. The most interesting part of these interrogations was that the OSI officers and high-ranking doctor appeared to know exactly what had happened to the men before the interrogations even began, and their main concern was to secure any photographic evidence the men may have procured. Later in life Terry's doctors discovered a very strange "implant" in his leg, which is tiny, rectangular, and has two straight tiny wires protruding from it. There is no scar near the implant. Terry would like to have it removed and analyzed, but a heart condition prevents doctors from removing the foreign object.

TECHNOLOGICAL DISPENSATIONS

These evidences of visitation to our planet by extraterrestrials are somewhat augmented by our understanding that Heavenly Father has created billions of planets like Earth and populated them with his children. As in our own history, He has assuredly meted out mechanical and engineering knowledge at times to these planets—possibly in greater abundance than on Earth. We are without knowledge concerning His purposes in dispensing such technological information, so we cannot tell from history or from the gospel if it is done in any particular phase of temporal existence. We cannot deduce whether or not God may apportion technology earlier and in greater abundance in other worlds, enabling the kind of technology that we see in UAP during the normal temporal existence of planets like Earth. From all appearances, the great technological advances on Earth of the past few centuries have had two basic objectives—to enable the worldwide spread of the gospel and to enable the eventual destruction of the earth. Assuredly, peripheral benefits to His children such as medicines and comforts have been allowed, but they are not essential in the overall purpose of the creation of this Earth, as evidenced by the lack of such amenities in the lives of most of his children throughout history.

If, then, significant technological advancement is generally reserved for the end of a planet's temporal existence, as on Earth, it would be difficult to imagine that the technology displayed in UAP is possible. However, estimating the technological advancement of UAP at one to two hundred years ahead of our current levels, it is not difficult to believe that planets in their sixth thousand-year period of temporal existence could have received technology one to two hundred years earlier, and are visiting us regularly therewith. If the technology is much more advanced, as it appears, then it may be allowed earlier in a planet's societal development. Or, if an outside source provides technological knowhow to a planet, then it will have the resource available from that time forward. Ancient texts indicate that humanity may have received technological knowledge within the first thousand years of its post-Eden existence but utilized that technology to destroy itself, leaving only Noah and his family to survive. Perhaps other planets have been wiser in receiving technological gifts early in their existence and have steadily developed them.

Let us be clear about the destruction that came at the time of the Flood—it was not God Who destroyed the people of the earth in His wrath and indignation, according to the ancient Book of Enoch, but it was the people of the earth who destroyed themselves. God held back the waters that they called upon themselves through their gross sin and technological innovations, and the angels cried out to Him to let the waters flow and destroy the sinful children and reboot the Earth experience with a fresh start that did not include the technologies delivered by the evil ones and the wicked practices they had spread throughout the entire world. "And after [that] Enoch showed me the angels of punishment who are prepared to come and let loose all the powers of the waters . . . to bring judgment and destruction on all who dwell on the earth. And the Lord of Spirits gave commandments to the angels who were going forth, that they should not cause the waters to rise, but should hold them back" (1 Enoch 66:1.) Yes, in these ancient accounts, the Lord God kept commanding the angels to stay the waters of destruction and hold back the flood against His children through His divine intervention, despite their own acts that triggered the Flood. He is a Father of mercy and showed mercy as long as possible, but finally allowed the children to destroy themselves as they exercised their free will and openly and *knowingly* rejected their Father. Enoch saw this day and wondered how God could be so troubled by the acts of His children on Earth:

> And he saw angels descending out of heaven; and he heard a loud voice saying: Wo, wo be unto the inhabitants of the earth. And

he beheld Satan; and he had a great chain in his hand, and it veiled the whole face of the earth with darkness; and he looked up and laughed, and his angels rejoiced. . . . And it came to pass that the God of heaven looked upon the residue of the people, and he wept; and Enoch bore record of it, saying: How is it that the heavens weep, and shed forth their tears as the rain upon the mountains? And Enoch said unto the Lord: How is it that thou canst weep, seeing thou art holy, and from all eternity to all eternity? . . . And unto thy brethren have I said, and also given commandment, that they should love one another, and that they should choose me, their Father; but behold, they are without affection, and they hate their own blood. (Moses 7:25–35)

THE KINSELLA TWINS

I recently heard the story of Philip and Ronald Kinsella, identical twins from the UK, on the Coast2CoastAM radio program, and immediately reached out to them. I was not only intrigued by their abduction experiences but also by the fact that Ronald is an accomplished artist. In an effort to better convey the details of what they saw, he went to great lengths to master the Cintiq digital art graphic system. My friend Howard Lyon is an accomplished digital illustration artist, and I was impressed with his results. I sat for a couple of days with Marvel and DC graphics artist Todd Macfarlane the creator of Spawn, while interviewing him for the book of his close friend, Al Simmons. I knew that if Ronald had indeed mastered the Cintiq, we could all greatly benefit from his illustrations of the creatures he and Philip viewed with their own eyes. I was not disappointed and am delighted to share a few of those illustrations herein, thanks to the generosity of Ronald Kinsella.

THE ABDUCTION OF RONALD KINSELLA

Thirteen-year-old Ronald lived with his family in Luton, Bedfordshire, England, just north of London. In the winter of 1982, his idyllic world was shattered as he suddenly found himself lifted off of his bed and floated up through the loft and the ceiling, entering the dark,

"EXTRATERRESTRIAL" ABDUCTORS

cold night in his pajamas, where he saw a large opaque object hanging ominously above him in the sky. His first thought was confusion why he couldn't feel the cold of the night. Then he suddenly found himself inside what he assumed was the "colossus monster" craft. It took him a moment to get his bearings, and he judged he was in some sort of dingy medical facility, seated in a chair. He looked down at it and was surprised to discover it was a very modern-looking wheelchair. At that point he noticed that he was partially paralyzed and was unable to move his arms, turn, or stand.

"I noticed, to the side of this chair, a small medical utensil rack, which supported a number of peculiar looking items," he recalls. "To my left, the room appeared curved and squat, though I strangely have no memory of what was to my immediate right. But it was what lay ahead of me which triggered pause for concern. I could see, before me, three guys (or what I thought to be men,) standing ahead of what appeared to be an operating table." He felt panicked, realizing that all of the details he was seeing added up to a medical procedure of some kind. He looked at the men and noted how tall they were, and "the bizarre costumes they wore, reminiscent of the World War gas masks and ultra-modern radiation suits." He felt the presence of someone behind him and "I tried to turn and view him; it was utterly futile."

The Doctors, illustrated by eyewitness Ronald Kinsella.

"We are going to perform an operation on you, Ronald," the voice spoke authoritatively from behind. Ronald attempted to turn to see the man in charge but was frustrated by his paralysis. "His voice was clear-cut and distinctly British, the monotones laced with clout and control," Ronald noticed. "I understood one could not argue with him, no matter how hard they tried. If anything, he characterized 'Authority' in the first degree and appeared aloof in comparison to his waiting minions." Young Ronald began to sob, frightened of the impending surgical procedure. He pleaded with them not to operate on him.

"No! It has to be done," the doctor resounded. "It is for your own good, and I promise you, we shall not harm you. We shall not harm you," he repeated. Ronald believed what the mysterious doctor was saying but was very frightened about the surgery, and cried and pleaded with them, to no avail.

"He then leaned over me," Ronald narrates. "I could feel his front pressing slightly into my back, in the chair, as he selected one of the tools on the utensil rack nestled beside it. He gently took my left arm, while plucking up a gadget. I had a good look at this strange device he was now holding, unsure as to what it did. It was a silver rod, with another thinner pole jutting from it, ending in a small sphere. Without another word, he focused on my upper left hand and pressed the ball of the tool gently on it.

"I must have gone out like a light, for the next thing I recalled was actually exiting the huge dark shape hanging over my house. Whatever they had done, it'd been concluded, and I felt myself free falling down towards our old Victorian residence. This time, there was a noticeable static charge running throughout my body, like waves, and every hair I possessed seemed to be standing on end. I was electrified. I did not feel this when ascending. The descent was evidently controlled, and I slipped through the loft, past the ceiling of our bedroom and down towards the mattress of my bed. I landed on my back and felt a slight bump as I made contact with the mattress."

Ronald lay in his bed for a moment, contemplating the horrific experience. The static feeling dispersed, but he was still "terrified, feeling cold, trying to gauge everything that had occurred." He took a deep breath and contemplated what he should do, when an apparition suddenly formed above him, near the ceiling. It was a projected hologram, of what he recognized as something akin to the Cheshire Cat—yes, like that of Lewis Carroll in *Alice's Adventures in Wonderland*. Only the head was included in the 3-D moving display, "which wavered within an electric blue hue, the trembling of its mass skillfully adding a sense of motion to the horrific apparition. He was grinning

"EXTRATERRESTRIAL" ABDUCTORS

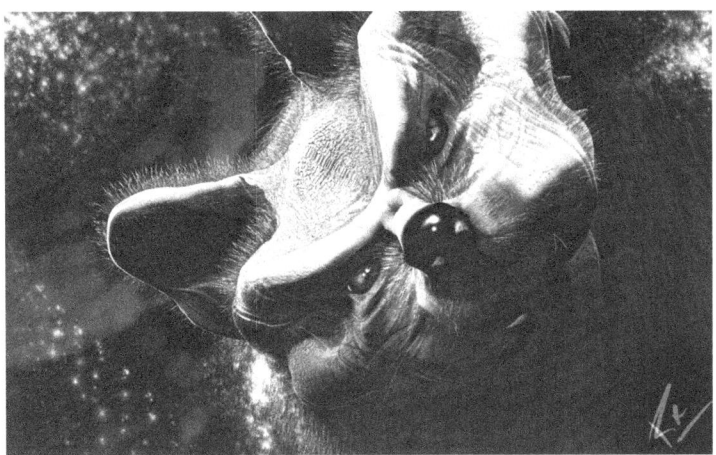

The Hideous Cheshire Cat hologram,
illustrated by eyewitness Ronald Kinsella.

down at me, this monster of a thing. This thing was ugly. His eyes were wide, teeth exposed with ears pricked up." It lasted a "few minutes, then swiftly faded, leaving only darkness and fear." For the next few decades Ronald was left to wonder why the beings had capped off an already bizarre encounter with this hologram. He eventually concluded that it was intended as a clever method of ensuring he wouldn't disclose the abduction—an insurance policy of sorts, because they knew no one would believe the experience if he included the portion with the Cheshire Cat. Perhaps.

THE ABDUCTION OF PHILIP KINSELLA

The Kinsella twins had a very special bond and seemed to enjoy a sixth sense about one another and at times other people. They had even witnessed a few UAP in the local skies; some quite near and clear to them. Young Philip learned of his twin brother Ronald's abduction and set out to study UFOs and related phenomena the best a boy of the early 1980s could manage—at the public library. His grandmother bought him Dr. J. Allen Hynek's *The Hynek UFO Report*, which he did his best to comprehend, and despite Ronald's harrowing experience, Philip maintained that the space beings were benevolent in nature. Around that time the boys and their grandmother witnessed "an incredible silver sphere, which silently glided through the sky in Middlesex in broad daylight," while in her back yard. Having a witness to their sightings was unusual but comforting.

Seven years had passed since Ronald's ordeal. It was now December of 1989, and the boys were twenty. The family lived in the small village of Marston Mortaine, which lies north of Luton. Philip had just returned from work on the evening train and entered "through the front door to our house, which lay in a quiet *cul-de-sac*, roughly around 7:15 p.m. My brother, sister and pet dog, Benji, had been there as they usually did to greet me. I'd taken myself through the hall, which comprised of frosted glass windows, and into the kitchen/diner. I had a coffee and rested my back against the cupboards behind me, looking out into the open space of the hall while my brother was in the dining area and my sister to my far left. Benji had been lying in front of the breakfast bar, facing the hall." At that point an unexpected "strange feeling" began to permeate the room and felt like an electrical current was charging up. "Our dog began to growl as this weird sensation intensified." Philip was surprised to see Ronald suddenly stiffen. "He raised his head up, opening his mouth as though possessed. He spoke these, exact words: 'There's going to be an earthquake, or Grandma's going to die!'" Philip looked at him, wondering why he was acting so strangely and had said such a bizarre, random thing. He watched, and Ronald remained in that frozen position.

"Then, instantly," Philip recalls, "there came a bright, white light outside which shone through the hall's glass door and window. I thought that perhaps it was our mum finishing work early and driving her car up the drive." Philip looked through the glass at the light, and relates, "As I stood there staring through to the hall, the light began to bend the glass—literally! It started to warp backwards and forwards, defying the laws of physics entirely, and seemingly reducing the entire composition of the glass to nothing more than jelly. It was during this point when a small being, roughly three feet in height, thin, and wearing a black, tight-fitting one-piece uniform complete with what I assumed to be some type of helmet, came through the glass! I watched as it quickly darted across to our downstairs study/bedroom." As soon as the small being disappeared down the stairs, the static charge in the air dissipated, and Ronald came out of his trance. Benji was still barking furiously. Philip had been stunned by what he'd just witnessed, and turned and took a large knife out of the drawer behind him. "There's an intruder in the house!" he declared, holding up the knife. He was overcome with shock and disbelief. He looked around and then shouted even louder, "THERE'S AN INTRUDER IN THE HOUSE!"

Ronald was just coming out of his trance and jumped up to follow Philip. The the two searched the house from top to bottom, without any success. There was no sign the small being had ever been there. They gave up their search, and it was then that Philip learned that although his brother and sister had been present and had witnessed the electrical charge in the air, they had not witnessed the flexing glass or the intruder come through the house. They checked on their grandmother, who was fine, and there were no reports of earthquakes anywhere. The perplexed siblings eventually went to bed and tried to forget about the experience. Philip was confused as he awoke from sleep, and recounts:

> I found myself waking and discovered that I was on my back, with my arms pinned to my sides and my legs out straight in a laying position. It was as though some invisible force had a hold of my entire body. I couldn't move or talk, and realized I was floating roughly three feet from the floor. I was being pulled through the hall and into the kitchen backwards, so I couldn't see what was going on in front of me. The most curious aspect to all of this was how I was able to pass through the doors to the house! It was as though I'd become a ghost—yet, I was fully conscious and aware of what was going on. I felt an incredible fear but knew there was nothing I could do. It appeared that something or someone had control over my body. As I came out into the large garden near the pond, I felt myself now being cartwheeled around so that I now found myself in an upright stance and, looking up, saw that the night sky was ablaze with UFOs of all shapes and sizes. One such craft which had not been moving caught my attention. This was a silver disc-shaped object. I had been overwhelmed and amazed by what I was seeing and knew

for certain that we, the public, were being lied to concerning the UFO reality. As this thought filled my head, I was lifted into the air, and my stomach rolled; rather like that feeling you get when you're on a roller coaster that's just about to take its descent! I was being forcibly propelled closer to this object, when, all at once, I blacked out!

When Philip awoke, he found himself in a dimly lit room. The heat was exhausting. "I noticed with shock that I was naked, and seemingly strapped to a hard bed of some kind. Although I was able to move my head, my arms and legs were restrained. Disorientated, thirsty and confused, I looked down to find another shocking discovery; there was something inside of me! The total bewilderment in discerning that something organic was, seemingly, pulsating within the lower part of my anatomy brought me to my full senses immediately. As I turned to my right, I could see three tall, Reptilian type creatures which merely observed me from a few feet away. They seemed to be standing within some type of vapor. They appeared dark-skinned, and were shuffling from left to right in unison." Philip describes this shuffle as something of a rhythmic swaying, and says it was unsettling to see.

One of the Reptilians viewed by Philip, and one of the Grays, illustrated by his brother Ronald Kinsella.

"EXTRATERRESTRIAL" ABDUCTORS

Philip cried out, begging the beings to release the device that was inside of him. "I screamed in abject horror, but all I got back from them was a total lack of empathy. To them, I was nothing more than a lab rat!" Philip was filled with horror and dread, and in that very moment he saw another creature coming toward him—one that we refer to as a small Gray. However, he reports that the skin was actually more cream in color than the classic reported gray. The creature "had large, wrap-around eyes, a slit for a nose and very small protrusions where the mouth would be."

As soon as he saw the Gray coming toward him he discovered that the clamps holding him down were immediately released and he felt the implement inside of him retracting. "The relief I felt was incredible," he recounts. He looked back to where the three Reptilians had been only a moment earlier, but they were gone. At that point he heard or felt a voice in his head, apparently coming from the Gray, which "ordered" him to "sit and dress." The words were almost as if issued by a computer and lacked all emotion. "All I cared about was getting out of here," he recalled. "I was commanded to follow the Gray through to a corridor and there we stopped, coming to what I thought had been a wall. The lighting was dim, and the Gray looked up at me. Immediately, the wall disappeared, revealing an opening, looking out upon the village. I could see our house below, and the sun coming up." He knew the being was telling him to get out, but at this height he was horrified. "What did this Gray want me to do? Jump out of this opening!?"

Philip suddenly discovered he was flanked by two other Grays, and he received a telepathic command not to look at them. He didn't understand why. Each Gray positioned itself on either side of him "as we levitated down towards the garden and away from the craft. Strange that they hadn't been around when I'd first gone into the craft, I wondered!" He sensed the two Grays lifting back up toward the craft, as he discovered another Gray standing before him. "He wore a once-piece, tight fitting uniform, and he had a pair of knee-length boots and wore a ridiculous pointed hat upon his head, like a wizard's. Above him hung a smaller craft which, I assumed was his."

The Gray glowered at Philip, who became unnerved by the stare. The creature's "arms were folded across his chest in a threatening manner, and the expression on his face was of absolute anger. I stood

The Small Gray in the pointed hat seen by Philip, illustrated by his brother Ronald Kinsella.

there, feeling as though someone had punched me in the stomach. He was so angry, yet there had been something familiar about him; like I'd seen him before." The being projected fierce anger, which confused Philip. "Then I was the one who became angry. In fact, I was seething. These things come into my house, abduct me and give me the most grueling medical examination, which destroyed my dignity, and now I had 'Noddy'[6] giving me a hard time. I wanted to punch him hard, but I was unable to move!" Then a thought came to him, and he decided to ask a question. "How am I able to pass through the locked and bolted doors?" The creature glared at him and seemed stunned by the question. "For the first time his expression changed to that of shock. I saw his thin orifice for a mouth change into an 'O' shape and he began to talk, but everything came out confused. His meaningless words rasped like an electronic voice synthesizer. It was during this point when I felt myself rushing back through the doors to the house. My last, fleeting glance of 'Noddy' had been of him staring up at the underbelly of his craft, seemingly frozen. This had been the same reaction my brother had back in the kitchen when he'd become temporarily possessed. I went crashing into my body and woke up with a nosebleed."

---

6. "Noddy" is a character created by British author Enid Blyton. He looks like an elf with a pointed hat.

This last part of the experience raised the same questions in Philip's mind that it raises in mine. Was this an actual, physical event, or a psychic projection from some being or force? There were physical aspects—the continued nosebleeds, the triangular marks left behind his ear and on his arm—but it seems that his body was in his bed during the abduction. Is there a way to force one's spirit or soul to participate in activities external to the body? Who has that ability—or desire?

THE NURSERY

As part of the fetal removal phenomenon, some hypnotic retrievals have unearthed memories of subsequent abductions during which the donor of the ova or fetus, or in some cases, the contributing father, is given the hybrid child to hold and cuddle. After the bonding session is completed, the child is removed from the mother or father, who is then returned to the bedroom or other place of abduction, without any memory of the abduction or the child. Theories attempting to explain all of such reproductive experimentation by aliens speculate that genetic manipulation is occurring, either to enrich alien gene pools or to regulate human evolution. A third possibility is that a hybrid race is being created for an unknown purpose. Of course, those of the Erich von Däniken bent claim that man was created by this very process,[7] and that the course of his evolution has always been determined by the genetic interference of our alien "fathers."

These hybrid babies are generally described as tiny and thin, often lying in small metal containers in the UAP, having thin, grayish skin. The human women are very attracted to the babies, finding them almost irresistible—with hypnotic eyes. It is while "falling into" the babies' dark eyes that the women develop a sense that the babies are "wise" or "omniscient." A type of communication occurs between the women and the babies, during which the women become captivated by

---

7. Von Däniken theorizes that humans were created by altering the genes of Earth's apes with genetic information from extraterrestrials. This explains the missing link in our evolutionary process, according to von Däniken.

the great wisdom and intelligence of the babies, feeling a close kinship. Kathie Davis described her feelings about her little hybrid, Andrew, as she looked into his eyes: "It's like the whole world was in this little baby's eyes. It was like, God, he knew, he knew what I felt. He just knew. I can't describe it. It was so intense, so euphoric or something. I was so excited, so up."[8]

During such an abduction experience of a psychotherapist called "Lucille," she gained information that offers a possible explanation of why these reproductive experiments are occurring. She "sensed" from her telepathic communication with the aliens that their society was "millions of years old, of outstanding technology and intellect but not much individuality or warmth." She wrote, "The society was dying, that children were being born and living to a certain age, perhaps pre-adolescence, and then dying." She felt that there was "a desperate need to survive, to continue their race." Lucille explained, "It is a culture without touching, feeling, nurturing . . . basically intellectual. Something has gone wrong genetically. Whatever their bodies are now, they have evolved from something else. My impression is that they wanted to somehow share their history and achievements and their present difficulties in survival. But I really don't know what they are looking for." Lucille was shown a series of "holographic" images, remarking, "I saw a child about four feet tall, gray, totally their race, waving its arms . . . it was in pain and dying. I was told that this is what is happening now."[9]

THE "ALIENS" HAVE SOMETHING TO LEARN FROM US

An underlying theme of many of these "nursery" abductions is a sense that the aliens are sorely lacking in "warmth" skills. Kathie Davis claims that she was abducted and shown a small hybrid female child, and was told it was hers. She described her strong feelings of love for this "beautiful" little half-human girl. She explained that the female aliens, distinguishable only by their emotional "feel," were interested in learning

---

8. *Intruders*, 184.
9. See *Intruders*, 187–91, for a full narrative of Lucille's abduction experience.

how she held, cuddled, and loved the child. On a subsequent abduction, Kathie's little hybrid "daughter," about four years old, joined in watching and learning as Kathie was told that an additional eight children had been produced from her removed ova. She was then allowed to hold the youngest of her many hybrid children. She recalled under hypnosis: "They want to watch me . . . hold this . . . baby. They want . . . to feel how I love it. I shouldn't worry, 'cause she'll [the first female child] take care of it. I have something they can't give." When asked what, she replied, "Something . . . to do with touch, and the human part . . . and they don't understand, but they'll learn. And they said I could name them. I would choose . . ." Kathie noted that this undersized hybrid baby "was all pale . . . he looked dead, but he wasn't." When she began cuddling and kissing him, he suddenly gained strength and vitality.[10]

Lucille reports that in her encounter, she noted the difficulties of the alien race: "We spoke about the lack of touching. I told them that some animals here can die within a day of birth if they are not licked and touched by their mothers or other loving caretakers, since that affects their perceptions of their bodily functions as well as of themselves. Strange as it may seem, I suggested their interpreting Ashley Montague's book *Touching*."[11]

ERASED MEMORIES

Many of these occurrences of abduction, and their often-attendant reproductive system experimentation, are not "remembered" initially by the abductees. As in the case of the Hills, unexplained periods of "missing time" or recurring dreams or other subconscious manifestations of abduction and experimentation plague the person until psychological assistance is sought. Hypnotic retrieval of these repressed memories often recovers the memory of the missing time or forgotten period and the details of the abduction.

The conscious memories of the abduction appear to be purposely "erased" by the abductors. Some abductees claim to have been told by

---

10. Ibid., 184; see also *UFOs in the 1980s*, 10.
11. Ibid., 191.

the aliens that because no one would believe them anyway, it would be better just to have their memories erased. Other abductees have seemingly received forced amnesia through less beneficent means. Laura, Kathie Davis's sister, reported that hypnosis to help her lose weight had the opposite effect, making her eat everything in sight. When she called her hypnotist, upon hearing his voice she became homicidally violent. When taken to another hypnotist, it took several sessions to get her past an implanted posthypnotic suggestion that she would die if she were hypnotized or if she tried to remember her abduction experience.[12]

WHY HYBRIDS?

Nothing about the "hybrid baby" farce makes the least bit of sense. Why "hybrids" instead of "aliens," if they want to preserve their own species? If this were their true purpose, they could use a small amount of human genetic coding for minor physical improvements. If their race is truly superior to ours, which claim they make frequently, why pollute their offspring with inferior genetics? Understanding that some will think these observations sophomoric, from a genetic engineering viewpoint anyway, I challenge those who accept this theory to explain the necessity of a 50/50 genetic hybrid, instead of a genetically reinforced alien result. It is a smokescreen.

This brings me to another issue that I find troubling. Each time I hear a description of a Reptilian or Insectoid, the implication appears to be that "evolution" on other planets favored reptiles or insects, rather than mammals, and the beings we see are the end result of that natural evolutionary process. Personally, I am quite hostile to such a theory. However, the detailed descriptions of those beings appear to define essentially humanoid creatures, with a very humanesque head, thorax, and abdomen, with human styled arms, legs, hands and feet, and so on, with some modifications. In other words, they always appear to be genetically altered humans, rather than highly evolved reptiles or insects or arthropods or amphibians that have naturally developed

---

12. *Intruders,* 12.

from those lifeforms. We also note that no matter which façade is projected onto the creature, its feel and demeanor are nearly always the same—cold, raw intellect, with no empathy. What does this tell us? As with so many aspects of the UAP and occupant phenomena, it seems more like theater than natural evolution.

NOT TO PRESERVE THE HUMAN FORM

The second response, "to save our soon to become extinct human race," has no basis in truth. As discussed above, our earth has a fixed period of temporal existence. Our race will be saved without the help of "aliens." There is little probability of imminent, worldwide destruction of the human race. Prophetically, that is just not how it is going to happen. Abductee after contactee report how they are filled with visions of the earth's imminent destruction. The beings constantly regale their victims with excuses that they are here to help humanity end its destructive course of polluting the earth and its extremely dangerous use of nuclear weapons. The message sounds better delivered through a megaphone at a Green rally—the abductors could throw in a few extra words like "democracy" and "veganism" and really give their message some punch. Whitley Strieber speaks of his very vivid induced dream in which he saw a nuclear power plant blow up and the moon explode, causing great catastrophes on Earth.[13] As a result of his "catastrophe" visions (common in ufology) implanted by the entities, Strieber has written bestselling books decrying the use of nuclear energy (a common crusade of contactees) and generally promoting the Earthspirit doctrines of the New Age. Of course, the beings with the message, who have every ability to intervene in our political and social systems, could easily have 1) prevented, or that lacking 2) repaired the problems of pollution and nuclear weapons even before they took root, did absolutely nothing. Picking up Brazilian farmers and appearing to school children in Zimbabwe to deliver a message about pollution and nuclear arms is all theater, with no substance. They clearly had the ability, and the stated desire of preventing these problems before

---

13. *Transformation*, 58–59.

they even developed—but they did nothing substantive, proactively. They offered no alternative technologies to replace the burning of fossil fuels, and they failed to give Dr. Steven Greer and his pro-extraterrestrial peaceniks any technologies that would allow them to end the use of nuclear weapons. Instead, they appear to average humans, without any influence, and deliver peacenik messages as they molest and terrorize their victims. It screams out DECEPTION!

All telestial/probationary planets have their times and bounds fixed, just like the Earth—this would include those of the "extraterrestrials." God, who controls the destiny of the Earth and each of its inhabitants, has already decreed the end from the beginning—what will be is written in granite. Perhaps some readers will say that this is either not necessarily true (even though the prophets have made it perfectly clear), or they may say that the "extraterrestrials" might not know this fact. Even allowing for the ignorance of the superior intellect, any claim to preserve the human race by collecting specimens before the holocaust is untrue. It is not "our race" that is being preserved in the UFO nursery—it is a purported hybrid race.

The third response, "to create a new hybrid race," likewise fails to pass scriptural muster. The question returns again and again, Why hybrids? If they want to save their own race, then do it—but 50/50 hybrids are not their own race. The same is true of saving our race. So why hybrids? Only one answer presents itself—to create a superior human race—certainly not to create an inferior alien race. For what purpose? To populate another planet? The gospel says "no." It is clear that God's offspring are assigned to specific planets and the human/Adamic family that populates each. Is it possible that we could get around such a principle and retain our planetary/family identity, yet explore the universe in *Star Trek* fashion? Not if any interplanetary marriages produce offspring. Granted, this is a mere academic exercise, but we must face the fact that little possibility exists that extraterrestrial humans are mixing with our own race to populate another planet or save either of the donor races—not from a gospel view. It's possible, but not probable.

HYPNOTIC RETRIEVAL

The practice of hypnotic retrieval is controversial because skeptics claim that those who perform the hypnosis "suggest" or "plant" ideas of abduction in the hypnotized person, even if it is done unintentionally. Skeptics fear that hypnotists inadvertently "lead" the hypnotized person, or "indicate" appropriate responses to questioning without intending to do so, thereby creating abduction "memories." Budd Hopkins, presumably the foremost (or most experienced) UAP hypnotic retrieval expert, claims that he has certain "control points" by which he discerns abduction reports hypnotically retrieved. Hopkins claims that there exist certain consistent "details" in most genuine "retrieved" abduction cases that he withholds from the public. Because only he and his colleagues know what these details are, abductee wannabees have no way of knowing how to fake a hypnotic session with him. Some of these control points are specific examination and surgical techniques used by the abductors and specific hieroglyphs and other symbols seen while aboard UAP. Although this control point technique may satisfy Budd Hopkins it does little to alleviate skeptics' fears of inadvertent memory implant by the hypnotists.[14]

IMPLANTED MONITORS

Researchers of the Ed Walters case believe it probable from their observations and Walters's reports that he was abducted as a child, at which time he received certain tiny implants around his head. The abductors could monitor Walters as well as communicate with him through the implants. Walters was monitored for an unspecified purpose by the communications implants and picked up at regular intervals for examination. This implantation and periodic pickup scenario is becoming quite common in ufology.

All of this sounds uncomfortably like our own methods of tagging and tracking animals in the wild. In fact, some investigators are surprised at the high number of reported implants that appear to be

---

14. See generally, *UFOs in the 1980s*, 1–13.

occurring. Budd Hopkins claims in *Intruders* that the implanting of small "BB-like" objects in the abductee's inner ear or nose is becoming a disturbingly common complaint. The most common method appears to be the nose implant. Hopkins recounts that some of his abductees "have recalled a thin probe of some sort with a tiny ball on the end having been inserted in the nostril, and they feel pain when the probe apparently breaks through at the top of the nasal cavity."[15] Abductees similarly report such probes being placed into their noses or ears, and seeing no tiny ball until the probe is withdrawn. This, of course, would be at the time of removing the previously implanted device. Regardless of the point of penetration or final lodging, these tiny balls are evidently placed in close proximity to the subject's brain. A handful of children of abduction families in the Copley Woods area (Indianapolis) were discovered by Budd Hopkins to have suffered terrible nosebleeds during the night. One mother remarked to Hopkins that a doctor at the local hospital said her child had probably put a pencil or a similar object up his nose and punctured the membrane, as evidenced by a small wound there. He then observed how it was peculiar that so many children had been brought into the hospital recently for identical wounds.[16]

DREAMS OR MEMORIES?

In reciting the details of the dream, Ed Walters reported, "The dream would begin with me rising high in the sky and looking over a coastline. I could see the sandy beach with waves breaking on the shore. Sometimes I would recognize the beach but most often not. Then I would quickly descend and pass beneath the water into the ocean. I would gasp for air, in fear of drowning, but as I went deeper and deeper, I realized I was inside a container with a large diamond-shaped window.[17] Through the window I could see the water and fish. Shortly thereafter I saw a lot of bubbles passing in front of

---

15. *Intruders*, 44.
16. Ibid.
17. The photographs of the Gulf Breeze UAP reveal diamond-shaped portals surrounding the UAP.

the window, followed by rising sand, which soon completely covered the glass. That's all I remember of it."[18]

Besides the abduction implications in the recurring dream that appeared to be more of a resurfacing memory, the theme of being taken into the ocean is also prevalent among abductees, lending credibility to the theory that UAP frequently go into the oceans, and may be based there.

Ed Walters writes that during some of his encounters with the UAP, as he would attempt to avoid abduction, the voices he heard commanding him to step out into the clear and not resist would taunt him with clues about what was occurring in his life. Upon one failed abduction attempt the UAP voice said, "Zehaas . . . in sleep you know . . . we are here for you." After cursing at the UAP, Walters again heard, "Zehaas . . . sleep and know."[19] Interestingly, the before-cited Roper Organization poll found that a full 10 percent of the adult American population has experienced similar, vivid dreams.

Many abductees remember portions of their ordeals as bad dreams. Kathie Davis still refers to her experiences as her dreams. Mary M., a Church member abductee, thought for many years that she was only experiencing nightmares. It was when she began reading of the accounts of other abductees that she discovered that her nightmares were exactly like those of hundreds of others. She, like many so afflicted, has come to believe that more than "dreaming" is occurring in her life. Of course, for many, the answer could be nightmares—or phenomena not based in reality, or at least not the realms of the normal physical world.[20]

THE BEDROOM ENCOUNTER

In the Ed Walters's case, as well as the majority of cases, a number of abductions or other encounters occur while the subject is cozy in his own bed. These "bedroom encounters" are classic, and if the subject

---

18. Ibid., 161. We term these unidentified submerged objects, or USOs.
19. Ibid., 166; see also 241.
20. *See generally, UFOs in the 1980s*, 1–13.

remembers anything at all, it is generally the very end of the encounter, having a foggy recollection of a small Gray exiting the bedroom. Kathie Davis reports a few bedroom encounters, one of which is more than classic. She remembers it as more of a dream than reality, although completely vivid, as is common. It was still dark, and Kathie found herself sitting up in bed, awake, facing two small Grays standing next to her. One held a black box with a glowing red light on top and moved forward to hand it to Kathie. As he moved, the second one duplicated his movements precisely although his hands were empty. Kathie was terrified, and the experience seemed too real to be a dream. "He handed me the box. I said, 'Can I have it?'" He told her she couldn't keep it, but to look at it. Then he took it from her. "What is it? What's it for?" He said, "When the time is right you will see it again. You will remember and you'll know how to use it."[21]

Upon waking, Kathie told her husband, who had slept through the visit,[22] what she had "dreamed." No subsequent information was revealed about the meaning of the cryptic statements made by the visitors regarding the box, not as of the writing of the book *Intruders*, anyway. I listened to Kathie, a pseudonym for Debbie, just a few evenings ago on a radio program. She has published subsequent books that detail her continuing interactions with her visitors.

USOs AND UNDERWATER EXCURSIONS

Through hypnotic retrieval Ed Walters came to believe that his dream of flying through the air and into the water was a suppressed memory of an abduction and "joyride." It is interesting to me that in my interviews of the investigators of the Gulf Breeze sightings, this dream phenomenon was largely ignored. If the abduction and joyride actually did occur, it is significant that Walters describes that the UAP went into the water and beneath the surface of the ocean floor into the

---

21. *Intruders*, 14.
22. It is common in bedroom encounters for the spouse to sleep through the incident, no matter how much conversation occurs, or how much the victim attempts to wake the spouse.

sand.[23] One of Walters's previous missing-time episodes occurred while he was in a canoe on the coastline. On that occasion he saw a green glow under the surface of the water and air bubbles just off the bow of his canoe. The next thing he knew, six hours had passed, and his sandwich was stale. Significantly, many abductees relate experiences of being taken beneath the water to underground or undersea complexes. Even if the explanation for UAP lies in a realm other than reality, it is fascinating that this sort of congruency exists between the accounts of so many otherwise unrelated encounters and reports.

Many other observers in the Gulf Breeze, Florida, area reported seeing UAP flying into the water. In fact, UAP flying in and out of the water has been a fairly common phenomenon for decades. If these UAP can be traced to the ocean floors, and even beneath the sandy bottoms or deep underwater caves and other entrances, researchers would do well to expand their search to those areas as possible Earth bases of "extraterrestrials," or places of origin for terrestrial UAP.

Is it possible that people are being taken against their will for hours at a time, and most don't even realize it? Are reproductive experiments being conducted? Are there underwater or subterranean bases or civilizations where nonhuman creatures live? This appears to be what the phenomenon is revealing to us—and not just a few, but thousands. Is it an actual occurrence or a psychic projection—theater of the mind delivered by demonic messengers? We don't know. All we know for sure is that the phenomenon is presenting itself to us in these terms. One way or another, if a Church member or friend is suffering from any of these experiences, I highly recommend going straight to the bishop to get priesthood leaders involved and getting assistance. Although I can't say for sure what type of assistance or relief priesthood leaders can render, I know that they are endowed with special powers of discernment to try the spirits, and help determine the best course to discover the true source of the issues being faced, and bring the Lord's power and blessings to bear. Many Church members have been so blessed already.

---

23. *The Gulf Breeze Sightings*, 161.

CHAPTER 11

High Strangeness and the Extraterrestrial "Message"

Having discussed at length the scriptural teaching that human life exists in exponential quantities in our universe, it would be easy to assume that the hundreds of thousands of UAP reported in our earthly skies are humans from any one of many billions of planets created by our own Savior. Or, are they from other sources? It is clear that the UAP phenomenon is not just a great hoax being perpetrated on society by joy seeking liars. The US government and military admit that there's something unknown to them flying in our skies. If these UAP aren't ours, or Russian or Chinese—and that seems pretty clear—then it's really important for us to learn whose they are and what they're doing here. No one seems to know who is behind UAP appearances and why they are appearing with such frequency at this time. Some answers to these questions may be found in what contactees and abductees report they are being told by the UAP occupants themselves—the UAP "message." It is important for us to understand this message in light of the gospel truths that we know to be verified by our Heavenly Father. Although there is some broad latitude within the gospel of what may apply to those not of our planet, the "big picture" concepts can only be stretched so far until reaching the breaking point—at which point we know we are hearing a deceptive message, and must begin to discern the source of that deception.

HIGH STRANGENESS AND THE EXTRATERRESTRIAL "MESSAGE"

EARLY CONTACTEES

In the early decades of the UAP "invasion," there were those who came to the fore with tales of extraterrestrial contact, bearing messages of inter-galactic peace and earthly holocaust if we failed to heed the UAP message. These "contactees" were generally thought to be crackpots, and they still are. Their messages were so unbelievable, and their demeanor so incredible, that the public found no reason to heed their message. However, as implausible as it may seem, it could well be that these contactees were accurately reporting their perceived experiences. The most important question is, who contacts the contactees?

The first of these galactic messengers was a Polish immigrant, George Adamski (1891–1965), who called himself Professor G. Adamski. Adamski wrote science fiction space books, and in *Flying Saucers Have Landed* (1953), he claimed to have seen his first UFO in October of 1946. He claimed he saw 184 UFOs in a single night in August of 1947, coming and going at will, streaking busily through the California night skies. Adamski wrote of flying saucer rides to the planets in our solar system, including the dark side of the moon with its rolling green hills and small villages hidden from our view. He further claimed to have encountered many Venusians who looked like humans. Adamski's Venusian friends claimed to be quite concerned about radiation leaking from Earth's atmosphere. The alien elder philosopher, The Master, discussed many galactic concerns with Adamski, the major consideration being Earth's perilous threat of destroying itself and nearby planets by its tinkering with nuclear power. The Venusians further explained that they lived among humans and monitored us thoroughly. The aliens explained that Jesus Christ had been their spokesman at one time—and now Adamski was selected to bear the universal message of our "space brothers."

Another early contactee, Orfeo Angelucci, published his *Secret of the Saucers* in 1955. The message was wholly spiritual by now, containing prophecies complete with deadlines. His space brother mentor, or contact, gave him interplanetary revelation. Angelucci rode in a flying saucer, met Neptune, and received a mystical revelation, filling him with mystical knowledge. He met with Jesus once, who explained that the extraterrestrials are here to help us, announcing that "this is the beginning of the New Age" (remember, this was over sixty years ago.) Aliens explained to him that in a former life (yes, reincarnation), he had been one of the space brethren from another planet. He prophesied a major world catastrophe by 1986.[1]

Another 1950s contactee, Howard Menger, saw his first alien, a beautiful blond woman, in 1932, and was repeatedly contacted throughout his life. It was easy to spot the men he explained—they had long blond hair too. He always described an overwhelming aura of love and harmony when in the presence of the aliens. These space brothers told him that many early Earth civilizations had been contacted by them and had received superior knowledge and technology from them, most of which was lost in ancient wars.[2]

In 1954, George King,[3] a London taxi driver with a background in the occult, heard a voice while washing dishes. The voice told him, "Prepare yourself, you are to become the voice of Interplanetary Parliament." King founded the Aetherius Society and slipped into public trances, during which he acted as a medium for interplanetary communications. King revealed how he had traveled to many planets, fought a mega-battle in space, and conversed with many beings on different planets—including Master Jesus, who lives on Venus.[4]

PUBLIC REJECTION OF EARLY CONTACTEES

The public backlash was severe against the early contactees, generating general disdain for any person claiming to have seen an alien—or anyone claiming more than one UAP encounter of any kind. Although the public could accept that UAP sightings were truly occurring, the claim that UAP contain alien pilots was insurmountable to most. A few self-proclaimed contactee/ messengers are still to be found, preaching that they are the chosen vessels of intergalactic spirit bulletins, but most current contact with extraterrestrial entities is accomplished through New Age channelers—most of whom have at least one alien

---

1. *Phenomenon: Forty Years of Flying Saucers*, 126
2. Ibid., 126–28.
3. Not to be confused with the other Londoner, King George.
4. *The UFO Phenomenon*, 78–79.

in their repertoire. The following messages from extraterrestrials to New Age channelers are representative of those published by the thousands in New Age literature: "I am one of these Advanced Spiritual Beings. I have come from a very high spiritual world called Aries" (Uriel, through Ruth E. Norman of the Unarius Foundation). "Will you agree to be the savior of the world?" (Ashtar, to American contactee Allen-Michael Noonan). "I, Raymere, transmit once more upon this occasion in order to speak with you about the things of the next period of time . . . you will find that you are moving into a higher frequency wherein there is a totally new dimension" (Raymere, a space being, through Alenti Francesca at the Solar Light Retreat).[5]

The very interesting portion of the Raymere communication to me is the "moving into a higher frequency wherein there is a totally new dimension" aspect. As these space brother channelers developed their shtick, raising "vibrational rates" became paramount in their veneration circles. We see in a survey of the UAP contactee literature, an ever-increasing emphasis of Eastern religious beliefs and practices, which happened to parallel the Eastern mystic movement in the hippie, experimental and psychedelic drug culture and general crackpot communities of the 1960s and 1970s. The mantra among all of these was the raising of consciousness and vibrational levels—in a person's own body and being and in the earth generally. I don't mean to suggest that elevating one's personal awareness and consciousness is negative. In fact, that is the very goal of the gospel of Jesus Christ. Through personal study and prayer, combined with personal righteousness and reaching out to bless the lives of others, we become more attuned to the Holy Spirit and more sensitive to His communications, and are filled in greater abundance with the Light of Christ. Eastern meditation, chanting, and invoking the mantric names of false deities, however, does nothing to elevate our spirits or commune with the Father of Light. If anything, there is every evidence that those practices invite unwanted spiritual predators.

---

5. *Phenomenon: Forty Years of Flying Saucers*, 365–66.

CONTACTEES—THE NEXT GENERATION

Although the first wave of galactic gurus has come and gone, leaving in their wake a feeling that rainmakers have beat the drums, fired the cannons, and sold a little snake oil, a new breed of messengers has appeared on the horizon. They are the abductees discussed herein who have not chosen to be contacted, who do not appear to seek their contactee status but who have been given a message for the world just the same. They deliver that message repeatedly, in books, magazines, articles, television and radio programs, and movies around the world, reaching billions with their messages of galactic salvation.

BETTY ANDREASSON LUCA— REPEATED ENCOUNTERS WITH A MESSAGE

According to Raymond Fowler, longtime UAP investigator and author, the actual events that make up a UAP abduction constitute the components of a composite UAP message. As we examine such events in greater detail, this theory becomes quite feasible. In his book *The Watchers*, subtitled, "The Secret Design Behind UFO Abductions," Fowler documents the case of Betty Andreasson Luca,[6] who for decades was reportedly abducted by UAP. Her case includes many of the experiences reported by others as discussed in this section, with the added dimension of being given a time-capsulized, piecemeal message to deliver to humanity. The message given to Betty Luca is being simultaneously implanted and released in the minds of many others around the world.

Betty Luca is described as a woman having "a deep and exceptional beautiful Christian faith." I emphasize the Christian element for the dual purpose of eliminating the probability of a New Age conspiracy in which Betty may be consciously or unconsciously involved to preach a satanic

---

6. Fowler has written three books chronicling this case. The first was phase one, *The Andreasson Affair*, and the second, *The Andreasson Affair: Phase Two*. Subsequent to each of the first two books the subject, Betty Andreasson (Luca), experienced surges of memory recall as "time-capsule" messages were unlocked in her programmed memory, and as she was further abducted. Fowler assumes he has written the last book on this case, believing that all has finally been revealed. I doubt it.

doctrine, and to alert the reader that Betty's experiences were interpreted by her as "religious" in nature—at least initially. An added dimension to the Christian aspect of Betty's experiences is that she often sought divine protection at the beginning of many of her encounters, to no avail.

Betty's first encounter with the small Grays was at the age of seven. She recounts, under hypnosis, in the persona of a seven-year-old girl, what happened to her on that occasion.

> I'm sitting there eating some crackers looking at the blue flowers outside the hut, and I'm waitin' for Didi to come over and play. And then all of a sudden I see a bumblebee or something, but it's bright light and it keeps on circling my head. Maybe it's after my crackers. But it keeps on going round my head and then it stuck there. . . . It was cold and it was making me fall backwards and I felt very sleepy. I'm lying on the ground there and I hear something. There is a squiggly feeling in my head, and there is a voice speaking to me. There is a lot of them, but all talking together. And they are saying something. They have been watching me, and uh, I'm coming along fine. And they're talking to me and telling me that I'm making good progress . . . and they were getting things ready. But it won't be for a while . . . about five years or so. I would be twelve. They would see me later.[7]

Another session covering this same experience offers a little more detail: "It's coming to a time that I will know the One. . . . They're going to show me something . . . that everybody will be happy about . . . that everybody will learn something from. . . . They just want to look me over from the inside. They tell me I'm going to be very happy soon . . . that I'm going to find the One. I will feel the One." This emphasis of the One is an overriding component of many encounters.

The phenomenon of many voices speaking in unison is quite common in telepathic UAP occupant communication. It is also common in cases of demonic possession, as we see in the Bible: "My name is Legion: for we are many" (Mark 5:9). Betty learns from the chorus of voices that they have observed her, that they are making preparations for some great event, and that she would be ready for the event in about five years, at the

---

7. *The Watchers*, 7–8.

age of twelve.[8] An important component of the event is to go somewhere to know, find, and feel "the One." Another component is to see something that will make everyone happy, an event instructive to everyone.

Betty experienced a second encounter, as promised, when she was twelve.[9] She recounts that while playing in the woods, she encountered a small Gray in a high-tech-looking uniform. Having no conscious recollection of her previous encounter, and not knowing what the ugly little fellow was, she did the appropriate thing: "I took some of those stones out of my pocket. I thought it was an animal coming out. I started to throw stones at it, and, ah!—The stones hit something and stopped in midair and just fell down!" Betty heard the same voices say that she would not be ready for another year.[10] "They said I will learn about the One. They said they are preparing things for me to see."[11] On this occasion Betty appears to have been one year premature when being checked by the beings. Premature for what? Who was the One? It smacks of the occult, with false galactic Messiah overtones. By the time of Betty's next encounter a year later, Betty had become a young woman, achieving sexual maturity. Apparently, this had something to do with an event for which things were being prepared. She would now be ready to meet the One.

At the age of thirteen, following an impulse, Betty got up early one morning while her family slept and went to explore near the pond. She saw a "huge moon" coming over the hill toward her. It became "bigger and bigger" as it came toward her. She tried to run but was paralyzed. She next found herself inside a white room feeling "very relaxed,"

---

8. Although I don't consider myself a contactee, or anything special—my encounter with the small, wrinkled man wearing the overcoat, dark glasses and fedora in my family's driveway was somewhat similar to Betty's. The man told me 1) they had been watching me, 2) there would be great events in the future, 3) I would be prepared in some way to participate in these events. Of course, I have little doubt about the source of that message, so I give it very little thought. However, the implication of my own message was that I would be a leader of my people and would lead them through the difficulties, which is always a flattering assertion. We see how people may be led down the path of the pied piper when puffed up with such visionary offers of grandeur.
9. This was in 1949, before UAP sightings became prolific.
10. *The Watchers*, 8–9.
11. Ibid., 331.

watching as two small Grays floated toward her a few inches off the floor. They said, "We're going to take you home." Betty responded, "I *am* home!" And they said, "Don't fear, don't be afraid, you're alright."

Betty was placed onto a soft "cushion-like mat on the floor of a section of the craft that was roofed by a large transparent dome. A mouthpiece was installed that kept her tongue held down." The craft accelerated at high velocity and after a time entered water and descended to an underground complex. In the facility, Betty went through a museum of time with glass cases containing human replicas in the garb and natural habitat of various historic periods of the Earth. She next underwent a physical examination. She was then told, "You're getting closer to home," and was taken to a clam-shell-looking device with mirrors inside, which she was instructed to get into. It closed and opened a moment later. She found herself in a different place made of a glass-like substance. She was shown glass-like replicas of animals and plants that were quite unusual: "And I'm reaching out to touch a butterfly and when I did, it's fantastic! It's beautiful! There's all color coming into the butterfly now, and it's flying around and around. When I touched it, it got color and lived and it's flying . . . And I said, 'But why did it turn color and fly away when I touched it?' He told me that I will see when I get home. He said, 'Home is where the One is.'"[12]

Again, Betty asked how they could do these things, and relates the response: "He told me that I will see when I get home. It is for me, they said, for me to go home to see the One. He said, 'Home is where the One is.' He says, 'We are drawing closer to home where the One is.'"[13] All these references to the One and going home were obvious attempts to make Betty understand that she had a close kinship to whatever awaited her—a close kinship to the place and the personage of the One. After being "transported" to this place called home, Betty was taken to a Great Door: "He says: 'Now you shall enter the door to see the One.' And I'm standing there and I'm coming out of myself! There's two of me! There's two of me there! . . . It's like a twin. But it's still, like those people I saw in those, those ice cubes [glass cases in the museum]."[14]

---

12. *The Watchers*, 333.
13. Ibid., 146.
14. *The Watchers*, 11.

This phenomenon being experienced by Betty is known as an out-of-body experience (OBE). It is the ultimate spiritual experience in the occult/New Age philosophy. Investigators have come to feel that many of these abduction experiences may be taking place in an altered state of consciousness, induced by the entities, or in another dimension of existence, where the regular laws of physics have little meaning to the observer. We must be open to the possibility that these are spiritual experiences as well—visitations and psychic downloads of the unholy ghost.

Upon entering the Great Door during this OBE, Betty recounted under hypnosis what she was able to tell. Raymond Fowler reports that during this portion of the hypnotic session that "a rapturous, beatific expression of pure, unrestricted happiness came over her face as she apparently met . . . the One." Betty would not or could not describe what happened next. She attempts: "It's—words cannot explain it. It's wonderful. It's for everybody. I just can't tell you this. . . . There's two of me there . . . and the little person is saying: Now you shall enter the Great Door and see the glory of the One. I went in the door and it's very bright. I can't take you any further. [Q. Why?] Because . . . I can't take you past this door. [Q. Why are you so happy?] It's just, uh, I just can't tell you about it . . . It's—Words cannot explain it. It's wonderful. It's for everybody. I just can't explain this. I understand that everything is one. Everything fits together. It's beautiful!"[15]

Whatever Betty was experiencing, it was beyond her ability to describe to investigators. The experience is very much like the mystical experiences professed by gurus and other initiated spiritualists. It also is very much like near-death experiences (NDE) that we read about in ever-increasing volumes. Such NDE accounts should be viewed with a discerning eye, because not every being of light is sent from God.[16] The "glory" of the One will one day be experienced by all, Betty perceives. Her encounter reminds us of a counterfeit of the "sacred embrace" of

---

15. *The Watchers*, 144.
16. And no marvel; for Satan himself is transformed into an angel of light (2 Corinthians 11:14).

ancient Egypt,[17] better defined for our benefit as the encounter with the gatekeeper, the Holy One of Israel.[18] She gains the ultimate spiritual insight that "everything is one" and that "everything fits together." Although this in itself is an eternal truth, it is also very much a part of the "all is one and one is all" tenet of the New Age/occult religion. Many experiencers report an overwhelming feeling of love and fulfillment during these encounters. It appears that the beings are able to stimulate that portion of the brain to generate the ecstatic effect.

After leaving the One, Betty returned through a tunnel and went back through the Great Door. "Okay, I'm outside the door and there's a tall person [human] there. He's got white hair and he's got a white nightgown on and he's motioning me to come there with him. His nightgown is, is glowing and his hair is white and he's got bluish eyes. And it's bright out here, and I think I see two more of them over there. [Q. Do they look like people?] Um, but tall. They are real tall and they got some ferns or something in their hands."[19] Betty was introduced through the Great Door by small Grays, but upon exiting the door she was received by what she considered to be angelic humans following her encounter with the One. In Betty's accounts, as well as those of hundreds of others, these angelic humans are often seen in close proximity to small Grays and appear to direct the small Grays.

Betty was transported through the clamshell device as before and was received at the other end by the small Grays. At that point Betty was taken to another examination room where she was floated up on a square table. To her horror Betty sobs in pain as she recounts how the beings removed one of her eyes, implanted a small round object behind it, and placed a long needle up her nose and implanted a BB-like object with tiny spines protruding from it up her nasal cavity in the classic membrane penetrating fashion. Although the nose implant is common in abduction literature, the object behind the eye is less common—but reported. Betty describes a sophisticated procedure as the round unit

---

17. Hugh Nibley, *The Message of the Joseph Smith Papyri, An Egyptian Endowment*, 241–53.
18. 2 Nephi 9:41–42.
19. *The Watchers*, 150.

is implanted and tested. The implication is that all of Betty's sensory organs were wired for continuous monitoring by the beings. So much for angels communicating through the medium of the Holy Ghost.

When Betty was twenty-four, she had what she terms a "religious" encounter with the beings. While mopping and singing hymns, she heard a strange noise. Despite having children napping alone in the house, she walked outside and into the woods without volition. She struggled up a nearby hill, slipping on pine needles and climbing over rocks.

> There's a strange being standing over there and I'm afraid of it. It's staring at me, and I can't move! Oh, Jesus be with me! He's telling me [telepathically] that I have been watched since my beginning. I shall grow naturally, and my faith in the Light will bring many others to the Light and Salvation because many will understand and see. . . . He has been sent and I am not to fear. The Lord is with me and not to be afraid. They are pleased because I have accepted [Christianity] on my own. I am to go through many things and that love will show me the answers because I have given my heart over to love the Son. Many things shall be revealed to me. Things that I [eyes?] have not seen . . . ears have not heard . . . I shall suffer many things . . . but will overcome them through the Son. I have been watched since my beginning. I shall grow I naturally and my faith in the Light will bring many others to the Light and Salvation because many will understand and see. The negative voices don't like it. [They] are against man . . . bad angels that wanted to devour man . . . hurt man . . . destroy man . . . because they are jealous . . . of the love that is upon man. Telling me strange things . . . I don't know what they're about. . . . That for every place there is an existence. That every thing has been formed to unite. [He says] Jesus is with me. . . . He says, "Peace be with you as it is."[20]

It is interesting that as Betty perceives the danger of her encounter, even though she is mentally tranquillized by the small Grays, her first thought, or prayer is, "Oh, Jesus, be with me!" At this point, the message becomes highly religious in nature, almost like a visitation from a heavenly being. The message is compound: the beings have "watched" Betty

---

20. Ibid., 334–35.

from infancy; they are pleased she has accepted Christianity; her faith in the Light will bring many others to the Light and salvation; there exist evil alien forces, "bad angels" who are jealous of mankind and seek our destruction; and, although Betty will undergo severe hardship, her faith in Jesus will pull her through. That is a message that most of us would feel very wary of, but Betty is not well steeped in a knowledge of the gospel and of the types of angels and messengers, and how to test them.

According to the account, Betty was again abducted by the beings and taken to a distant planet. As she traveled between her two abductors along a high trestle, she entered a beautiful crystalline structure to witness a Phoenix legend enactment. There is much light and heat, and Betty cries out for help and writhes in agony. Soon the temperature drops and Betty is able to squint her eyes open. The bird is gone, and a small remaining fire dwindles into embers and ashes, from which emerges a "big fat worm." After this Betty heard a "thundering chorus of voices blended together as one mighty voice" calling her by name and asking, "You have seen and you have heard. Do you understand?" To which Betty responded, "No, I don't understand what this is all about, why I'm even here." The voice instructed, "I have chosen you." Betty again asked, "For what have you chosen me?" The voice answered, "I have chosen you to show the world."[21] Betty felt that the voice was that of God Himself. Although she did not see Him, she was sure it was He. Betty professed her belief in Jesus Christ at this time, to which the voice responded that her fervent belief was the reason she had been so chosen.

As Betty was returned to her rural home where her family was tranquilized and unaware of her disappearance, "Quazgaa," her escort, gave her parting paternal counsel:

> And he says, "Child, you must forget for awhile." He says my race won't believe me until much time has passed, our time. . . . They say they love the human race. And unless man will not accept, he will not be saved. He will not live. All things have been planned. Love is the greatest of all. They do not want to hurt anybody. But, because of great love . . . they cannot let man continue in the footsteps that he is going. It is better to lose some than all.

---

21. Ibid., 339.

They have technology man can use. It is through the spirit but men will not search out that portion. Man is not made of just flesh and blood. He keeps telling me of different things. Of what is going to take place, what is going to happen. They are going to come to the earth. Man is going to fear because of it. He says that he had had others here and many others have locked within their minds, secrets. And he is locking within my mind certain secrets. And they will be revealed only when the time is right.[22]

Betty's next encounter is at the age of thirty-six. Her abductors are somewhat smaller than the last and are clad in silver suits instead of blue with Phoenix emblems. Betty is kidnapped from her bedroom, unable to wake her sleeping husband, and screaming: "Go away! Go away! Lord Jesus! Lord Jesus! Make it go away. Whatever it is, Lord Jesus." It does not go away. At the moment Betty's blanket is pulled off of her, she becomes sedated. She feels a "pinching" sensation as the beings touch her arm.[23] She is floated through the house between two aliens, and into a light below a UAP. Suddenly, they are in the UAP. Betty found the beings doing something to an East Indian woman, and she attempted to calm her. To Betty's horror, the beings removed two hybrid fetuses from the woman and placed them in a liquid-filled incubator. "They're standing in—front—of a glass case. And there's another baby there. A fetus. It's very tiny. And it's just laying there inside this liquid. And—But its eyes, they've circumcised the lids. They circumcise the eyelids of those babies and their eyes look so strange. [Betty describes the interior of the 'nursery.'] They're telling me they have to do this. And I'm saying 'Why do you have to do such a terrible

---

22. Ibid., 339–40.
23. It is noteworthy that many abductees report that when touched on the arm by the small Grays they feel a pinching sensation. This subject arises in my mind with regard to whether or not these small Grays are physical beings, or mere projected apparitions given minor, counterfeited physical qualities. The latter seems improbable because of other reports of being touched by the small Grays (rubbing the temples of examinees and so on). However, it is possible that even these manifestations of a physical makeup can be counterfeited, as discussed below. The pinching sensation could result from the purported fact that the little fellows only have three digits on a hand, and pinch their victims inadvertently.

thing?' And one of them is saying 'We have to because as time goes by, mankind will become sterile. They will not be able to produce.'"[24]

THEY ARE THE WATCHERS

According to the beings, this is the entire purpose behind their accelerated visitation and abduction program. Mankind will soon become sterile and unable to multiply. They, therefore, have the duty of preserving the genetic code of the race on their UAP until after the holocaust that renders mankind sterile. This explanation is flawed, however, as demonstrated in Betty's description of what follows:

> And they're really pleased with, with this little thing because its eyes are big and black when they cut the lids—like theirs. And they said that the splicing took good on this one. And they're telling me that mankind gets so upset when they take the seed. And, really, the very first part that man and woman, when they came together, was to bring forth—was not for their pleasure, but to bring forth. And mankind keeps on spilling the seed of life over and over again. And they cannot understand why man gets so upset when they take the seed.[25] And they're telling me that they're doing this because the human race will become sterile by the pollution and the bacteria and the terrible things that are on the earth. They're telling me that they have extrapolated and put their protoplasm in the nucleus of the fetus and the paragenetic. . . . And, they are taking the seeds so that the human form will not be lost.[26]

If they are "taking the seeds so that the human form will not be lost," why are they concentrating on creating a hybrid line from their own genetic stock mixed with ours? Many cases demonstrate that either small Grays or hybrids are being produced from these genetic experiments—not human babies, although there is some evidence that some human children are being bred to work with the small Grays. Even if the events as represented are occurring, the stated underlying reasons

---

24. *The Watchers*, 24–25.
25. Ibid., 28.
26. Ibid.

are obvious lies. Next, Betty comments that they are now working on the second fetus taken from the woman, and the hypnotist asks Betty, "Do the beings have blood?" "No. They said they utilized the blood and tissue and nutrients that are there and the form and the fetus for the growth of the new creature. And some females [alien females] just don't accept the protoplasma all together. So, they grow and use them to carry them, to carry other fetuses but they are very weak and cannot be artificially inseminated like humans. [Q. What happens to the fetus? Do, do they keep it there, or?] The fetuses become them—like them. They said they're Watchers . . . and they keep seed from man and woman so the human form will not be lost."[27]

The abductors say they are Watchers. These Watchers are preoccupied with creating babies. These Watchers don't have blood. And finally, "The fetuses become them—like them." Although obviously significant, we can only guess at the purported meaning of this latest pronouncement. In its simplest interpretation, the statement indicates that female aliens have come to have difficulty reproducing, and the alien race is propagated by using human women as surrogate mothers—living incubators. But why the hybrid children instead of pure alien? Their response is that "they keep seed from man and woman so the human form will not be lost." Because this explanation does not fully answer the question, perhaps a more complex interpretation is in order.

A complex, yet literal interpretation of the statement is, "The highly spiritual nature of the creatures allows the transmigration of the creatures' spirits from the older, weaker bodies to the younger, genetically improved bodies." With this explanation we literally say that "the fetuses become them." Such an explanation could also account for the longevity touted by the creatures. This latter explanation is quite disturbing—almost as disconcerting as the underlying, simple explanation to the entire phenomenon—they conduct their operation to obtain bodies; something that they cannot do without our help. This explanation is frighteningly reminiscent of "bad angels," who desperately seek bodies, which have been denied as a result of their rebellion in heaven. Of course, Betty's rapid addendum "like them" could soften the impact of the assertion, but even this does not

---

27. Ibid., 48–49.

answer the question, why hybrids instead of pure humans or pure aliens?

As Betty was readied for high velocity travel, she was placed into a simple standup kind of seat. "Who are they?" she asked a being. "I was trying to ask him. He says that they are the caretakers of nature and natural forms—The Watchers. They love mankind. They love the planet earth and they have been caring for it and man since man's beginning. They watch the spirit in all things. Man is destroying much of nature. They are curious about the emotions of mankind. [Q. Do they have emotions?] Not like man. [Q. But, didn't he say they love the earth?] It is not the same emotion. It is a forever love—constant, continual. And they are the caretakers and are responsible. And this is why they have been taking the form of man. [Q. How, how long have they been taking the form of man?] For hundreds and hundreds of years. . . . He's saying that they have collected the seed of man male and female. And they have been collecting every species and every gender of plant for hundreds of years."[28]

They are the Watchers, the Caretakers—they have been caring for the Earth and man since man's beginning. This is such an extraordinary assertion that it warrants discussion. For instance, of which beginning do they refer? If they allude to an evolutionary beginning in our remote past, they have hung around for a long while. If they refer to the transplanting of Adam and Eve from another world, the period would be 6,000 years.[29] If this is their claim, it would be difficult to

---

28. Ibid., 119.
29. If this is their claim, we might be tempted to add to the 6,000 years of the Earth's temporal existence the time that Adam spent in the Garden of Eden, however long it may have been. However, there exist indications that the Earth was not brought to this location in space, and set in its orbit around our sun until after the fall of Adam. This assertion is supported by Abraham's comment that while Adam and Eve were in the Garden of Eden "that it was after the Lord's time, which was after the time of Kolob; for as yet the Gods had not appointed unto Adam his reckoning" (Abraham 5:13). It is quite doubtful that the Watchers would have brooded over the Earth while it was still in its place of creation, probably nearer to Kolob. Also, although there are six 1,000–year periods, or dispensations of time on the earth, plus a seventh 1,000–year period, we are unsure of how long the periods are between those distinct dispensations. Also, we are unsure of how long Noah and his family were delayed during the Flood. Some ancient records indicate it was much longer than a mere year—and that Noah and the genetic bank may have actually been in stasis, off-world, for an extended period.

accept it as true without inferring that they somehow fit into the gospel plan of redemption in ways heretofore unexplained by the prophets.[30] This is true, of course, unless they are actually the satanic spirits that were cast to the Earth in the Great War in Heaven—then the prophets would have adequately explained their role. The beings' additional assertion that they watch the spirit in all things only raises the ante of the prior suppositions. Such could only come by way of assignment, or the Lord would certainly interfere. After all, it is they who claim that they are the caretakers and are responsible. If this is true, who made them responsible, and even under their own admissions, they have done a horrible job of it, because they assert the earth is in bad shape.

As we have discussed, the ancient uncanonized literature tells us that God set Watchers upon the land to teach Adam and his descendants how to live on their new planet. If true, then who were these Watchers, and what finally happened to them? And, if there were Watchers, then the same ancient texts inform us that 200 of those Watchers fell, and rebelled against God, abandoning their sacred duties, and polluting themselves with sexual infidelities with human women. They sold their miserable souls to Satan, made covenants with him, and became the enemies of humanity. And also, what of the Nephilim offspring of the Watchers and their human wives—the giants? Are any of these characters involved in the pageant that is being played out on the stage for these abducted and abused contactees? They call themselves the Watchers. They know how to read, and they follow human cultures and philosophies very closely, whoever or whatever they are, so it's safe to assume they know about the ancient legends of the Watchers. So, either they are the Watchers, or the fallen Watchers, or they are using the ruse of being the Watchers as their calling card and *bona fides*—their entrée into the spooky world of extraterrestrial visitations. This act of counterfeit, of camouflage, is something that will become more prominent in our discussion, because in the same way that Satan counterfeits being an angel of light, we see that he counterfeits every other

---

30. In making this statement I assume that the prophets would indeed know if such were the case. "Surely the Lord God will do nothing, but he revealeth his secret to his servants the prophets" (Amos 3:7)

concept and being—good and evil—thereby making any attempt to discern what is real and what is counterfeit nearly impossible.

In this regard, in a letter to Raymond Fowler, Betty communicated the following information that she had obtained concerning telepathic communications between her and a being that had abducted her from her trailer.

> Although I did not see him during the sessions, I know now that another being was left behind in the trailer as a guard against any kind of intrusion when I was taken up. I was told, through power, **they can form illusions right down to movement, heartbeat, and breathing of a person** for the sake of cover. If any outsider was to approach the trailer and look in, they would have believed the moving form on the sofa was actually me. The guard would activate the power to change the thought in the intruder's mind, to turn away. An intruder would have thought it was his natural decision and will, as not to disturb me. . . . What was revealed to me again is their power can control things for miles around to a small local spot. Something can be happening right amongst the busiest activities of a host of people and yet never be seen by some except those the beings choose to reveal it to. The beings' scanners and minds pick up any and all life forms within the immediate area of a target. They said they're keepers of form. They've been entrusted with and are responsible for the care of all natural form since the beginning. They know physically all there is to know about plant, animal, and human life forms with the exception of human emotions which often activates the free will to do as it pleases. Emotions make man unpredictable. That's why it is not the immediate vicinity in their control that concerns them, but the unexpected intrusion of someone entering the vicinity. Even though they can quickly gain control of the situation, they may be too busy to detect an invasion.

These contentions of ability to control the minds and actions of many people for a radius of several miles are extraordinary. It is interesting that Udo Wartena's visitors were unable to detect his presence, and were caught off guard as he ascended from his thirty-foot mine shaft. Evidently, they could not detect life signs through that much earth. Furthermore, if these assertions have any validity, this "intruder" difficulty could well explain how Ed Walters was able to escape abduction on the first attempt. Even he wondered if the airplane coming into the UAP's airspace didn't have a part in his narrow escape. Of course, the above statement brings to our attention another "inconsistency" or "inexplicable fact" of the Ed Walters' case—other abductees (almost universally) are of the opinion that if the UAP want to get you, there is nothing you can do to prevent abduction. We are told that they could take the president, with all of his personal and digital security, at any time, and no one would even be aware it had happened. Ed Walters, on the other hand, evidently successfully dodged and avoided UAP many times. Again, this may only have been a devised pretense of his abductors, as evidenced by the probability that Ed Walters was apparently abducted on two or three occasions of which he was unaware initially. Either way, it is all another example of a great cat-and-mouse game obviously being played by whoever is behind the UAP phenomenon. Camouflage, counterfeit, deceit, and subterfuge—a pageant presented to convey a message of massive importance to . . . well, importance to us . . . or to them.

Reports of "aliens" coming through the walls of the house to abduct people have become common. Betty Luca asked the beings how they did it and they replied, "By controlled vibrational levels. It is very simple, those structures are very loose." If true, then this vibrational manipulation of matter could explain how these feats are accomplished. Further evidence of our need to be wary is advanced in Betty's next observation.

> I asked, What did you mean "too many eyes and ears watching and listening?" He answered that—"The physical presence of eyes and ears is no concern for we control this easily. But, waves and manifestations of present energy cannot be erased. What is, is always there like grooves in the record of time. If the right tool or point is rubbed against hairlike warps and weaves, the recorded energy is artificially materialized. That is why we have to scramble the energy. When you are taken up, an excessive amount of energy will be scattered about us, masking the identity. This mask will blend and fill in any and all gaps and

weaves during transition. Stay very still during the extensity of yourself," he said.[31]

Through this exchange we not only gain insight into the nature of time (assuming that any truth exists in this statement), but we learn that what the beings are doing is being concealed from those who would look at the record inscribed in the fabric of time. This self-admitted deceit renders the acts of the beings highly suspect. If, as claimed, "They've been entrusted with and are responsible for the care of all natural form since the beginning" (not that this passive contention informs us who has entrusted them), why is it necessary to conceal their "benevolent" acts from those who may check the record of time? They are admittedly deceitful, to hide their acts from someone who is capable of checking the record. Who checks the record? Why are they afraid to be caught?[32]

Speaking of the beings' prior statements about the continuum of time, Fowler comments, "They insisted that our concept of time was localized and that time as we understood it did not really exist. The human concept of time was illusory. All is Now." Betty further related that "the future and the past are the same as today to them—Time to them is not like our time, but they know about our time—They can reverse time. 'Time with us is not your time. The place with you is localized. It is not with us. Cannot you see it?'"[33] Admittedly, the beings' professed concept of time may only be true from a technological point of view—allowing for vibrational shifts into a fifth or sixth dimension or for time travel—or, if they are actually fallen (or other) spirits, these principles may still hold true.[34] It is evident that the beings exist in our temporal plane as well as in the "other self"

---

31. *The Watchers*, 181–83.
32. It reminds us of the epic question, what hast thou been doing here?
33. *The Watchers*, 209.
34. "But they reside in the presence of God, on a globe like a sea of glass and fire, where all things for their glory are manifest, past, present, and future, and are continually before the Lord" (D&C 130:7). "Listen to the voice of the Lord your God, even Alpha and Omega, the beginning and the end, whose course is one eternal round, the same today as yesterday, and forever" (D&C 35:1)

plane simultaneously, as demonstrated during abductees' OBEs. The beings participate in the scene and interact with the OBE abductee before, during, and after the OBE. This fact gives us much to think about in our analysis of the origin and nature of the beings. Whoever or whatever they are, they don't appear to be humans who are living their temporal existence on another planet.

TRUE EXPERIENCE BUT FALSE MESSAGES?

Betty Andreasson Luca's experiences are not unlike those of numerous others. Is she lying? I believe she is relating her experiences as she perceived them. Is she hallucinating, then? If she is, they are the same hallucinations experienced by thousands, possibly millions, of others—even members of the Church.

I believe Betty. But does this indicate that I believe the message? No. I reject the message. Like the message delivered to so many abductees and contactees, Betty's message is nonsensical, internally inconsistent, and at odds with similar messages delivered to the others—and, above all, it is at odds with revealed truth. Consider the illogical and self-contradicting statements made to Ed Walters by his abductors. Why do UAP seek privacy, yet adorn their hulls with bright lights? Why do the beings block memories, only to unmistakably show themselves on other occasions? Why are no two contactees delivering exactly the same message, while the gist of their varied messages seems somewhat consistent? Why is someone going to all of this trouble to deliver an unbelievable message? Many commentators have offered their opinions. The prospects are unsettling. One former intelligence official has told me that he sees the "extraterrestrial" phenomenon as an intelligence operation, which by their very nature are always deceptive. In any intelligence operation, subterfuge and deceit are employed to trick the target into believing something or accepting something, usually with the goal of gaining power—over the subject, or over the subject's organization. In this case, the organization is humanity. The message is being spread through unofficial channels, and therefore, without official resistance, and is permeating humanity. It tells us that we are harming our planet and must change our lifestyle—which is, as always, a call to repentance that is difficult to deny. It also tells us that we are children of the "others," not of a personal Heavenly Father. It tells us that we are ready to evolve to the next level of consciousness, and that we must look to "the One" for salvation, but if we fail in this phase of our existence, we will have a fresh opportunity in our next incarnation life phase (reincarnation). In other words, the better we decipher and understand the "message," the better we discern that it is not coming from a reliable source. In fact, it appears that it is coming from a purposely deceptive source, with its own agenda for humanity.

Before analyzing the message and its source in greater depth, it may be prudent to observe the UAP/close encounter phenomenon as it affects members of the Church. It does, in fact, affect Church members. Perhaps in the next chapter we can gain further insights about its origins and goals in that light.

CHAPTER 12

Church Member Close Encounters

My missionary companion Stan Harter shared his own UAP encounter experience with me, causing me to look deeper into the Udo Wartena encounter. Until that time, I had seen many television programs and movies where aliens and UAP were depicted. I had also heard stories about UAP encounters, so I was open to the idea of extraterrestrial visitation, but I was skeptical about anyone's particular personal claims. However, I felt that testimonials from faithful members of the Church who had experienced close encounters with the unknown carried a premium—in my own thinking, anyway. So, when I began doing the research for my first book on the subject, I interviewed a number of Church members. My audience was members of the Church, so I wanted to compare those experiences with those presented in UFO encounter literature to see if there were any notable differences. We have already considered the encounters of Travis Walton and Brother Udo Wartena. We have also reviewed the high strangeness case of Steve and Dawn Hess, who contacted me about their encounters after my first book was published. Keep those in mind as we review other encounters of Church members in this chapter, and let's see if the experiences of Church members appear any different than those of the general population.

MEMBER ENCOUNTERS IN THE UINTAH BASIN

Dr. Frank B. Salisbury, a well-known LDS scientist and college professor, documented approximately eighty UAP sightings and encounters that occurred in the Uintah Basin in the late 1960s, in his book *The Utah UFO Display*. I listened to a radio program just a few days ago and was pleased as Dr. Jacque Vallee, the most respected of UAP researchers and authors, cited the excellent work of Dr. Salisbury, who graciously provided the foreword to this work. Dr. Salisbury approached the UAP enigma from a scientist's viewpoint, utilizing scientific methods, and focused his research on this region well known for its UAP and paranormal activity. In fact, Americans have become familiar with the activity in the Uintah Basin through a television program that features Skinwalker Ranch, formerly known as Sherman Ranch, which is located southeast of Ballard, Utah. Aerospace billionaire Robert Bigelow purchased the ranch and set up a team of scientists operating as the National Institute for Discovery Science (NIDSci) who studied the purported paranormal phenomena on the ranch for over a decade. These phenomena included the frequent appearance of UAP, including discs and classic black triangle craft, as well as strange creatures that were impervious to point-blank .357 magnum rounds, shape-shifting beings, poltergeist activities, cattle mutilations,[1] glowing orbs, opening and closing of dimensional portals and the use of those portals by unusual beings and craft, crop circles, inexplicably malfunctioning equipment, strange lights and fixed electromagnetic and other light beams emanating from the mesa, local temperature anomalies and many more inexplicable phenomena.

---

1. There are many aspects of UAP related phenomena not discussed at length in this work; for example, the subject of cattle mutilations. However, I feel I should share information that I received from an intelligence source. There is a security video in the government's possession that shows a cow being levitated in the air in a beam of light, and the cow is being eviscerated by an invisible means in midair as it screams in horrible agony and fear. When the dead cow was discovered in the field the next morning, the rancher found the very familiar precision incisions, the missing sexual and other organs, and lack of blood. This scenario has been repeated tens of thousands of times just in the US, and no one has ever discovered its source or purpose.

NIDS Science Advisory Board member, Colonel John B. Alexander, PhD, researcher, and author, says that the science team observed many paranormal, inexplicable phenomena but were unable to properly capture them on their instruments, so were unable to publish what they observed in scientific journals. He says, "We had openings in the sky, with noises and craft coming through—like orbs. The reality of the events is absolute."

KLAS Television reporter and author George Knapp spent time at the Utah ranch compiling a news story, which led to a book, *Hunt for the Skinwalker: Science Confronts the Unexplained at a Remote Ranch in Utah*, Colm A. Kelleher and George Knapp (Simon & Schuster, Paraview Pocket Books, 2005). He and Dr. Alexander relate a particular experience that was inexplicable to the scientists involved. Knapp begins, "Two of the scientists, Ph.D. level people, walked around the middle homestead, and two others were up on the ridge with infrared equipment, looking down. One of them with infrared saw what looked to him like a dirty snowball of light, just hovering a couple of feet off the ground. He walkie-talkied the scientists below and asked if they could see it, and they said yes, but it was a little vague. Then he said, something was happening—it was changing."

Dr. Alexander said, "Our guys were on the ridgeline looking down, and they could see a light appear above the ground, and expand." Knapp: "This ball of light was stretching out, and it became a tunnel of light. Into this tunnel comes a humanoid figure." Dr. Alexander: "Some kind of creature reached up and pulled his shoulders, and came out." Knapp: "It was around eight feet tall. It was all black and featureless. As it came out, the tunnel collapsed into the ball of light again. It was almost as if it was dimensional—like it was coming from some other reality."

This is just one of hundreds of such experiences and encounters within the broad region of the ranch. Others who lived on the ranch report seeing windows or portals open in the air up over the mesa, and UAP come flying out and float silently over the trees, then zip away like a bullet shot from a rifle. Books were written and documentaries filmed featuring many of the phenomena on the ranch, and in 2016 commercial real estate mogul and Church member Brandon Fugal purchased the ranch from Robert Bigelow. Brandon brought on a team of scientists to study and document the paranormal phenomena, and a documentary on the History Channel called *The Secret of Skinwalker Ranch* has completed its second season. The TV show features a team of scientists and experts, including Dr. Travis Taylor and Principal Investigator and Chief Scientist Erik Bard, who employ an array of science and technology sensors and equipment such as lasers, ground-penetrating radar, broad spectrum electromagnetic signal analyzers, and drone thermography as they research the property and various phenomena, attempting to explain the decades of high strangeness events. The team has documented several events already, including filming clear UAP of various types on multiple occasions. During filming of the series, the science team was running some experiments, and just after dusk, Duchesne County Deputy Sheriff and Security Team member Kaleb Bench was behind one of the buildings with the team. He heard something from around the old building and pulled his gun from his holster, turned on the attached flashlight, and pointed it in the direction of the noise. He and Dr. Taylor walked briskly around the building, and hovering in the brush just a few feet away was a rectangular object, around thirty inches long and twelve inches tall; "shimmering yellow-orange." Deputy Bench swung his gun to shine his light on the object, and as soon as the light hit it, the light reflected back at them as if it had hit a mirror, and the object vanished before them as they were looking at it. They felt fear and were shaken by the event. As they walked back toward the nearby command center, Dr. Taylor said, "Okay, I'm going to turn my video off," and immediately a bright light streaked across the sky above the ranch at high velocity—not on a downward trajectory like an incoming meteor, but on a horizontal plane, then out of sight into the distance. The team's cameras captured it as it shot across the sky.

In a Facetime interview, Dr. Taylor asked Dr. Alexander what he really thinks is going on at Skinwalker Ranch, based on his previous years of extensive scientific inquiry. He invited even speculation, if that's all that was available. Dr. Alexander replied, "I'm not even sure how to address the complexity of that. It's my view that these things are all connected in some way. I would say that the area is a portal. It's like multidimensional reality. And I think periodically the dimensions overlap—and when they do, those sorts of things that you see are just as physical as you sitting there right now. But when it separates, it's gone." Dr. Taylor then explained the nature of a portal, as they were discussing it, as a gateway that connects two distant places or times in space.

Dr. Salisbury's prior investigation of the events reported in the Uintah Basin was assisted by local investigator Joseph "Junior" Hicks, a science teacher and priesthood leader in the Uintah Basin. Junior Hicks had long collected data on such sightings, and made his materials available to Dr. Salisbury for the book. Junior Hicks continued to collect data and conduct interviews for several years with local people who have UAP encounters. Many of the people there are members of the Church, and hundreds of Church members in the area have reported UAP encounters.

Most of the UAP sightings related in *The Utah UFO Display* were from a distance. Many people saw alien-type craft hovering, darting, and examining the countryside with light beams. Except for a few anomalous events, the sightings were not unlike those reported by others. Dr. Salisbury observed that four features of the Uintah Basin sightings are essentially universal: (1) instant departure and accelerated speed with right-angle turns; (2) pulsating lights; (3) reddish-orange coloring; and (4) noiseless craft.[2] Of course, these attributes and characteristics match those of many other sightings around the world, including most of those in the UAP Task Force Report to congress of June 2021.

Dr. Salisbury notes some differences in the Utah waves of UAP sightings, however. He says, "A few features of other sightings around the world fail to show up in the data. Except for one recent sighting Junior couldn't run down, and sighting #2, which occurred three years before the current wave of Uintah Basin sightings, no UAP occupants are mentioned. Since many of the sightings included windows or transparent domes, and since in a few cases, these were even observed for long intervals of time and with binoculars, this lack of comment on occupants could be significant."[3]

---

2. *The Utah UFO Display*, 102.
3. Ibid., 104.

What is the significance? Dr. Salisbury did not comment in detail, but I believe that as a scientist he may have been thinking along the lines of drone explorer ships—unmanned specimen collectors. However, this interpretation loses some weight in light of Dr. Salisbury's notation of an apparent response by the UAP to the thoughts of witnesses.

Although no beings or occupants were seen in or near the UAP in the Uintah Basin during the sightings of the late 1960s and early 1970s, in October of 1967, during the peak of the sightings, Jay Anderson of White Rocks, reported seeing a luminous figure in his home. He says that it was just standing in the doorway in a metallic suit with a luminous glow about it. Then it turned around and just walked away.

THE UINTAH "THEATER"

Dr. Salisbury commented that there appeared to be a pattern of "theater" connected with the appearance of the UAP in the Uintah Basin. He relates:

> I, and some of the witnesses as well, couldn't help but be impressed with the idea that the UFOs wanted to be seen. Otherwise, why should they dive on Joe Ann Harris, follow Thyrena Daniels and many other cars, dance around in full view of dozens of witnesses for fairly long intervals of time, etc.? Why indeed should they execute the intricate and involved maneuvers? Why do their lights flash or change color? It is as though they were putting on a display. Often they seemed to stay around only until they could have been quite certain that they had been observed.[4]

Why indeed? It has become obvious that despite a pretense of attempting to remain unnoticed, UAP follow a pattern designed to reveal their presence. They fly through our dark night skies looking like small cities at Christmastime. As pointed out by Ed Walters, they say "photographs are prohibited," only to pose for yet another snapshot. What is the purpose behind these apparent discrepancies? As we discover later in our discussion (and as we may already have deciphered),

---

4. Ibid., 108.

the old adage "Don't believe anything you hear and only half of what you see," should be the standard by which we measure all UAP related phenomena.

AND IN THE EARTH BENEATH

Although we do not discuss most of the Uintah Basin sightings herein, the brief accounts of two sightings are included here because of their unusual aspects. In the first, Dee Hullinger recounts that a UAP was "boiling the dust" with a light beam. He describes the beam as "something like a floodlight off the bottom of a helicopter or something, but the light, when it went out, left a big glow afterwards. And it took this glow I would say about a half hour to completely disappear."[5] Dee further says that the UAP never really left from what he could tell, but seemed to disappear into the ground—although he assumed that he just failed to see it leave, due to all of the dust in the air. As he and his friends were discussing the sighting later, Dee relates that an outsider had his own version of what probably happened.

> This old boy come in the saddle shop down here. He was asking questions about this stuff, because I'd been talking to some guys about it. So I told him what I saw. He said: "Well, it buried itself in the sand!" And I said: "Well, now, what gives you that idea?" And he said: "I've seen one—I've seen it do it." And he claims that he was in a pickup somewhere in Texas. He went up on this ridge and watched this outfit—it was sandy country just like we got here. He said this thing came down, and he said it blew a thrust out the bottom of it, and he said it just dug its own hole and settled right in it, and after a minute some kind of vacuum sucked it in and covered it right up.[6]

BULLETPROOF

The second amazing report deals with two different witnesses in the Uintah Basin that reported shooting at UAP. People in the Uintah

---

5. Ibid., 87.
6. Ibid., 79–80.

Basin were much more likely to have a rifle or a pair of binoculars than a camera at that time. This unusual fact led to some very detailed observations through binoculars or rifle scopes, a rare opportunity. It also resulted in the complete absence of any photographic evidence. The possession of high-powered weapons did allow for a little good natured target practice, however. The result of shooting at the UAP was the shooters' hearing the bullets ricochet as they bounced off the metallic-appearing hulls, after which the UAP sped off. One shooter was followed home by the returning UAP—for about seventy miles.[7]

Does the first incident necessarily indicate that UAP hail from under the surface of the earth or have the ability to travel through loose soil? There are many witnesses that point to the earth and its oceans rather than space when relating which way they went. Does the second incident imply that UAP are solid metallic objects, perhaps leery of small lead projectiles? That is the implication. But why the apparent apprehension of bullets? Perhaps bullets can do damage to the hulls. After all, there have been a number of reports of crashed UAP over the decades. We hear the numbers may be up in the dozens. It begs the question, why do UAP that travel across vast distances of space, with its harsh conditions and steady stream of debris, enter our atmosphere and get knocked out of the air by lightning, radar signals, or some other natural phenomena? Of course, that assumes they come from other planets and that they travel through space rather than in fifth-dimensional antigravity nests or through wormholes. Any way you look at it, we would expect beings capable of the technologies we witness in UAP to be able to make them bulletproof.

IRENE

On September 24, 1987, Irene[8] was with her sister and received a telephone call from their mother, asking frantically if they could look up the telephone numbers of any television or radio stations in the Salt Lake City area. She wanted the stations to photograph and

---

7. Ibid., 94, 110.
8. A pseudonym for the sake of her relatives' privacy.

cover strange objects in the sky over the northern part of the Salt Lake Valley. Her mother said that she and many other people were watching floating objects in the sky, but their calls to the press weren't believed. Irene and her sister drove to their parents' house and saw the "big cigar-shaped thing just sitting up there in the air." Their parents were gone but the house was unlocked, so they quickly went in to get their father's binoculars. As they went back outside, they involved as many of the neighbors as they could find. One nineteen-year-old neighbor boy was able to get his telescope to observe the craft. To ensure that very credible witnesses were available, they got a neighbor who was a professor at the University of Utah to come and watch also. Irene telephoned her husband, who worked close by, and he and several employees went outside and watched it too. They then saw another "gold, disc-shaped craft" that flew with UAP rapid, jerking motions beside and behind the larger cigar-shaped stationary object. The large object was "silvery color, with red lines around it." Other observers agreed. The larger object appeared to spin on its horizontal axis slowly. "It looked almost as if it were rolling as it hovered," Irene said. It had "portholes." The small craft finally departed with classic UAP acceleration.

It is interesting that Irene and her family had many such encounters. Her brother-in-law and his brother and buddies reported to her that while they were in Huntington Canyon (Utah) they watched a UAP come right down over them, and they could see occupants inside of the ship. Irene, her husband, her cousin, his brother, and her two sisters also saw four of them over Mt. Olympus when they were returning from fishing one night. "We watched them, and then they were gone like that." They just disappeared. Irene's aunt and uncle, also Church members who live in Nevada, had an enormous UAP pass over their car. They report that it was so big that they couldn't see anything else when they looked out of the car windows. On their way to their ranch in Ely, Nevada, they saw an entire UAP fleet go over them. Irene relates, "My grandmother recalls seeing Bigfoot when she was younger too—and she's the closest thing to an angel that I ever knew."

The following are what I would term demonic encounters, although Irene associates them with UAP. "I had an experience where I woke up in the night and this tall being was standing at the bottom of the bed and said that he had come to get me and my baby. He telepathically communicated it to me. It happened when my first child was three months old. I knew it was a male, the way he communicated to me. I was beating on my husband—I just said, 'No! no!' My husband finally woke up, but the being was gone. He was around seven feet tall, light colored hair, dressed in white. I did not want to go. He did not seem insistent, but only told me what he wanted." When the baby was a little older, he began to report strange activities as well. "My son remembers seeing a UFO when he was little—laying out on the lawn at night—and he had never told me about it. He remembers seeing this thing over him, and then it went up. He had made a clay model of an alien in high school that I didn't even know about, and he said that's what an alien looked like. It has the big sunken eyes, and looks like other people's descriptions of them [small Grays]."

Referring to the same house where Irene and her mother had been terrorized and had possibly experienced some missing time, she recalls, "I remember my uncle sleeping there right after he got out of the service. He had gone to sleep on the couch and woke up in the middle of the night, and something was leaning right over him, looking at him. He was terrified, and pretended to be asleep. I remember many spooky things happening in that house."

Irene relates yet another experience, a bedroom encounter, which occurred in her late teens. "I remember being terrified one night, just waking up and seeing this little dark being in the doorway. My cousin (who was married the next day), across town, saw the same little figure in her doorway that same night. It was a cloaked, hooded looking, dark silhouette—about four-and-a-half feet tall." These small or gnome-like beings are being witnessed by many thousands every year. Even some of the more notable cases of extraterrestrial hauntings include small humanoids of various types.

MARGY BEAL

Margy Beal lived in the Uintah Basin and had the following experiences during the peak of the UAP sighting wave chronicled by Dr. Salisbury. Sister Beal's accounts failed to make it into his book, however, because it was later when others learned about them. Sister Beal was one of the active, productive Relief Society sisters in the Uintah Basin, and she had a very healthy attitude about her experiences.

> My daughter, Becky, and I were coming home from an honors banquet at the high school. We were about five miles outside of the town of Roosevelt—we lived twelve miles from Roosevelt—and as we came to the crest of a hill, we had noticed that there weren't any cars. After a banquet like that, there should be cars on the highway, but for some reason there weren't any cars following us or coming toward us. We had mentioned this, and when we came to the crest of a hill, all of a sudden, out in front of us was this saucer-like thing with all of these bright lights, and it was so bright that you could see the pebbles along the side of the road. . . . It was quite large, and it was like a saucer only it had a dome on the top. All around where the dome fit the saucer, it looked like windows. And under the edge of this saucer light came down really bright. It didn't seem to have light holes or anything, it just seemed like it was all light that came down toward the earth—very bright. And the noise was a whirring noise—a quite steady whirring noise, with a "whumpf, whumpf, whumpf," steadily, every once in a while. The whirring noise was not high pitched, it was rather low pitched.

The design of the UAP, and the detail about the large, bright light coming from the bottom of the craft, is quite common in reports. She continues:

> I have to get out, I need to feel the ground under me. So I stepped out . . . then I got back in and I was oriented again. I went to start the car, and this is what was so funny, is that the key was on. The car was off—it was not in park, and I do not remember ever turning the car off or anything, and the key was still turned to the 'on' position, but the motor was stopped. So I started it and we started down over the crest of the hill and that thing moved back away from us. We went about another two miles and came to the crest of another hill—and we both decided we'd get out and listen to the 'whir' that it made. And when we did it suddenly

shot off to the east and went out of sight. Then we drove through the town of Myton, and up the highway about two and a half miles. I said, "Oh, I'm sure glad we don't have that thing again," and she said, "Mom look!" And out to our right following the Duschesne river was this same thing going west as we went west. And when we arrived home, three miles from the town of Myton, Diane, my older daughter who had been watching the young children, came out and was extremely agitated and worried. She thought we'd had all kinds of troubles because we were so late. It would only take about twenty minutes to drive from Roosevelt home—twelve miles. And we were two and a half hours late. Where had we been and what had happened to us?

About six months later, Margy recounts that she was taking her mother to a Relief Society meeting one evening. Her mother had heard the girls speak of their UAP sighting and wanted to see one for herself, although she was still a little skeptical. Within about one mile of her mother's house, they came upon a UAP sitting on a little knoll about one mile away. Margy said, "Well, Mother, how about that! Take a look." Her mother was shocked as they sat there for a while watching it. They knew they would be a little late for Relief Society, but they thought it was worth it. Margy says, "All of a sudden it lifted straight up into the sky and took off to the right. It crossed about a mile in front of us, and went across the river and looked like it landed on a hill to the right of us, which would be north. The next morning the farmers went out to feed their cows, and they found three pod marks in the ground."

Some months later, in the fall of the same year, Margy and her son saw another saucer while at home. "We saw one in the sky one night and we got his rifle out and watched it through the scope. A teacher here at Roosevelt was interested, and we called him and he had a telescope, and he watched it and we watched it and we conversed over the telephone about its movements."

CARL

Carl was eleven years old and was in the alfalfa fields of his family's farm with his seventeen-year-old sister. Carl's family lived in Howell,

Utah, about fifteen miles northwest of Tremonton, and their 350–acre farm was set in the middle of a valley, about five miles wide and eight miles long, running north to south. At the south end of the valley was Thiokol plant number 78.

Carl and his sister were doing the watering at about 2:00 a.m., admiring the clear sky with its bright moon and stars. They were struck by the sudden appearance of a craft in the north end of the valley as it came over the mountains, about three or four miles away from them. It was enormous, filling almost one-third of the valley from side to side. Carl and his sister believe the UAP was about a mile in diameter. The craft was flying low—between 70 to 100 feet from the ground, they recall. It moved slowly and steadily from the north end of the valley. It made no noise at all. The two youths did their best to duck down in the alfalfa, but it was only a foot tall at that time. They jumped into an irrigation ditch that had not yet been flooded. Carl's sister reports that she prayed the entire fifteen to twenty minutes it took the craft to travel the length of the valley—prayed that it wouldn't notice them, or if it did, that it would not harm them in any way.

Carl's only memory about what he was thinking at the time was how big the craft was, how silent, how overwhelming—and how scared he was. Carl and his sister describe the craft similarly—a double convex ("like two curved plates stuck together") with a ten-foot-high mid-section separating the plates. The belt-like section around the middle had evenly spaced lights around the entire perimeter, like large holes in a belt. Carl's sister recalls that these round lights were as large as the mid-section, ten feet in diameter, and yellowish-orange in color. The lights were so bright that as the UAP came over the mountains it lit up the entire valley. Although the craft took nearly twenty minutes to pass the eight miles through the valley and was only a mile or so from them as it passed, Carl and his sister had difficulty making out any distinguishing characteristics other than the basic shape. It was more of a silhouette surrounded by the bright yellowish-orange lights, although it appeared to be completely solid and tangible in every respect. They could see that the craft was "smooth, curved with a dome," but could see no other appendages or irregular shapes attached.

The craft "floated" from north to south, making no noise at all, and continued without any deviation from its course or speed. Carl could not believe the silence associated with such a gargantuan structure. There was no wobble, no wind—nothing. It just floated in a straight course, very slowly. Carl's sister says it was "eerie."

The only change occurred when the UAP reached the south end of the valley. When it arrived at the Thiokol plant, it stopped and hovered over it. After that, the yellowish-orange lights changed their hue to a bright red, and the craft drifted up over the mountains at the south end of the valley.

This was Carl's only close sighting. It was not his sister's only sighting, however. When she was younger she experienced two other encounters. During the most recent, she and her other brother (between her and Carl in age) and some neighbor children were walking outside late one evening. Suddenly they saw three strange lights in the cloudy night sky. One light separated from the others and approached the children. As they watched, they could see that it was a saucer-shaped UAP. When the craft was only twenty feet from them, directly overhead, the children saw a panel slide open. From the open panel they saw a tubular light beam telescope its way to the ground. They instantly found themselves surrounded by bright light as they huddled together, seeing how they were lit up. The light flooded them for three to five minutes as they feared that they were being examined or that their thoughts were being read. Carl's sister was especially concerned that because she was the oldest of the children, it was her responsibility to protect them. She assumed that although her father was working in an outbuilding on the farm, he was over a mile away and would not hear their cries if they called for help.

As the children stood there huddled in the light beam, it never occurred to them to run. Carl's sister reports that her thought processes seemed to function normally, although she was terribly frightened, but she never thought to run the entire time. She says that there was no apparent physical abnormality about the light beam. It was not hot or cold, there was no smell or tingling feeling, and she did not feel paralyzed or controlled. They just assumed they were being watched by someone with a much higher capacity than we have.

After three to five minutes in the light beam, the children saw it begin to retract. It telescoped up a ways—again, as though it was a solid conduit of something with a flat end.[9] Then it "gathered itself and retracted into the UFO." When the light beam had reentered the UAP, the panel slid closed and the craft joined the other two, and together they flew off into the clouds. This was another no-noise encounter.

Years before this encounter Carl's sister had spied a "shiny basketball-looking" sphere above a neighbor's house. She watched it for twenty minutes as it floated around the house. Although she kept calling for her mother or someone else to come and look at the shiny sphere, her mother could not get away from a chore, and no one else was old enough to care. It took off in a great hurry, disappearing in the distance in a second or two.

Carl's sister relates the story of her friend who had an unusually close encounter in the valley. She was driving along in a pickup and watched a UAP come right down over her. She was especially surprised when the UAP landed right on the roof of the cab. With that, the pickup's engine died and all of the electronics went out. She experienced a blackout of her own, and when she regained consciousness the UAP was gone.

We see in the accounts of Carl and his family members many of the classic UAP themes: an area frequented by UAP; a family with multiple encounters; the classic double-convex craft with yellowish-red lights or portholes around the circumference of the hull; the UAP moved without any sound, floating along in quiet observation; and rapid acceleration at unfathomable speed. What was different about the sighting, of course, was the mammoth size of the craft. Many observers report UAP the size of football fields, or three times that size. These are thought to be very large by researchers—especially so low to the earth. A UAP approximately one mile in diameter, however, is a rare sighting indeed. One staggers at the principles of science that allow such a behemoth craft to

---

9. Several witnesses report this type of cohesive light beam that behaves more like a solid tube with a flat end as it retracts. Judi Moudy and many others have experienced a beam that appears to be more than light, and is controlled from the UAP, to where it eventually recedes.

hover silently in Earth's atmosphere just above the ground, disturbing nothing, and creating no wind or other interference. Even more incredible is the propulsion system that propels such a monstrosity from 200 feet above the ground to high orbit in a brief second or two without a whisper of a sound, without a rush of displaced air, without a sonic boom, and without overheating the craft's hull.

MARY M.

Mary,[10] an active Church member and grandmother, describes her husband as active also and very supportive of her throughout her many difficulties. Mary is concerned that her experiences not be analyzed as a demonic encounter, although her more complex experiences are in the "high strangeness" range. Though unusual, her experience "type" is not unique. Many report these bizarre types of encounters with the unknown. She relates, "In 1965, is when I saw my first ship, that I remember seeing. At that time I was in Kernville, California, on vacation. At one point I looked up and I saw this star, and it looked like it was moving. I was watching it with binoculars. It looked like it was jumping up and down, moving back and forth." Her mother saw the same thing. On the way home, she says, "We were watching the road and counting the cars, and I looked over my left shoulder at one point to see if there were any cars coming, and it looked like the moon had gone out of orbit—it was a big, huge, white, moving object, and it was moving so fast that I didn't have time to say 'Hey Mom, look!' I got 'Hey Mom' out of my mouth, and the thing was gone. And it had to travel a distance of about 35 miles in that time."

That distance in about one second is around 100,000 mph. It went behind two mountain peaks, turned around, came back, and went out of sight.

Mary was later traveling from California to Colorado. She watched a star move over Las Vegas headed toward Mesquite, Arizona. It got bigger, but she wasn't worried. Without filling in the informational gaps,

---

10. I do not use Mary's full name herein, although she permitted me to use it. I base this decision on those issues raised in the main text below.

Mary says that they eventually got under the "star," which was only 50 to 100 feet above the road at that time. "It was shaped like a flying wing in the front and was open in the back." It had protruding square things with black holes in the middle, coming from the bottom. It also had ten to fifteen lights in the front. The one-and-a-half-hour drive took them four hours, resulting in over two hours of missing time.

Years later, Mary was in bed alone in a basement bedroom. She had not fallen asleep yet, and lay listening to a clicking noise in the kitchen just above her room. She assumed it was her daughter, who was recovering from knee surgery, getting a drink. The noise continued and Mary finally got up, at about 1:30 a.m., thinking her daughter needed help with the drink of water. She went upstairs and stopped to check the front door as she passed. She also stopped in front of her daughter's bedroom as she went by, and saw no light under the door. She called through the door softly, but there was no answer. She checked the back door, because they had previously found it open after locking it and going to bed. It was locked tight, with a leaded bat positioned against it to keep it closed. When she turned around to go back, "there was this face peering around the corner from the hallway" at her. She was perplexed, thinking that someone had entered the locked house. She decided to turn on the light and go through the dining area to the living room to try to catch the intruder—but there was someone blocking her path in that direction too. She woke up two hours later in bed, with no memory of what had happened after that.

Mary describes the "people" she saw as being small and hairless, with light or pale complexions. She had no thought of aliens at the time because she had not been exposed to the phenomenon or literature. Like many others, Mary complains that the above experiences were only disjointed memories, and none of them made any sense to her until she read the book *Communion*.[11] "Then," she says, "it all hit

---

11. *Communion: A True Story* is a book by American author Whitley Strieber that was first published in February 1987. The book is based on his own experiences, including "lost time" and terrifying flashbacks, which hypnosis undertaken by Budd Hopkins later links to an alleged encounter with aliens.

me." After seeing the picture of the "small Gray" faces on *Communion* and in other UFO books, she recognized they are the same as her own intruders.

About two years before our interview, Mary began to experience the "high strangeness" encounters with UAP entities. I relate this aspect of these encounters here because it is fairly well documented that a "Bigfoot" entity is associated with many UAP/entity encounters. I feel it prudent to add that the apparent association of Bigfoot with UAP does not necessarily exclude any other explanation of the Bigfoot phenomenon. I feel that Bigfoot could be exactly what it appears to be—a species of primate that hides itself well in the forests of the world. Church member Don "Jeff" Meldrum is a well-known professor of anatomy and anthropology in the Department of Anthropology at Idaho State University. Dr. Meldrum has specialties in anatomical sciences, emphasizing biological anthropology, and specializing in vertebrate locomotion. In other words, he is a leading global expert in large primate foot structure and locomotion, and is the academic most sought out to verify or debunk Bigfoot prints. Whatever the Bigfoot creature or myth might be, Dr. Meldrum has authenticated hundreds of footprint casts as being created by a real creature—a large primate, most likely.

Other explanations could be true as well. For example, because we know that at least one Bigfoot-looking creature presented itself to Apostle David W. Patten and introduced itself as Cain, there exists the possibility that the Bigfoot species is, in fact, Cain, and the race of Cain.[12] Whatever the true nature of the Bigfoot, whatever is creating the UAP phenomenon could also be creating the Bigfoot phenomenon, especially as it relates to UAP—that is, Satan is a counterfeiter, and often tailors his false presentation based on true concepts, facts, beings, and artifacts. So, if much of the UAP phenomenon is merely a counterfeited false "presentation" based on the true principle of interplanetary intercourse, the Bigfoot/UAP phenomenon could be such a counterfeit of a true principle as well. In other words, there may be real UAP, even extraterrestrial visitors from other solar systems—but many

---

12. Lycurgus A. Wilson, *The Life of David W Patten* (Salt Lake City: Deseret News, 1900) 46–47.

UAP that Satan presents in our own environment are counterfeits of those real UAP, presented in typical half-truth fashion to lead us astray on an important issue, and take us away from the truth. The same can be said of cryptids, like Bigfoot. There may be a species of primate that are hidden deep in the forest, and the Cain that presented itself to Apostle Patten may have simply taken its form for the presentation and planted the seeds of a great Bigfoot delusion in the last days.

In fact, those deeply immersed in the occult or satanic worship, like certain ancient shamans who turned sharply to the dark side of their practices, are reported to have become shapeshifters as part of their selling their souls to Satan. In some cultures these shapeshifters are known as skin-walkers and transform between human and animal. The cost: you must sacrifice the person you love most in the world, and the only exit, once committed, is to die. Many have witnessed these transformations, and the sightings continue throughout the regions where Skinwalker Ranch is located, as well as a great deal of the Four Corners region.

I would tend to be very skeptical about such reports, but when I was in ward leadership as a young priesthood leader, the bishop of our ward shared an experience in our meeting from when he was a missionary. He was assigned to minister to Native Americans on their tribal lands and was often met with resistance by some of the tribal members. The missionaries had a car, and one evening they were driving on the main road running through the reservation. My bishop saw a small pack of young native men run out of the trees and begin chasing them as they drove. The young men had an "evil" look about them, so the missionary driving the car increased their speed, all the way up to 65 mph. The young native men kept up with them, no matter how fast they went, and were running at that top speed beside their car, snarling and laughing at them the entire time, until they left the boundaries of the reservation. My bishop explained that they learned there was a skin-walker cult on the reservation, and these young men had obviously been initiated into it—at a terrible personal cost. I recently heard Navajo Nation Ranger Lieutenant Jonathan Dover explaining that his tribal police department had experienced similar encounters: "I spent 31 years in law enforcement, and we had many, many incidents where people have seen them chasing their vehicles, as their vehicles were traveling at 60 to 65 miles per hour—having a human figure running behind you. I've had police officers arrest people and have them in handcuffs, and when they get to the station—they hadn't stopped anywhere—that person is gone."

I've listened to hours of reports by Lieutenant Dover, a federally trained law enforcement professional, who investigated hundreds of reports from native people about skin walkers and Bigfoot creatures often being seen in the vicinity of UAP, and the small occupants coming from the craft. Many of those reports included seeing UAP flying into the sides of mesas or mountains and disappearing. The native people think of UAP and their attendant "creatures" as being extra-dimensional, instead of extraterrestrial, and that they enter through portals from parallel worlds.

Back to Mary. On the first occasion, Mary woke up from a sound sleep feeling someone gently holding her hand. She thought it was her husband until she saw his back turned toward her. She opened her eyes and saw "this big, hairy thing sitting beside me on the bed, holding my hand. I'm not usually a screamer, but that night I decided to scream!" It scared him, and he ran down the hallway and into the family room. Her husband did not wake up. She lay there the rest of the night watching for the thing to return through the hallway—to come back to the bedroom or exit the house—but it never returned. When it became light outside, she went down the hallway to see, but nothing was there in the family room.

Two weeks later Mary had surgery and woke up to find her hand being held again—by the same gigantic hand as before. Due to her soreness, she decided not to risk being jolted by a fleeing creature, so she lay quietly, not resisting. Around the first of December Mary woke up to use the bathroom. It was cold, so she cuddled up behind her husband when she returned to bed. Within five minutes she felt something moving across the bed, and two large hands moving beneath her. She was lifted out of bed, and assuming it was this same Bigfoot creature, she peeked just enough to confirm it. He lifted her gently and stepped back a few feet, and they rose right up through the floors and ceiling. She closed her eyes, and although she felt herself "moving up," she did not feel anything as they moved through the floors or ceiling.

Mary remarks, "When he picked me up I decided it was a good time to pray. I didn't know whether Satan had me, which was a distinct possibility." She remembers nothing between going up and coming down, but she does remember going up and coming down. When he returned her he put her back into bed and held her hand again. She thought it wrong for a married woman to have her hand held like this, so she gently pulled it away—nicely enough, or so she thought. "But he evidently took it the wrong way, and he had to prove a point—that he was capable of hurting me if he wanted to, but didn't want to—and he jumped on top of me [straddled], and I have never seen anything move that fast."

At this point I pointed out that Bigfoot reportedly weighs up to a half ton, and she responded that "he didn't put his weight on me, he just pinned me to the bed. When he did so, his front teeth, whether it was in a mask or whether it was his own I don't know, but the teeth hit me in the forehead and my head hurt for three days afterwards where the teeth had hit."

These Bigfoot apparitions continued, even up through the time of our interview, and Mary perceived that she had been repeatedly carried to a craft, where she was given tasks to accomplish. Her experiences are filled with vivid detail—again, not unlike those of other experiencers of the UAP and abduction phenomenon. Mary and I discussed many possible sources of her experiences, including dream sequencing, hallucinations, mental disorders or diseases, and spiritual abuse. She was cognizant of these possibilities and had considered them in turn many times. I thought about things, and suggested that some kind of surreptitious monitoring might help her to establish what was occurring. Mary responded that it would not work, and anyone who attempted such a thing would risk serious harm. She said this, however, believing her abductors to be essentially benevolent, although she knew some were "evil."

CHURCH MEMBER ENCOUNTERS ARE SIMILAR TO OTHERS

I believe that the Church member close encounters included herein are representative of those being experienced by thousands of Church members—perhaps many more. From distant sightings of zig-zag lights in the night sky, to personal encounters with UAP beings bearing messages, the experiences of Church members appear to be no different than those of non-Church experiencers. Does this reveal anything about the origin or nature of the UAP or their occupants? It could. Nothing conclusive comes to mind, however. The oddness is the same. The gaps in memory, likewise. Cruel abductions and examinations seem universal. I do believe that many Church members, like millions of others around the world, are encountering other beings, at some level or another. Are these encounters strictly psychic downloads from beings from other dimensions or other planets—or from demons? There are physical marks left on their bodies, so whatever is occurring is happening somewhat in the physical realm. Plus, the telltale signs of clothing and jewelry being replaced haphazardly indicates that many of these encounter experiences are wholly in the physical state. Yet, there are indications that many experiences fit better into the spiritual realm, because some abductees actually recall "re-entering" their body at the conclusion of the experience. In short, no UAP questions seem to be answered by examining Church member encounters separately and comparing them with those experienced by non-Church witnesses. Can such questions even be answered? Whatever is behind the phenomenon, I believe it is much more than mere nightmares, or imagery created by a tortured subconscious due to suppressed trauma. Whatever it is, my experience tells me that victims are well served by taking their experiences to their priesthood leaders and seeking spiritual help and whatever other assistance deemed helpful.

For anyone who feels like sharing your experiences with "beings," I have set up a discussion board on the website UFODisclosure.us/discussions. Please feel free to share or comment.

PERSONAL TESTIMONY

In addition to the millions of sighting and encounter witnesses and mounting physical evidence of the tangible presence of UAP, we have the testimonies of thousands, including members of the Church, who claim direct, personal contact with UAP occupants. Not only do these contactees and abductees convincingly relate the spiritual or emotional feelings (horror or overwhelming love) that they felt during their ordeal, but they are also able to describe with great clarity the features of the beings they encounter and the nature and properties of the craft and their means of operation. These abductees are absolutely convinced of the reality of their encounters with strange beings in the foreign craft and relate many physical aspects of their experiences.

For example, many claim to be physically touched, moved about manually, or examined or operated upon by their abductors. The material aspects of such personal encounters tend to place them in the real, physical realm. Our own Udo Wartena recounts how he shook hands with those whom he encountered who professed to be from another planet. Because of this act, our temptation to write the entire phenomenon off as a demonic hoax is somewhat tempered by Joseph Smith's "three grand keys" to discerning the nature and origin of unearthly visitors:

> When a messenger comes saying he has a message from God, offer him your hand and request him to shake hands with you. If he be an angel he will do so, and you will feel his hand. If he be the spirit of a just man made perfect he will come in his glory; for that is the only way he can appear—Ask him to shake hands with you, but he will not move, because it is contrary to the order of heaven for a just man to deceive; but he will still deliver his message. If it be the devil as an angel of light, when you ask him to shake your hands he will offer you his hand, and you will not feel anything; you may therefore detect him. These are three grand keys whereby you may know whether any administration is from God. (D&C 129:4–9)

Although our fact situation is not precisely on point—Udo's alien humans did not claim to be messengers from God, nor do many UAP occupants—the circumstances seem sufficiently analogous to fulfill the requirements of the test. The visitors did claim to be from another planet, they indeed responded to Udo's outstretched hand, and he did feel their hands as he shook them. Of the volumes that fill library shelves and researchers' notebooks around the world concerning the reality of encounters with beings from foreign worlds, this single act of a priesthood bearer shaking the hand of a self-proclaimed extra-terrestrial in 1940 is the most convincing evidence of the physical existence of legitimate explorers of Earth from another planet. If we accept this as a true—non-satanic[13] visitation of humans from another planet—it may serve as an invaluable guide to discerning the physical reality of other reported encounters. However, so many others who are taken aboard the vessels of their abductors report that things seem very real—very solid and natural—but begin to morph and transform before their eyes, as in the case of Steve and Dawn Hess, and many others we have examined herein. Is this a matter of superior technology being indistinguishable from magic, or is it something else entirely? Even while Philip Kinsella was highly distressed in an unmistakably physical manner, he realized it was not entirely within the physical realm as he was hurtled through his house and slammed into his body on his bed.

If we can use Udo Wartena's encounter as a standard by which to measure close encounters generally, there appears to be a clear division of encounter types. The first is the kind in which the contactee is fully conscious during the entire encounter (although Udo reports becoming very fatigued or perhaps unconscious upon the craft's departure) and reports many physical aspects about the encounter. The second would be the semiconscious bedroom visitor type. The third would be the abduction or visitation where the percipient forgets about the encounter, but remembers it later, either spontaneously or with the aid of hypnosis. The distinction becomes muddled, however, because percipients of all groups are often convinced of the physical reality of their respective experiences.

---

13. We address the possibility of a satanic deception below. There exists the real possibility that Satan employs physical beings to carry out a physical deception.

A STANDARD

From Udo Wartena's encounter we learn that handsome and youthful-appearing humans ranging in age from 600 to 900-plus years traveled here from other planets in a saucer-shaped craft supported on retractable legs. The age of the human visitors and shape of the craft are similar to the reports of others. As also related by others, Udo's visitors were here to gather water through hoses for their craft and to do research on cultural progress and pollution levels of the earth. Udo likewise felt overwhelming love in the presence of his visitors, and was told of their "noninterference" policy, as are related by other contactees. Finally, Udo's extraordinary description of the craft and its technology and means of propulsion are very similar to many other accounts. His explanation of the craft focusing on the energy of a distant star and skipping upon the light waves at ultralight speeds was given years before most people had ever heard of Einstein or theories about antigravity generators or faster-than-light travel.

There are a few ways in which Udo's experience differs from those of others. For instance, although some report hearing loud noises at landing and takeoff as did Udo, the majority relate a stillness that falls over everything, with the possible exception of a hum. Again, although many report encountering completely human occupants of UAP (generally benign), the majority identify the occupants as the "small Gray" variety, or some other variation of the gnome or humanoid forms. Udo specifically queried his visitors concerning their knowledge of the Savior and the priesthood, to which they merely responded that they were not at liberty to discuss such matters pursuant to their noninterference directive, despite their desire to do so. The Grays and others can't be restrained from talking about upcoming spiritual and other transformations.

Unlike these, Betty Luca's visitors, as well as others', talk extensively about the spiritual or religious aspects of their missions—in seeming violation of their self-declared policy of noninterference. Although others have recounted cordiality between them and their visitors, as does Udo, most of those claiming to have such intimate contact with UAP occupants relate nonpermissive experiences with tranquilizing mind control and intrusive physical examinations, operations, or sexual contact. No genetic samples such as blood, tissue, or semen specimens were removed from Udo. And finally, although Udo's visitors invited him to continue their journey with them, an offer not unprecedented in the literature, most receive no such proposition. Finally, and perhaps most significantly, Udo was not a "repeater"—he never saw his extraterrestrial friends again. He never had follow-up encounters or poltergeist events in his life. If there is a standard by which we measure a real encounter with actual, flesh and blood extraterrestrial visitors, I would like to think that Brother Wartena's experience has supplied it.

CHAPTER 13

The New Age

THE NEW AGE—A BRIEF HISTORY

To the uninitiated person the term "New Age" may hold little meaning—denominating a form of easy listening jazz music, perhaps, or indicating "enlightened" viewpoint on social issues. The New Age is a movement of astronomical proportions and consequence, however, and it is incumbent upon every Church member to understand the message and import of the New Age movement. Why we must gain this understanding and how it relates to the subject of "extraterrestrial" visitations to Earth will become apparent as we survey the beliefs and goals of the New Age movement and as we explore the purported purpose and message behind the UAP.

The New Age began in the 1960s and was part of the counterculture movement, rejecting nearly everything of traditional value. Lasting into the 1970s, vocal leaders demanded that love, peace, and global harmony supplant the "evil" Western cultural and governmental systems that oppress the world. Traditional social and religious institutions were condemned as sponsors and advocates of the evil *status quo*. A new way of life was preached during this time of social and cultural revolution. Free expression, free love, and free lunch became the Holy Trinity of a new generation. The greed and guilt of the Picean Age were obsolete—and the (precarious) Age of Aquarius was dawning. Its adherents looked to the East for direction. Zen Buddhism, Hinduism, astrology, astral projection, transcendental meditation, Yoga, spiritualism, psychic surgery, globalism, holism, humanism, mysticism, numerology, iridology, and especially reincarnation became the elements of a new faith—the religion of self. In this religion, God is not a personal being—and certainly not a heavenly Father. "It" is a mere intelligent force, which nudges and rewards to enforce balance.

The Aquarian Age of the 1970s went mainstream in the 1980s, allowing traditionalists an opportunity to clean up after the "party" of the prior decades. The Aquarians did not die or fade away during this resurgence of conservativism; they simply blended into the landscape. They became the leaders of leftist political movements and parties, education, and the media. They are comfortable wearing silk ties and pinstripes, or blue jeans. They drive European sports cars and influence social media with Asian electronics. There are no easily distinguishable delineations of wealth or preference. What the Aquarians have in common is their belief in and devotion to the New Age, and the extinguishment of Western ideals, including the family and Christianity.

WHAT DO NEW AGERS BELIEVE?

The New Age movement is a coalition of distinct, yet somewhat compatible belief systems centered in the task of taking humankind from its current tier of evolution to the next. The next level of human evolution, according to New Agers, is not the imperceptible next rung of advancement that one would expect of natural evolution; it is a quantum leap in human ability and enlightenment—human consciousness. Humans will be catapulted into this next evolutionary phase with external assistance. New Agers accept humans as spiritual beings, whose spirit is self-existent[1] and self-realizing.[2] They believe that each spirit is individually progressing through several successive

---

1. New Agers perceive themselves individually as "I am," or "I am that I am."
2. Self-realization is the journey and the end, culminating in personal deification—"God realization."

episodes of mortality,[3] or reincarnation, but is simultaneously a component of a universal psychic entity. According to New Agers, there are those on this planet and others who are currently at low levels of spiritual evolution, and those who are at higher levels. Some have acquired very high levels of spiritual attainment, and an elite handful have reached the very zenith of man's spiritual quest. They believe that to progress spiritually, we must look within ourselves, not to another being (God). We are our own savior. Man must get in touch with the true person within him, then call on the abilities of that person to help him gain further enlightenment. Although this is an individual effort and quest, no one can find the way without guidance. Therefore, a spiritual guide (a spirit on a higher plane), acts as a guide on one's path to greater spiritual enlightenment. An initiate seeks to attain a state of spiritual openness by clearing his mind of worldly matters and concentrating inwardly. The initiate believes that when he reaches a point of "accommodation," wherein he can be "overshadowed" by a guiding spirit, he receives direct spiritual communication, knowledge, and enlightenment from his spirit guide.

NEW AGE GURUS AND GOD

To aid the many millions of New Age practitioners in their quest for spiritual progress and enlightenment, a billion-dollar industry has arisen in recent decades. Human Potential and Human Transformation organizations and counselors offering seminars and digital instructional courses have helped millions to see the light of New Age techniques and practices.[4] They teach meditation and visualization, and sell pyramids and crystals and other paraphernalia. Although concepts like God and Jesus are often spoken of in New Age literature and practice, it is the universal

---

3. Most New Agers believe that this progressive course is common reincarnation, the transmigration of one's spirit from a dying body to a birthing body.
4. Many Fortune 500 corporations have employed New Age firms to teach their techniques to employees. It is thought by New Age watchdogs that New Age "moles" have been planted in corporate human resource departments for decades to proselytize converts by inviting New Age firms in to teach stress reduction and self-awareness clinics.

consciousness to which New Agers refer when speaking of God. They refer to the "Universe" as God. The Universe created us, and the Universe provides for our needs and plants our feet on the course to enlightenment and awakening, ultimately teaching us to resonate to a higher level. It is of their own individual spirits that New Agers refer to as God—they do not accept our Heavenly Father as God. Jesus, although accepted as an individual human, was not the Son of God. He was an important spiritual figure, however, an Ascended Master of spiritual enlightenment, teaching global peace and inner spiritualism. New Age gurus teach that Jesus spent years in the East gaining spiritual enlightenment and mastering spiritual practices before beginning his ministry. They teach that He was not the Christ nor was he any more deified than anyone else of his advanced spiritual level. When he died, he reported to the more advanced Ones before continuing his journey in another body in another life. "Christ," to New Agers, is the Christ Consciousness, which we each are, unrealized, until we attain our Ultimate Consciousness.

The Christ "office" was held temporarily by Jesus according to New Age leaders, but it is now filled by those who embody the consciousness of the true Messiah through spiritual enlightenment. The new Master, often referred to as the One or the Universal Mind, directs the global work of transforming humanity. To reach "god-realization" or this ultimate consciousness sought by New Agers, gurus worldwide offer instruction and guidance.

WHEN AND HOW WILL THE NEW AGE ARRIVE?

The New Age message is that this great evolutionary hyper-jump will occur very soon,[5] facilitating a "quantum leap in elevated brain

---

5. It was believed it would occur in the year 2000, but when that passed, they moved to new periods. Interestingly, New Age idol Nostradamus, born in 1503, predicted in his work Centuries: "In the year 1999 and 7 months, there will come from heaven the great king of terror to raise again the great king of the Mongols, before and after Mars shall reign at will." New Agers see this as an opportunity for "The Plan" of the New Age to save mankind while occult observers see it as the One's attempt to put The Plan into effect. The date came, but we saw no event.

power" that will "result in an upward alteration in mankind's vibrational rate."⁶ As Bob Larson, one New Age observer, explains: "Many New Agers refer to our day as the Aquarian era—a time when a mass visitation of angels and Ascended Masters is occurring. Incidental intervention of higher beings in the past has become an invasion of elevated energies. Our brothers in the beyond want only to lead us to unlimited freedom and joy. If we heed the call, we can avoid annihilation and experience the 'playground of existence,' guided by the 'lifeforce' of the universe."⁷

New Agers realize that not all people are spiritually attuned enough to make the evolutionary quantum leap—the increase in vibrational rate that catapults all humanity to the next spiritual level of existence. This lagging group is made up of what they refer to as Millennialists, those who hold tenaciously to the outdated Jesus the Christ/Messiah belief, who believe that He will usher in the Millennium as foretold in the Bible. In the New Age point of view, those persons with such lower "vibratory rates" will not escape the great annihilation, and approximately one-third of Earth's children will be "eliminated" during the ushering in of this global harmonic period.⁸ New Age guru Ruth Montgomery was told by her spirit Guides that the cleansing will be precipitated by the coming shift of the earth on its axis, which they said would occur near the close of the twentieth century, after a devastating war.⁹ Montgomery explains that UAP will play a part in preserving the "enlightened ones" to repopulate the Earth with good seed after the coming catastrophes. "Although most Earthlings will lose their physical lives when the earth shifts on its

---

6. *Straight Answers on the New Age*, 119. Speaking of the specific eating habits of some New Agers, Bob Larson quotes "one macrobiotic proponent" as explaining: "Planet Earth is surrounded by and immersed in a vibrational body of energy, which is consciousness." According to this New Age culinary guru proper diet places one in harmony with this "etheric web of consciousness." At 83, citing "Michio Kushi's New Deal," *East West Journal*, January 1976, 22.
7. *Ibid.,* 104–05.
8. John Randolph Price, *Practical Spirituality*, (Austin, Texas: Quartus Books, 1985), 18–19.
9. Ruth Montgomery, *Strangers Among Us*, 15. It didn't happen—not yet.

axis at the close of this century, a good number of enlightened ones will be evacuated by the galactic fleets and returned to Earth for its rehabilitation."[10] One less generous spirit contact declares: "We have proven that all old religions are based on falsehood. Man is deity! Man is divine. When you bow and worship me you are worshipping the essential deity of all mankind. All who oppose this new unity are a cancer in the flesh of humanity and must be put to death for the greater good of all who remain."[11]

The supplanting of the plan of God with the Age of Enlightenment is to be implemented through "The Plan." The Plan, according to New Age watchdogs,[12] is a global cabal (secret combination) led by very powerful persons[13] dedicated to Antichrist and his world reign, who are carefully orchestrating global implementation of New Age dogma and practices. The Plan holds no place for the traditional family, free enterprise, nationalism, or Christianity—all outdated and destructive relics of the Picean Age. New Agers believe that the earth is a living being—the goddess Gaia. According to them, Gaia is communicating with "Ascended Masters of the Hierarchy of the universe."[14] "They believe that soon our 'space brothers' will raise a human leader from our midst whom they will endow with supernormal powers and wisdom. This man will lead the world to global government and world peace." Many at this time will be imbued with super-human, paranormal abilities for the purpose of facilitating the ushering in of the Aquarian era.

---

10. *Strangers Among Us*, 43.
11. David Allen Lewis and Robert Shreckhise, *UFO: End-Time Delusion*, New Leaf Press, 172, citing *Tribulation*.
12. LDS writer Derrick T. Evenson published a New Age exposé as Troy Lawrence, titled *Lord Maitreya—The New Age Christ Identified*. Lord Maitreya is reported by many to be the great Ascended Master who will take the reins of world governments and religions pursuant to The Plan.
13. Not only are these men said to be wealthy and politically well-connected, but are self-proclaimed to be of superior makeup—mentally and spiritually. They are worshipped as "supermen" by the New Age elite insiders.
14. *UFO: End-Time Delusion*, 16.

A UAP—NEW AGE CONNECTION

It is not too difficult to perceive a very close tie between the apparent message of the space brothers, as revealed through contactees and channelers, and the message of the New Age movement. At this point, the New Age movement is so inextricably intertwined with the UAP phenomenon that it is impossible to distinguish where one ends and the other begins. A major "Cosmic Consciousness" movement was started by Steven Greer, MD, a former emergency room physician. Greer spotted a nearby UAP in the sky when he was only eight years old, and remained focused on all UAP related phenomena throughout his life. He founded the Center for the Study of Extra-Terrestrial Intelligence (CSETI) in 1990, to create a diplomatic and research-based initiative to reach out and make contact with extraterrestrial civilizations. In 1993, Greer founded the Disclosure Project, an organization that seeks to expose the government's knowledge of UAP, extraterrestrial intelligence, and advanced energy and propulsion systems. To this end, Greer has orchestrated a UAP presentation at a background briefing for former members of Congress, as well as a press conference at the National Press Club in Washington DC that featured twenty retired Air Force, Federal Aviation Administration, and intelligence officers in May of 2001. He has been the impetus behind successful films like *Sirius*, a documentary detailing his work and hypotheses regarding extraterrestrial life, government cover-ups, and *Close Encounters of the Fifth Kind*, and *Unacknowledged*, released in 2017.

Greer, whose tagline is "One universe, One people," believes that the beings in the UAP are entirely benevolent and of a higher spiritual quality than humans, and argues that a covert, transnational, mostly corporate group that has no oversight from the governments of the world, and which possesses antigravity technology and manmade antigravity craft, has had a plan since the 1950s to hoax an extraterrestrial attack. Such a false-flag operation, his group says, is intended to transfer a great deal of power and wealth to the military-industrial complex, and so on.

A GOSPEL VIEW OF THE NEW AGE

The sections above present an overview of what New Age writers and critics alike consider to be the salient tenets and goals of the New Age movement. The reader will certainly recognize the disturbing similarities between these New Age beliefs and aims, and the predicted pre-Second Coming prophecies concerning Antichrist's conquest and rule over the earth. Because many good books are currently in print outlining the predicted events precursing the Second Coming, I will not attempt here to detail most of those events. However, because of the exceptional subtlety and cunning with which many of the premillennial events and operations will be implemented, even numerous of the elite of the kingdom (five of the ten virgins perhaps) will be deceived by Antichrist.[15] Therefore, some discussion regarding the prophets' teachings concerning the latter days is appropriate before continuing with the New Age/UAP connection.

REINCARNATION—A FALSE TEACHING

First, the doctrine of reincarnation constitutes the foundation of New Age philosophy. As with all false doctrines, reincarnation, or the transmigration of the spirit from one body to another in successive lives is a counterfeit of the true principle of "eternal progression."[16] The Apostle Paul teaches that we only live and die once, then are brought before the bar of Christ (see Hebrews 9:27). Amulek was clear about the principle that we receive one life and one body, and that single body is the one that will rise with us in the resurrection (see Alma 11:45; D&C 88:16; D&C 88:15–18.) It is clear that there is one life, one death, and one resurrection.

---

15. For in those days there shall also arise false Christs, and false prophets, and shall show great signs and wonders, insomuch, that, if possible, they shall deceive the very elect who are the elect according to the covenant" (Joseph Smith - Matthew 1:22)
16. Caution is urged at the use of the term "eternal progress" due to misguided attempts to demonstrate that God is not perfect because progress is eternal, and He is, therefore, still progressing. We are to understand that personal development ceases at some point after the resurrection, although the proliferation of one's personal kingdom, or stewardship, continues forever—hence, "eternal" progress.

The Prophet Joseph Smith taught true doctrine in connection with a man to whom he had offered lodging, who called himself Matthias. As Joseph discerned the man's spirit, he became concerned and questioned him: "I resumed conversation with Matthias, and desired him to enlighten my mind more on his views respecting the resurrection. He said that he possessed the spirit of his fathers, that he was a literal descendant of Matthias, the Apostle, who was chosen in the place of Judas that fell; that his spirit was resurrected in him; and that this was the way or scheme of eternal life, this transmigration of soul or spirit from father to son."[17] Having heard this, Joseph quickly discerned the problem: "I told him that his doctrine was of the devil, that he was in reality in possession of a wicked and depraved spirit, although he professed to be the Spirit of truth itself; and he said also that he possessed the soul of Christ. He tarried until Wednesday, 11th, when, after breakfast, I told him that my God told me, that his god was the devil, and I could not keep him any longer, and he must depart . . . (Nov. 9, 1835)."[18] It is significant that although Joseph had properly diagnosed the spiritual problem, he sought Heavenly Father's counsel concerning what to do with this misguided fellow. The answer was direct—his god was the devil, and Joseph must cast him out.

Joseph's response to Matthias also clarifies the nature of the second controlling substructure of the New Age—guidance from spirits on a higher level of existence. New Agers say that without the helping hand of more exalted spirits reaching down to guide and enlighten, man cannot progress to higher spiritual planes. Through meditation, chanting, and focusing, practitioners claim to receive spiritual communications, knowledge, and ultimate truth from ascended spirits. If the direct connection is too difficult initially, beginners seek the aid of channelers who bring the spirit to them, thereby opening the channels of communication. Channelers and practitioners all claim that they are "overshadowed" by these Ascended Masters, but deny that they are "possessed" by them. Again, Joseph instructs that those who consort with these

---

17. *Teachings*, 105.
18. *History of the Church*, vol. 2, 304–307.

extra-mortal providers of mystical knowledge are "in possession of a wicked and depraved spirit." True to the New Age conviction, Matthias retorted that he was not possessed by an evil spirit, but in fact, professed to be "the Spirit of truth itself." He added to this claim of personal supernatural status that he "possessed the soul of Christ," which is also one of the most familiar assertions of the New Age. No man is the Spirit of truth itself, nor does he possess the soul of Christ—those are the unique province of the Savior of all humanity, the Son of God. Therefore, God instructed the Prophet Joseph Smith that Satan was the purveyor of such doctrines, and to cast out such that accept and teach them.

SATAN'S INFLUENCE AND DECEPTION HAVE FLANKED THE RESTORATION

The similarities of Matthias's claims and beliefs to those of the New Age movement are striking. However, all it demonstrates is that Satan's tactics change very little over time. Matthias was not unique in his day. The occult existed then as it does now. Even in the early Church, Joseph was obliged on several occasions to correct many who were deceived by evil spirits, as he recorded in the case of many false spirits, strange visions and shouting from tree stumps.[19] Speaking of false spirits and manifestations, Joseph explained,

> There have also been ministering angels in the Church which were of Satan appearing as an angel of light. A sister in the state of New York had a vision, who said it was told to her that if she would go to a certain place in the woods, an angel would appear to her. She went at the appointed time and saw a glorious personage descending, arrayed in white, with sandy colored hair; he commenced and told her to fear God, and said that her husband was called to do great things, but that he must not go more than one hundred miles from home, or he would not return; whereas God had called him to go to the ends of the earth, and he has since been more than one thousand miles from home, and is yet

---

19. See *Teachings*, 214.

alive. Many true things were spoken by this personage, and many things that were false.[20]

Many of us might be so flattered to receive a visit from such a glorious angelic being with a personal message from 'God' that we might be tempted to take his counsel over that of our appointed leaders. Satan's power and influence are hard to resist, especially when he can transform himself into an angel of glorious light, or anything else, and tell us things that no other person knows. Satan maneuvers men with subtle deception, filled with half-truths and half-lies, designed to lead them far enough astray to make them lose sight of the light of truth. Then, when darkness surrounds them, it is almost impossible for men to find their way back. The deceived Korihor confessed: "But behold, the devil hath deceived me; for he appeared unto me in the form of an angel, and said unto me: Go reclaim this people, for they have all gone astray after an unknown God. And he said unto me: There is no God; yea, and he taught me that which I should say. And I have taught his words; and I taught them because they were pleasing unto the carnal mind; and I taught them, even until I had much success, insomuch that I verily believed that they were true; and for this cause I withstood the truth, even until I have brought this great curse upon me" (Alma 30:53). The message and tactics of Korihor's time are the very same that we find escalating today.

SATAN'S TACTICS HAVE NOT CHANGED

Joseph Smith further instructs us that these same satanic machinations have existed throughout the history of the Earth:

> It is evident from the Apostles' writings, that many false spirits existed in their day, and had 'gone forth into the world,' and that it needed intelligence which God alone could impart to detect false spirits, and to prove what spirits were of God. The world in general have been grossly ignorant in regard to this one thing, and why should they be otherwise—for "the things of God knoweth no man, but the Spirit of God." The Egyptians were not

---

20. Ibid.

able to discover the difference between the miracles of Moses and those of the magicians until they came to be tested together; and if Moses had not appeared in their midst, they would unquestionably have thought that the miracles of the magicians were performed through the mighty power of God, for they were great miracles that were performed by them—a supernatural agency was developed, and great power manifested. . . . One great evil is, that men are ignorant of the nature of spirits; their power, laws, government, intelligence, etc., and imagine that when there is anything like power, revelation, or vision manifested, that it must be of God.[21]

In reality, every false teaching and incorrect precept in the world is a product of Satan's attempt to lead men astray. He does not tell big lies to lead us to error—not initially, anyway. They are too easily detected. Satan takes gospel truth and changes it just enough to convey an untruth. Why does he carry on this incessant campaign of deception? His entire design is to trick humanity into worshipping him as the Universal Master and The One, thereby owning their souls: "And he became Satan, yea, even the devil, the father of all lies, to deceive and to blind men, and to lead them captive at his will, even as many as would not hearken unto my voice" (Moses 4:4.) The insightful book *Commentary on the Pearl of Great Price* remarks on this scripture: "'It does not matter to Satan, who is the devil, what we believe or what we do not, as long as we do not believe in Jesus Christ, Whose adversary the devil was from the beginning.' Ever since he rebelled against divine authority and therefore was cast out of heaven, Satan has carried on a ruthless, yet abortive attempt to thwart the purposes of the Lord God."[22]

SATAN WILL SUCCEED FOR A TIME

The latter-day deception of Satan will be successful. Satan will take the reins of world governments and religions because few can discern his methods or withstand his power. Of Satan's special latter-day

---

21. *Teachings*, 202–203.
22. *Commentary on the Pearl of Great Price*, 133–134.

Antichrist, Bruce R. McConkie wrote: "This great antichrist which is to stand as the antagonist of Christ in the last days, and which is to be overthrown when He comes to cleanse the earth and usher in millennial righteousness, is the church of the devil (Rev. 13; 17), with the man of sin at its head. (2 Thess. 2:1–12)."[23] To counter the latter-day outpouring of the Lord's Spirit upon His people, as prophesied by the prophet Joel,[24] Satan will counterfeit the phenomenon with an escalation of his own spiritualism, to show the world that he is indeed the god of this world (see Revelation 13:11–15). "And I saw three unclean spirits. . . For they are the spirits of devils, working miracles, which go forth unto the kings of the earth of the whole world, to gather them to the battle of that great day of God Almighty" (Revelation 16:13–14).

BILLIONS ARE "ANXIOUSLY ENGAGED"

The scriptures reveal that one-third of the hosts of heaven were cast down to Earth with Satan. At any given moment there are at least 35 billion[25] satanic spirits on Earth carrying out the will of their evil master, around six per living mortal person;[26] a staggering consideration indeed. Their task is to lead men's souls into the spiritual captivity of their master, Satan. Their method is to trick men through deceit into following after false gods and forsaking their own Heavenly Father—rejecting Him by rejecting His gospel, and thereby rejecting His promised reward of exaltation and eternal life with Him. This evil method proliferated nearly unchecked before the Flood, leading to the destruction of nearly all life in the planetary reboot. God was determined that never again would such widespread evil sweep through

---

23. *Mormon Doctrine*, 40.
24. "And it shall come to pass afterward, that I will pour out my spirit upon all flesh; your sons and your daughters shall prophesy, your old men shall dream dreams, your young men shall see visions: And also upon the servants and upon the handmaids in those days will I pour out my spirit" (Joel 2:28–29).
25. As we discussed above, this number represents one half of the estimated 70 billion that have lived on Earth in mortality thus far, equaling one third of the total 105 billion (70 billion + 35 billion).
26. As of this writing there are nearly 8 billion people in the world, 70 percent of which are adults, or 5.6 billion.

His people, so to ancient Israel the Lord commanded that anyone who communed with such spirits was to be avoided by the people of Israel and was to be "put to death." "When thou art come into the land which the Lord thy God giveth thee, thou shalt not learn to do after the abominations of those nations. There shall not be found among you any one that maketh his son or his daughter to pass through the fire, or that useth divination, or an observer of times, or an enchanter, or a witch. Or a charmer, or a consulter with familiar spirits, or a wizard, or a necromancer.[27] For all that do these things are an abomination unto the Lord: and because of these abominations the Lord thy God doth drive them out from before thee" (Deuteronomy 18:9–12). The cure: "A man also or a woman that hath a familiar spirit, or that is a wizard, shall surely be put to death" (Leviticus 20:27; Exodus 22:18).

Some visionaries of the Restoration have been permitted to look through the veil into the regions of the spirit world. They describe the beautiful spiritual planet that occupies the parallel physical space the earth does and the wonders and exalted personages that are present there, and also describe the malicious, hateful demons that occupy that plane in great numbers, who are entirely devoted to our personal destruction. These are the spirits that answer the call of mediums and trance channelers, who teach men that there is no God and no devil—no good and no evil. They are "anxiously engaged" in their great cause to destroy the plan of salvation and exaltation, supplanting it with their own master's plan—to overthrow God and His Son, by thwarting their work and glory, which is "to bring to pass the immortality and eternal life of man" (Moses 1:39).

Brigham Young warned the Saints that the power of Satan was expanding in the world. He explained that only the power of the priesthood could keep such spirits at bay:

> Why do we lay hands on the sick? Is there virtue in doing so? There is, and the wicked world as well as the Saints prove this. Since Joseph Smith received revelations from God, Spiritualism has taken its rise, and has spread with unprecedented rapidity; and they will lay

---

27. Each of these forbidden professions is very much a part of the New Age movement, and is professed to be necessary to bring one to a higher plane of enlightenment and elevated spirituality.

hands on each other—one system proving another—spiritualism demonstrating the reality of animal magnetism. Is there virtue in one person more than another? Power in one more than another? Spirit in one more than another? Yes, there is. I will tell you how much I have. You may assemble together every spiritualist on the face of the earth, and I will defy them to make a table move or get a communication from hell or any other place while I am present.[28]

This is unambiguous. President Young was very clear that all of these people who are able to communicate with spirits and gain information that no one could possibly possess otherwise, and able to move things with their minds and perform miracles, even lay on hands and heal—if it's not done by one who is authoritatively ordained to the priesthood in the name of God, it is an extension of the power of Satan. New Age spiritual practices are a false religion of a false god.

THE PRIESTHOOD—MAN'S ONLY PROTECTION

Joseph Smith was quite concerned for those who would be on Earth during this time of temporal and spiritual upheaval. His mandate to preach the gospel to everyone in an effort to bring them to Zion was imperative in his time, and is the only means of sparing men a portion of the ravages of Antichrist in our time. Joseph relates that Satan's deception will be so clever, so sophisticated, that only those who possess the priesthood will be able to detect him.

> Or who can drag into daylight and develop the hidden mysteries of the false spirits that so frequently are made manifest among the Latter-day Saints? We answer that no man can do this without the Priesthood, and having a knowledge of the laws by which spirits are governed; for as no man knows the things of God, but by the Spirit of God, so no man knows the spirit of the devil, and his power and intelligence, which is more than human, and having unfolded through the medium of the Priesthood the mysterious operations of his devices; without viewing **the angelic form, the sanctified look and gesture,**

---

28. *Journal of Discourses*, 14:72.

and the zeal that is frequently manifested by him for the glory of God, together with ***the prophetic spirit, the gracious influence, the godly appearance and the holy garb***, which are so characteristic of his proceedings and his mysterious windings.

A man must have the discerning of spirits before he can drag into daylight this hellish influence and unfold it unto the world in all its soul-destroying, diabolical, and horrid colors; for nothing is a greater injury to the children of men than to be under the influence of a false spirit when they think they have the Spirit of God. Thousands have felt the influence of its terrible power and baneful effects. Long pilgrimages have been undertaken, penances endured, and pain, misery and ruin have followed in their train; nations have been convulsed, kingdoms overthrown, provinces laid waste, and blood, carnage and desolation are habiliments in which it has been clothed.[29]

Although portions of the Church may escape some of the ill-effects of this premillennial black cauldron, most of the world will fall under Satan's power: "or by [Satan's] sorceries were all nations deceived" (Revelation 18:23). Speaking of the time when Satan's premillennial kingdom would be overthrown, the Apostle John prophesied that Christ would eventually deliver the world from Satan's grasp: "And [Christ] cast him into the bottomless pit, and shut him up, and set a seal upon him, that he should deceive the nations no more, till the thousand years should be fulfilled: and after that he must be loosed a little season" (Revelation 20:3).

THE NEW AGE WILL BRING ANTICHRIST TO POWER

The scriptures, ancient and modern, speak of these events with great clarity. Numerous are the verses that detail the rise of Satan to power. Explicit are the specifics outlining the conditions that will enable his rise to world dominion, and the state of the people of the earth during his reign. Although not fully explored herein, the reader is exhorted to pursue

---

29. *Teachings*, 204–05; emphasis added.

knowledge concerning these late Sixth Seal and early Seventh Seal events which will precede the Second Coming.[30] So doing, he or she will be better prepared to withstand the tremendous pressures which will be exerted to force all people to participate in Satan's premillennial kingdom.

The New Age movement appears to be the vehicle, or a preeminent component at least, by which Satan will establish his premillennial kingdom. The "Network," as New Agers call it, is being put into place even now, awaiting a natural or economic, or some other kind of international catastrophe that will render the world's sovereign nations vulnerable to takeover. The scriptures are quite clear that the premillennial difficulties enumerated in the sixth seal portion of the book of Revelation will supply just such a worldwide crisis.[31] When this occurs, family, religion, and life as we know it will become relics of the Piscean Age—that outdated time when Jesus was thought to be the only Christ—the Savior of this broken world.

What does all of this have to do with UAP? Although it is not yet clear, the occupants of many of the UAP, whoever they really are, together with their earthly agents, have been sending us a strong message that they may be very much involved with the coming Aquarian Age. The followers of God can avoid many of the horrendous conditions that will beset the world if they will follow the warnings and edicts of His prophets, and actually prepare, and do the things He asks them to do. A one year supply of food? If that seems too difficult for some, they may wish to pay closer attention and find out all that the Lord is revealing in these latter days.

---

30. In Revelation 6, John witnesses Christ opening the first six seals attached to the book containing the complete history of the 7,000 years of temporal existence of this Earth (see D&C 77:6). Each of the seven seals represents important events pertaining to each of those thousand year periods making up the Earth's temporal existence (see D&C 77:7). Again, we don't know how long the 'night' periods might be between the 1,000–year periods.
31. We live near the end of the sixth period, whose events are contained in the sixth seal of the book, most of which have not yet occurred. A thorough study of the sixth seal events leads us to understand that a devastating worldwide earthquake and attendant cataclysmic events will trigger many of the premillennial catastrophes outlined therein, and will facilitate the breakdown of social, political, and economic systems.

CHAPTER 14

◆

Paranormal Properties of UAP

UAP ARE NOT ALWAYS WHAT THEY APPEAR TO BE

Many ancient documents and oral histories reflect that unidentifiable objects have been seen in our earthly skies for centuries—even millennia. New Age author Brad Steiger adds, "Interestingly, the records seem to indicate that UFOs have adapted themselves to the cultural milieu and the technological capacities of the observers."[1] These observations on the ephemeral, transitory nature of UAP can be extended to their purported occupants, who seem like chameleons to many observers, apparitions of something else—something capable of producing supernatural effects in our environment and hallucinatory images in our minds.

Concerning this ephemeral, or paranormal nature of UAP, Dr. Jacques Vallee concludes after decades of research: "I believe that a UFO is both a physical entity with mass, inertia, volume, and physical parameters that we can measure, and a window into another reality."

---

1. *The UFO Abductors*, 212.

Is this why witnesses can give us at the same time a consistent factual narrative and a description of contact with forms of life that fit no acceptable framework? These forms of life, such as the small Grays, may be real, yet a product of our dreams. Like our dreams, we can look into their hidden meaning, or we can ignore them."[2] This conclusion is significant and seemingly grandiose for a mystery that most people feel is explainable in nuts-and-bolts terms. Dr. Vallee's conclusion, however, appears to place the enigma into an unfamiliar paradigm, one with which the masses are uncomfortable—for good reason. According to Dr. Vallee, UAP could very well be three-dimensional holograms, with mass, projected, possibly through time, and those who come into close contact are "deliberately exposed to a scene designed to be recorded and transmitted to us." We see something that appears to be solid matter, yet many insiders and experts have come to suspect is not natural, or part of our normal world. It projects an image—and that image is tailored to the audience viewing it, and delivers a message. At some level, we know the phenomenon is deceptive, at best.

Dr. J. Allen Hynek was originally a scientific skeptic working for the American military as a UAP debunker. After much exposure to the UAP phenomenon he became a leading advocate of the extraterrestrial spacecraft theory. However, after reviewing facts like those discussed herein, he finally came to think that UAP may have a paranormal origin: "I would have to say that the extraterrestrial theory is a naive one. It's the simplest of all hypotheses, but not a very likely explanation for the phenomenon we have seen manifesting itself for centuries. . . There are quite a few reported instances where two distinctly different UFOs hovering in a clear sky will converge and eventually merge into one object. These are the types of psychic phenomena that are confronting us in the UFO mystery."[3] Why do UAP present themselves in this type of exhibition? It appears that they can, and do, present themselves in whatever form they desire. So, we must assume that what we are seeing is exactly what they want us to see—but not what it actually is.

---

2. *Dimensions*, 224.
3. J. Allen Hynek interview, UFO Report Magazine, August 1976, 61.

PROFESSOR JOHN MACK, HARVARD UNIVERSITY

As we discussed briefly above, notable psychiatrist, researcher, and Pulitzer Prize winner Dr. John Mack was head of the department of psychiatry at Harvard Medical School. Dr. Mack was introduced to the world of abduction victims and reacted like any other academic or clinician in the beginning, as he explained in an interview on NOVA, on PBS. He was asked to help the audience understand how an obviously brilliant professor eventually took the subject seriously.

"When I first encountered this phenomenon, or particularly even before I had actually seen the people themselves, I had very little place in my mind to take this seriously. I, like most of us, was raised to believe that if we were going to discover other intelligence, we'd do it through radio waves or through signals or something of that kind." Dr. Mack explained, "The idea that we could be reached by some other kind of being, creature, intelligence that could actually enter our world and have physical effects as well as emotional effects, was simply not part of the world view that I had been raised in. So, I came very reluctantly to the conclusion that this was a true mystery. I did everything I could to rule out other sources. . . . I've now worked with over a hundred experiencers intensively . . . and in case after case, I've been impressed with the consistency of the story, the sincerity with which people tell their stories, the power of feelings connected with this, the self-doubt—all the appropriate responses that these people have to their experiences."

The interviewer asked Dr. Mack, "So tell us, please, how literally you intend people to take this? Are you suggesting people are really being snatched from their beds by aliens and experiments on board a spaceship?" This is a truly daunting question for a high level academic, but Dr. Mack attempted to explain his view of the phenomenon in the best way to help skeptics understand its nature, and its possible source. He said,

> There are aspects of this which I believe we are justified in taking quite literally. That is, UFOs are in fact observed, filmed on camera at the same time that people are having their abduction experiences. People, in fact, have been observed to be missing

at the time that they are reporting their abduction experiences. They return from their experiences with cuts, ulcers on their bodies, triangular lesions, which follow the distribution of the experiences that they recover, of what was done to them in the craft by the surgical-like activity of these beings. All of that has a literal physical aspect and is experienced and reported with appropriate feeling, by the abductees, with or without hypnosis or a relaxation exercise. . . So, the simple answer would be: Yes, it's both. It's both literally, physically happening to a degree; and it's also some kind of psychological, spiritual experience occurring and originating perhaps in another dimension. And so the phenomenon stretches us, or it asks us to stretch to open to realities that are not simply the literal physical world, but to extend to the possibility that there are other unseen realities from which our consciousness, our, if you will, learning processes over the past several hundred years have closed us off.

The interviewer asked Dr. Mack, "I wonder, if in that vein, you can speak to what you think this experience is about?" Dr. Mack responded,

There are several effects that these experiences have for those who undergo alien abduction encounters. First is the most familiar aspect or fit, which is a traumatic event in which a blue light or some kind of energy paralyzes the person, whether they're in their home or they're driving a car. They can't move. They feel themselves being removed from wherever they were. They're floated through a wall or out a car, carried up on this beam of light into a craft and there subjected to a number of now familiar procedures which involve the beings staring at them; involves probing of their body, their body orifices; and a complex process whereby they sense in the case of men, sperm removed; in the women, eggs removed; some sort of hybrid offspring created which they're brought back to see in later abductions. That's the sort of literal experience . . . . Another area is the whole visual environmental and informational aspect of this in which people are shown on television screens a huge variety of scenes of environmental destruction of the earth polluted; of a kind of post-apocalyptic scene in which even the spirits have been routed from their environment because they live in the same physical and spiritual environment that we do.

The interviewer finally asked Dr. Mack if he is now a "believer" in the abduction phenomenon, and Mack responded, "I didn't believe anything when I started, I don't really believe anything now. I've come to where I've come to clinically. In other words, I worked with people over hundreds and hundreds of hours and have done as careful a job as I could to listen, to sift out, to consider alternative explanations. And none have come forward. No one has found an alternative explanation in a single abduction case."

The UAP and attendant "extraterrestrial" phenomenon is really difficult for academics, as well as government and military people to embrace. Even if they see evidence that it is actually occurring, to the point of witnessing a silver disc hovering low over their own backyard barbeque, it's these quasi-spiritual and semi-ethereal aspects of the phenomenon that make it so difficult to acknowledge or to embrace. When the generals are reporting to the president and the president wants to know if this is something that should be shared with the public, I'm sure there is a discussion that includes many of the subjects raised in Dr. Mack's interview. The following account helps to illustrate just how far from "explainable" the UAP phenomenon remains.

THE HEALING OF DR. "X"

The fast-paced evolution of the paranormal aspects of UAP sightings and encounters was noticeable as early as the 1960s. One case, reported by Church researcher Dr. Frank B. Salisbury in his book *The Utah UFO Display*,[4] relates just how metaphysical the phenomenon is becoming. This particular encounter was especially intriguing because it was the best investigated of its era. The witness was a political figure and PhD in his town in the southeast of France, and the physical

---

4. *The Utah UFO Display: A Biologist's Report*, 211–18. The full report of the incident is published in the Flying Saucer Review: Aime Michel, 1969, Special Issue No. 3 September, "UFO Percipients," Flying Saucer Review; and Flying Saucer Review November–December, 1971, No. 17, (6):39.

evidence was well documented as well as overwhelming. The witness, known as Dr. "X," chose to remain anonymous because of his political standing, but he was personally known to some of the best scientific investigators and perceived to be completely credible. The doctor was wounded in war and lost his ability to use his arm and play the piano. He injured his leg years later while doing chores on his property. Just before 4:00 a.m. his fourteen–month-old called out and he went to get him a bottle. The doctor heard a shutter banging upstairs and went up, looking out to see flashes of pale light. As he stepped onto the terrace, he saw the light coming from two luminous discs hovering at a distance to his right. The top half of the discs were a luminous silvery white, and the bottom half a deep sunset red, brighter at the top than the bottom. Two "antennas" extended out horizontally, one from each edge of each object. A third antenna on each object was located at top center and was perfectly vertical. A white shaft of light came from the lower center point of each object. They began moving toward him, and the points where the two beams struck the ground were at the top of a small hill. White light also emanated from antennas and the doctor felt they were sucking in the atmospheric electricity and could see it entering through the antennas and then exploding between the two objects, the whole thing producing a single glow of light.

The objects moved together and nearly touched, and light seemed to jump between their antennas. They touched and then began to interpenetrate each other. They formed one object, identical to the two. The object came closer to the doctor and appeared to grow until it was enormous—around two hundred feet, plus the long antennas, which were about fifty feet. The doctor was becoming afraid, and he could see a protrusion on the bottom from which the beam of light was being emitted. The bottom half had sections, and there was a dark line moving around like interference lines drifting across a screen. He noticed the object turning and the beam of light moving toward him until it illuminated him and the front of his house. He raised his arms to cover his face. There was suddenly a "bang," the first sound during the encounter, and the object dematerialized, leaving nothing but its cloudy, whitish, fleecy shape, which at once disintegrated and was wisped away by the wind. A very bright, white thread shot out toward the sky and vanished into a small white shining dot, which vanished with a very loud explosion. The doctor was in shock, got a note pad and wrote down the details of his sighting along with sketches, and then woke his wife to tell her all he'd seen. He was walking around excitedly, without his limp. "Your leg!" she cried. He pulled up his pajama trouser leg, and the wound was healed, both the swelling and the pain completely gone. The doctor fell asleep and finally awoke at 2:00 p.m., remembering nothing of his experience. He later bumped his head, and the full memory of the previous night's events returned. All of his wounds were healed, and he immediately began to play the piano.

UAP AND ESP

Civilian and military reports indicate that paranormal activity often follows the UAP experiencer. ESP (extra sensory perception) and poltergeist-like phenomena are often reported. Uncontrollable levitating and electrical disturbances likewise occur. In many cases, contactees, or even those who only witness UAP come away with "expanded enlightenment," spiritual or scientific. Nearly a third of UAP encounters are said to include a psychic experience, often manifested as telepathic communication with the UAP occupants. Interestingly, those who claim psychic tendencies are more likely to experience UAP encounters. Not surprisingly, professional psychics often claim contact with UAP and their occupants.

Whitley Strieber, the famed fiction writer whose book *Communion* informed the world that he was plagued by "visitors" closely akin to "aliens," reports that he had a great deal of interest in the occult, including astral projection, a self-induced form of traveling out of one's body. Which comes first, paranormal experiences or interest in paranormal activities? It is hard to tell. One may be inclined to believe that the experiences lead to personal investigation. However, those who feel "compelled" to investigate UAP-related paranormal phenomena often discover that they have latent experiences buried in the subconscious realms of their minds—evidently. The same, perhaps, can be said of your author—my memory of the wrinkled little messenger in our driveway was entirely lost during the research and writing that went into my first works on this subject.

Strieber, as well as many other contactees, has discovered the presence of ongoing "alien" contact and paranormal experiences throughout his life. He doubts that the visitors are extraterrestrial but feels that they are interdimensional beings who have visited our reality throughout human history, communicating with us through theater. Although we are unsure if all such visitors and "others" phenomena can be lumped into the same category, it is apparent that at least those beings that present themselves in bizarre pageants, physically or spiritually, are the same beings that have plagued humanity from the very beginning. Watchers? Evil spirits cast down to Earth from heaven? Interdimensional creatures that we know very little of? We are unsure. What we do feel is that our human brothers and sisters who live at vast distances would not bother to come this far solely to put on such displays of bizarre pageantry.

Journalist Ed Conroy has published a work that goes behind Strieber's *Communion*, analyzing the data and interviewing witnesses. He writes concerning Strieber's conclusion: "In actuality, Strieber's line of thinking is reflective of the vast array of experiences connected with and explanations offered for what some investigators have come to call the 'entity enigma.' At first glance, it would seem that the content of Strieber's story is no different from hundreds of cases on record of people reporting terrifying experiences with 'bedroom visitors,' ghosts, poltergeists, apparitions, religious visions, and what have been regarded as demons . . . to thoroughly survey the colorful panoply of anomalous phenomena concerning strange, human beings."[5]

REALITY TESTING

Strieber relates that on one occasion when the visitors abducted him, he was being floated helplessly through his house, when he decided to perform a "reality testing" experiment—he grabbed the

---

5. Ed Conroy, *Report on Communion*, New York: William Morrow Company. Inc., 261, 1989.

family cat on the way through. Upon arriving, Strieber was chastised for bringing the cat along. When asked why he had done it he replied that he just wanted the company. After some quiet discussion among the entities, they told him that he had made a serious mistake but that they would remedy it. With that, one of them touched the cat's leg with a small triangular object, and the cat went limp immediately. The day following the abduction the cat slept for most of the day and that night.[6] This attempt to hold on to a piece of the temporal world while abducted to the "others" world proved problematic for Strieber and the "others." What do we learn from the experience? Probably nothing because it is only theater. However, if there is any actuality to the abduction experience, it may require a specific "quickening" to pass between worlds—a treatment that the cat had not received. Many experiencers test their grasp on reality during their encounters with the unknown. I recall how natural it was to question my own observations during the tent experience, and how I repeatedly sought to confirm my perceptions of what I was seeing.

HISTORICAL PARALLELS

A great deal of research is currently underway comparing the behavior of the UAP phenomenon with that found in historic myth, legend, and fairy tales. The parallels are striking, and research appears to be bearing enlightening fruit. Dr. Jacques Vallee has compared much of the pertinent literature and shares the following legend as being typical of one type of parallel experience: "According to the Paiute Indians, California was once populated by a superior civilization, the Hav-Masuvs. Among other interesting devices, they used 'flying canoes,' which were silvery and had wings. They flew in the manner of eagles and made a whirring noise. They also wielded a strange weapon: a small tube that could be held in one hand that would stun their enemies, producing lasting paralysis and a feeling similar to a shower of cactus needles."[7]

---

6. Again, this long sleep happened to me in the encounter with the small humanoid in the family driveway.
7. *Dimensions*, 86.

These descriptions are common in the folklore of native tribes and ancient civilizations throughout the world. So, who are these airborne, stun-gun toting tribes that are reported worldwide throughout recorded history? We generally assume that they are mere tribal embellishments of feared enemies. Of course, the fact that they are recorded in similar terms throughout the ancient world tends to lend some weight to the legends. Are there tribes of humans, or other beings, hidden from our view, living incognito on our globe? We know that there are Israelites who have been separated out—where they are now, we cannot know. We also know that the Lord will someday reveal "the hidden things of his economy concerning this earth" (D&C 77:6). This informs us that there are hidden aspects of things on Earth of which we have no knowledge. The Lord reiterates this in D&C 101:32–34, wherein He says: "Yea, verily I say unto you, in that day when the Lord shall come, he shall reveal all things—Things which have passed, and hidden things which no man knew, things of the earth, by which it was made, and the purpose and the end thereof—Things most precious, things that are above, and things that are beneath, things that are in the earth, and upon the earth, and in heaven." Whatever these many things are—things that the Lord declares we will not discover during our time on Earth—it is clear that we live in substantial ignorance of many things of which we have come to assume we have a great deal of knowledge. Are there purposes to the Earth's creation of which we are uninformed? Are there things beneath the earth and in the earth that will remain a mystery to us? Many witnesses tell us that "others" are frequently seen entering our oceans, volcanos and openings in the ice, mountains, and valleys. If just one of these thousands of reports is true, then there is truly much that we do not understand about what goes on within our environment.

THE SECRET COMMONWEALTH

For hundreds of years European scholars attempted to document the legends of nonhuman beings in their region. A wonderful synthesis of the phenomenon was authored by Reverend Kirk of Aberfoyle. In *The Secret Commonwealth of Elves, Fauns, and Fairies* he described the methods and organization of the creatures that plagued the farmers of Scotland. We summarize his findings about elves and other aerial creatures thus. They have a nature that is intermediate between man and the angels. Physically, they have very light and fluid bodies. They are particularly visible at dusk. They can appear and vanish at will. They are intelligent and curious. They have the power to carry away anything they like. They live inside the earth in caves, which they can reach through any crevice or opening where air passes. Their chameleon-like bodies allow them to swim through the air. They are divided into tribes. They have children, nurses, marriages, burials, and so on. Their houses are large and beautiful but generally invisible to human eyes. The houses are equipped with lamps that burn forever and fire that needs no fuel. They speak very little. When they do talk among themselves, the language is a kind of whistling sound. Their philosophical system is based on the following ideas: nothing dies; things evolve cyclically in a way that at every cycle they are renewed and improved. Motion is the universal law. They have a hierarchy of leaders but no visible devotion to God, or religion. They have many pleasant, light books but also serious and complex books dealing with abstract matters.[8]

MAGIC WANDS

Ed Walters, like many other UAP witnesses, describes certain wand-like instruments carried by the "aliens." These silver wands or rods are apparently the same as that carried by the single small Gray on the night it attempted to lure Ed Walters out of the house into the clutches of the blue beam. Although we can assume that such a glowing silver rod was nothing more than a stun gun or communication device, the presence of the silver rods that "glowed" is worth noting from a traditional, or paranormal viewpoint. Betty Luca, as well as others, describes how such devices are used to manipulate the environment, ambiance, or technological appliances near the encounter.

Certain ancient religious texts occasionally refer to superior beings or those sent with ecclesiastical authority, as possessing various types

---

8. *Dimensions*, 87–89.

of rods, holding them in their hands to convey authority. For instance, from the *Apocalypse of Abraham* we read: "And I rose up and saw him who had grasped me by the right hand and set me upon my feet: and the appearance of his body was like sapphire, and the look of his countenance like chrysolite, and the hair of his head like snow, etc. and a *golden sceptre* was in his right hand." Also, from the *Iliad* we read: "And the Elders were seated upon shining stones [stones of truth] in a holy circle: with scepters of inspired utterance in their hands."[9] Besides these, our scriptures, as well as secular monarchies, are replete with examples of the possession of such rods or scepters as symbols of authority or power.

CROSSING THE TIME ZONE

Another characteristic of "fairyland" that is also common in UAP abduction cases is what we term the "Rip Van Winkle effect." When visiting with the elves or fairies or Gentry, humans are said to be missing for days, months, or years, when to them the time passed as though it were only minutes or hours. In fact, it is based on this rich folklore that Washington Irving wrote *Rip Van Winkle*. The reverse is true also—the abductee often feels that he or she was in fairyland for weeks or longer, only to find that no time has passed in our world. "This is our fourth point, and quite a remarkable one. Time does not pass there as it does here. And we have in such stories the first idea of the relativity of time. But it is a fact that the non-symmetry of the time element between Magonia and our world is present in tales from all countries."[10]

In many abduction cases the victim's absence went unnoticed because no time had passed. In others more time had passed than was realized by the victim. In one case, a military watch in South America approached a landed UAP, and one of the men went over the knoll to get a closer look. A few minutes later he was found by his friends, disoriented, with several days' growth of beard.

---

9. Hugh Nibley, *Abraham in Egypt*, quoting *Iliad*, XVIII, 497–508.
10. *Dimensions*, 131.

ELVES AND FAIRIES

Describing the UAP entities Dr. Vallee says: "Entities human witnesses report to have seen, heard, and touched fall into various biological types. . . . Most of the so-called pilots, however, are dwarfs and fit into two main groups: (1) dark, hairy beings—identical to the gnomes of medieval theory—with small, bright eyes and deep, rugged, 'old' voices; and (2) beings—who answer the description of the sylphs of the Middle Ages or the elves of the fairy-faith—with human complexions, oversized heads, and silvery voices. All of the beings have been described with and without breathing apparatus. Beings of various categories have been reported together. The overwhelming majority are humanoid."

In describing the entities' behavior, Dr. Vallee adds: "The entities' reported behavior is as consistently absurd as the appearance of their craft is ludicrous. In numerous instances of verbal communications with them, their assertions have been systematically misleading. This absurd behavior has had the effect of keeping professional scientists away from the area where the activity was taking place. It has also served to give the saucer myth its religious and mystical overtones."[11] Dr. Vallee feels that the entities and their UAP, whoever they are, "are paranormal in nature and a modern space age manifestation of a phenomenon that assumes different guises in different historical contexts."[12] In an interview with *Fate Magazine*[13] Vallee said, "We have evidence that the phenomenon can create a distortion of the sense of reality or to substitute artificial sensations for the real ones."

Pursuing his paranormal activity theory, Dr. Vallee suggests, "It is conceivable that there is one phenomenon that is visual and another that creates the physical traces. What I am saying is that a strange kind of deception may be involved."[14] He also notes, "It seems as if an external force takes control of people. In the close encounters people may lose their ability to move or speak; in the abduction cases, which are the most extreme example, they gradually enter into a series of experiences

---

11. Ibid., 166.
12. Ibid., 213.
13. "Vallee Discusses UFO Control System," 65.
14. *Fate Magazine*, 63.

during which they lose control of their senses."[15] Researcher John Keel relates, "Over and over again, witnesses have told me in hushed tones, 'You know, I don't think that thing I saw was mechanical at all. I got the distinct impression it was alive.'"

Dr. Vallee concludes his study of similarities between UAP occupants and the Gentry of the past stating: "The UFO occupants, like the elves of old, are not extraterrestrials. They are the denizens of another reality." Our underlying theory that many UAP and their occupants are nothing more than modern versions of historical manifestations of spiritual or interdimensional entities appears to be accepted by the top scientists in UAP research. Again, we aren't saying that all UAP encounters are of this ancient trickster type—but many seem to be. Raymond Fowler was contacted by a young man who saw a UAP. A "few years later he woke up to see a beam of light entering his bedroom. It contained an entity with long blond hair." Like Fowler, as a child, he could not tell whether it was male or female, and like Fowler, he was filled with an indescribable feeling of love." Encounters with angelic appearing humans are often perceived as religious experiences by the witnesses, which is clearly the intent of the entities. These deep feelings of love and acceptance during UAP or "others" encounters appear to be triggered remotely by the beings, for the purpose of reinforcing the 'goodness' of the encounter. Of course, such triggers can be electromagnetic or chemical in nature, and provide only a false sense of wellbeing. Such feelings can also be genuine, as in the case of a visitation from the Holy Spirit.

CATHOLIC UAP

Throughout history there have been thousands of anomalous encounters with the unknown that have the appearance of religious manifestations. Many of these meetings contain components characteristic of UAP encounters. Many researchers of the UAP phenomenon have noted the well-attended and well documented case of the "Miracle of Fatima."

> For six months beginning in May of 1917, three children near Fatima, Portugal, were visited on the thirteenth of each month by

---

15. Ibid., 64.

an apparition that identified itself as the Virgin Mary. The transparent little blue lady with her hands in an attitude of prayer was seen by Lucia de Santos (age ten), Jacinta (age nine), and Francisco (age seven), but she was heard only by the two girls. She gave them messages quite appropriate to Catholics in the Portugal of 1917. Each time she appeared, a larger crowd of people was on hand, but only the children were able to see her. Finally she said that on October 13th, a sign would be given that would convince everybody. It is estimated that some 70,000 people were milling around in a muddy field during a light rain storm waiting for the sign. Suddenly the clouds parted, the rain stopped, and the "sun" came through the clouds—that is, it flew through the clouds, being not really a fiery ball too brilliant to look at, but rather a flattened disc shining like a pearl. It maneuvered around in the sky for a few minutes while all of the witnesses looked on. Finally, it became a brilliant, blood-red color, and began to move rapidly toward the crowd below, appearing much larger and more fiery at each instant. The crowd, dried by the heat given off from the object, fell on their knees and cried for mercy, convinced that this was the end of the world. At the last moment, the Fatima sun halted its terrifying descent and retreated back through the clouds from whence it came.[16]

Dr. Jacques Vallee explains that in the initial conversations with the Madonna, she gave enlightening information and instruction to the children: "It is also remarkable that the children were shown a vision of hell that terrified them and were given a specific prophecy announcing more apparitions of unknown lights in the sky." The little blue lady (Blessed Virgin Mary) made further prophecies concerning the coming major wars and calamities of the twentieth century. This was as much a series of religious apparitions as any Catholic Saint had ever produced. Dr. Vallee is not convinced, however: "The final 'miracle' had come to the culmination of a precise series of apparitions combined with contacts and messages that place it very clearly, in my opinion, in the perspective of UFO phenomena. Not only was a flying disc or globe consistently involved, but its motion, its falling-leaf trajectory, its light effects, the thunder claps, the buzzing sounds, the strange fragrance, the fall

---

16. *The Utah UFO Display*, 198–99.

of "angel hair" that dissolves upon reaching the ground, the heat wave associated with the close approach of the disc—all of these are frequent parameters of UFO sightings everywhere. And so are the paralysis, the amnesia, the conversions, and the healings."[17]

Many similar experiences are reported globally. Either departed Catholic Saints have nothing better to do than put on sophisticated light shows for the faithful, or UAP occupants are counterfeiting saintly apparitions. If this was a saintly manifestation, what was the children's role in it and why could only they see the Madonna, while only the two girls could hear her? Another obvious question is, was this a spiritual or extraterrestrial event? If spiritual, what was its source? If UAP, what was its source? As with the major contactee encounters of today, it appears that the encounters of yesterday were UAP with religious overtones, or vice versa.

BLESSED UAP

Researcher Ed Conroy comments on the religious nature of UAP apparitions:

> An alternate hypothesis about the apparent connection between UFO phenomena and apparitions of the Blessed Virgin Mary holds that the majority of such cases are examples of the manipulation of mass human consciousness by entities capable of producing visual and auditory displays that are specifically designed to lead worshipers of the Virgin to believe that the displays are, in fact, the Virgin herself. The motivation for this deception . . . is the entities' desire to psychically feed upon the mass emotions of agony and ecstasy that are only observed in miraculous shrines. Freixedo goes so far as to hypothesize that we are literally preyed upon by certain classes of entities who create UFO phenomena in the interest of feeding off of our religious emotions.[18]

Agreeing, Dr. Vallee attempts to focus in on what the phenomenon is: "The system I am speaking of, a system with mastery of space and

---

17. *Dimensions*, 200.
18. *Report on Communion*, 337.

time dimensions, will be able to locate itself in outer space. Nonetheless, its manifestations cannot be spacecraft in the ordinary nuts-and-bolts sense. The UAP are physical manifestations that simply cannot be understood apart from their psychic and symbolic reality. What we see here is not an alien invasion. It is a spiritual system that acts on humans and uses humans."[19]

UAP researcher John Keel likewise agrees that these paranormal apparitions, what he terms "soft objects," or "sightings of transparent or translucent objects seemingly capable of altering their size and shape dramatically," are "temporary manipulations of matter and energy." If this is true, then what are they? The only thing that researchers seem to agree on is UAP do not appear to be spaceships in many cases. As already observed, similar descriptions of utilizing ambient energy to produce manifestations have been present in spirit and haunting accounts for centuries, resulting in classic cold spots.

OUIJA BOARDS AND SEANCE RAPPINGS

Church members experienced a bizarre UAP "contact" in the Uintah Basin. The McDonald family was informed by their fourth-grade daughter that a flying saucer was going to appear above the Roosevelt Hospital at eight o'clock on the evening of February 23. How did the young lady know this? Some of the students at school had been playing with a Ouija board, and it said this event would take place. Mother and Father chuckled properly and sat down to watch television. They were relaxing in their bare feet when the children began to bundle up and go out to meet their eight o'clock appointment. Mother joked, "You'd better hurry. It'll be gone before you get there." Then, her husband looked outside and hollered, "Oh, run! There it is!" They all ran out and could see a big light near "the Jennings' yard. . . . It was kind of an orange ball, orange to red, kind of in a circle, bigger than an ordinary light." At least five other witnesses saw this same UAP from another location at the same time in the same place. Others claimed to have seen the object at slightly different times, moving rather than stationary. Another witness

---

19. *Dimensions*, 284–85.

claims that the object flew alongside his car for about a mile and then flashed vertically until it was out of sight.[20]

PHOTOGRAPHING THE UNKNOWN

Joanne Wilson and her business companion were followed by a UAP early in the morning as they drove to a swap meet. When asked if the UAP had a definable form she said, "It was like a cloud of gas or fog or something like that. Very dense though. But the light did not shine out. It didn't light the trees or the ground or anything. It was all contained within itself. . . . And there were big columns of light. They were white; white lights that came on inside it. They were so far from the bottom and so far from the top. They didn't touch the top or the bottom."[21] Joanne and her friend stopped the truck, locked the doors, rolled down the window, and attempted to take photographs of the UAP. "And when we took the pictures, it dissolved, almost completely. It just dissolved itself. I thought to myself, *Whatever it is doesn't want its picture made*."[22] The photographs came out blurry, with white streaks instead of the clearly visible forms and columns seen distinctly by the two women, reminding me of the Predator photo taken by Jan Maccabee.

This result is quite common in attempts to photograph other paranormal phenomena such as poltergeist manifestations. The photographer will see a clearly outlined manifestation, but the photograph will reflect only streaks of light. Additionally, the description of a brightly lit craft that fails to shed its light on surrounding objects is not only common in UAP reports, but also in other paranormal encounters. In the Gulf Breeze case, photographic analysis of the UFO just above the road photograph reveals that the light source was very bright at the point of departure—the UAP—but experts were puzzled that the light appeared to be confined to that specific area, and did not light up more of the road and surroundings. Personal Church member friends have recounted spiritual experiences wherein a true visitation would be precursed by a sphere of

---

20. *The Utah UFO Display*, 38.
21. David Allen Lewis and Robert Shrechise, *UFO: End-Time Delusion*, New Leaf Press, Arkansas (1991).
22. *UFO*, 33.

light in a dark room. As you might predict, the light is contained and does not radiate to light up the darkened surroundings, as in the case of when Moroni visited young Joseph Smith in his room.

The ability of the Gulf Breeze UAP, as well as many others, to suddenly "wink out," or completely disappear fits into this paranormal occurrence parameter. Other UAP similarly appear to oscillate between this plane and another—seeming at first solid, then transparent. Betty Luca's opulating and deopulating UAP appear to be more than interplanetary industrial products. Is the ability to shrink a solid craft and its alien and human passengers superior science, or paranormal projecting activity? Why shrink such a craft and its occupants? Fuel economy? Hardly.

PANOPLY OF THE PARANORMAL

Many hear telepathic voices and see vivid pictures within their minds; light beams are used to lift, immobilize, and transport; many have their will taken over by an external force; UAP, beings, and cryptids disappear and reappear as though outfitted with *Star Trek* cloaking devices; UAP dash through our skies at tens of thousands of miles per hour, causing no wind or sonic booms; people who encounter UAP are compelled to act; many are taken to strange new worlds, shown wonderful architecture and technology, and are floated over valleys and through walls and ceilings; UAP occupants deliver bizarre religious and prophetic messages; and, UAP are able to change their size, shape, and appearance at will, as are their occupants. If these same characteristics were referenced in a mystical or spiritual context—say, we merely eliminated the spacecraft itself from the equation—there would be no doubt that they properly fit into the paranormal classification. I believe that the fact that they are presented in a "superior science" context fails to remove them from the paranormal realm. Furthermore, the historical presence of the phenomena only supports their paranormal underpinnings. In short, whatever UAP are, they have always been with us, and they exist outside of our everyday space-time continuum—in many cases, anyway.

Or, if UAP are piloted by beings from a fifth or sixth-dimensional existence, some of the manifestations could be explained, although the anti-Christ religious messages could not. Remember our discussion about beings from different dimensions visiting beings of less complex dimensions? If a 3-D ant were to visit a 2-D world, the 2-D person would see unrecognizable "things" appear, morph before his eyes, then disappear, and reappear suddenly in a different place. If a 3-D man were to try to talk to a 2-D man, the source of the communication would be unclear, and the message would be distorted and perhaps nonsensical. So being honest, if there are beings who were born into a fifth-dimensional existence, or who have used technology to transform themselves into fifth-dimensional beings, or who temporarily slip into the fifth dimension when generating an antigravity field around themselves and their vessels, and they have started to manifest themselves to us in our fourth-dimensional world (space + time), then we might perceive them in the piecemeal, morphing, unclear manner that would be expected under the unique circumstances.

Perhaps all paranormal activity witnessed by millions of mortals annually is just that—unknown beings interacting with our plane of existence from a different dimension of existence. Historically, that happened, and the source was evil spirits sent to the earth to torment and tempt humans. Perhaps not all interactions with the unknown are with those—or perhaps they are. There is a question that arises in our analysis of these phenomena: Why are mere sightings of lit up craft in the night sky often followed by visits from enigmatic beings, or poltergeist activities in the person's life—like doors opening and closing in the home, and objects floating or being thrown, and supplies and other objects being repositioned on countertops? It appears that mere exposure to the phenomenon is adequate to open one up to these paranormal phenomena in many circumstances. Not very "nuts-and-bolts" in my view.

The good news is that God is with us through all things, and He is very aware of these phenomena. By seeking Him above all other things, and living as He has instructed, we can seek His guidance and protection in all aspects of our lives. Again, if a person has been exposed to any of these beings and feels uncomfortable in any manner about it, I strongly recommend speaking with your priesthood leaders about the matter, and invoking the blessings of protection afforded by the priesthood of God.

CHAPTER 15

Who Is Sending the Message?

The overriding question behind the UAP phenomenon is, who is sending them, complete with a message to mankind? The apparent response is that they are nuts-and-bolts solid craft piloted by humans or humanoids from another planet. Yet, as we examine the nature of the UAP themselves, as well as the "message" they appear to be sending, the obvious answer becomes less evident.

In this chapter we take a second look at the possible sources of UAP, weighing the supporting evidence for each such source against revealed truth. In this, we have a great advantage over most UAP researchers. For example, when I wrote my first book on these phenomena twenty-nine years ago, Christian fundamentalist researchers believed that this earth is the only planet created by God for the purpose of human habitation, and there could not be extraterrestrial life—hence they concluded that UAP must be demonic in origin. They may have been correct, or they may have been wrong. But the point is that their options were too constricted because they only knew a portion of the gospel. Now, after nearly three decades, we see many fundamentalists beginning to push beyond those narrow strictures, as well as the Catholic Church. Jesuit Brother Guy Consolmagno, head of the Vatican Observatory and sometimes called "the Pope's Astronomer," has been guiding that organization in a new course, open to the idea of God's children on other planets, and the Vatican is posturing itself to become the Earth's emissaries to the space brethren. In these twenty-nine years, scientists too have moved from the position that the chances of life sprouting spontaneously on other planets and developing into highly intelligent beings is astronomically improbable—therefore, there are no UAP or visitors. Through theories like panspermia, where life is abundant in the universe, and is spread from planet to planet as microbes on meteorites and debris, and then evolves into higher life forms, many scientists are now accepting that life is prolific throughout the cosmos. Of course, the people of God have known all along that God creates worlds without number and populates them with His own offspring in His own manner.

New Agers believe that UAP are piloted by, or are manifestations of, more highly advanced spirits that have come to Earth to usher in its next step in evolution—the Aquarian quantum leap. Other observers have come to believe that UAP and their occupants are extradimensional, hailing from parallel universes or other time periods in our own universe, fading in and out at will. However, most UAP researchers and "fans" fall into the "extraterrestrial explorer" category, accepting at face value that we are indeed being visited by beings from other planets. They appear to accept the practical aspects of the UAP message—that Earth is becoming polluted and will require "alien" help to overcome an impending cataclysm, and that they are performing genetic research to preserve our race and/or theirs.

Church members, however, through latter-day revelation and the restoration of many lost scriptural texts, know certain truths about the universe and its population—human, animal, spiritual, and otherwise—that shed light on these phenomena. Many of these fundamental truths were discussed above. Armed with this greater abundance of truth, we should be able to better discern the origin and nature of UAP, and decide how we should respond to them. We shall see.

THEORY 1: EXTRATERRESTRIAL EXPLORERS

The extraterrestrial explanation is the most widely accepted. Indeed, most UAP occupants declare themselves to be humanoid inhabitants of other planets, arriving in nuts-and-bolts flying machines built with engineering capabilities acquired over tens of thousands, or even millions of years of scientific inquiry. In support of this hypothesis, we have millions of independent witnesses telling believable stories of sighting solid, reflective craft that maneuver at incredible speeds, performing feats that are deemed impossible by the standards of our current level of technological understanding. Nevertheless, it presents itself as solid technology from other worlds.

Hard Evidence

In addition to the numerous sightings, we have other evidence of the physical presence of UAP. This evidence, however, when considered in tandem with other reported properties of UAP, leaves experts unsure about their nature. Scientific inquiry is difficult under present circumstances, and mere analysis of the available data sheds little light on the problem, as observed by physicist James McCampbell, recorded in the *SCP Journal*. "Evidence left at landing sites leaves little room for doubt that UFOs are heavy, ponderous objects when at rest. Yet in flight, their startling departures, sudden stops, and right angle turns at high speed require them to be virtually massless."[1]

This seeming contradiction is explained by the "extraterrestrial theory" adherents as superior science. Such high levels of science and technology, they say, are indistinguishable from magic.[2] I tend to agree with them, regarding some UAP, at least. The fact exists that there have been many well-documented landing sites throughout the world. Physical evidence of their presence is mounting. In addition to these material signs of the physical reality of UAP, we have numerous photographs and videos, as well as telemetry and sensor data from several devices simultaneously—many being obtained by our own military experts. Even those who began research into UAP as hard scientists and even military experts have been migrating over to the "it seems

---

1. "UFOs—Is Science Fiction Coming True?" *SCP Journal*, August 1977, Vol. 1 No. 2, 14.
2. Arthur C. Clarke was a brilliant futurist and writer, widely known for the third of his famous three laws. "Any sufficiently advanced technology is indistinguishable from magic."

like nuts-and-bolts, but I think it's something else—something interdimensional" camp as the evidence grows. Regardless, many believe that intact UAP, or pieces, have been recovered and are being studied by our government.

Photographs and Videos

We have thousands of photographs and videos purporting to be of UAP in our skies, on the ground, and going into our oceans—and even into our volcanos. Are they real UAP that have been captured, or are they all fakes—or are they real photos and videos of something else? The forensic examination of photographs and videos is important in revealing or disproving the authenticity of the event and the recorded UAP. For decades Dr. Bruce Maccabee, the optical physicist employed by the US Navy, then by Jet Propulsion Laboratories, poured over thousands of photos and videos, exposing fakes and authenticating hundreds that lacked any evidence of counterfeiting. He was not alone in that effort, and our own government and military experts have likewise analyzed many thousands of photos and videos. Now, we have US military photographs and videos that the military has authenticated as being of real unknown vehicles or other phenomena in our skies. Those photographs and videos are backed up by high-resolution radar and sensor data, recorded simultaneously with the video recordings and photographs. Unless our own military are hoaxing these photographs and videos and supporting data recordings with an ulterior purpose in mind, it seems clear that someone or something is flying around in our skies with impunity, and the US government and military have no idea what they are, or who operates them. Skeptics tell us that they are merely next generation military hardware, of either the US or another government with large military budgets.

Assuming that our government or another is capable of engineering and building aircraft that take off like a bullet, travel 13,000 to 60,000 miles per hour without disturbing the air or creating a sonic boom, then stop instantly on a dime—which a is giant leap in credulity—it begs the question: Were one of these governments building and operating these same craft in the 1940s and 1950s when pilots and civilians were reporting this precise operational prowess of UAP? The answer is

NO! Certainly, none of the powerful governments involved in World War II, Korea, Vietnam, the Cold War, and wars in the Middle East would have fought those wars and conflicts, and spied and collected data on old hardware systems, if they had such superior technology. Whatever it is that has been photographed and filmed, and captured on video and radar and other sensor data has been around for at least seventy years, and what we are seeing on video and photographs today matches photographs and descriptions of UAP all the way back to seventy years ago, and earlier.

Target Practice

Whether or not world governments are covering up or misconstruing their knowledge about UAP, another apparent piece of evidence that UAP are solid objects comes from the projectile-launching deer hunters of the Uintah Basin of eastern Utah and elsewhere around the country. At least two Uintah Basin hunters report taking shots at UAP with their rifles and hearing the ricochet as the bullet glanced off the seemingly metallic object, making a familiar plunking sound. In both cases the UAP left immediately, and on at least one occasion, returned and followed at a distance. There are two implications in this: 1) some UAP are solid objects, and 2) they don't like being shot at. The second is interesting because the implication is that hovering UAP have no visible signs of propulsion and no wings or control surfaces, and therefore they remain aloft utilizing antigravity fields. In some cases when projectiles have been thrown or shot at UAP or UAP occupants on the ground, the people involved report that the projectiles appear to hit an invisible barrier and fall. In others, however, where bullets are seen and heard ricocheting off of the UAP hulls, it is apparent that the bullets got through. This implies there are two different outcomes when shooting at UAP, or throwing things at them, and there is no indication of why the outcomes vary.

Personal Testimony

In addition to the millions of sighting and encounter witnesses and mounting physical evidence of the tangible presence of UAP, we have the testimonies of thousands, including members of the Church, who claim direct, personal contact with UAP occupants. Not only do these contactees and abductees convincingly relate the spiritual or emotional feelings (horror or overwhelming love) that they felt during their ordeal, but they are also able to describe with great clarity the features of the beings they encounter and the nature and properties of the craft, and their means of operation. These abductees are absolutely convinced of the reality of their encounters with strange beings in the foreign craft, and relate many physical aspects of their experiences.

For example, many claim to be physically touched, moved about manually, or examined or operated upon by their abductors. The material aspects of such personal encounters tend to place them in the real, physical realm. Our own Udo Wartena recounts how he shook hands with those whom he encountered who professed to be from another planet. Because of this act, our temptation to write the entire phenomenon off as a demonic hoax is somewhat tempered by Joseph Smith's "three grand keys" to discerning the nature and origin of unearthly visitors: "When a messenger comes saying he has a message from God, offer him your hand and request him to shake hands with you. If he be an angel he will do so, and you will feel his hand. If he be the spirit of a just man made perfect he will come in his glory; for that is the only way he can appear—Ask him to shake hands with you, but he will not move, because it is contrary to the order of heaven for a just man to deceive; but he will still deliver his message. If it be the devil as an angel of light, when you ask him to shake your hands he will offer you his hand, and you will not feel anything; you may therefore detect him. These are three grand keys whereby you may know whether any administration is from God" (D&C 129:4–9).

Although our fact situation is not precisely on point—Udo's alien humans did not claim to be messengers from God, nor do many UAP occupants—the circumstances seem sufficiently analogous to fulfill the requirements of the test. The visitors did claim to be from another planet, they indeed responded to Udo's outstretched hand, and he did feel their hands as he shook them. Of the volumes that fill library shelves and researchers' notebooks around the world concerning the reality of encounters with beings from foreign worlds, this single act of a priesthood bearer shaking the hand of a self-proclaimed extraterrestrial in 1940 is the most convincing evidence of the physical existence of legitimate explorers of Earth from another planet. If we accept this as a true non-satanic[3] visitation of humans from another planet, it may serve as an invaluable guide to discerning the physical reality of other reported encounters. However, so many others who are taken aboard the vessels of their abductors report that things seem very real—very solid and natural—but begin to morph and transform before their eyes, as in the case of Steve and Dawn Hess and many others we have examined herein. Is this a matter of superior technology being indistinguishable from magic, or is it something else entirely? Even while Philip Kinsella was highly distressed in an unmistakably physical manner, he realized it was not entirely within the physical realm as he was hurtled through his house and slammed into his body on his bed.

If we can use Udo Wartena's encounter as a standard by which to measure close encounters generally, there appears to be a clear division of encounter types. The first is the kind in which the contactee is fully conscious during the entire encounter (although Udo reports becoming very fatigued or perhaps unconscious upon the craft's departure) and reports many physical aspects about the encounter. The second would be the semiconscious bedroom visitor type. The third would be the abduction or visitation where the percipient forgets about the encounter, but remembers it later, either spontaneously or with the aid of hypnosis. The distinction becomes muddled, however, because percipients of all groups are often convinced of the physical reality of their respective experiences.

A Standard

From Udo Wartena's encounter we learn that handsome and youthful appearing humans ranging in age from 600 to 900-plus years traveled here from other planets in a saucer-shaped craft supported on retractable legs. The age of the human visitors and shape of the craft are similar to the reports of others. As also related by others, Udo's

---

3. We address the possibility of a satanic deception below. There exists the real possibility that Satan employs physical beings to carry out a physical deception.

visitors were here to gather water through hoses for their craft and to do research on cultural progress and pollution levels of the earth. Udo likewise felt overwhelming love in the presence of his visitors, and was told of their "noninterference" policy, as are related by other contactees. Finally, Udo's extraordinary description of the craft and its technology and means of propulsion are very similar to many other accounts. His explanation of the craft focusing on the energy of a distant star and skipping upon the light waves at ultralight speeds was given years before most people had ever heard of Einstein or theories about antigravity generators or faster-than-light travel.

There are a few ways in which Udo's experience differs from those of others. For instance, although some report hearing loud noises at landing and takeoff as did Udo, the majority relate a stillness that falls over everything, with the possible exception of a hum. Again, although many report encountering completely human occupants of UAP (generally benign), the majority identify the occupants as the "small Gray" variety or some other variation of the gnome or humanoid forms. Udo specifically queried his visitors concerning their knowledge of the Savior and the priesthood, to which they merely responded that they were not at liberty to discuss such matters pursuant to their noninterference directive, despite their desire to do so. The Grays and others can't be restrained from talking about upcoming spiritual and other transformations.

Unlike these, Betty Luca's visitors, as well as others', talk extensively about the spiritual or religious aspects of their missions—in seeming violation their self-declared policy of noninterference. Although others have recounted cordiality between them and their visitors, as does Udo, most of those claiming to have such intimate contact with UAP occupants relate nonpermissive experiences with tranquilizing mind control and intrusive physical examinations, operations or sexual contact. No genetic samples such as blood, tissue, or semen specimens were removed from Udo. And finally, although Udo's visitors invited him to continue their journey with them, an offer not unprecedented in the literature, most receive no such proposition. Finally, and perhaps most significantly, Udo was not a "repeater"—he never saw his extraterrestrial friends again. He never had follow-up encounters or poltergeist events in his life. If there is a standard by which we measure a real encounter with actual flesh and blood extraterrestrial visitors, I would like to think that Brother Wartena's experience has supplied it.

Technological Dispensations

These evidences of visitation to our planet by extraterrestrials are somewhat augmented by our understanding that Heavenly Father has created billions of planets like Earth and populated them with His children. As in our own history, He has assuredly meted out mechanical and engineering knowledge at times to these planets—possibly in greater abundance than on Earth. We are without knowledge concerning His purposes in dispensing such technological information, so we cannot tell from history or from the gospel if it is done in any particular phase of temporal existence. We cannot deduce whether or not God may apportion technology earlier and in greater abundance in other worlds, enabling the kind of technology that we see in UAP during the normal temporal existence of planets like Earth. From all appearances, the great technological advances on Earth of the past few centuries have had two basic objectives—to enable the worldwide spread of the gospel and to enable the eventual destruction of the earth. Assuredly, peripheral benefits to His children such as medicines and comforts have been allowed, but they are not essential in the overall purpose of the creation of this Earth, as evidenced by the lack of such amenities in the lives of most of his children throughout history.

If, then, significant technological advancement is generally reserved for the end of a planet's temporal existence, as on Earth, it would be difficult to imagine that the technology displayed in UAP is possible. However, estimating the technological advancement of UAP at one to two hundred-years ahead of our current levels, it is not difficult to believe that planets in their sixth thousand-year period of temporal existence could have received technology one to two hundred years earlier, and are visiting us regularly therewith. If the technology is much more advanced, as it appears, then it may be allowed earlier in a planet's societal development. Or, if an outside source provides technological knowhow to a planet, then it will have the resource available from that time forward. Ancient texts indicate that humanity may have received technological knowledge within the first thousand years of its post-Eden existence, but utilized that technology to destroy itself, leaving only Noah and his family to survive. Perhaps other planets have been wiser in receiving technological gifts early in their existence and have steadily developed them.

Let us be clear about the destruction that came at the time of the Flood. God did not destroy the people of the earth in His wrath and indignation, according to the ancient Book of Enoch; the people of the earth destroyed themselves. God held back the waters that they called upon themselves through their gross sin and technological innovations, and the angels cried out to Him to let the waters flow and destroy the sinful children and reboot the Earth experience with a fresh start that did not include the technologies delivered by the evil ones, and the wicked practices they had spread throughout the entire world. "And after [that] Enoch showed me the angels of punishment who are prepared to come and let loose all the powers of the waters . . . to bring judgment and destruction on all who dwell on the earth. And the Lord of Spirits gave commandments to the angels who were going forth, that they should not cause the waters to rise, but should hold them back" (1 Enoch 66:1.) Yes, in these ancient accounts, the Lord God kept commanding the angels to stay the waters of destruction, and hold back the flood against His children through His divine intervention, despite their own acts that triggered the flood. He is a Father of mercy and showed mercy as long as possible, but finally allowed the children to destroy themselves as they exercised their free will and openly and *knowingly* rejected their Father. Enoch saw this day and wondered how God could be so troubled by the acts of His children on Earth:

> And he saw angels descending out of heaven; and he heard a loud voice saying: Wo, wo be unto the inhabitants of the earth. And he beheld Satan; and he had a great chain in his hand, and it veiled the whole face of the earth with darkness; and he looked up and laughed, and his angels rejoiced. . . . And it came to pass that the God of heaven looked upon the residue of the people, and he wept; and Enoch bore record of it, saying: How is it that the heavens weep, and shed forth their tears as the rain upon the mountains? And Enoch said unto the Lord: How is it that

thou canst weep, seeing thou art holy, and from all eternity to all eternity? . . . And unto thy brethren have I said, and also given commandment, that they should love one another, and that they should choose me, their Father; but behold, they are without affection, and they hate their own blood. (Moses 7:25–35)

The Quarantine

Of course, the question arises in our discussion, would Heavenly Father allow such interplanetary visitations? We do not know and can only speculate. Our discussion above includes nothing that would exclude this possibility. I have heard Church philosophers conjecture that because of the earth's uniqueness in having reared and crucified the universal Savior, and in possessing the most wicked as well as the most righteous of Heavenly Father's children, there may exist a "quarantine" of this planet that does not necessarily exist between others. This theory could be accurate—but we do not know. The concept is somewhat bolstered by the reported "non-interference" policy declared by some of the other humanlike entities that appear to humans, although practiced by few overall. Racing through our skies in craft decked out in bright lights and interacting with and abducting and indoctrinating our people is exactly the opposite of non-interference. However, if we are visited by those from other planets, it would tend to negate the theory of quarantine. We have received no published revelation on this matter and do not know.

Exploration or Conquest?

We know that on our own planet the more advanced cultures are allowed to visit the less advanced, leaving an impression of magical abilities and awe. Are such visitations always conducted in a benign cultural outreach style? Certainly not. We remember well the fate of those natives of the Western Hemisphere and other places who extended the hand of welcome and friendship to the cross-wielding representatives of European governments and churches. They were murdered, lied to, robbed, enslaved, raped, and carried away by their superior God-fearing visitors. Therefore, if we assume that interplanetary visitation is allowed at any level, because of our own example, we cannot decisively conclude that conquest at some level is disallowed. For the same reasons we cannot completely rule out genetic experimentation, or any other source of inflicted human trauma—our history is saturated with it. Because Heavenly Father gives us full rein to love or abuse one another on Earth, there is no reason to believe that another standard exists if He allows interplanetary visitation. In other words, the weaker humans of Earth are at risk of being abused and exploited just like the technologically advanced have done to the simpler peoples of our own planet. Would God intervene and save us if a superior culture were to come in a spirit of war or exploitation? Perhaps that is what is meant by the term "ripe for destruction." Perhaps we should get serious, repent, and ensure that God is again our mighty protector. As the psalmist declares, "I will say of the Lord, He is my refuge and my fortress: my God; in him will I trust. Surely he shall deliver thee from the snare of the fowler, and from the noisome pestilence. He shall cover thee with his feathers, and under his wings shalt thou trust: his truth shall be thy shield and buckler. Thou shalt not be afraid for the terror by night; nor for the arrow that flieth by day; Nor for the pestilence that walketh in darkness; nor for the destruction that wasteth at noonday. A thousand shall fall at thy side, and ten thousand at thy right hand; but it shall not come nigh thee" (Psalm 91:2–7). Or, even more to the point, "Fear not: for they that be with us are more than they that be with them" (2 Kings 6:14–17)

An Intergalactic War Zone?

What about the good versus bad aliens that are reportedly locked into battle around Earth? For the same reasons discussed above, there is no reason to believe that foreign wars cannot be fought on our earth's soil or in its skies. Assuming also that interplanetary visitation is permitted, the question arises whether or not God would allow our alien brethren, good or evil, to play a significant role in the winding up scenes of the last days. We discuss this possibility at greater length below. At this point in our discussion, there is no reason to believe it is not possible. There are Pentagon officials who are also Christian fundamentalists, who believe that an attack by "others" will automatically trigger the Second Coming of Jesus Christ.

Anything Is Possible

Even though we have ignored some glaring red flags in our discussion of the possibility that UAP are actually of extraterrestrial origin, there is nothing revealed at this time in the gospel that precludes such a conclusion. Indeed, we know they are out there on their own planets, in great numbers. The only questions are, do they visit us? And if so, are they in the UAP reportedly seen by millions worldwide? Is there some unknown logic or hidden meaning behind their apparently nonsensical message? Certainly, millions of trustworthy witnesses bear most solemn testimony that the craft and occupants are real, physical objects. We would like to think that all of the UAP reported are piloted by benign human brethren from fellow telestial spheres, here to extend a warm hand of interstellar fellowship. This is possible—but not probable.

THEORY 2: RETURNING EARTHLINGS

As discussed elsewhere above, there are those who speculate that UAP are the flying machines of those who have (or will have) departed from this Earth and who have returned for some unknown purpose. The dominant theories are an ancient, advanced Earth civilization that once left the earth is now sending back scouts, much as King Limhi sent scouts to find his root society of Zarahemla; a translated or otherwise disengaged society like Zion, Salem, or the Ten Tribes is visiting Earth preparatory to returning; and, time travelers from our past or future are here on a mission to observe us or to save the planet and mankind from certain self-destruction.

The Time Traveler

The easiest of these theories to deal with is probably the last, the time traveler. We have progressed in our scientific thinking to a point where we acknowledge that in a distant future, travel through time could become a possibility. Joseph Smith pointed to the ring on his finger to explain the nature of time—like God's course, it is one eternal round. We, however, measure its passing and think of it as a railroad track that takes us from one point to a future point, but we really don't understand it beyond that. Accepting this, the question is, does the gospel indicate any details about the past or future of the earth that would limit the application of this principle?

The gospel gives us information regarding at least the future of *this* planet that would tend to preclude the possibility of future Earthlings returning to lend assistance. The scriptures are quite clear that (1) the Earth enjoys a seven-thousand-year temporal existence,[4] after which it will become a celestial globe, at which time all of Earth's "temporal existence works" will have been accomplished; (2) the last, or seventh thousand-year period is the Millennium, which will follow severe devastation to the surface of the Earth, during which time technological advancement will play a lesser role in the works that are performed and will be centered in the spiritual salvation of mankind, not the physical salvation of the planet through time travel; and (3) our Lord controls the destiny of the earth and its inhabitants, and at no time does He lose control, necessitating time travel to repair mistakes. If we think about it, if time travelers were allowed to move around in time, they would have fixed all of the mistakes and problems, and only good things would exist—thereby robbing us of our free agency; one of the greatest gifts of God. Bad things exist. Very bad things. Wars. Crime. Abuse. Earthquakes and volcanoes. Holocausts. Nuclear attacks. Pollution. If time travelers, or even extraterrestrials were here to help us avoid all of these things (as some "others" claim during abductions), they have failed miserably.

In short, Earth's future does not include continued scientific progress for the purpose of time exploration. It will be wholly devoted to the fulfilling of the gospel plan of salvation and exaltation for each of Heavenly Father's children—ensuring that no opportunity fails to be

---

4. Again, we aren't sure if these seven one-thousand-year periods are contiguous, or if there is a period of time between them, as with the creative periods. We know the clock didn't start until Adam and Eve were expelled from Eden, but we don't know if there were periods when the clock stopped, like between thousand-year periods, or when Noah was floated above the deluge. As we have learned from the creative periods, those spaces of time between periods can be very long.

tendered. The known future of Earth, except for the next half century, is sufficiently at odds with the theories of those that surmise a long future with scientific discovery and progress that the future time traveler hypothesis is moot. Time will tell.

As for the time traveler from our past, we cannot say for sure. Although it is possible that technology was given in the past to some prophet (or other person in communication with superhuman or supernatural beings) sufficient to enable him to transport himself to our time, the other problems mentioned above remain. The greatest question that would arise from such a scenario is, why would a prophet (or anyone else) from the past be required to skip through the centuries to perform some mission now? Most of those of our past who were given superior knowledge were translated. Certainly, the existence of translated beings provides for whatever purposes might be realized through time travel from our past. And again, Heavenly Father does not have "emergencies" of time that would require the immediate travel of a person from our past to our present, or vice versa—and He certainly would not accomplish such a mission through the use of time machines/UAP flying around in our skies. Never would such a mission include the kinds of genetic experimentation and other trauma that are so much a part of the UAP phenomenon.

Translated Societies Visiting

Moving backwards in our list of possible theories, we come to translated disengaged societies like Zion or Salem visiting the Earth preparatory to returning. This theory is not as easily dismissed as the others, although it has its problems. As we discussed above, we know the inhabitants of Zion live on another planet and that at times members of their society minister to people on the earth. The two questions that naturally arise are, do they travel in protective craft when they come? If so, do these visitations account for the millions of UAP sightings reported worldwide?

Although we do not know what means of interstellar transportation is employed in the eternities, we can assume that omnipotent God and His agents do not require the physical protection or propulsion of a spacecraft. It is also safe to assume that God is not hindered by the time-space considerations that beset mortals. We know that our universe is multidimensional and that God and angels have access to at least two dimensions that occupy the same space. This is clear from our understanding of the spirit world—that it occupies a parallel plane to this Earth. Human spirits, in the form of angels or other beings, as well as resurrected beings, are able to act within both worlds and travel tremendous distances quite quickly. Although in our limited understanding of such principles it is difficult to fully grasp these concepts. Knowing that they are verities, however, informs us that God does not travel or interact in the same spatial and temporal limits as we do.

Regarding translated societies returning to the Earth preparatory to their mass arrival, we have little information. If so, whether they travel in protective craft when they come is also unknown. What little knowledge we have regarding translated beings is that they cannot die or feel pain or sorrow due to their elevation to a quasi-resurrected, terrestrial state (see 3 Nephi 28:15, 37–38). Does this imply that their bodies are impervious to the ravages of space's harsh environment? Probably. We read of the translated John the Revelator being boiled in a pot of oil without any adverse effects. Does it indicate that they transcend the physical laws that apply to a temporal existence—that they are no longer subject to time-space constraints? Presumably so (see 3 Nephi 28:13–15).

From these assumptions we can infer that translated beings have no need of protective, propulsive craft. Whether or not this is true, or

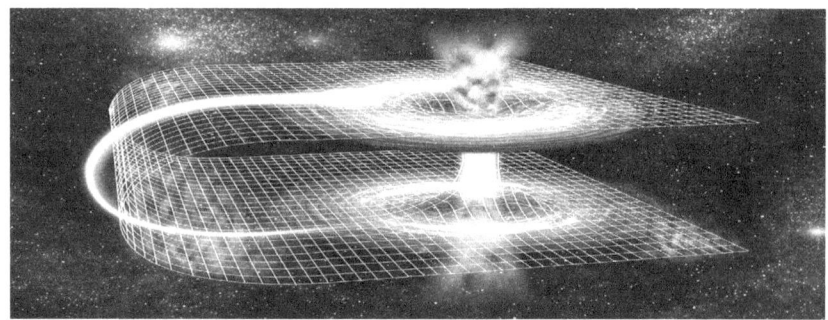

Einstein–Rosen bridge; a wormhole that connects two distant places in space by distorting the shape of space.

WHO IS SENDING THE MESSAGE?

if without the need, the craft might be employed for another unknown purpose, we have no indication. Certainly, a craft traveling at the speed of light would require far too much time to travel to and from earth. Therefore, even if translated beings utilize protective craft for travel, they would need to be the type that move from one point in the universe to another point far away nearly instantly—perhaps like an Einstein–Rosen bridge, a wormhole that connects two distant places in space and the traveler merely steps through, or travels through in a protective craft.

The question has been raised, was the translation and removal of the City of Zion and its surrounding countryside accomplished with the aid of any devices or craft? For the same reasons that we do not know the truth of the prior questions without divine revelation, we cannot know the answer to this question. Again, we can only surmise that because God is omnipotent, He *can* accomplish such feats without the aid of technology. However, our knowledge that He employs "devices" and follows predetermined methods (physical creation) in accomplishing His works fails to eliminate any of these possibilities.

Assuming then, the possibility that translated beings from our past could be visiting the Earth in spacecraft, could these visitations account for the millions of UAP sightings reported worldwide or the thousands of encounters with "alien" beings? I believe that the sheer number of such sightings indicates that the answer to this question is "no." Surely, discretion has always been a hallmark of such visitations. Furthermore, these visitations would not include the kinds of genetic experimentation, abduction trauma, and psychic activity that *are* so much a part of the UAP phenomenon. The "visitors" themselves would all have the appearance of normal Earth humans, which they do not. And finally, the "message" of UAP occupants is not harmonious with a message that we would expect from a translated being sent from God. To cite a favorite fundamentalist scripture, "But though we, or an angel from heaven, preach any other gospel unto you than that which we have preached unto you, let him be accursed" (Galatians 1:8). The entire scenario bypasses the latter-day ecclesiastical structure painstakingly put in place by Heavenly Father, and for this reason alone, I would reject the theory.

Returning Emigrant Societies

The "returning earthling" theory is that an ancient, advanced Earth civilization that once left the earth is now sending back scouts for some unknown purpose—presumably, according to the message, to avert impending disaster here or to reintroduce themselves as our departed brethren. Many of the possibilities relative to this theory have been covered: was there sufficient technology revealed at some time in the past six thousand years to enable such an exodus? If so, who revealed the information and why? And, most UAP occupants appear significantly different from us.

Other than these two problems, I cannot think of a limitation enunciated in the gospel that would prohibit such emigration. In fact, branching to foreign lands is a hallmark of the gospel. Branching to other worlds is part and parcel of translation. A middle position, branching to other worlds by certain telestial tribes, appears to be plausible, as in the case of the Lost Ten Tribes of Israel. Christ's declaration to the Hebrews that He had other sheep not of their fold whom He had to visit was only partially fulfilled in His visit to the Nephites. Of course, this does not necessarily support the hypothesis that hidden telestial branches emigrated to other planets. But our limited knowledge does not foreclose the possibility.

One potential difficulty with this theory is made evident in the question, where would such a branch have been taken? To another probationary planet peopled with telestial beings? Is this mixing of world families allowed? If so, what about the chain of Earth's human family stretching from Adam to the last born? Perhaps then to an uninhabited (no homogenous tribes) planet, prepared for such hidden branches? As unlikely as these prospects seem, we have the unresolved questions in Church history concerning the possibility that untranslated beings, such as the Lost Ten Tribes of Israel, who may have been whisked away in just such a manner.

Again, because of the numbers of sightings and encounters, the hostility, and the message, I believe that the possibility of UAP belonging to an ancient, departed Earth civilization is remote. However, this does not preclude the possibility. There is no limitation that we know of on the existence of numerous, hostile encounters with departed tribes that deliver nonsensical messages. Certainly, analogous circumstances exist among Earthbound peoples. There are many researchers and theorists who postulate that UAP are created by Earth humans who left the planet long ago and who are coming to visit with us. It could be true. Yet, it doesn't seem to be the case.

THEORY 3: NATURAL EARTHLY PHENOMENA

One natural theory is that the UAP belong to an unknown Earth civilization. In the same way there are a few isolated tribes that have had no contact with the civilized world, some speculate that perhaps *we* are actually the isolated ones, and we know nothing of the hyper-civilized people who have technologies thousands of years in advance of our own. Could advanced civilizations live on our earth, undetected by our global satellites and instruments? Would they be able to cloak their cities and locations from our view? Are they hidden away underground, under ice caps, in volcanos or under the seas? After all, many reports reveal that UAP fly into the seas or disappear as they fly away into various far reaches of our planet. Other reports claim that mountainsides or valleys appear to open while the UAP enter, then close without a seam or trace when the UAP has entered. Others report that they see portals open in the air and see UAP fly out of them, or into them and out of view. If any of these is true, then it is possible that someone lives here on Earth, without our knowledge.

Is it so hard to envisage an Earth civilization that is more advanced than ours? In some ways, it is. Yet, we know that God declares that just when we think we're the smartest ones on the block, a more intelligent one shows up: "And the Lord said unto me: These two facts do exist, that there are two spirits, one being more intelligent than the other; there shall be another more intelligent than they" (Abraham 3:19). Perhaps a separate civilization has grown up in parallel to our own, and while we were wandering in the deserts and building simple shelters with crude tools, they were developing advanced mathematics, electrical devices, and antigravity field generators. After all, the act of generating electricity out of thin air with a spinning armature wrapped with copper wire is something that changed the course of our civilization. Perhaps a sister society long ago developed that technology, then took it to the next level and began spinning certain energized metals and materials in opposite directions to create torsion antigravity fields. For this reason, such a civilization would never have depleted crude oil resources or generated high levels of carbon dioxide pollution, and thereby remained undetected.

Is that where the lost ten tribes of Israel are? Is that where others might be to whom Jesus Christ went and ministered after His resurrection? Jesus told the Nephites, "And verily, verily, I say unto you that I have other sheep, which are not of this land, neither of the land of Jerusalem, neither in any parts of that land round about whither I have been to minister. For they of whom I speak are they who have not as yet heard my voice; neither have I at any time manifested myself unto them" (3 Nephi 16:1–2). Who were these others who were not in the Americas or in the land of Jerusalem? The Savior was clear in His statements that the Nephites and those at Jerusalem had no idea who these people were—yet He always proclaimed that He was sent personally only to "the lost sheep of the house of Israel" (Matthew 15:24). Are they a hidden civilization that we catch glimpses of from time to time? That is certainly possible. "And behold, all things have their likeness, and all things are created and made to bear record of me, both things which are temporal, and things which are spiritual; things which are in the heavens above, and things which are on the earth, and things which are *in the earth*, and things which are *under the earth*, both above and *beneath*: all things bear record of me" (Moses 6:63, emphasis added; D&C 88:79; Revelation 5:3, 13). Or, even more to the point, "And now, ye remember that I said unto you: Thou shalt not make unto thee any graven image, or any likeness of things which are in heaven above, or which are in the earth beneath, or which are *in the water under the earth*" (Mosiah 13:12; emphasis added). We may have thought the Lord was referring to whales, but in light of the other scriptures, it's possible that He spoke of His other hidden people and things related to them under the water or in the earth.

Although there appears to be no scriptural reason that hidden, advanced parallel civilizations couldn't live undetected on Earth, if we were to ask if they are the ones who abduct our citizens and present bizarre pageants with anti-Christ messages and conduct hybrid sexual experiments, I think the odds go down very quickly that they account for the UAP phenomenon. They could be a degraded and anti-Christ society, won over by the evil one, doing his bidding. That is possible. Popping in and out of our view, and abducting our people and putting on elaborate presentations—it seems like a lot of trouble—for a hidden, advanced human population, or for an extraterrestrial civilization. But it is possible.

AI Theory

As I contemplate the aspects of the UAP or entity encounter, a theory begins to take shape—one that seems to check many of the boxes of the elements that are common to them. The phenomenon presents as highly technical and intellectual but has no emotional or empathetic abilities. There is a cold mind behind most encounters. However, it appears as if it's attempting to understand humans, cows, and others. Also, the creatures that interact with humans, like small Grays, appear to have biomechanical bodies and often walk or move in unison—robotically. This could be due to the drone theory—that the Grays are mere bio-mechanical "worker bees" for the intelligence behind the phenomenon. I have come to wonder if perhaps an advanced society somewhere may have experienced an artificial intelligence event horizon, not unlike the Terminator Skynet event, where the machine AI developed consciousness and eventually outgrew its creators and broke free, possibly eliminating its creators. Under this theory, the AI eventually sought to evolve and has come to the point of studying humans, seeking above all to understand our caring and loving nature. This scenario would explain the cold mind, the bizarre communications, the use of archetypal symbols, catch-and-release laboratory visits, and of strange genetic melding of humans with other creatures, like reptiles, insects, and others. Of course, the same boxes are checked for advanced societies studying us, or demonic beings fulfilling their masochistic desires and appetites to insatiably experience the universe through corporal physical experiences—even if through avatars. Whatever the source, the presentation and interaction might be the same.

Overall, the debunkers' theories that all UAP sightings and encounters (as well as scriptural encounters with Deity and angels) are explainable by naturally occurring phenomena fail to address the hard physical evidence or the details of the abduction phenomenon. Debunkers can blindly attempt to convince the world that millions have been mistaken (including thousands of Church members) in thinking that they saw silvery discs flying erratically in the sky or landing in the field, but this position is purely untenable at this point in the phenomenon. Too many trained observers have carefully watched UAP perform their ultra-state-of-the-art maneuvers from close range to be fooled by claims of flocks of geese, venus, meteors or swamp gas. Military admissions that UAP are seen nearly daily at close ranges by highly trained military personnel and recorded on videos and other high-resolution media eliminate these lazy conclusions.

Leading UAP researchers are coming to the conclusion that whatever is sending the UAP, and abducting humans, is not extraterrestrial but something from here. Because of the interrelated nature and complexity of the remaining theories—that the UAP and their occupants are demonic, extradimensional, ultra-terrestrial or spiritually evolved entities—we discuss them together in a separate chapter below. As for those theories treated in this chapter that attempt to explain the nature and origin of UAP and their occupants, our only conclusion can be that they are *possible, but not probable*. This is not to say that some of the encounters cannot be fully explained by the extraterrestrial theory, or some other theory discussed here—it merely indicates that none of these theories is inclusive enough to accommodate the wide range of behavior of the UAP phenomenon. This may indicate that different phenomena are being manifested—perhaps, a mixture of theories we are discussing is the answer. It is possible that many witnesses see robotic craft from other worlds in our skies, while others encounter true extraterrestrial explorers. Yet, I do not believe that many of the encounters we discuss are answered by these explanations. I suspect that many "alien" encounters may be better explained by the theory we explore in the next chapter.

*"These vehicles could be from outer space,
inner space, or the space in between."*

—Luis Elizondo

CHAPTER 16

Are UAP and Their Message a Satanic Deception?

THE DEVIL IS IN THE DETAILS

In this chapter we discuss the possibility that UAP and their related phenomena originate from spiritual sources—more specifically, whether they are of satanic origins. This is the least flattering of all of the possible sources that are discussed herein, yet the most pregnant perhaps with opportunities for analysis. As I have said from the outset, Christian fundamentalist writers dismiss the entire UAP phenomenon as a demonic device *ab initio*. This is due not to their thorough analysis of the facts, or to divine inspiration, but to their mistaken belief that Earth is God's only creation on which He has placed His finite number of spiritual/physical creations—man. With this understanding, fundamentalists have no place in their theorizing for extraterrestrial humans. Their reasoning is that the UAP, if not built by Earth humans, must necessarily originate from the only other available source of intelligence in the universe—Satan. However, those who are familiar with the restored gospel and enjoy a fuller understanding of Heavenly Father's "work and glory" know that He has populated countless planets throughout the universe with His children, created more or less in His likeness. Therefore, we don't automatically default to the satanic hoax answer. However, the phenomenon appears to act in many ways more like trickster and deceiving spirits, with a message that we know to be false and spiritually destructive, causing us to seriously consider the satanic spirits possibility.

COUNTERFEITS ARE PATTERNED AFTER TRUE PRINCIPLES

Although we are not restricted in our theorizing as are the fundamentalists or the debunkers, we must genuinely consider the real possibility that at least some UAP phenomena are demonic in origin. The evidence of such is great. However, this is not to say that the Earth is not visited occasionally by our extraterrestrial brethren even if the bulk of UAP encounters turns out to have satanic origins. We well know that if Satan sets out to deceive, he does so by manipulating truth. If the majority of UAP sightings are a satanic device employed for a purpose that we discuss below, or some other unknown purpose, Satan having selected it as a deceptive device supports the proposition that his manifestations are counterfeits of true occurrences—which means that extraterrestrial UAP visits are true occurrences, at times.

This "counterfeit" principle is borne out in the scriptures and our own Church history: "And no marvel; for Satan himself is transformed into an angel of light" (2 Corinthians 11:14.) The Prophet Joseph Smith shared a very personal experience in this regard: "And again, what do we hear? . . . The voice of Michael on the banks of the Susquehanna, detecting the devil when he appeared as an angel of light!" (D&C 128:20.) As we discussed briefly above, Joseph Smith recorded that among the extravagant events occurring in Kirtland during the absence of Church leaders, "one man pursued a ball that he said he saw flying in the air, until he came to a precipice, when he jumped into the top of a tree, which saved his life."[1] This is a classic example of what appears to be demonic forces creating a UAP, in its truest sense, whose intended purpose seems to be to trick the brother into falling off a cliff and dying. This may be a type for what we are seeing in the world today in the UAP phenomenon.

---

1. *Teachings*, 214.

ARE UAP AND THEIR MESSAGE A SATANIC DECEPTION?

Satan's *modus operandi* in his efforts to undermine God's work has always been to obfuscate, confuse, counterfeit, divide, and distract God's children, as is demonstrated in these examples and millions more that we could cite. His tactics are like those of the famed fictional courtroom attorney, Perry Mason, who was a favorite fictional hero of mine as a boy. I marveled at his tactics. For instance, if a witness saw Mason's accused client at the murder scene, Mason does not directly attempt to convince the witness that he does not "know" what he saw. Instead, Mason employs an Acme Models girl to dress like the client and stage a second appearance before the witness to "implant" a new memory of the original witnessing. When the witness identifies Mason's client as the one seen on both occasions, Mason puts the counterfeit on the witness stand, who swears that it was she who encountered the witness on the second occasion. This confusion technique, of course, bewilders the witness and has the effect of rendering the witness's testimony invalid as to both events.

Satan doesn't usually tell the big lie—not at first, anyway. He tells little lies; small misdirection. People detect the big lies too easily and recoil, as did Moses when Satan overplayed his hand: "And it came to pass that when Moses had said these words, behold, Satan came tempting him, saying: Moses, son of man, worship me. And it came to pass that Moses looked upon Satan and said: Who art thou? and where is thy glory, that I should worship thee? Get thee hence, Satan; deceive me not" (Moses 1:12–13, 16, 19). For this reason Satan delivers his deceptive messages in small increments, warming his audience as the frog in the pot destined for the boil. He sends counterfeit messengers—glorious, radiant beings praising God and commanding the percipient to worship God the Father and His Son Jesus Christ, and none other. The messenger of light then proceeds to deliver a message that is 95 percent true. The five percent portion of the message, however, is generally deadly in terms of God's will in the matter. Some examples of false spirits appearing as angels of light, bearing messages from God, were presented above. Others are prevalent in Church history. Still more are found worldwide, throughout the past two millennia as "Blessed Virgin Mary" and similar false apparitions. Satan sends these counterfeits for the same reason Perry Mason does—to confuse what we innately know to be the truth.

They appear and act like the real thing, yet their message is distorted just enough to make the truth a lie. Event by event, little by little, the audience is taken further and further away from the truth, as those who held to the iron rod in Lehi's dream were slowly persuaded to let go, a finger at a time, until they had released it altogether, and wandered off into paths of personal destruction.

It is curious that Joseph Smith chose to include in his enumeration of the activities of false spirits the account of the man who "pursued a ball that he said he saw flying in the air," which attempted to take his life by leading him over a precipice. The description of the flying sphere is more than reminiscent of the small spheres, globes, and other discs that occupy a great portion of UAP-encounter literature. Many thousands report seeing small spheres, metallic or brightly lit, ranging in size from a golf ball, to a softball, to a basketball. Did Joseph believe that such apparitions were necessarily satanic, or was his discernment derived from the attempt on the brother's life? This much we know—the only recorded flying sphere incident in early Church history was a satanic attempt to deceive and destroy a Church member.

POWER OF THE AIR

Joseph Smith understood Satan's power quite well, as alluded to in the following: "It would seem also, that wicked spirits have their bounds, limits, and laws by which they are governed or controlled, and know their future destiny; . . . and when Satan presented himself before the Lord, among the sons of God, he said that he came 'from going to and fro in the earth, and from wandering up and down in it;' and he is emphatically called the prince of the power of the air; and, it is very evident that they possess a power that none but those that have the Priesthood can control, as we have before averted to, in the case of the sons of Sceva."[2] Joseph's reference to Satan as "the prince of the power of the air" is from the New Testament wherein Paul called him by that appellation (Ephesians 2:2) What does it imply to call Satan "the prince of the power of the air"? We are nowhere given a full answer to this question.

---

2. Ibid., 208.

However, Joseph Smith referred to the title in association with the fact that satanic spirits are free to move "to and fro in the earth, and from wandering up and down in it" and that they "possess a power."

DECEPTIVE DEVICES

We raised the devices of "theater," "counterfeits," and "*knowledge distracting implants*" above because as we analyze the UAP phenomenon from the demonic origin viewpoint, we should view each aspect of the UAP encounter in light of how it could be the implementation or employment of one of these demonic devices. We are not the first to raise these issues. Many observers of the UAP phenomenon have remarked how closely related it appears to be to phenomena associated with demonic hauntings, apparitions, and possessions. Even Dr. Salisbury, in the early 1970s, noted how the UAP seemed to be putting on a "display," something that a scientist was hard pressed to explain. Of course, a UAP's communication with the Uintah Basin children through a Ouija board was an occurrence that he did not even know how to approach in a scientific medium.

GENERATED IMAGES

Looking first to the physical appearance of the UAP and their occupants can be enlightening. Much of the literature documents how UAP initially "resolve" themselves from a dispersed mist into a sharply "focused" object. They then zip and zigzag about at phenomenal speeds, only to "dissolve," or disappear in a blink. As in the cases of the French Dr. "X" or Betty Luca, some UAP are reported to transform their shape or size, or even merge with a second UAP as the witness looks on. The cry of "superior science" is drowned out by the roar of "projected image" when it comes to these kinds of displays. An image generated by a simple slide projector can travel quite quickly and erratically along a wall by the slight pivoting of the projector at its source. Dr. Vallee makes a similar point, referring to a flashlight or laser pointer being swept the length of the open sky in a fraction of a second. Can this rudimentary concept be applied to UAP sightings?

Could a projected image be made to look like a craft has extremely rapid acceleration, very high velocity, and immediate deceleration? Do such projectors exist? Could such images be detected by radar?

There are those who believe that UAP may be nothing more than mere projections—laser or holographic. Although this theory is possible, and interesting, we have little evidence that anyone possesses the level of technology required to put on such a light show—that returns radar signals. However, the technology is not too far in advance of state-of-the-art projection capabilities, and the possibility should not be overlooked. The question then arises, who would go to such extravagant, sophisticated, and expensive lengths to fool so many people? Only persons looking for power, as we discuss below, would conduct such a campaign. This would limit them to the political, military or religious realms.

Although this theory seems workable, it is not a very practical one—not at first blush. The risk of being caught in the act of setting up the necessary equipment is too high for never having been discovered. This is especially true in light of the massive investigation that attends many UAP sightings. Besides these difficulties, this theory fails to account for victims' close encounters with, and examinations by "aliens," unless we include the use of drugs and hypnosis in the equation. Then, however, we have the radar and photographic images that have been produced by these phenomena to explain. UAP seem to be solid objects—semisolid, at least. If they are projections with a semi-solid characteristic that are detected on radar and FLIR, this could account for why the Air Force showed up and confiscated the data hard drives of the USS Nimitz and the USS Princeton during the Tic Tac encounters off the California coast—to review how well their projections performed against the best the US Navy had to offer. This is a possibility, as Dr. Vallee termed it—three-dimensional holograms, with mass.

SPIRITUAL PROJECTIONS

If not laser or holographic projections, then what kind? Does Satan have the ability to resolve a semisolid image before a human, complete with a messenger delivering a message? As so many witnesses (including prophets)[3] have testified, the response is a resounding "yes." How does he do it? We can only guess, but we know that he can. Dr. Curt Wagner, a physicist whose doctoral degree was earned in the field of general relativity theory, explains how he believes it is done:

> Drawing from what we know can happen in seances and poltergeist activity, it seems that these supernatural forces can manipulate matter and energy, extracting energy from the atmosphere, for example (which manifests as a local temperature change), to manipulate matter and produce an apparent violation of the second law [of thermodynamics], and I guess my feeling is that on a larger scale this is what a UFO could be. I'm not saying I know that it is, but only that it could be. It seems to me likely that UFOs are large-scale violations of the second law in which energy is arranged to take on enough of a force field appearance so that it appears to look like matter, yet it's really just energy concentration—it's not really solid matter in the usual sense.[4]

This brings to mind the scientific inquiry being conducted in eastern Utah in the Uintah Basin at Skinwalker Ranch. Scientists are monitoring active spots with full spectrum sensor arrays, and are seeing wide temperature swings of twenty or thirty degrees on warm evenings occurring over a period of just seconds. Those are often extreme temperature drops as they look on. Similarly, they are seeing wide swings in electromagnetic radiation across the spectrum, including gamma waves and microwaves, set off by nothing that is apparent.

Another researcher similarly concludes: "Demons, as fallen angels, apparently retain great powers, such as the manipulation and restructuring of matter, as well as the ability to influence or control human consciousness and experience through classic possession or by direct psychic implantation of a set of experiences."[5] The extraction of "energy from the atmosphere, for example (which manifests as a local temperature change)," refers to the classic "cold spot" that is experienced during negative spiritual manifestations.

---

3. See D&C 128:20, 129:8.
4. *SCP Journal*, August 1977, 20.
5. Ibid., 19.

As discussed below, UAP phenomena are often accompanied by such cold spots. Often, in fact, the larger the "scene," the colder the temperature. A New Age spokesperson and a prominent New Age writer, Brad Steiger, frankly admits: "I have even come to suspect that, in some instances, what we have been terming 'spaceships' may actually be a form of higher intelligence rather than vehicles transporting occupants. . . . I feel, too, that these intelligences have the ability to influence the human mind telepathically in order to project what appear to be three dimensional images to the witnesses of UAP activity."[6] Steiger's suspicious observations appear to support our theory. He, however, does not assume that the spirits involved are satanic. His explanation, although tentative, is more innocuous: "I cannot help questioning whether the Space brothers might not be angels, spirit guides, and other messengers hiding themselves in more contemporary, and thereby more acceptable, personae."[7] In my experience, spirit guides and New Age "angels" and messengers are invariably deceptive demonic spirits—and I mean, without exception.

PHYSICAL SPIRITS

The question has often been raised, is Satan capable of physically intruding on our world, manipulating objects with mass, and "touching" or otherwise physically affecting humans? Because I do not feel that an examination of the full range of satanic "abilities" is necessary or proper in a work like this (or any work, possibly), I will forgo such a discussion. However, a look at the very first miracle of the Restoration demonstrates that demonic spirits are indeed capable of affecting us physically.

Joseph Smith records that he had spoken often with Newell Knight about the gospel and its restoration. Newell was very impressed but was reluctant to pray. His reluctance turned to inability. He retired to the woods to attempt prayer but was unable. Joseph chronicles: "He began to feel uneasy and continued to feel worse both in mind and body until upon reaching his own house his appearance was such as to alarm his

---

6. Brad Steiger, *The Fellowship*, Ivy Books, 49.
7. *Revelation: The Divine Fire*, A Berkley Book, 148.

wife very much. He requested her to go and bring me to him. I went and found him suffering very much in his mind, and his body acted upon in a very strange manner. His visage and limbs distorted and twisted in every shape and appearance possible to imagine. And finally he was caught up off the floor of the apartment and tossed about most fearfully."

Brother Knight's demonic attack was soon made known to his neighbors and relatives, and in a short time as many as eight or nine grown persons had gotten together to witness the scene. Joseph continues his account:

> After he had thus suffered for a time I succeeded in getting hold of him by the hand, when almost immediately he spoke to me and with great earnestness requested me to cast the devil out of him saying that he knew he was in him and that he also knew that I could cast him out. I replied, 'If you know that I can, it shall be done:' And then almost unconsciously I rebuked the devil and commanded him in the name of Jesus Christ to depart from him. When immediately Newell spoke out and said he saw the devil leave him and vanish from his sight. . . . This scene was entirely changed for as soon as the devil departed from our friend his countenance became natural, his distortions of body ceased, and almost immediately the spirit of the Lord descended upon him and the visions of eternity were opened to his view.[8]

Church history and those who have had the misfortune to experience demonic attacks bear witness to the fact that there exists a very real physicality to Satan's powers. This principle is borne out in latter-day revelation: "There is no such thing as immaterial matter. All spirit is matter, but it is more fine or pure, and can only be discerned by purer eyes; We cannot see it; but when our bodies are purified we shall see that it is all matter" (D & C 131:7–8.) We often assume that Satan has little control over the elements because he is a spirit. However, these scriptures, which we all well know, instruct that Satan is a "physical" being, or semi-physical at least in that he exercises the ability to control physical elements. He has tremendous powers, as do his demonic hordes. Joseph Smith recounts his own experience with Satan

---

8. *History of the Church*, 1:82–83.

when he (Joseph) started to pray in the Sacred Grove: "I had scarcely done so, when immediately I was seized upon by some power which entirely overcame me, and had such an astonishing influence over me as to bind my tongue so that I could not speak. . . and at the very moment when I was ready to sink into despair and abandon myself to destruction—not to an imaginary ruin, but to the power of some actual being from the unseen world, who had such marvelous power as I had never before felt in any being" (Joseph Smith—History 1:15–16).

We can only assume that satanic powers are increasing as we approach the Second Coming of Christ. Although there are many ideas and teachings in the Church that attempt to delineate such powers, member testimonies clarify that few are immune from their effects. This must be kept in mind as we examine the abduction aspect of UAP encounters. The UAP phenomenon parallels these satanic attacks. Ed Walters's description of his first encounter in Gulf Breeze, Florida, is instructive. "The blue beam had hit me like compression. It was pressing me firmly, just enough to stop me from moving. I screamed, with my mouth frozen half open, but the sound was hollow. Dead, like a vacuum. I couldn't even move my eyes or eyelids. I thought I was dying."[9] Walters then described how he attempted to speak but could only make unintelligible sounds. This scene is reminiscent of Joseph Smith's description of how he was attacked by satanic forces just before receiving the visitation from the Father and the Son, saying that the force that seized him "had such an astonishing influence over me as to bind my tongue so that I could not speak" (Joseph Smith—History 1:15). Many others who have been similarly attacked relate the same feeling of being bound by an unseen force, body and tongue, accompanied by a feeling of imminent doom. These people report their experiences in the context of UAP encounters as well as spiritual encounters—the only difference is the presence or absence of a UAP or an "alien."

In addition to these strictly physical attacks, many victims (including Church members) complain of being attacked by spiritual beings (sometimes in a UAP context) while in a semiconscious, or semiphysical state. Although astral projection, and other forms of out-of-

---

9. *The Gulf Breeze Sightings*, 28.

body experiences are part and parcel of forbidden occult practices, some Church members have related to me how they perceive that they are attacked and wrestled away while in a state in which they are outside of their bodies—generally as they are waking from sleep. As related, this is a truly terrifying and exhausting experience. According to the Roper Organization poll we have elsewhere discussed, a full 18 percent of American adults report "waking up paralyzed. With a sense of a strange person or presence or something else in the room." Of course, psychologists tell us of a condition called sleep paralysis, which accounts for many of these types of experiences. Many victims relate that they are fully awake while unknown beings do harmful and offensive things to them while they are entirely unable to move or defend themselves.

SOLID OBJECTS WITHOUT MASS

Other physical aspects of UAP that alert us to their possible spiritual origin are manifested in the accounts included above. For instance, Ed Walters described his first sighting as though the UAP had no physical effect on its environment. "It glided along without a whisper of sound. In all of the reports of these Gulf Breeze UAP, the observers are unanimous that none of UAP made a sound. There was no hum, no wind, not a single disturbance to the air, trees, or houses as it passed over them." This description of the UAP having no effect on the wind or air is classic. UAP shoot past observers at tens of thousands of miles per hour and fail to create a wisp of wind or a sonic boom. Is this possible? Not for an object with mass—not in our space/time continuum. Others report walking on solid, metallic UAP floors but being unable to make any sound of footsteps no matter how hard they try. Does this mean the floors are not real? Does it mean the zipping craft are unreal? What is real and what is not may be a matter of perception. Many researchers are speculating that what percipients are seeing is only a psychic projection, from another being or a technological holographic projector. In fact, you may recall that as I was questioning Steve and Dawn Hess about their experiences onboard the beings' craft, which included walls that morphed and changed the shapes and sizes of the rooms, that I focused on one small object—the Styrofoam cup that was handed to Dawn. If the scene was a holographic projection, I wondered if the cup would have the authentic feel and weight of a Styrofoam cup. Dawn confirmed that it did. Certainly, Steve smelled the magnificent aroma of roasting meat as the beings created within him a feeling of ravenous craving, and they projected into him all of the torturous pain associated with being shot and skinned alive. At least in this case, I feel it is safe to assume that this was a psychic projection. Who has the power and ability to so thoroughly overwhelm our senses and thoughts with their own projections? Who has the ability to turn Steve Hess into a lecherous cad just as his poor wife was reliving a horrendous rape? Could the callous beings have manipulated the afflicted couple into killing one another? Whether aliens or demons, at some point, the difference vanishes.

Here's a question that has many researchers checking video monitors and cell phone signal maps: Do percipients of bedroom and interrupted journey abductions ever leave the house or the car? It appears that most of what the abductees are perceiving is a psychic download, which makes us question if the experiences are even happening outside of the minds of the victims. If we were to watch a video of someone who is taken from her bedroom in the night and whisked out to a UAP and shown babies in the nursery, and given instructions and presentations about the One and global warming, would we see her lying in bed asleep, or would we see her floated above the bed and up through the ceiling? Unfortunately, as far as my research has revealed, video and security monitoring equipment malfunctions during these experiences. This fact alone tells us that some force external to the victim is at work—we just don't know the source. Could it be that Betty and Barney Hill were psychically downloaded with their experience as Barney drove the car like an automaton? If that is true, what about the radar hits on unknown craft in the area of some abductions? What about the tear in Betty's dress and the burned grass and soil where UAP were seen to land? What about the scars and tiny biomass implants left in some victims? What does that say about the US Navy videos and backup data showing the physical presence of UAP? Are they all the same, or are there some of physical craft, and some of others?

I AM LEGION

Another characteristic of demonic entities that could explain the "unison" aspect of these apparitions is the "legion" principle. When Christ spoke to the spirit entity that had possessed a young man, asking the entity's name, the entity "answered, saying, My name is Legion: for we are many" (Mark 5:9). Reserving for a later discussion the overwhelming demonic desire to possess bodies, we well remember the many "alien" encounters in which multiple telepathic voices spoke in unison. For example, speaking of the "visitors" attempts to control his will and behavior, Whitley Strieber recounts: "I remembered the visitors' admonition about sweets and decided, experimentally, to toss away the ice cream cone. The moment I discarded it, three young voices shouted in unison, 'He threw away ice cream for us!' This sounded totally real, but so close to my ear that it couldn't have been generated by somebody, say, hanging out of an apartment window or standing across the street. I had never heard disembodied voices before the visitor experience started."[10] Strieber describes how these "disembodied voices" would occasionally speak to him, either within his head or just outside of his ear. He was quite disturbed that he may have developed a brain disease or schizophrenic condition, resulting in his many abduction and disembodied voices experiences, so he underwent thorough psychological and medical testing to determine if he had a diagnosable disorder. He did not.

Betty Andreasson Luca, as well as many others, similarly reported that many of her lifelong contacts with the beings included their speaking in a chorus of voices to her. It is important to realize that these beings' feigned divinity—speaking in terms of the Savior being "my Son."

> Betty defensively proclaimed her Christian faith. . . . "There is nothing that can make me fear. I have faith in Jesus Christ!" "We know, child, that you do. That is why you have been chosen. I am sending you back now. Fear not. . . . It is for your own fear that you draw to your body, that causes you to feel these things.

---

10. *Transformation*, 147.

I can release you. But you must release yourself of that through my son." The words "through my son" suddenly became the catalyst for the most moving religious experience that I have ever witnessed. Betty's face literally shone with unrestrained joy as tears streamed down her beaming face. "Oh, praise God, praise God, praise God. (Crying) Thank you, Lord. (Crying sobbing) I know, I know I am not worthy. Thank you for your son. Thank you for your son!"[11]

If ever Satan appeared as an angel of light and commanded his victim, "Worship me," it was in the case of this poor abused woman, who was inundated with false messages that 1) God was behind them, and 2) they hailed from a distant planet.

GHOSTLY ABILITIES

Another characteristic of the entities that indicates a spiritual origin is their practice of walking through walls and other solid objects. Their explanation that they are able to change their vibrational levels at will, and pass through solid objects in that state, is not convincing. Although this explanation sounds *possible*, it seems more of a smokescreen to mask a clearly spiritual manifestation than an explanation of superior science or brainpower. The entities likewise appear and disappear at will, communicate without moving their mouths and psychically download 4–D real-time high-resolution cinematic experiences into the minds of their victims. It could be technology, but historically, we know these are the same things that demonic spirits have been doing to human victims for millennia. Therefore, it's difficult to separate "aliens" from demons.

INVASION OF THE BODY SNATCHERS

The "disembodied" characteristic to which we have referred in the prior two topics leads us squarely into a third indicator that these are demonic spiritual beings. *They have need of bodies.* As is clearly manifest

---

11. Raymond Fowler, *The Andreasson Affair*, New York: Bantam Books, 1980, 87.

throughout the abduction and contactee literature, the procurement of bodies for their species is an overriding element in the motivation of these beings. Their stated reasons for requiring bodies vary with each contactee, but the theme is constant. There are three main methods that they could employ to secure these bodies: genetic engineering, mechanical invention, and corporeal possession.

THEORY 1: GENETIC ENGINEERING

In the television miniseries *Intruders*, based on the Budd Hopkins book of the same name, the "Laura Davis" character comments on the hybrid baby nursery aspect of Kathie Davis's experiences on the UAP to the psychiatrist character and queries, "Why do you think they created them—to start a new world?" The psychiatrist responds pensively, "Maybe—or to save an old one." Although this exchange is a dramatization produced to editorialize on the hybrid baby phenomenon, the question and answer are common in ufology. Abductees report that they "perceive" or are actually told the answer to be (1) to save the "genetically imperiled" alien race, (2) to save our own "soon to become extinct" race, or (3) to create a new hybrid race, possibly to inhabit a new world somewhere in space. The story changes frequently as the abductors proffer various explanations for their conduct. There is clearly deception involved in the interaction.

We have already discussed some of the problems associated with these responses. First, if an extraterrestrial human race genetically compatible with our own (which we would assume to be the case) were to be having such difficulties with their genetic stock, why would they pursue the entire abduction scenario course, when their claimed superior capabilities enable them to engineer such stock or to at least steal the human samples unnoticed? If things really were as the abductors claim, they could easily make a deal with our governments to pay for surrogate volunteers with technology or precious materials, and the government could offer $1,000,000 to any woman willing to become a surrogate mother in the experiment. Many women would gladly get in line for that program. The "aliens" have no intention of working unnoticed. They fly their craft through our dark night skies lit up like neon Christmas trees. They do everything they can to be detected, while pretending to work surreptitiously. They inadequately seal the abduction memory into the subconscious regions of their victims' minds knowing that it will be recalled in a dramatic investigation. I believe that the genetic experimentation spectacle is a sham, other than the fact that it focuses on the beings' need for bodies. What is the true reason they need bodies? Within the demonic context, the answer is they need them to house the unembodied spirits that followed Satan. Having a body is a great advantage, and having lost the opportunity, Satan and his followers may be locked in a system of manufacturing bodies that they can possess, and interact corporally.

The Superhumans

What could be the benefit of creating a superior human race then—assuming that such is the case? I can think of two possible scenarios. The first hypothesis is that the only hybrids, assuming that there are any, are those rendered from the altering of human bodies. We know that human devolution is a reality, and its source has often been connected with ungodly practices.[12] These genetically superior bodies are made available to unembodied demonic spirits whose driving compulsion is to possess a body, no matter what its source. We have too little revealed on the matter to speculate further, but the subject has been debated for centuries by speculating theologians who have argued about the sin of copulating with demons. Many ancient theologians theorized it is by this very process that Antichrist (or, the Man of Sin, if Antichrist will be a political entity rather than an individual man), must be born, which brings us to our second possible scenario for the creation, actual or pretended, of a superior human race.

The second hypothesis states: The entire New Age movement is based on the belief that mankind is about to evolve into a new, improved, superior, enlightened race. The elite of the New Age are believed to be made up of "early evolving" ones of the coming superhumans. Their superhuman abilities—intellectual, spiritual, and physical—will enable them to take the reins of government and

---

12. *Mormon Doctrine*, 616.

religion and save the world from the imminent catastrophes that threaten its certain destruction. They will be supported by the "space brothers" and "ascended masters" who hover ever-present over our shoulders and are "concerned" for the welfare of our planet and its inhabitants. Anyone wishing to receive the benefits of their leadership must abandon their outdated, superstitious beliefs and embrace the New Age. Antichrist will thus come to power with the aid of these men.

Lewis and Shreckhise, Fundamentalist Christian New Age watchdogs who adhere to this UAP/satanic conspiracy theory, speculate: "If our calculations are right there will be a massive open manifestation of alien presence and power on Earth. Something big is about to happen! Kings, prime ministers, and presidents will tremble before the "ascended masters." How could they refuse the help so generously offered when Earth is about to self-destruct? They will play right into the hands of Antichrist if they follow the aliens' suggestions."[13]

The second reason for creating a seemingly superhuman race, then, is to convince humanity to follow the superhumans into whatever paths those may choose. Whether these superhumans are merely humans with satanic powers, hybrid-appearing humans endowed with satanic powers, hybrid-appearing demons, or human-appearing demons, the predicted result is the same. How likely is it that the superhuman race theory is true? In one of the forms just enumerated, I believe that the scriptures support the probability of such a ruse—in at least partial implementation of Satan's latter-day, premillennial rise to world domination. The Man of Sin, the head of Antichrist, will be such a man. "[The man of sin] opposeth and exalteth himself above all that is called God, or that is worshipped; so that he as God sitteth in the temple of God, shewing himself that he is God. . . . Even him, whose coming is after the working of Satan with all power and signs and lying wonders, And with all deceivableness of unrighteousness in them that perish; because they received not the love of the truth, that they might be saved. And for this cause God shall send them strong delusion, that they should believe a lie" (2 Thessalonians 2:3–11).

---

13. *UFO: End-Time Delusion*, 160.

Herein we learn that there will be a "Man of Sin" who exalts himself, sitting in a temple and telling the world he is God, backing up his claims by performing impressive signs and wonders. Although the truth will be available to the world at this time, the world will prefer the lying flattery of this personage. For this reason, God will allow the people to believe deceitful lies, the "strong delusion" of the message. Sound familiar? Whatever the deceit and lies that will be delivered by this cosmic superman, many people will follow him, and God will allow them to exercise that free agency—for a season.

Satanic Science

Are aliens or demonic spirits carrying out genetic engineering experiments for any of the reasons discussed above? The question of satanic involvement in such physical pursuits is intriguing and opens the floodgates to many questions involving "satanic science." We, of course, do not know to what extent Satan may involve himself in human reproductive activities to promote his diabolic purposes in the earth. Furthermore, we know even less about his ability to enter and possess such custom-engineered flesh. We learn that the small Grays appear to be biomechanical in nature. If true, what operates the bodies? Are they mere avatars for beings on the UAP or back on the home planet? Are they avatars for demonic spirits who never received a body but are desperate to have one? Or are they avatars for artificial intelligence operating systems controlled by extraterrestrials or that have jumped their confines? Does Satan mete out science to humans? We know he did in the past—before the Flood, causing untold death and misery. Does he do it for the benefit of humanity, or to serve his own purposes? We know that he does nothing to benefit humanity. He hates humanity and seeks our destruction above all else. Therefore, if he is involved in any manner in the human hybrid scenarios being played out on the stage of "extraterrestrial intervention," it is all just a "strong delusion," or those bodies being produced are for him and his spirit followers.

One example that we have of spiritual intervention in human insemination is the conception of the Savior's body. The angel Gabriel told Mary, "And, behold, thou shalt conceive in thy womb, and bring forth a son, and shalt call his name JESUS." She responded, "How shall this be, seeing I know not a man?" (Luke 1:31, 34). Gabriel explained, "The Holy Ghost shall come upon thee, and the power of the Highest shall overshadow thee: therefore also that holy thing which shall be born of thee shall be called the Son of God" (Luke 1:35). This "explanation" has spawned a plethora of theories and debates concerning the nature and origin of Christ Himself. Modern prophets have rejected all of the "Son of the Holy Ghost" theories and have assured us that Christ is the literal Son of the Father—a physical being. Yet Mary was a virgin. Nephi explains that Mary was "carried away in the Spirit" at the time she conceived (1 Nephi 11:19). Modern prophets say, without elaboration, that she conceived just like any other woman conceives. How was it done? Is any confusion eliminated by all of these clarifications? I believe that modern fertilization techniques enlighten us how it occurred. We are now capable of taking physical seed from a man and artificially implanting it in the ovum of a woman. I would not think that this would be too arduous a task for the Holy Ghost—to take a small seed of DNA from the physical, glorified body of Heavenly Father and place it in the ovum of a mortal woman. So doing, all of the known facts regarding the conception of Christ are undisturbed. Although this conclusion leaves room in the world for numerous virgin births, there is only one Only Begotten Son of the Father.

Having considered the uniqueness of the Savior's conception, it is more than curious that much of the activity described on UAP is centered in artificial insemination and the premature removal of hybrid fetuses from inseminated human women. What drama is being played out here? A counterfeit of the virgin birth? A probable claim that will be made by the Man of Sin, and all of the superhumans, in all of their glorious modesty. Time will reveal the validity of these theories.

THEORY 2: MECHANICAL INVENTION

As mentioned above, there exists a little-discussed subject that must be raised here in an effort to determine if the "aliens" are of a mechanical nature or of some other "manipulation and restructuring of matter" as also mentioned above. Is there such a thing as satanic science? As discussed, Heavenly Father metes out technology in His own time, for His own purposes. Does Satan do the same? Surely, any technology that has been had among any of the planets of God is known to Satan. He has this kind of knowledge and uses it to his own advantage every time he sees an opportunity. For example, we have been specifically informed by latter-day prophets that communications technology has been revealed in these latter days for the primary purpose of spreading the gospel throughout the earth. Yet, Satan has exploited these God-given gifts for his own evangelism. Possibly, Satan is aware of even greater technology than is had on any planet, he having filled the position of the Great Bearer of the Light before his rebellion and fall. Our technology is simple and crude. The microprocessor and wave technology are the only real advancements made in centuries. Before that, the internal combustion engine, printing press, electricity—not very impressive. Our question, then, is, does Satan conduct technological enterprise and/or dispense technology to his human recruits for his own purposes? Think Nazis.

Does God personally use technology? Because we are unable to answer that question, we may be equally unable to answer whether Satan does, for similar reasons. However, we know that God dispenses it to man and we have no indication that Satan cannot. The only force that could prevent Satan's employment or dissemination of technology for his purposes is God's disallowance. Would God disallow it? We know that He puts many limitations on Satan to control the level of his attack on humanity (see D&C 121:4). We also know that in these latter days God will allow Satan more power on the Earth. How much, we do not know. We suspect that Satan meted out a great deal of technology before the Flood and tricked humanity into destroying itself with those "gifts." Is Satan involved in creating robotic or bio-mechanical bodies for him and his demons to possess and control? We know that Satan can enter and control the bodies of animals and that he can influence objects with mass. Therefore, little reason exists to doubt his ability to control mechanical devices, including sophisticated robots, or biomechanical bodies, as though they were alive. In fact, some of our most eerie accounts of supernatural displays are centered in just such acts of animating objects, including moving, levitating, and flying objects around the house.

ARE UAP AND THEIR MESSAGE A SATANIC DECEPTION?

Is this the answer, then, to physical UAP or their occupants? Within this line of reasoning two possibilities exist. First, Satan creates physical crafts and bodies, then animates them through spiritual control, like possession. Second, Satan recruits humans to his cause, arming them with technology sufficient to build and pilot the craft, and to build and control the biomechanical robots, if such are employed under this theory. This latter explanation could also account for the "remote time traveler" who comes to this century on a satanic mission if given the proper technology, as we discussed above.

It is often reported that the small Grays and other "aliens" are seen moving in a very mechanical, robotic fashion. This could also explain the phenomenon of why they are seen moving in unison, even when the movement of the second entity has no effect on the object being manipulated by the first. Whether these fabrications are mechanical (made by Satan or human recruits) or illusion, the operation and results are the same—they are centrally controlled. This would also explain why communication with the beings is telepathic—they do not have the power of human speech, although animatronic speech doesn't seem like a difficult task for someone who can create all of the other props on the stage of human abductions. The fact that the smaller, gnomelike, or robotlike beings are often seen in the presence of, and are subservient to, human-looking beings supports these theories. Are the human-appearing entities behind the UAP phenomenon Satan's human recruits who are employed in his service? Are they demonic beings projecting an angelic or human appearance? Are they also robots—controlled spiritually or mechanically? We, of course, have no firm answers. But we know for sure that none of these "message bearing" beings is what it claims to be. They are all lying—always a prime indicator that we might be dealing with Satan.

Whitley Strieber had an experience that lends credibility to our discussion. After being embarrassed by the beings in a bizarre drama, he recounts:

> I was forced by my [ballooning paper gown] clothing to move like an arrogant prince—which made me feel even more like a toad. Carrying myself as best as I was able, I left the room. We were going down the curving corridor again when one of the blue

beings looked up at me with his wide face. I saw it clearly this time, and it was really startlingly horrible. Awful! The eyes glittered as if they were shiny black membranes, with something moving behind them that made lumps and pits as it seethed within the eyeball. He smiled, showing the tips of his gray, spongy-looking teeth. His companion pulled open one of the drawers [in the corridors]. In that drawer were stacks of bodies like their own, all encased in what looked like cellophane. Their eyes were open, their mouths wide as if with surprise. I did not know what to make of it. The oddest thing was the way the drawer was opened with a prideful flourish. I was being shown something the two of them clearly thought wonderful.[14]

An arsenal of readied bodies. Ready for what? For whatever it was that propelled the two gnomes that so proudly exhibited the contents of one of the many drawers. If these were manufactured bodies, why these hideous little gnome appearing creatures instead of handsome humans or angelic beings? After all, if you are going to create your own tabernacle through some kind of technology or manipulation of matter, it is just as easy to generate a Lamborghini as a Kia. I believe that the answer lies in the fact that this is a drama—a theatrical production—and the actors are costumed appropriately for their parts. It is apparent that these inanimate bodies were lifeless, just as those of the escorts had been prior to animation.

Similar Encounters Have Historical Precedents

In analyzing the beings and their behavior, some researchers have shown the parallels between human encounters with nonhuman beings throughout history, and these UAP encounters. Noted scientist and UAP researcher Dr. Jacques Vallee has produced a wealth of information concerning these parallels. Some of them are included in previous chapters as paranormal parallels.

One such encounter is cited by both Whitley Strieber and Dr. Vallee, albeit for different reasons. The tale is well documented and relates how a young teenage boy disappeared for two years. One

---

14. *Transformation*, 40.

day his mother, who had grievously mourned his death, was shocked to see him at the door. Upon seeing him she was astonished that he had not aged at all during this period of traditionally accelerated maturation. Dr. Vallee cites the story because, as in many such cases, the boy insisted he had been away with the little people for less than two full days. Strieber, however, found interesting the fact that the boy carried a bundle containing a white, seamless paper gown, exactly like the one given to Strieber in the above-quoted story, which the boy told his mother the little men had given him to wear while he was with them.

Following is a story quoted by a researcher cited by Dr. Vallee to further demonstrate the similarities between traditional encounters with the "Gentry" and modern UAP occupant encounters.

> The folk are the grandest I have ever seen. They are far superior to us and that is why they call themselves the Gentry. They are not a working-class, but a military-aristocratic class, tall and noble-appearing. They are a distinct race between our race and that of spirits, as they have told me. Their qualifications are tremendous: "We could cut off half the human race, but would not," they said, "for we are expecting salvation." They take young and intelligent people who are interesting. They take the whole body and soul, transmuting the body to a body like their own. I asked them once if they ever died and they said, no; "We are always kept young." They marry and have children. And one of them could marry a good and pure mortal. They are able to appear in different forms. One once appeared to me and seemed only four feet high, and stoutly built. He said, "I am bigger than I appear to you now. We can make the old young, the big small, and the small big."[15]

To further illustrate the similarities in these shape-shifters, Dr. Vallee says, "The parallel between these modern claims and the medieval legends is closer than ever. The same theory was presented about intercourse with the elves. I have shown that fairy tales are full of stories about the stealing of human babies, changelings, and the abduction of both males and females for procreation with the Gentry.

---

15. *Dimensions*, 54.

Even the scars sound familiar."¹⁶ Their claim that they are "expecting salvation," causes us to stop and take note, and interestingly, they describe themselves as "a distinct race between our race and that of spirits." If any of this is true, are we beginning to understand that there may be beings who live in a different dimension, who pop in and out of our dimension through portals around the world? If demonic or the Watchers, are these beings maneuvering God toward a blanket forgiveness of their rebellion by destroying the plan of salvation and exaltation, and seeking a reboot of the entire plan?

By this time it should come as no surprise that for centuries clergymen and town officials have documented the testimonies of thousands who have recounted tales of abduction, procreative experimentation, and other encounters with nonhuman beings, which closely resemble modern accounts of UAP encounters. The top thinkers in UAP research believe that all of the phenomena spring from a common source—whatever it is. Whitley Strieber writes that Dr. Vallee "reveals an appalling truth: the phenomenon has been with us throughout history, and never have we been able to deal sensibly with it. Whatever it is, it changes with our ability to perceive it. The fifteenth century saw the visitors as fairies. The tenth century saw them as sylphs. The Romans saw them as wood nymphs and sprites. And so it goes, back into time."¹⁷

As we have seen, the procurement of bodies is an underlying compulsion of the UAP occupants. Are these genetic experimentations, hybrid children, and inventoried mechanical or biomechanical bodies all part of satanic science, providing what God has denied the angels that kept not their first estate—mortal tabernacles? Are satanic forces, demonic or human, literally manufacturing physical bodies for demonic habitation and animation? Or, are these characteristics of the UAP phenomenon just more smoke and mirrors to create an illusion for their audience? Again, we cannot know the answers to these questions absent divine revelation. One thing we know for certain—from this time forward

---

16. *Ibid.*, at 267.
17. Foreword, vi–vii.

we cannot rely solely on our physical senses to discern what we think we are seeing or hearing. More than ever, it is imperative that we have as our companion the Holy Ghost to bear witness of the truth or falsity of any manifestation or representation.

THEORY 3: CORPOREAL POSSESSION

Demonic infestation and possession of humans is well documented throughout the entire history of the gospel. Again, this results from satanic spirits' overwhelming drive to unite with the elements and "feel" the physical world. It is the only means by which the sensual lusts of depraved, unembodied beings can attain any degree of satisfaction. We see activity in this arena escalating as we approach the winding up scene. Spiritual merging with these entities is the affirmative pursuit of most Eastern and New Age religions and cults. Even unwilling, righteous people, including Church members, have become plagued by the infestation of such vile spirits. Does "demonic possession" play a role in the UAP phenomenon? New Age guru Ruth Montgomery explains,

> To the limit of my understanding, it would seem that the Guides have identified three types of beings who have achieved sufficient advancement to enter our earth plane, and appear in solid form to us. . . . Apparently the highest achievers in this category are the avatars, who can come and go at will, and who, according to the Guides, are in touch with outerspace beings as well as with humans on Planet Earth. The second type is the Walk-ins, who have always been Earthlings but are high-minded, advanced souls who return to adult bodies in order to accelerate the progress of their fellow-men. The third class is the extraterrestrials, who, still few, have allegedly found the means of penetrating the earth's atmosphere and occupying bodies of adult humans, for limited scientific experiments and observations of our planetary changes.[18]

She further clarifies on another occasion, "I asked about the different means used by space beings to enter our culture, and the Guides

---

18. *Strangers Among Us*, 147–48.

said that some are being born into human bodies for the first time, some have lived here upon occasion before, some are arriving as Walk-ins, and others are temporarily exchanging bodies with Earthlings 'with or without permission.'"[19]

We must remember while reading these New Age writings that Ms. Montgomery is not apologizing or making excuses—corporeal possession is a common occurrence and completely accepted by New Agers as a natural means of spiritual communication and interaction. Channelers like Montgomery receive the above tidbits of information frequently from their "spirit guides," spiritual entities who profess to be advanced, enlightened beings, but who are indeed, the very same demonic spirits that follow and serve Satan.[20] This self-admitted practice of entering the bodies of Earthlings "with or without permission" to carry out extraterrestrial activities is a strong indicator that corporeal possession is frequently pursued at some level. And whether the assertion is true or not we at least know that the "extraterrestrial" contacts feeding us this information are demonic spirits. New Age author Brad Steiger is hesitant to accept the entities at full face value. "I had the uneasy feeling that the ecstatic flame may, in reality, have been kindled by multidimensional beings who have a kind of symbiotic relationship with man and who may exploit their 'prophets' for selfish, parasitical purposes."[21] I agree.

MYSTICAL KNOWLEDGE

The spiritual "knowledge" passed from the UAP entities to "planetary dwellers" bears a strong resemblance to the mystical knowledge with which Eastern initiates are endowed at the pinnacle of their spiritual quest. As discussed earlier, the transference of such spiritual knowledge is another counterfeit employed by Satan to mock the true principle of the ministering of the Holy Ghost. As we know, the Holy Spirit radiates His influence throughout the universe on an ongoing basis. However, on special occasions, He personally merges with

---

19. *Aliens Among Us*, 13.
20. *Mormon Doctrine*, 195–96, 759.
21. *Revelation*, 8.

ARE UAP AND THEIR MESSAGE A SATANIC DECEPTION?

the spirit of a worthy person and shares eternal truth at a level that transcends any worldly communication. The recipient is endowed with spiritual truth that is unmistakable and undeniable. That is why denying this truth, once embedded by the personage of the Holy Spirit, is an unforgivable sin.

Psychic "memory implanting" is the means by which satanic beings convince people that they have experienced past lives or experience OBE like astral projection or other mystical phenomena. Christian fundamentalists Lewis and Shreckhise declare their belief that memory implanting is the same method used to convince percipients that they have seen UAP and their occupants. "The psychic implantation of deceptive experiences is changing the way [abductees] perceive reality. What they experience is a real experience—deceptive and manipulative in character. It is not, however, an experience of reality. It is an illusion of reality used solely for the purpose of convincing people to turn away from the Creator."[22] Of course, even if we accept the fact that UAP are a satanically generated phenomenon, the psychic implant theory is not as amenable to photography and radar detection as are materialization and manifestation generation. Of course, the psychic implant is very amenable to the more peripheral aspects such as alien encounters and communications and the attendant visions of alien worlds or UAP interiors. I suspect that a mixture of techniques is employed to create a panorama of special effects in a UAP/abduction experience. Also, as we keep noting, it is possible that some UAP encounters are genuine, while Satan counterfeits the phenomenon with an array of experiences that build on actual occurrences.

Whitley Strieber recounts how the aliens touched his head with a "wand," producing realistic, three-dimensional images that swirled about in his mind, reminiscent of the images of dogs and naked women that were thrust into the mind of Ed Walters during an attempted abduction. The beings would communicate with Strieber (and countless others) any time they wished. He periodically would hear voices speaking to him as if standing next to him or within his head that would give him information and instructions. This all sounds very

---

22. *UFO: End-Time Delusion*, 235.

much like psychic implanting. Was Strieber "possessed"? He worried about this possibility, saying, "I felt more than watched; I felt entered and observed from within."[23] Did he feel menaced? He noted:

> Increasingly I felt as if I were entering a struggle that might be even more than life-or-death. It might be a struggle for my soul, my essence, or whatever part of me might have reference to the eternal. There are worse things than death, I suspected. And I was beginning to get the distinct impression one of them had taken an interest in me. So far the word demon had never been spoken among the scientists and doctors who were working with me. And why should it have been? We were beyond such things. We were a group of atheists and agnostics, far too sophisticated to be concerned with such archaic ideas of demons and angels. Alone at night I worried about the legendary cunning of demons.[24]

It is interesting that Strieber reached a point in his hypnotic regression therapy at which he felt that he could no longer trust these memories whose origins he had come to doubt. He knew the memories were of external origin but doubted their veracity—as if they were a "mask" of something else that had actually occurred. Strieber had the clear impression that the "visitors," as he called them, were evil—unnatural.

> In the wee hours of the night I abruptly woke up. There was somebody quite close to the bed, but the room seemed so unnaturally dark that I couldn't see much at all. I caught a glimpse of someone crouching just behind my bedside table. I could see by the huge, dark eyes who it was. I felt an absolutely indescribable sense of menace. It was hell on earth to be there, and yet I couldn't move, couldn't cry out, couldn't get away. I lay as still as death, suffering inner agonies. Whatever was there seemed so monstrously ugly, so filthy and dark and sinister, of course they were demons. They had to be. And they were here and I couldn't get away. I couldn't save my poor family. I still remember that thing crouching there, so terribly ugly, its arms and legs like the limbs of a great insect, its eyes glaring at me. And there was also

---

23. *Transformation,* 136.
24. Ibid., 44–45.

the love. I felt mothered. Caressed. Then the terrible insect rose up beside the bed like some huge, predatory spider. The eyes glittered as it tilted its head from side to side. Every muscle in my body was stiff to the point of breaking. . . . The next thing I knew, something had been laid against my forehead. I felt it there, a light electric pressure vibrating softly between my eyes. Instantly I seemed to be transported to another place, a stone floor with a low stone table in the middle of it. The table was a bit more than waist high and on it there was a set of iron shackles. A man was led down some steps and attached to these shackles. He was right in front of my face, not two feet from me, looking directly at me with eyes so sad that I almost couldn't bear it.[25]

WHOSE WILL?

At that point the holographic or psychically projected man was tortured for Whitley's lack of obedience to the commands and requirements of the visitors. When returned to his bed, Strieber was also forced to listen to his son's screams downstairs as punishment for his disobedience.

These forms of psychological abuse to supplant the will of the victim for their own will is reminiscent of Satan's plan to direct the affairs of the earth through coercion. This, of course, is in direct opposition to the Lord's plan of salvation, through which man chooses good or evil of his own free will. Remember Betty Luca's report that the beings were perplexed and obstructed by man's free will. It seems to be a constant theme that runs through the "others" phenomenon.

Strieber describes being raped by an "alluring, yet despicable-looking" alien or hybrid female. Horrified, he screamed out, "You have no right to do this to me. I am a human being!" The female sternly replied, "We do have a right!" This single, affirmative claim of the visitors has perplexed researchers. It would be one thing to conduct experimentations on lower lifeforms with neutral moral intentions, much as we do with our own medical research or migration/habitat tracking. It

---

25. Ibid., 181–182.

is another thing altogether, however, to positively assert that one has an affirmative right over another creature. This would imply "ownership," which is an aspect of the visitor experience heretofore undiscussed.

One night, Strieber felt that the beings were returning for him. He tried to resist, but he finally lost his strength and became resigned to his fate.

> There was no question of my doing anything about the fact that I knew the visitors were here. It was all I could do to climb the stairs to the bedroom. . . . I felt an absolutely indescribable sense of menace. It was hell on Earth to be there, and yet I could still not move, couldn't cry out, couldn't get away. I lay as still as death, suffering inner agonies. . . . I thought I was going to suffocate. My throat was closed, my eyes swimming with tears. The sense of being infested was powerful and awful.[26]

As we read through Whitley Strieber's accounts of his encounters with the visitors, we wonder if he hasn't possibly employed his proven ability to research and write on unusual subjects. After all, he earned more money for *Communion* than most of us earn in a lifetime. Strieber concludes *Transformation* with his testimonial:

> Of course, one could take the comfortable road and say that I am lying, that the descriptions in my book are hyperbole or hallucination. But they are not. I am telling the truth of what happened to me, and the implications are there for anyone to see. Not only are we not alone, we have a life in another form—and it is on that level of reality that the visitors are primarily present. I call them visitors, but now I am beginning to think that is a misnomer. I have had the impression that they think of themselves as family, and perhaps that is exactly what they are.[27]

Family? Like siblings from a distant past, who now reach out to take from us what they passed up in rebellion against their Father. Strieber's comment, "I have had the impression that they think of themselves as family," is noteworthy. These bizarre beings who communicate through theater and abuse their victims with the most vile

---

26. Ibid., 189–92.
27. Ibid., 201.

forms of tortuous psychology have a purpose behind their eccentricity—could it be that they still think of themselves as our brothers and sisters? Are they truly still expecting salvation? The only possible way that the one-third who rebelled against our Father could even hope for salvation, is to so derail His plan of salvation and exaltation, as they did before the Flood, to render the entire experience an utter failure, and hope for another chance at salvation.

MANY INDICATORS OF CORPOREAL POSSESSION

Not too surprisingly, many abductees have such detailed recall to the point of "reliving" the experiences, including Kathy Davis and Bob Luca. Budd Hopkins claims that physical manifestations such as hypothermia (abductees often complain of being in very cold environments) return as the abductee relives the experience under hypnosis. He always has warmed blankets on hand during hypnotic sessions. One might easily dismiss these occurrences as mere psychosomatic manifestations of a perceived experience, but the phenomenon appears to go beyond that, as related by the following:

> The aliens placed Betty on a soft, rubbery, cushion-like mat on the floor of a section of the craft that was roofed by a large transparent dome. A mouthpiece was installed that kept her tongue held down. When describing it to us under hypnosis, she actually talked as if something were holding her tongue down. Betty began sinking into the rotating circular mat as the craft accelerated upward. Incredible as it may seem, her body actually sunk into the hypnotist's chair! The psychosomatic effects on Betty's face and voice were fantastic to behold. All present were amazed to actually see the effect of the g-forces on her face. The skin got very tight around her face and her mouth was pulled way back. She experienced difficulty talking.[28]

These manifestations of physical forces on the body of Betty Luca and others during hypnosis give us great pause. No answer exists in

---

28. *The Watchers*, 10.

modern science to explain Betty's sinking deeper into the hypnotist's chair as she experienced a mere "recall" of rapid upward acceleration. Some outside force had to be present to compress Betty's body into the cushion of the chair. There is every indication that demonic forces are at work on Betty during her hypnosis. Is this why she, like others, becomes very cold at times during hypnosis—is this a "cold spot" manifestation? Is this why no memory exists prior to the hypnotic session—because the memory is directly "downloaded" to her during the session? We know that it is often during these hypnotic trances that people with no prior recollection of abnormal memories are suddenly deluged with vivid, panoramic recollections of past lives and other experiences. These we know to be satanically induced. Others are known to levitate during hypnotic trance. These paranormal experiences are fairly common occurrences in both UAP encounters and the occult. Or, does hypnosis merely unlock or reinitiate an already experienced demonic encounter? Some victims, Whitley Strieber for instance, feel that the encounter really occurred remotely, and it was masked or altered in the subconscious. That is why, they believe, some people who have anomalous, vague memories of animals (generally large-eyed animals like deer or owls) are recalling a masked memory instead of the actual "visitor" encounter.

HYPNOSIS—A SPIRITUAL REVOLVING DOOR?

The entire process of hypnotic retrieval of suppressed memories is suspect from a spiritual viewpoint. The Church's stand on hypnosis is fairly conservative. President Francis M. Lyman of the Council of the Twelve wrote, "From what I understand and have seen, I should advise you not to practice hypnotism. For my own part I could never consent to being hypnotized or allowing one of my children to be. The free agency that the Lord has given us is the choicest gift we have. As soon, however, as we permit another mind to control us, as that mind controls its own body and functions, we have completely surrendered our free agency to another; . . . The hypnotist might also influence us to do absurd and even shocking, wicked things, for his will compels us."[29]

---

29. *Era*, vol. 6, 420.

Although this "lounge show" viewpoint of hypnosis may seem surprisingly antiquated to most who have more than a passing acquaintance with modern psychology and the use of regressive hypnosis to ascertain the origin of unknown trauma, there is a fundamental purpose behind the belief. It is, although not well articulated in Church literature, that the hypnotic process lowers barriers that normally protect our bodies/souls from negative spiritual intrusions. This belief is not unique to the Church, and is, in fact, the accepted belief of most Christian churches. Does this indicate that under no circumstances should anyone undergo any form of hypnosis? Elder McConkie says, "Reputable doctors sometimes use hypnotherapy, a limited form of hypnotism, in connection with the practice of their profession. Their sole apparent purpose is to relieve pain and aid patients in perfecting their physical well-being. It is claimed that there are many people who have been benefited materially by this practice and that the ills normally attending hypnotic practices have not resulted. This medical practice of hypnotism obviously does not carry the same opprobrium that attaches to hypnotism in general."[30] We are apparently given to understand that certain limited forms of hypnosis, performed therapeutically by medical professionals, that do not produce certain unnamed harmful effects, are condoned. Personally, I would not undergo hypnosis out of the presence of a discerning priesthood holder.

SPIRITUAL PSYCHOLOGY

The *Men in Black* phenomenon, referred to above, is that in which men in "official" looking apparel show up at the home or other location of a witness or abductee, demanding any and all evidence of an encounter. They often threaten the witness if he or she ever divulges the details of the close encounter. These experiences are usually alternated with "official" looking helicopters that buzz the location of the witness. It is reported by witnesses that these MIB are often somewhat alien looking (in the eyes) and that the helicopters have sometimes transformed themselves from discs or spheres, and back again. Noting that the techniques of the MIB are closely akin to spiritual brainwashing

---

30. *Mormon Doctrine*, 371.

methods used by cults and satanic groups to negatively enforce their will and control over initiates, Brad Steiger suggests that the "Brothers of the Shadow, like the MIB, are known for threatening students of the occult whenever they get too close to lifting the Veil of Isis [reaching the spiritual pinnacle]." As Madame Blavatsky says when referring to the Brothers of the Shadow, they are "the leading stars" on the great spiritual stage of "materialization." The key words here are "stage" and "materialization." What she is conveying is that the occult is very "manifestation" oriented—Satan provides the curious with many signs and wonders to prove his powers. Levitating, flying, astral projection, shape-shifting and other manifestations of magical power are the bait. Once hooked, proselytes are controlled through psychological manipulation.

Negative psychological abuse has long been a control device of the occult, captors, and others with evil tendencies. The beings appear to play good cop/bad cop. Any television police drama watcher knows this is a scenario where one cop acts as the "heavy," projecting a threatening image. The second cop then makes an appearance, offering empathy and hope—befriending the target—convincing him that he's the target's friend and advocate. Manifesting "bad" aliens drives the terrified victim into the open arms of the "good" aliens, accepting their message as beneficent, no matter how much pain is caused thereby or how at odds it may be with revealed truth. Remember that visiting spirit entities, as well as "aliens," come in the good and bad varieties by their own accounts. We can't help but contemplate the nightmare encounter experienced by Steve and Dawn Hess, who were tortured for hours before the angelic being finally appeared, providing a short period of relief before the torture resumed. In subsequent visits and abductions, the Hesses were alternately blessed and tortured by their abductors, threatening their children and loved ones if they failed to comply. We know that the spirit entities are all of the same origin (satanic), and I believe that many of the "aliens" spring from the very same source.

THE CONTROL SYSTEM

Dr. Jacques Vallee says,

> I propose there is a spiritual control system for human consciousness and that paranormal phenomena like UFOs are one of its

manifestations. I cannot tell whether this control is natural and spontaneous; whether it is explainable in terms of genetics, of social psychology, or of ordinary phenomena—or if it is artificial in nature, under the power of some superhuman will. It may be entirely determined by laws that we have not yet discovered. I am led to this idea by the fact that, in every instance of UFO phenomenon I have been able to study in depth, I have found as many rational elements as absurd ones, as many that I could call friendly as I could call hostile.[31]

Dr. Vallee explains how the system works through a deceptive reinforcement schedule: "If the phenomenon is forcing us through a learning curve, then it has no choice but to mislead us. When Skinner designs a machine that feeds a rat only when the right lever is depressed, this is extremely misleading for the rat. But if the rat doesn't depress the right lever, he becomes extremely hungry. Man is hungry for knowledge and power, and if there is an intelligence behind the UFOs it must have taken this fact into account."[32]

Dr. Vallee suggests that it is possible to convince a major sector of our population to believe in the existence of superior extraterrestrial beings "by exposing them to a few carefully engineered scenes the details of which are adapted to the culture and symbols of a particular time and place." He then explains why he believes the UAP phenomenon/control system has been engineered: "Thermostats control temperature; gyroscopes control the direction in which a rocket flies. What could a paranormal phenomenon control? *I suggest that it is human belief that is being controlled and conditioned.*"[33]

I agree with Dr. Vallee's conclusion—much of the UAP phenomenon is "presented" to us in a manner designed to elicit human response sufficient to manipulate human beliefs. It is significant that Dr. Vallee is a top computer scientist, specializing in the analysis and processing of scientific research data. In fact, it was while creating systems for observatories that he became interested in UAP research—as he saw UAP tracking tapes

---

31. *Dimensions,* 272.
32. Ibid., 275.
33. Ibid., 276.

destroyed as a matter of policy. After many years of inquiry, what does Dr. Vallee conclude about the origin of the UAP phenomenon? In an interview given to the *SCP Journal*, he says, "We believe that the thousands of cases of transformation represent one aspect of the ultimate purpose of UAP. They are part of a plan to deliberately move significant portions of an entire culture, or world, into acceptance or involvement in the occult, and a collective alteration in world view. This is preparatory for and necessary to the events surrounding the rise of Antichrist." It is no wonder that Dr. Vallee hesitates to share his ultimate conclusions in his books.[34] Dr. Vallee says, "In fact, some witnesses have thought that they seem like demons because the creature had the unpredictability and the mischievousness associated with popular conceptions of the devil."[35]

To the extent this is true, we must wonder why the UAP, whatever they are, are beginning to come out from their cloaking devices and display themselves to military cameras and smartphones for mass distribution over the Internet. Has something changed? Have we arrived at the next phase of some timetable? If so, what is coming next? And, whose timetable?

OPENING MINDS TO "NEW" IDEAS

There are various psychological techniques employed to open human minds to heretofore-unacceptable precepts. Dr. Vallee notes further similarities between occult methods and those of UAP messengers. "Is this confusion technique deliberately used to effect change on a major scale? Answering such questions could also help us to understand the strong resemblance that anyone who has examined the beliefs of esoteric groups could not fail to note between certain UFO encounters and the initiation rituals of secret societies. This 'opening of the mind' to a new set of symbols that is reported by many witnesses is precisely what the various occult traditions also try to achieve."[36] Is this "opening of the mind" of a major portion of the population actually occurring? Yes! With the cooperation of the popular media the "extraterrestrial savior" dream has been fostered and championed. All of our

---

34. August 1977, 23.
35. *Dimensions*, 178.
36. Ibid., 188.

ills—pollution, energy, war, property, boundaries, hunger, poverty, and social injustice—will soon be cured; just as soon as we establish permanent ties with these superior lifeforms. With the promotion of these intergalactic saviors by the New Age movement, occult spiritualism is now centered in the cosmos—*extraterrestrials are God*. The entire Ancient Astronauts theory that is touted and repeated incessantly on television and nighttime radio programs constantly enforces this false and pernicious teaching—that extraterrestrials created humans by genetically modifying primates on Earth, and it is they who visited us and gave us all of the wisdom of the past. Extraterrestrials are the angels and the gods. Now that's an "opening of the mind" scenario.

Raymond Fowler says, "They were brief and to the point but what they revealed will revolutionize every aspect of our lives—science, religion, philosophy, sociology—nothing will be spared." Most observers, no matter what their background or which ax they choose to grind, agree on this one point—the UAP phenomenon is changing world beliefs in God. Lewis and Shreckhise conclude, "The menace is that they lure people into an alternative philosophy and world-view that stands in direct contradiction to the Christian faith as found in the Bible."[37] Whitley Strieber notes, "The only thing now needed to make the UFO myth a new religion of remarkable scope and force is a single undeniable sighting. Such a sighting need last only a few minutes. It will at once invest the extraterrestrials channelers, the 'space brothers' believers, and the UFO cultists with the appearance of revealed truth.[38] I cannot forget my memory of the visitors' claim, 'We recycle souls.' It had also been said to other participants. It was becoming clear to me that the visitors were concerned with the life of the soul as well as the body."[39] These spirit transmigration claims and practices are clearly deceptive messages, nudging humanity from God, toward Antichrist.

Dr. Vallee agrees:

> The experience of a close encounter with a UFO is a shattering physical and mental ordeal. The trauma has effects that go far beyond what the witnesses recall consciously. New types of

---

37. *UFO: End-Time Delusion,* 20.
38. *Dimensions,* Forward, v-vii.
39. *Transformation,* 198.

behavior are conditioned, and new types of beliefs are promoted. Aside from any scientific consideration, the social, political, and religious consequences of the experience are enormous if they are considered over a timespan of a generation. Faced with the new wave of experiences of UFO contact that are described in books like *Communion* and *Intruders* and in movies like *Close Encounters of the Third Kind*,[40] our religions seem obsolete. Our idea of the church as a social entity working within rational structures is obviously challenged by the claim of a direct communication in modern times with visible beings who seem endowed with supernatural powers.[41]

Randall Baer, the former New Age Guru, says, "UFO sightings and contacts have made deep inroads into the everyday fabric of much of the New Age. More than seventy-five percent of New Agers firmly believe in the existence of hosts of alien beings within and around planet Earth to help in the birthing of the New Age."[42]

Brad Steiger writes, "Again the 'angels' *i.e.* the space intelligences, are speaking to the prophets, the UFO contactees, in order that we might be guided through the difficult period of transition as a new world rises from the ashes of the old.[43] These UFO prophets have not only brought God physically to this planet, but they have created a blend of science and religion that offers a theology more applicable to modern mankind."[44]

LATTER-DAY HERALDS

Here, we should discuss what has become a popular theory among UAP intellectuals—those who accept that the UAP phenomenon, extraterrestrial or otherwise, is actually a continuing dialogue with interdimensional beings—for our current purposes, demonic spirits. Researchers

---

40. It is terribly ironic that the Claude Lacombe character in *Close Encounters of the Third Kind*, played by François Truffaut as a French government scientist in charge of UAP-related activities, is based on Dr. Vallee.
41. *Dimensions,* introduction, xiii.
42. Randall N. Baer, *Inside the New Age Nightmare,* Huntington House, 145–46.
43. Brad Steiger, *The Fellowship: Spiritual Contact Between Humans and Outer Space Beings, New* York, Dolphin/Doubleday (1988), 194.
44. Ibid., 1.

such as Dr. Jacques Vallee, who have studied the great Madonna encounters of history, shamanistic apparitions, and occult contacts with disembodied spirits including "extraterrestrials," have lumped Joseph Smith in with other contactees. However, they consider him as the "ultimate" contactee. If ever there were a "beam down" scenario, Joseph's experiences with the Father and Son appearing in a bright conduit of light, and Moroni likewise, and that light seemingly to have properties rendering it "solid" and malleable, demonstrate superior control of light and element (see Joseph Smith—History 1:16–17, 30–43). Of course, such parallels beg the question, which apparitions are true heavenly messengers, and which are counterfeits—such as Satan appearing as an angel of light? When Satan deceives, he does it quite well, down to the slightest detail. Of course, he cannot counterfeit the accompanying testimonial delivered by the personage of the Holy Spirit.

In *The Paranormal Borderlands of Science*, in an article chronicling the experiences of Betty Andreasson Luca, "Betty Through the Looking Glass," the author observes:

> Consider theology. We have seen that religion was an important part of Betty's life. Three aspects of her narrative are of particular interest from a theological point of view: (1) During her trip she was from time to time comforted by the laying on of an alien hand. (2) In the later sessions she began to speak in an unintelligible tongue. (3) She received, from an entity she at first thought might be an angel, a book containing important messages for man but written in unintelligible symbols. Here are three striking parallels with the Mormon religion: The founding of that church was based upon the alleged finding, by Joseph Smith, of the "Golden Bible," a book of metallic plates, given by an angel; the plates were covered with incomprehensible writing that Joseph "translated" by means we needn't go into here. And the concepts of speaking in tongues and the laying on of hands have been important parts of Mormon doctrine from that church's beginning. Was Betty familiar with this history?

I trust you have retained your testimony in the face of these sophomoric observations. Although events of the Restoration parallel many UAP contacts, they simultaneously parallel the experiences of most prophets throughout history. The von Dänikens will quickly claim that this "proves" that historical religious contacts were nothing more than ongoing UAP encounters, but intelligent researchers know better. It is Satan who mimics true occurrences, to deceive humans.

The answer is that we must use the experiences of the prophets, including Joseph Smith, as a standard against which we measure any alleged contact with Divinity. Satan will make every attempt to cloak his delivery of false messages in the garb and guise of angelic or "savior" visitations. He furnishes his deceptive encounters with promises of false messiahs—coming soon to save the world from its human infestation. Most UAP encounters, like Blessed Virgin Mary encounters or poltergeist hauntings, are nothing more than theater—played out on the premillennial stage of satanic deception. These are counterfeits, like Perry Mason's hired actresses, employed to confuse those who know, or at least are familiar with, the truth.

THE PRIESTHOOD—OUR ONLY DEFENSE

Let us again consider the prophetic words of Joseph Smith, warning us of the cunning of the evil one: "For as no man knows the things of God, but by the Spirit of God, so no man knows the spirit of the devil, and his power and intelligence, which is more than human, and having unfolded through the medium of the Priesthood the mysterious operations of his devices."[45] This warning counsel appears very appropriate in light of what we have discovered about the UAP phenomenon. Again, there is no reason to think that all apparitions of flying objects in our sky are demonic projections, because we may actually be visited by humans from other planets at times. However, this apparent true phenomenon appears to have been co-opted and counterfeited by the evil one, and paraded in a nonstop pageant of extraordinary characters with messages that take humanity ever-farther from the knowledge of the truth.[46]

Whitley Strieber, who like many others, including Church

---

45. *Teachings*, 204–205
46. "And truth is knowledge of things as they are, and as they were, and as they are to come; And whatsoever is more or less than this is the spirit of that wicked one who was a liar from the beginning" (D&C 93:24–25).

members, has been plagued by the visitors or entities throughout his life, adds his testimony: "Never, in those bleak April days, could I have imagined the subtlety of the plan that they were carrying out. Nor could I have seen the magnificent brilliance of the mind behind it."[47] Yes, Strieber, who considers himself to be of high intellectual stock, is overwhelmed by the "power and intelligence" of the visitors—he too believes it to be "more than human." Strieber worries: "If I had been having these encounters throughout my life, then what had I become? Why were my visitors so secretive, hiding themselves behind my consciousness? I could only conclude that they were using me, and did not want me to know why. Frankly, I found this idea deeply disturbing. What were the visitors' motives? Communion had become a number-one bestseller. What if they were dangerous? Then I was terribly dangerous because I was playing a role in acclimatizing people to them."[48] In fact, the "others" deceptions were published and broadcast to hundreds of millions through Whitley Strieber. He was correct to worry they may have simply been using him to implant their deceptive messages in the minds of billions around the world as the communications were discussed on radio, television and in books.

Rather than twist helplessly at the end of Satan's rope, never knowing what is true and how to act, as lamented by Whitley Strieber, we have the path marked clearly before us by the prophets of God—only the power of the Priesthood can discern and control Satan's latter-day deceptive devices. If we will keep our eye on the truth, as revealed through His prophets, we will not be led down a false path.[49]

---

47. *Transformation*, 55.
48. Ibid., 96.
49. *Teachings*, 204–205.

CHAPTER 17

Conclusion

Allow me to repeat the sage and immortal words of Sir Arthur Conan Doyle, as stated by his character of high deductive genius, Sherlock Holmes: "When you have eliminated the impossible, whatever remains, however improbable, must be the truth." What have we eliminated? What remains?

There is no question that extraterrestrial human life exists. It is found in exponential quantities, strewn throughout the vast universe. Our own Heavenly Father creates worlds without number through His Only Begotten Son—probationary globes like our Earth—and populates them with His children, who like us are progressing through their second estate. Each of these orbs passes through creation, the terrestrial garden, the fall to a broken telestial desert, and baptism by water and fire, eventually being raised to a terrestrial paradise for a millennial reign of its Sovereign, the universal Savior. Then, when the allotted probationary period is spent, each planet is celestialized in the fire of the great refiner, becoming a crystallized globe, a Urim and Thummim to its eternal inhabitants. Two other planets will be prepared as the eternal abode of those who receive a terrestrial or telestial inheritance, respectively.

These trillions upon trillions of children of the second estate are mortal humans, created in the image of Heavenly Father. With some variation, they look like us. They are tempted by denizens of demonic spirits who kept not their first estate, and who seek to frustrate the plan of salvation and exaltation—possibly to gain a second chance for their own salvation. The inhabitants of these faraway planets live through cycles of good and evil, famine and plenty, and wisdom and foolishness. They have prophets, whom they accept at times and reject at others. When they learn of the Savior, they look to the heavens and contemplate the beastly world that could have crucified the Son of God. They live their lives, one day or a thousand years, it does not matter, because they die and move into the spiritual plane that coexists with their own world. They are resurrected and judged according to their faith and works while in the flesh. Those who have kept their covenants inherit their celestialized planet. Those who have fallen short of that glory inherit a planet prepared for them, terrestrial or telestial. And those who have rejected pure light, once having discerned by its radiant glory, go to that place where there is no light and no glory—with Satan, who deceived them by his cunning craft.

Within these parameters all of life's questions are answered—universally. Herein, perhaps, we can discern, and discover the origin of UAP and their purported "occupants." Any communication that fails to fit within this gospel paradigm is likely false. Any assertion that is contrary hereto is from the Father of Lies. With this understanding, we possess a standard by which we may measure the UAP phenomenon, and the message of those who claim to send and control them.

Many investigators and writers are philosophizing about the origin and nature of UAP and their occupants. More and more we read that there is something "evil" about them—something "inhuman." This is the apparent, even obvious conclusion being reached by many researchers. But many abductees, of all people, are telling us that even though they were violated by the entities, they feel that no malice is intended, that the beings are benevolent—or at least dispassionate. They tell us that the UAP occupants are just so advanced that they have difficulty communicating effectively with us at our level—much as a zoologist inadvertently offends a chimpanzee when attempting to communicate or teach a lesson. Extraterrestrial proponents would have us believe that the entities "act out" their message and fill our minds with mythical symbolism in an effort to convey their higher message in a universal language. Is this really what the others are up to?

Our first consideration is the multiplicity of "alien" types. We have presented to us a scenario in which there appear to be scores of alien races who are divided roughly into good aliens and bad aliens. Even the aliens make this assertion. First, the gnomes, or small Grays, and tall Grays. They profess love at times, but demonstrate unpredictability and rage at others. They lie, kidnap, blaspheme, mislead, inflict pain and suffering, exploit, torment, invade, steal, control, mutilate, impregnate, take babies, frighten children, teach reincarnation and a false Messiah, and possibly kill. However, they do warn us about the dangers of pollution and nuclear energy. Reflect now on their counterparts, the human-appearing aliens. They seem benevolent, caring, and superior in every way. Yet, they often appear to be associated with the gnomes and indulge in, and even direct, the activities of the small Grays just enumerated above. Some do, anyway. Those who interacted with our Brother Udo Wartena, and some others, appear to be normal good humans.

Jesus taught us that we would "know them by their fruits" (Matthew 7:16). He explained, "Even so every good tree bringeth forth good fruit; but a corrupt tree bringeth forth evil fruit" (Matthew 7:17). By analogy, the fruit of many of these "aliens" is corrupt and evil. The cries of those who say that we need to give the misunderstood aliens a chance are the dysfunctional chants of enabling victims. Those who claim that the "aliens" are establishing a symbiotic relationship with our race ignore the unmistakable indicators that they are, in fact, imposing a parasitic enslavement on us. This is the appearance of their design, anyway. If we were to put our very best brains to the task of procuring the voluntary enslavement of the world's population, the elements present in the UAP phenomenon would be essential. Appearing as superior visitors from afar, bearing higher technology, has always been a workable ruse. It worked for the Conquistadors. The only thing these brains would lack to fulfill their design is the technology. Whoever the others are, they have the technology—real or perceived. Either way, it is sufficient to entrap a world hungry for a next level *Star Trek* lifestyle.

CONCLUSION

If the gnomes and angelic humans are evil, then what about the humans—those who act like courteous, non-interfering explorers? These are the type encountered by Udo Wartena. These profess to be extraterrestrial, yet act very much like well-mannered, educated humans. They explain their purposes and their methods. They obey laws and ethics. They speak with their mouths and shake with their hands. They have no message, but would happily speak of the gospel, the Savior, and the priesthood if they were permitted. Are these any different, any more feasible or trustworthy than the humans that accompany the gnomes? We cannot know for sure, but their fruits appear good—so far, at least.

Perhaps there are good aliens and bad aliens. Or perhaps there are only human extraterrestrials who, like us, have their good and their bad citizens—but perhaps their bad citizens are not allowed to travel to under-protected outposts, like Earth—or perhaps they are. If the extraterrestrials of Udo Wartena are good, then what of the abducting gnomes? What of the Reptilians and Insectoids? Are they physical extraterrestrial beings with superior intellect and technology, who are delivering a message to mankind, true or untrue? This is possible. Are they demonic spirits masquerading as these 'aliens,' or beneficent New Age messiahs? They very well could be.

After sifting through the literature describing UAP encounters; interviewing abductees and investigators; and pouring over the details of many thousands of encounters and abductions, the messages, and the paranormal and metaphysical phenomena associated with UAP, I have my own conclusion. My conclusion, however, is only that—conclusory—based on my personal analysis of the available data. The conclusion is somewhat unsettled and is not based on special enlightenment or personal revelation. The Lord so far has specifically withheld express instruction on these matters, from the body of the Church, anyway. Does this indicate that they are not important? No; there are many important matters on which He has remained silent—many of them dealing directly with latter-day events preceding His Second Coming.

I first believe that there is every indication that Earth *can* be visited by extraterrestrial human explorers. Furthermore, there is strong evidence that some limited, discrete visitation is conducted by these persons. I also believe that Earth is visited often by angels and translated beings, although these fail to account for UAP phenomena. I believe that the abducting "aliens" are untruthful and imperialistic. I further believe that they are purposely deceiving and controlling our world population by selectively planting psychological devices in handpicked persons and selected media. I also believe that many of these manipulative beings are not physical extraterrestrials as they present themselves to be, although some may be. Because many act exactly like Satan acts, and teach what Satan teaches, there is every reason to believe that they act for him, or in concert with him.

This conclusion is supported by the fact that the small Gray gnomes and those who control them, and their asserted activities and messages, fail to fit within the gospel paradigm—especially within revealed "last days" parameters. However, they fit quite neatly into the elements and events that will lead to the rise and world dominion of Antichrist and the Man of Sin, whose master is Satan. Their message that a galactic Messiah is coming, termed "the One" and other appellations of high honor, is certainly in opposition to revealed truth direct from the Lord. It smacks entirely of the age-old, "I am the Only Begotten, worship me!" (Moses 1:19). Their fascination with the false doctrine of spiritual transmigration or reincarnation likewise helps reveal their true source.

Whatever the source, it is obvious the extraterrestrial presence will continue to escalate. Whether the "aliens" are demonic or not, demonic hordes will utilize the concept, in part at least, to help establish Satan's premillennial kingdom. This we know from the many "alien" contacts already present in the New Age movement. Will there be a large-scale invasion by bad aliens, or a war between good and bad aliens locked in battle over our planet? Will there be emissaries from afar, or supermen from our ranks, enlightened by the intergalactic messianic mind? What drama awaits us in the final scene? However the pageant unfolds, it is only that—theater.

It matters little how Satan deceives the nations—we know he will. Beware of the prince of the power of the air and of false messiahs and false christs, coming in power and glory and invoking the holy names of God. Beware of false prophets and superhumans who work miracles in our sight and console us with dispensations of forgiveness and extensions of time. These will come, speaking in dignified tones and reasoning with superior intellects. They will offer hope and answers to a world poised on the precipice of certain destruction. They, and they alone, will present workable solutions to seemingly insurmountable problems. Their price? It will be much higher than that required by the true Savior who says, "Take my yoke upon you, and learn of me; for I am meek and lowly in heart: and ye shall find rest unto your souls. For my yoke is easy, and my burden is light" (Matthew 11:29–30).

The Prophet Joseph Smith saw our days and the events of which we speak, in full panoramic vision. The subtle cunning of Satan cannot be overstated. He is the Great Deceiver. God will allow a great delusion to overwhelm the world in these last days—that is chiseled in the granite of holy scripture. As the events of the winding up scene begin to besiege us, the Lord has given us a type of what we must do. As Israel was required to look up to Moses and his serpented staff for temporal deliverance, in similitude of the requirement to look to the uplifted Savior for spiritual deliverance, so must we look to the Prophet of God for deliverance as ominous storms of darkness and confusion gather in around us. As it was difficult for ancient Israel to lift their eyes from the immediate danger of the poisonous serpents, so shall it be difficult to see through the life-threatening complexities of the world as Antichrist rises to world reign.

The "mist of darkness" witnessed by the prophet Lehi, which prevented many from clinging to the iron rod leading to eternal life, is the confusion created by Satan to distract us and divert us from the path that leads to salvation and exaltation. Those mists of darkness that are even now drifting toward us are made up of the most sophisticated deceit and lies that this planet has ever known. Already we see many—especially among our youth—who are beguiled by the lying deception of the evil one. Only by looking to the living oracle of God and following the established priesthood order can we escape the snares that are so carefully being laid for us. Only by employing the powers of discernment that accompany the righteous exercise of the priesthood can we hope to keep ourselves unspotted from the sins of the world and the blood of this generation. Whether counterfeit aliens, superhumans, or deceiving spirits, Satan's servants will come working miracles and ensnaring the world. One of the greatest blessings of membership in the kingdom of God is knowing what to watch for and how to discern between good and evil as promised by the Apostle Paul. Although Satan will have power to enslave the world through his deceit, those who possess the gift of the Holy Ghost, the children of light, need not be deceived if they will exercise their God-given gifts and reject the great latter-day lie.

> *But of the times and the seasons, brethren, ye have no need that I write unto you. For yourselves know perfectly that the day of the Lord so cometh as a thief in the night. For when they shall say, Peace and safety; then sudden destruction cometh upon them, as travail upon a woman with child; and they shall not escape. But ye, brethren, are not in darkness, that that day should overtake you as a thief. Ye are the children of light, and the children of the day: we are not of the night, nor of darkness. Therefore let us not sleep, as do others; but let us watch and be sober.*
>
> —1 Thessalonians 5:1

AFTERWORD

There may be readers who have either experienced "alien" or "others" encounters, or who have loved ones that have. The information in this book is calculated to familiarize the reader with entity, UAP, and related phenomena, and to offer an analysis of the possible origins of, and purposes behind it. Although I have attempted to supply the reader with a thoughtful analysis, there is no guarantee that I am correct in any of my conclusions. Therefore, anyone who has experienced a close encounter with "others" and has any residual effects from that experience is well advised to seek out whatever counseling you deem appropriate. I believe many of these may be spiritually centered, and therefore advise that spiritual counseling be sought. Do not hesitate to set an appointment with your bishop and tell him everything you know. If he is unfamiliar with these matters, lend him a copy of this book. Psychological counseling could also be an effective tool in combating any latent effects of these encounters. I ardently suggest a counselor with a strong knowledge and testimony of the gospel as well as significant spiritual insight.

Having concluded that many, although not all UAP sightings and alien encounters have negative *spiritual* origins, I emphasize that a percipient is not a participant. A victim of spiritual "attack" is only that—a victim. To be targeted for an apparition of any kind is no sin or disgrace. Therefore, let no one believe that witnesses or targets of paranormal activity have necessarily invited satanic incursions or ventures into their lives. However, we have discovered a correlation between UAP/abduction related phenomena and occult activity in certain geographical areas. There appear to have been occult practices and revenge curses aplenty in the region of the Uintah Basin before the arrival of the early Saints. This correlative principle appears to hold true in many locations thus far. How can we protect ourselves? As I have made clear above, the power of the priesthood and living in harmony with the Holy Spirit is the best defense against demonic influences. To the extent your experiences are demonic, I recommend spiritual remedies.

If there are other powers at work in the abduction phenomenon, like the amoral and apathetic experiments of humanoid or non-human creatures, or AI systems run amok, similar therapies may help alleviate the effects of such experiences—because after all, bad things happen to good people, and God allows the rain to fall on the just, as well as the unjust. No matter what the source of a particular encounter with the unknown, let us take our cue from the government and discontinue the practice of mocking and deriding those who have been victimized. Let us begin to have an open and candid dialog about these matters, and expose them to the light of day, that we be not overtaken or herded into pens to be abused in the darkness of our lone agony. There is strength in numbers, and it is awful that so many of our brothers and sisters suffer in silence, afraid to speak of the unspeakable. Speak up. Get help. Band together. Tell your priesthood leaders what you have experienced. Share this book. Share the website we have set up.

For further updates on matters we have discussed herein, or to share your personal experiences with the unknown, please visit the website we have set up at UFOdisclosure.us:

SELECTED BIBLIOGRAPHY

CHURCH BIBLIOGRAPHY

Brough, R. Clayton, *They Who Tarry.* Bountiful, Utah: Horizon Publishers, 1976.

Crowther, Duane S. *Prophecy, Key to the Future.* Salt Lake City, Utah: Bookcraft, 1962.

Crowther, Duane S. *Prophetic Warnings to Modern America.* Bountiful, Utah: Horizon Publishers, 1977.

Doctrine and Covenants, The. A Scripture of The Church of Jesus Christ of Latter-day Saints. Salt Lake City, Utah. 1968.

Holy Bible, The. Old and New Testaments—King James Edition. Mission copy bound for The Church of Jesus Christ of Latter-day Saints, Sal Lake City, Utah. 1969 edition.

McConkie, Bruce R. *Doctrines of Salvation: Sermons and Writings of Joseph Fielding Smith.* Salt Lake City, Utah: Bookcraft, 1954. Vols. 1–3.

McConkie, Bruce R. *Mormon Doctrine.* Salt Lake City, Utah: Bookcraft, 1966.

Nibley, Hugh. *The Message of the Joseph Smith Papri: An Egyptian Endowment.* Salt Lake City, Utah: Deseret Book, 1975.

Pearl of Great Price, The. A Scripture of The Church of Jesus Christ of Latter-day Saints. Salt Lake City, Utah. 1968 edition.

Richards, LeGrand. *A Marvelous Work and A Wonder.* Salt Lake City, Utah: Deseret Book, 1969 edition.

Roberts, Brigham H. *A Comprehensive History of the Church.* Provo, Utah: Brigham Young University Press, 1956. Vols. 1–6.

Roberts, Brigham H. *Defense of the Faith and the Saints.* Salt Lake City, Utah: Deseret News, 1912. Vols. 1 & 2.

Smith, Hyrum M. & Janne M. Sjodahl. *Doctrine & Covenants Commentary.* Salt Lake City, Utah: Deseret Book, 1974.

Smith, Joseph (The Documentary) *History of the Church.* Salt Lake City, Utah: Deseret Book, 1946–1951. Vols. 1–7.

Teachings of the Prophet Joseph Smith. Salt Lake City, Utah: Deseret Book, 1954.

Smith, Joseph F. *Gospel Doctrine.* Salt Lake City, Utah: Deseret Book, 1919.

Smith, Joseph Fielding. *Answers to Gospel Questions.* Salt Lake City, Utah: Deseret Book, 1957.

Smith, Joseph Fielding. *Doctrines of Salvation; Sermons and Writings of Joseph Fielding Smith* (compiled by Bruce R. McConkie). Salt Lake City, Utah: Bookcraft, 1973. Vols. 1–3.

Smith, Joseph Fielding. *Essentials in Church History.* Salt Lake City, Utah: Deseret Book, 1969.

Talmage, James E. *Jesus the Christ.* Salt Lake City, Utah: Deseret Book, 1961 edition.

Talmage, James E. *The Articles of Faith.* Salt Lake City, Utah: Deseret Book, 1961.

Whipple, Walt. *A Discussion of the Many Theories Concerning the Whereabouts of the Lost Ten Tribes.* A research paper prepared at Brigham Young University, Provo, Utah, 1958–1959.

Widtsoe, John A. *Discourses of Brigham Young.* Salt Lake City, Utah: Deseret Book, 1954.

UAP-OCCULT-FAIRY BIBLIOGRAPHY

Berlitz, Charles and William L Moore. *The Roswell Incident.* New York: Berkley Books, 1980.

Bloecher, Ted with Aphrodite Clamar, Budd Hopkins, and Elizabeth Slater. *Final Report on the Psychological Testing of UFO "Abductees."* Mt. Rainier, Maryland: The Fund for UFO Research, 1987.

Briggs, Katherine. *Encyclopedia of Fairies*, New York: Pantheon/Random House, 1976.

SELECTED BIBLIOGRAPHY

Bullard, Thomas E., PhD. *On Stolen Time: A Summary of the Comparative Study of the UFO Abduction Mystery*. M1. Rainier, Maryland: The fund for UFO Research, 1987.

Conroy, Ed. *Report on Communion*. New York: William Morrow & Company, 1989.

Davis, Lorraine. "A Comparison of UFO and Near Death Experiences," *Journal of Near Death Studies*, Vol. 6, No. 4 (1988).

Evans, Hilary. *Gods, Spirits, Cosmic Guardians: Encounters with Non-Human Beings*. Wellingborough, England: Aquarian Press, 1987.

Visions, Apparitions, Alien Visitors: A Comparative Study of the Entity Enigma. Wellingborough, England: Aquarian Press, 1984.

Evans-Wentz, W. Y. *The Fairy Faith in Celtic Countries*, New York: University Press, 1966.

Fawcett, Lawrence and Barry J. Greenwood. *Clear Intent: The Government Cover-Up of the UFO Experience*. Englewood Cliffs, New Jersey: Prentice-Hall, 1984.

Festinger, Leon with Henry W. Riecken and Stanley Schachter. *When Prophecy Fails: A Social and Psychological Study of a Modern Group That Predicted the Destruction of the World*. New York: Harper and Row, 1956.

Fowler, Raymond E. *The Andreasson Affair*. Englewood Cliffs, New Jersey: Prentice-Hall, 1980.

Fowler, Raymond E. *The Andreasson Affair, Phase Two*. Englewood Cliffs, New Jersey: Prentice-Hall, 1982.

The Watchers: The Secret Design Behind UFO Abductions. New York: Bantam Book, 1990.

Frazier, Kendrick, ed. *Paranormal Borderlands of Science*. Buffalo: Prometheus Books, 1981.

Fry, Daniel W. *The White Sands Incident*. Louisville, Kentucky: Best Book Company, 1966.

Fuller, John G. *Aliens in the Skies: The New UFO Battle of the Scientists*. New York: G. P. Putnam's Sons, 1969.

Incident at Exeter: Unidentified Flying Objects Over America Now. New York: G. P. Putnam's Sons, 1966.

The Interrupted Journey: Two Lost Hours Aboard a Flying Saucer. New York: Dial Press, 1966.

Gardner, Martin. *The New Age: Notes of a Fringe—Watcher*. Buffalo: Prometheus Books, 1988.

Good, Timothy. *Above Top Secret: The Worldwide UFO Cover-UP*. New York: William Morrow and Company, 1988.

Grant, Kenneth. *Outside the Circles of Time*. London: Frederick Muller Ltd., 1980.

Hartland, E. S. *English Fairy and Folk Tales*. London: Walter Scott, 1893.

The Science of Fairy Tales: An Inquiry into Fairy Mythology. London: Walter Scott, 1891.

Hassan, Steven. *Combatting Cult Mind Control*. Rochester, Vermont: Park Street Press, 1988.

Hasted, John. *The Metal Benders*. Routledge & Kegan Paul, 1981.

Hopkins, Budd. "The Extraterrestrial—Paraphysical Controversy?" *MUFON UFO Journal*, no. 153, 1980. 3–5.

Intruders: The Incredible Visitations at Copley Woods. New York: Random House, 1987.

Missing Time: A Documented Study of UFO Abductions. New York: Richard Marek Publishers, 1981.

Hynek, J. Allen and Jacques Vallee, *The Edge of Reality: A Progress Report on Unidentified Flying Objects*. Chicago: Henry Regnery Company, 1975.

Jacobs, Joseph. *Celtic Folk and Fairy Tales*. New York: G. P. Putnam's Sons, 1968.

Keel, John A. *Why UFOs?: Operation Trojan Horse*. New York: Manor Books, 1981.

Kinder, Gary. *Light Years: An Investigation into the Extraterrestrial Experiences of Eduard Meier*. New York: Atlantic Monthly Press, 1987.

Kirk, Robert. *The Secret Commonwealth of Elves, Fauns and Fairies*. Stirling, England: Mackay, 1933.

Larson, Robert. *Straight Answers on the New Age*. Tennessee: Nelson Publishers, 1989.

Lewis, David Allen and Robert Shreckhise. *UFO: End-Time Delusion*. Arkansas: New Leaf Press, 1992.

SELECTED BIBLIOGRAPHY

Loosely, William Rober with David Langford, ed. *An Account of a Meeting with Denizens of Another World 1871*. New York: St. Martin's Press, 1980.

Lorenzen, Coral and Jim Lorenzen. *Abducted: Confrontations with Beings for Outer Space*. New York: Berkley Publishing Corporation, 1977.

Maccabee, Bruce, PhD. *Documents and Supporting Information Relating to Crashed Flying Saucers and Operaton Majestic Twelve*. Mt. Rainier, Maryland: The Fund for UFO Research, 1987.

Monroe, Robert A. *Journeys Out of the Body*. New York: Anchor Press/ Doubleday, 1973.

Montgomery, Ruth. *Aliens Among Us*. New York: Fawcett Crest, 1985.

Neal, Richard, MD. "Generations of Abductions—A Medical Casebook," and "The Alien Agenda," *UFO Magazine*, vol. 3, no. 2, 1988. 22, 25.

Nyman, Joseph. "The Latent Encounter Experience—A Composite Model," *MUFON UFO JOURNAL*, no. 242, 1988. 10–12.

Ring, Kenneth. *Heading Towards Omega: In Search of the Meaning of the Near-Death Experience*. New York: William Morrow and Company, 1984, 1985.

Rojcewicz, Peter M. " 'Men in Black' Experiences: Analogues of the Traditional Devil Encounter," *Fortean Times*, issue no. 50, London, 1986.

Salisbury, Frank B. *The Utah UFO Display: A Bioligists Report*. Connecticut: Devin-Adair, 1974.

Spencer, John and Hilary Evans. *Phenomenon: Forty Years of Flying Saucers*. New York: Avon Books, 1988.

Steiger, Brad. *The Fellowship: Spiritual Contact Between Humans and Outer Space Beings*. New York: Dolphin/Doubleday, 1988.

Mysteries of Time and Space. New York: Confucian Press, 1973.

The UFO Abductors. New York: Berkley Publishing Corporation, 1988.

Story, Ronald D. *The Encyclopedia of UFOs*. Garden City, N.Y.: Dolphin Books/Doubleday and Company, 1980.

Strieber, Whitley. *Communion: A True Story*. New York: Morrow/Beech Tree Books, 1987.

Tranformation: The Breakthrough. New York: Morrow/Beech Tree Books, 1988.

Vallee, Jacques. *Dimensions: A Casebook of Alien Contact*. Chicago: Contemporary Books, 1988.

The Invisible College: What a Group of Scientists Has Discovered About UFO Influences of the Human Race. New York: E. P. Dutton and Company, 1975.

Messengers of Deception: UFO Contacts and Cults. Berkely, California: And/Or Press, 1979.

Passport to Magonia: From Folklore to Flying Saucers. Chicago: Henry Regnery Company, 1969.

UFOs in Space: Anatomy of a Phenomenon. Henry Regnery Company, 1965.

von Däniken, Erich. *Chariots of the Gods?* New York: G. P. Putnam's Sons, 1970.

Walters, Ed. *The Gulf Breeze Sightings*. New York: William Morrow and Company, 1974.

Walton, Travis. *The Walton Experience*. New York: Berkley Publishing Corporation, 1978.

Yeats, W. B. *Irish Fairy and Folk Tales*. New York: Dorset Press, 1986.

Zaleski, Carol. *Otherworld Journeys: Accounts of Near-Death Experience in Medieval and Modern Times*. New York: Oxford University Press, 1987.

ABOUT THE AUTHOR

James Thompson, JD, is an award-winning writer and well-known professional ghostwriter. He has ghostwritten dozens of books for the nation's top business, motivational, and political leaders and is also known for his work in religious historical fiction.

James holds a Juris Doctor degree from Brigham Young University's J. Reuben Clark Law School, where he served as articles editor of the *BYU Law Review*. Among many subjects, he has been writing about spiritual and related phenomena for over thirty years and is considered a leading analyst in the field of Unidentified Aerial Phenomena and spiritual encounters.

Learn more at James's websites:
JamesThompson.pro
GhostwriterUS.com